Emerson & Eros

Emerson & Eros

The Making of a Cultural Hero

Len Gougeon

State University of New York Press

Published by
State University of New York Press, Albany

For information, contact State University of New York Press, Albany, NY
www.sunypress.edu

Production by Kelli Williams
Marketing by Susan M. Petrie

Library of Congress Cataloging-in-Publication Data

Gougeon, Len.
    Emerson and Eros : the making of a cultural hero / Len Gougeon.
        p. cm.
    Includes bibliographical references and index.
    ISBN-13: 978-0-7914-7077-0 (hardcover : alk. paper)   1. Emerson, Ralph Waldo,
1803–1882—Philosophy.   2. Emerson, Ralph Waldo, 1803–1882—Knowledge and
learning.   3. Emerson, Ralph Waldo, 1803–1882—Influence.   4. Literature and
myth.   5. Authors, American—19th century—Biography.   6. Transcendentalists
(New England)—Biography.   7. Social reformers—United States—Biography.
8. United States—Intellectual life—19th century.   I. Title.

PS1642.P5G64   2007
814'.3—dc22

2006023729

10 9 8 7 6 5 4 3 2 1

For Deborah,
who has always been
my first circle.

CONTENTS

Acknowledgments   ix

Prologue   1

Chapter 1
  Psychomythic Humanism: Re-centering Reality   21

Chapter 2
  The Spirit and the Flesh   45

Chapter 3
  "God's Child": Emerson in His Journals   75

Chapter 4
  "The Devil's Child": Emerson's Early Public Voice   125

Chapter 5
  The Call To Serve: Re-centering America   159

Epilogue   193

Notes   199

Works Cited   241

Index   255

ACKNOWLEDGMENTS

In the course of writing a book, one inevitably incurs many debts to those who provided help and encouragement along the way. After more than thirty years of writing about Emerson, I have accumulated an unusual number of these. Since it involved so many different aspects of Emerson's life and thought, this particular project was a special challenge. My journey into the depths of Emerson's inner self forced me to consider everything from his psychological development, to his spiritual crises, to his complex and, at times, conflicted relationships with church, family, friends, and community. It also necessitated a consideration of the sources of Emerson's remarkable creativity and the unique expression of that creativity in his lectures, poems, and essays. The philosophical sources of Emerson's thought and his place in a historical and intellectual continuum reaching back to the Neoplatonists of the third century and forward to the psychomythic humanists of the twentieth century presented yet another challenge. And so my debts are many. To name all of the persons who have contributed to my knowledge and appreciation of Emerson over the years would require more space than is available here. It would begin in graduate school with A. W. Plumstead and David Porter and continue on from there. And so I will not attempt it. Instead I will limit myself, first of all, to those individuals who were kind enough to read and comment on the manuscript of this study at various stages during the long period of its evolution. Among the earliest of these were Robert Habich, Wesley Mott, David Robinson, Alan Hodder, and Richard Geldard. Their many suggestions, as well as their encouragement, were invaluable. Later readers included Robert Richardson and Joel Myerson, both of whom possess a vast knowledge of Emerson and the period in which he lived and worked. Others outside of the Emerson circle were also extremely generous in providing much needed guidance. John Norcross, whose knowledge of modern psychology is second to none, was a tremendous help in preventing me from running off the tracks at various junctures. My philosopher friends and colleagues, John McGinley and Kevin Nordberg, performed a similar noble service, drawing from their considerable experience in teaching classical philosophy. And in my own English department, John Meredith Hill and Carl Schaffer, a poet and a creative writer, as well as humanists of the first order, offered sound advice on my "sound and sense." To all of these, I will be eternally indebted. There are, of course, a myriad of Emerson scholars whose works help to provide the necessary underpinnings for the present study, in addition to those already noted. Their names can be found in the list of works cited at the end of the text. Among these, especially, are Lawrence Buell, Ronald Bosco, Phyllis Cole, Albert von Frank, Barbara Packer, Laura Dassow Walls, and Sarah Wider. It is my good fortune that these scholars are also friends, and to them I offer my heartfelt thanks for the many conversations we have had and the works they have published, all of which contributed considerably to my own modest effort.

Finally, closer to home, I would like to thank Patrick J. Scanlon, a former graduate student whose enthusiasm for psychomythic criticism helped to rekindle my own, my daughter, Nadia Lynn Gougeon, who was kind enough to read and critique my manuscript in its various stages, and lastly my wife, Deborah, whose faith and patience were a constant resource throughout the long gestation of this study.

PROLOGUE

Give all to love;
Open thy heart;
Friends, kindred, days,
Estate, good-fame,
Plans, credit and the Muse,—
Nothing refuse.

—R. W. Emerson, *Give All to Love*

 This study began many years ago as an effort to answer a question. That question, however, must first be prefaced by a few observations. For the first thirty years of his life, Ralph Waldo Emerson was the epitome of upper-middle-class American gentility and conformity. Considered undistinguished as an undergraduate at Harvard (his younger brothers Charles and Edward were seen as the bright lights of the family), he graduated in the middle of his class and elected to attend the Divinity School at his alma mater, thus following in the footsteps of a long line of Emerson divines, including his father and grandfather.[1] His career in the Divinity School was as unremarkable as his undergraduate performance. Eventually, he completed his studies, married a young woman with the right social credentials and family background, and assumed a comfortable position in one of Boston's more prestigious Unitarian congregations, the Second Church. Nothing could possibly be more conventional and predictable. Indeed, as Lawrence Buell recently observed, in the first thirty years of his life, "Emerson did little to distinguish himself from respectable mediocrity."[2] Remarkably, however, before the third decade of his life was complete, he would suffer the death of his young wife, abandon the ministry, travel to Europe, and eventually, through an extraordinary series of publications and lectures, emerge as one of America's most gifted writers, speakers, philosophers, and social

1

reformers, a thoroughgoing revolutionary prophet who sought to "unsettle all things" in an effort to redeem and reform his world. An extremely creative and highly unorthodox thinker, his dynamic, idealistic, and supremely optimistic Transcendental philosophy would scandalize some but delight and enthrall many, especially the youth of America whose imaginations he captured. By the end of his long life, he would be revered as a veritable oracle, an American icon, a thinker and prophet of immense importance. He was recognized as a person whose vision helped to shape the destiny of his nation and the course of Western thought. The one hundredth anniversary of Emerson's birth in 1903 was celebrated in one form or another in virtually every major American city. He was memorialized by Charles W. Eliot, the President of Harvard, and Theodore Roosevelt, the President of the United States. By the end of the decade, his works had been translated into all major Western European languages, Swedish, Russian, and Japanese.[3]

Now, more than two hundred years after his birth, Emerson's reputation endures. In the decade of the nineties alone, nearly one thousand articles and books were published discussing his life, ideas, and his continuing influence.[4] His incisive aphorisms as well as quotes from his various poems, essays, and addresses routinely appear on insurance company calendars and in presidential addresses. The question, then, simply put is this; how did all this happen? How did a conventional preacher of modest ability, leading an utterly predictable and comfortable middle-class life, eventually emerge as his nation's foremost prophet, seer, and social reformer? And further, what was the source of the dynamic, mystical, and transcendent power that Emerson claimed to have discovered within himself that enabled such a dramatic transformation? In an effort to find an answer to these questions, I initially planned to examine Emerson's personal psychological, spiritual, and intellectual development. I soon found that it would also be necessary to relate that development to the special needs of the time and place in which he lived if I was to comprehend the enormous impact that he had on his society. Emerson's life experience, I discovered, involved a complex and, at times traumatic, inward journey that ultimately led to the source of his philosophy of personal transcendence, the discovery of what he called "the God within." Emerson's personal discovery provided the basis for his Transcendental philosophy which, in turn, offered vital answers to his society's most pressing moral and social problems. Emersonian Transcendentalism soon became an essential ingredient in the ferment of social change that would serve to characterize the period 1830–1860 as "the era of reform" in America.[5]

The middle decades of the nineteenth century, like those of the twentieth century, were a time of great tension and social alienation in America. For Emerson, the period was characterized by a constant and distressing emphasis on material progress at the cost of human dignity, meaning, and self-worth. The early stages of the Industrial Revolution and the rapid development of commercial enterprise were accelerating the pace of life and creating enormous wealth for some. In New England, much of this wealth was generated by the cotton-based textile industry, the raw materials for which were produced almost exclusively by southern slave labor.

The persistent pursuit of material gain during this period brought about the subordination of more humane values and created an alienating environment where, as Henry David Thoreau complains in *Walden* (1854), "men have become the tools of their tools." This inversion of values, where material worth outweighed human worth, is captured succinctly in Thoreau's observation that, "We do not ride on the railroad; it rides upon us."[6] Worse yet, in an environment characterized by endless commercial competition and the pursuit of the "almighty dollar," presumably free citizens had, in Thoreau's view, become "the slave drivers" of themselves. It is not surprising that in such a dismal and frantic environment, "The mass of men lead lives of quiet desperation."[7] Additionally, the subordination of women, the mistreatment of Native Americans, and the ugly fact of slavery, provided a searing indictment of America's growing materialism and corresponding disregard for basic human dignity.

Emerson saw this problem arising in the 1830s, at the beginning of his public career as lecturer and essayist. In his "American Scholar" address (1837), he describes a society rife with alienation where almost every person has been "metamorphosed into a thing." In such a world, spiritual life is virtually nonexistent, and "The planter, who is Man sent out into the field to gather food, is seldom cheered by any idea of the true dignity of his ministry. He sees his bushel and his cart, and nothing beyond, and sinks into the farmer, instead of Man on the farm. The tradesman," says Emerson, is no better off because he "scarcely ever gives an ideal worth to his work, but is ridden by the routine of his craft, and the soul is subject to dollars." Even the clergy have been compromised and literally de-humanized, just as most others have been. "The priest becomes a form; the attorney a statute-book; the mechanic a machine; the sailor, a rope of a ship."[8] A decade later, the problem had only grown worse, and in his "Ode: Inscribed to W. H. Channing" (1847), he proclaims,

> 'Tis the day of the chattel,
> Web to weave, and corn to grind;
> Things are in the saddle,
> And ride mankind.

In this context, the value of humanity itself had been greatly discounted in the ledger book of life. "Men are become of no account," Emerson observes. "Men in history, men in the world of to-day are bugs, spawn, and

are called 'the mass' and 'the herd.'"[9] In such a world, people blithely accept
the fact of slavery because of the usefulness of its products. As Emerson
notes, "What if it cost a few unpleasant scenes off the coast of Africa? That
was a great way off. . . . If any mention was made of homicide, madness,
adultery, and intolerable tortures, we would let the church bells ring louder,
the church organ swell its peal, and drown the hideous sound. The sugar
they raised was excellent: nobody tasted blood in it."[10] Everywhere, institutions of all types that had once provided a source of meaning, self-worth,
and human dignity were fast becoming enervated and generally dysfunctional, at least in a moral sense. At its worst, "the establishment," as Emerson would call it, now tyrannize over the hapless masses, and demanded a
dull conformity and acquiescence to a torpid and immoral status quo. As he
observes in "Self-Reliance" (1841), society itself has become a "joint stock
company," where "the virtue in most request is conformity." As a result, individualism is discouraged. There is little opportunity for personal growth
and development (Emerson called it "self-culture"), because "Society everywhere is in conspiracy against the manhood of every one of its members."[11]
There was scant concern for authentic spiritual values and religious vitality
in a world that did not look beyond the material reality of the senses. The
churches themselves were not immune from this general malaise. In his controversial "Divinity School Address" (1838), Emerson describes in painful
detail "the causes of that calamity of a decaying church and a wasting unbelief."[12] The primary deficiency of the age, he eventually discovered, was
its inability to connect with the primal, erotic, instinctive, and intuitional
element within, the affective side of humanity that connects us with divinity
itself and also binds us to one another. In short, the age was becoming increasingly heartless and, therefore, spiritually enervated. Emerson came to
believe that without feeling, there could be no faith, love, or harmony and
no perception of "higher law" or divinity in human experience. Without
dreams, there could be no vision of a better world. Under such circumstances, society ceases to progress and becomes an arid graveyard of repeti-
tious sameness. In place of a life-sustaining divinity, society worships at the
"sepulchers of the fathers."[13] Where emotional and imaginative vitality are
present, however, life and faith abound. The intuition of immortality and divinity brings redemption and renewal. As Emerson notes in his "Divinity
School Address": "A more secret, sweet, and overpowering beauty appears
to man when his heart and mind open to the sentiment of virtue. Then instantly he is instructed in what is above him. He learns that his being is without bound; that, to the good, to the perfect, he is born, low as he now lies
in evil and weakness."[14] This personal insight, however, came to Emerson
only after he completed a sometimes painful inward journey. Before he
could heal his society, he had to heal himself.

   Emerson experienced the dramatic collapse of his own world following the death of his young and beautiful first wife, Ellen Tucker, in 1831.

The young minister was cast back upon himself to find the meaning of his life. His formal Unitarian faith, he discovered, failed utterly to satisfy his acute emotional and spiritual needs. Suddenly deprived of the traditional supports of church and family, Emerson set out upon what would become a heroic, inward journey. Through a remarkable process of self-discovery, he eventually penetrated the very essence of his being. In the depth of his own inner sphere, Emerson eventually found what he believed to be the center and source of all life: an overarching, mystical and all-encompassing divinity which, like Augustine's God, possessed a center that was everywhere and a circumference that was nowhere. Eventually, he named this dynamic and transcendent force the "Over-Soul," but he also used other names such as Eros, the eternal One, the Reason, Love, or more traditionally, God. Unbeknownst to himself, he had actually been prepared for this discovery, in part, by his extensive readings in European Romanticism and the philosophy of Immanuel Kant, Samuel Taylor Coleridge, Goethe, and others, as well as his own Puritan heritage (represented to him directly by his oracular Aunt Mary Moody Emerson) with its emphasis on interior religious experience and the mystery of conversion. The death of his wife Ellen served as the catalyst that set these diverse influences into a dynamic and creative flux. The outcome of this dramatic inward journey was uniquely Emersonian. Eventually, it touched every part of his life and informed his deepest thoughts on the nature of divinity, art, time, history, language, culture, and the human social condition. Eventually this "new thing," as he once called it, became known to the world as Transcendentalism. He preached it throughout the rest of his life in lectures, addresses, essays, and poems.

Emerson's Transcendental philosophy, as it turned out, was exactly what his age required. It eventually provided a dynamic impetus to social reform that helped to fuel a veritable "second Revolution" of American culture. With its emphasis on the dignity and divinity of all people, the supreme importance of the individual, and the obligation of all to work for the greater good, Transcendentalism helped to bring about an end to slavery and also promoted the rights of women, Native Americans, the poor and oppressed, immigrants, and all other marginalized people. It insisted on the sacred right of all Americans to share in the promise of freedom, equality, and justice, regardless of race, class, or gender. Emersonian Transcendentalism countered the distressing dehumanization of society by re-centering the world around humankind, both individually and collectively. The major thrust of this movement stressed the importance of activating and utilizing humankind's natural instinctive, affective, and intuitional resources, which are themselves a manifestation of the power of divinity. Emerson insisted that this divinity is within every person. It is precisely this affective quality that Perry Miller identifies as the very heart of the Transcendental movement. "The real drive in the souls of the participants," he maintains, "was a hunger of the spirit for values which Unitarianism had concluded were no longer estimable." For Miller, Transcendentalism is essentially "a protest of the human heart against emotional starvation."[15] By emphasizing both the validity and the authority of divine intuitions, Transcendentalists embraced the spiritual and emotional energy that they believed united all of humanity and, ultimately, imparted dignity and meaning to life. By yoking the power of the affections and an intuitive perception of divinity with the conscious power of reason, Transcendentalism offered an effective and dynamic antidote to the sense of alienation and spiritual enervation that pervaded American society at the time. As Emerson observes in *Nature* (1836), "The reason why the world lacks unity, and lies broken and in heaps, is, because man is disunited with himself."[16] To look within and access the divinity that is part of every person's being, "the eternal One," is the first and most important step in personal redemption, as Emerson learned from his own experience. This, in turn, leads to the redemption of society through the recognition of basic and universal human rights and the obligation of all to promote social justice. The end result is a more noble life and a just society. Emerson offered his contemporaries a Transcendental vision of personal harmony and social coherence based upon mutual respect and brotherhood. He describes the concept in mythic terms in the "American Scholar." "It is one of those fables, which out of an unknown antiquity, convey an unlooked-for wisdom," observes Emerson, "that the gods, in the beginning, divided Man into men, that he might be more helpful to himself; just as the hand was divided into fingers, the better to answer its end." For Emerson, the source of this original unity is still with us. It is the power of Eros, the Over-Soul, the "divine Reason." "The old fable covers a doctrine ever new and sublime"; he asserts, "that there is One Man,—present to all particular men only partially, or through one faculty; and that you must take the whole society to find the whole man. Man is not a farmer, or a professor, or an engineer, but he is all." It became an article of absolute faith to Emerson "that man is one."[17] It is this essential concept that imbues even the oppressed slave with divine dignity. As Emerson observed in an early journal entry, "Democracy/Freedom has its root in the Sacred truth that every man hath in him the divine Reason. . . . That is the equality & the only equality of all men." He goes on to note that, because of the presence of this element of divinity in all people, slavery is an "unpardonable outrage."[18] By virtue of his Transcendental faith in the divinity of man, Emerson sought to effectively reverse the de-humanizing values equation of his time. He insisted boldly and confidently that "The world is nothing, the man is all."[19]

As noted earlier, Emerson represented this divinity within, the life-giving and life-sustaining force in nature and mankind, variously as the Over-Soul, the eternal One, the Reason, Love, or "Eros." He used this latter term in its most original, mythological sense, and this is the sense in which it is used in this study. According to Hesiod, Eros was the most ancient of all the Gods. Many held that he was the son of Erebus and the Night. His function was to coordinate the elements that constitute the universe. As such, he can be seen as a personification of the elemental force that "brings harmony to chaos," the first and most essential formative dynamic in the development of life.[20] Only in his later manifestations does Eros appear in a less cosmic context as the god of human love, passion, and feeling, but even in the diminutive form the cohesive and progenerative element is conspicuous. For Emerson, Eros represents the essential cosmic force, the glue that holds the universe and humanity together. His writings are infused with this dynamic spirit. Because this divine energy is the source of all harmony, it is Eros who shapes the vision of the Muse. These two provide the keys to all understanding and they are the source of all meaning. This connection is made explicit in Emerson's poem "Love and Thought."

> Two well-assorted travelers use
> The highway, Eros and the Muse.
> From the twins is nothing hidden,
> To the pair is nought forbidden;
> Hand in hand the comrades go
> Every nook of nature through:[21]

This unifying power of Eros, of Love, is also made explicit in the poem "Beauty." In an obvious reflection on his own prophetic role, Emerson here describes the creative experience wherein the poet is able to discern the essential harmony of a seemingly fragmented and painful world. Amid images of incipient chaos, "errant spheres," "quaking earth," "dens of passion, and pits of wo," the poet perceives "strong Eros struggling through" bringing order and thus "solving the curse."

> He heard a voice none else could hear
> From centered and from errant sphere.
> The quaking earth did quake in rhyme,
> Seas ebbed and flowed in epic chime.
> In dens of passion, and pits of wo,
> He saw strong Eros struggling through,
> To sun the dark and solve the curse,
> And beam to the bounds of the universe.[22]

Because they are the special conduits of this divine power, for Emerson the poet and the scholar (his dual vocation) displace the enervated priest. The ideal scholar is a person of insight, but also feeling; "He is the world's eye. He is the world's heart." Because of this, "He is to resist the vulgar prosperity that retrogrades ever to barbarism, by preserving and communicating heroic sentiments, noble biographies, melodious verse, and the conclusions of history."[23] Emerson described himself in describing his ideal scholar. He is one who must be open to all knowledge. He is an eclectic thinker who can entertain a wide diversity of thought and feeling through the medium of the heart as well as the eye. He is a visionary who can penetrate the surface and reveal, like "strong Eros," the one among the many, the *unus mundus*, the divine harmony of all things.

It is in the role of the poet, however, that Emerson most clearly serves as the harbinger of divinity. The poet will perform much the same function as the scholar, but with greater passion, and hence, much greater authority. "The poet," Emerson says, "is the sayer, the namer, and represents beauty. He is a sovereign, and stands on the centre. . . . Therefore the poet is not any permissive potentate, but is emperor in his own right." The power this "emperor" personifies and projects is that of the divinity that dwells within all humankind. This power transcends the staid limitations of the "joint-stock" world. Because poets facilitate a dramatic process of transformation by appealing to humanity's divine nature, and because for Emerson man in his current social state is "a god in ruins," poets function as "liberating gods" who, in effect, liberate gods, or demigods at least.[24] In this ideal form, both poet and scholar are avatars of the divinity within. They are representations of Emerson himself in the role he eventually assumed as Transcendental prophet and redeemer.

Emerson's message of divine liberation was, indeed, radical and revolutionary. By imbuing individuals with divine authority, he sought to emancipate them from the repressive strictures of America's corrupt obsession with "things." Not surprisingly, this soon led him into conflict with the conservative "fathers" of his society, who condemned his philosophy and his message as "the latest form of infidelity." Despite such harsh criticisms, Emerson persisted in his role as prophet and oracle throughout his lifetime, following his initial transformation. It is a role that he grew into gradually, sometimes with great reluctance, resistance, and even self-doubt. At times, especially in his antislavery crusade, like a wearied Christ, he wished that this cup might pass from him. In the end, however, he persevered through public ridicule and opprobrium to see his vision triumph.

In considering the overall trajectory of Emerson's life, it occurred to me early on that understanding the dramatic transformation that made his exceptional career possible would require both spiritual and psychological, as well as literary, insight. Fortunately, around the time of my first serious engagement with Emerson's writings, I came upon the works of a gifted group of eclectic thinkers who seemed capable of answering this need. These writers, Joseph Campbell, Erich Neumann, Mircea Eliade, and Norman O. Brown, appeared in many ways to replicate Emerson's own example in their quest for unity, meaning, and human understanding in an increasingly chaotic and threatening world. It is also significant that, writing in the mid-twentieth century, these "psychomythic humanists" (as they shall be designated here) confronted a major crisis similar to that faced by Emerson in the mid-nineteenth century, namely, a potentially catastrophic collapse of the prevailing cultural paradigm.

The middle of the twentieth century in America, as well as the Western world generally, like the mid-nineteenth century, was a time of rapid change. This was wrought though dramatic industrial and technological development, social and political conflict, and global warfare. The result was often fear, anxiety, and a feeling of alienation. Despite the decade of prosperity that followed it, for many, the First World War appeared to signal the general collapse of Western civilization, which, according to Ezra Pound in his poem, "Hugh Selwyn Mauberly," amounted to "two gross of broken statues," and "a few thousand battered books." A "lost generation" of American writers, including Ernest Hemingway, F. Scott Fitzgerald, John Dos Passos, and others attempted to find its way through bewilderment, disappointment, and depression. T. S. Eliot pronounced this failed and faltering world a "Waste Land" in his famous poem by that name. Following a decade of economic depression and hardship in the 1930s, the United States found itself involved in yet another devastating global war. This conflict included the unique horrors of the Holocaust and thermonuclear devastation. The Second World War demonstrated with stunning cruelty humankind's seemingly unlimited capacity for inhumanity. The euphoria that followed the successful conclusion of that war soon gave way with the advent of yet another war in June 1950, this one on the Korean peninsula. The Korean conflict, in turn, was followed by the growing and persistent paranoia of the Cold War. The very technology that brought the Second World War to a successful conclusion for the United States now seemed to threaten the annihilation of all humankind. The growing tensions over Civil Rights added yet another dimension to the generalized anxiety and sense of alienation of the 1950s and 1960s in America. Humanity's place in the scheme of things seemed uncertain at best. The notion of human dignity and self-worth was assaulted on many fronts. Conventional religious beliefs, as in the mid-nineteenth century, seemed inadequate to answer the needs of the time. It was difficult to maintain notions of brotherly love while constructing a family fallout shelter. It now appeared to many that all values were purely subjective at best and at worst a mere excuse for oppression. The seeds of postmodernism had been planted.

It was during this time of fragmentation, tension, and growing disbelief, that the psychomythic humanists considered here published some of their most significant works. Strongly influenced by the theories of Carl

Jung and, to a lesser degree Sigmund Freud, these thinkers attracted significant attention in academic circles and elsewhere. Joseph Campbell, Erich Neumann, Mircea Eliade, and Norman O. Brown all shared a deep interest in human psychology, as well as other disciplines. In significant ways, their collective thought bears a strong resemblance to Emerson's, as well as other nineteenth-century Romantics and Transcendentalists. One of the reasons for this is that they shared many common sources. Additionally, Emerson was himself an influence on all of these writers, both directly and indirectly.[25] Like Emerson, these writers are highly eclectic and draw upon a vast range of sources, from the mythic to the strictly scientific. The results are often provocative. Despite my fascination with these similarities and the possible guidance that they might provide in exploring Emerson's transformation, I put the matter aside for many years. I was instead drawn into a study of Emerson's public career as a reformer, especially his antislavery crusade about which so little of substance was then known. At least one of the reasons for my attraction to this topic was the fact that I grew up watching the Civil Rights Movement unfold on the black and white Sylvania TV in my parents' living room, and I was deeply moved by it. As a result, like many in my generation, I became interested in matters of social justice and race from an early age. It was, therefore, natural that I should be curious about Emerson's relationship to the greatest reform movement of his time. And so I began researching and eventually writing about the evolution of Emerson's increasingly active social role, and the long and difficult path he followed in emerging from the relative quietism of the 1840s to the turbulence of the 1850s and beyond. Throughout, I was impressed by the passion of his campaign for social justice. However, I was also curious about the source of his inspiration and the depth of his commitment to such a controversial but important cause as antislavery. There was also the question of the relationship of this very public crusade to his Transcendental philosophy, a philosophy which, in the eyes of many scholars, appeared to encourage an aloofness from public affairs. The pursuit of answers to these questions eventually brought me back to the psychomythic humanists. In my renewed desire to explore Emerson's inner life, I considered various current theories of personality offered by modern psychology, from Personal Construct Theory, to Existential Phenomenology, to Psychodynamic Social Learning Theory.[26] While all were interesting, and undoubtedly worthwhile in their own right, the purely psychological approach proved to be too restrictive to account for Emerson's many facets. Ultimately, I found that none spoke so well to him as the psychomythic critics that had made such an impression on me earlier. No doubt, one reason for this is the fact that they were responding to a similar cultural crisis. Also, of course, they had been touched by Emerson themselves.

Collectively, these psychomythic humanists provide a unique and revealing perspective on Emerson's life and thought. Although diverse in their thinking, their works reveal four common Emersonian characteristics, each contributing to a unifying vision of reality and humanity's central place in it. First, all found through their studies of psychology (as well as religion, myth, history, art, and anthropology) that certain patterns or "archetypes" of experience and behavior appear to be universal. These archetypes were discovered in various myths, stories, tales, histories, sagas, religious accounts, songs, and rituals, as well as iconography, among widely diverse populations and civilizations over vast periods of time. Second, each of these thinkers ultimately explained the ubiquity of these archetypes by suggesting that their common source was, in one form or another, a "collective unconscious" that resides in the psyches of all people everywhere. Their studies of such archetypes revealed a great deal about human nature as expressed in philosophy, art, history, anthropology, theology, and various other disciplines. For some, these mythic archetypes and the collective unconscious, which is their ultimate source, appear as a manifestation of, and a point of contact with, a universal and divine force that resembles what Emerson called the "Over-Soul," "Reason," "Eros," "Love," and "God."

The third characteristic these thinkers have in common is that they are all, like Emerson, extremely eclectic in their thinking and frequently cross several disciplines in developing their individual studies. Despite this eclecticism, however, like Emerson's ideal scholar, they tend to center their studies on an examination of human nature itself, albeit from a variety of perspectives. By placing humankind in this central position, as both perceiver and perceived, all experience is seen as originating from and intimately related to humanity, both individually and collectively. The result is that, like Emerson and other American Transcendentalists and Romantics, they find in the apparently chaotic nature of human experience an ultimately unified and meaningful reality. Humankind's universal participation in a collective unconscious suggests the essential unity of the human family itself. Clearly, psychomythic humanism responded in many ways to the critical needs of the time, just as Emerson's Transcendentalism had a century before. The need itself was similar: to therapeutically address the strong sense of fragmentation and alienation that resulted from an acute dissatisfaction with the present failed paradigm of meaning through the rediscovery of an ultimate source of harmony deep within the collective unconscious, the universal "soul" of humanity.

The fourth and final characteristic these thinkers share with Emerson is this; they all maintain that the general malaise of the civilized world derives from an overemphasis on consciousness (Emerson called it "the Understanding"). This situation is largely the result of a pervasive rationalism associated with the relentless march of science, technology, and material culture. In turn, the emphasis on consciousness results in ne-glect, or even repression, of the unconscious dimension of the psyche, the side that unites us with ourselves, with the divine, and with the rest of the human family. The result is a pervasive sense of alienation. Because of the remarkable similarities in their understanding of the psychological structure and essential needs of human nature, and because they were re-sponding to a cultural crisis similar in its effect to that experienced by Emerson, I found that the writings of these psychomythic humanists pro-vide a unique prism through which it is possible to view the interior land-scape of Emerson's mind. Their insights also allow us to trace the path that Emerson followed in reaching the spiritual source of transcendence that became the mainstay of his intellectual life as well as his public role as prophet, seer, and reformer.

It is curious that, despite the many provocative archetypal and psy-chological insights that appear in Emerson's writings, a comprehensive study of this psychological/archetypal/spiritual aspect of Emerson, as re-flected in both his life and his works, has never been attempted. Addition-ally, despite the strong presence of the affective, emotional element in Emerson's writings, as witnessed especially in such essays and poems as "Love," "Friendship," and "Give All to Love," as well as his numerous and often passionate antislavery addresses, this important element of Emerson's work and life has been largely ignored, or even denied. A brief overview of Emerson criticism to date suggests a possible explanation for this anomaly.

Sarah Wider's far-ranging and indispensable study, *The Critical Reception of Emerson: Unsettling All Things* (2000), reveals that, for the most part, studies of Emerson over the years have focused almost exclu-sively on his intellect and his intellectual contributions. This is certainly ironic, given the emphasis throughout his writings, both early and late, on intuition and sentiment.[27] Indeed, many critics seem to preclude the possi-bility that Emerson was even capable of psychological behavior, and by that is meant behavior stimulated by anything other than intellectual sources.[28] Consequently, a vital element so necessary to any truly humanistic study (and the sine qua non of the psychomythic approach) is missing; namely, a sense of the erotic, mystical, and intuitive Emerson, the passionate poet, philosopher, and visionary who feels as well as thinks. In fact, as we shall see, it is this very quality that is the source of his most creative and striking thought. Indeed, Emerson himself maintained that, "it is a law of our nature that great thoughts come from the heart."[29] An exclusively intellectual atti-tude, of course, is antithetical to the very impulse of psychological criticism. As Carl Jung points out, "one could pursue any science with the intellect alone except psychology, whose subject—the psyche—has more than the two aspects mediated by sense perception and thinking. The function of value—feeling—is an integral part of our conscious orientation and ought not to be missing in a psychological judgment of any scope."[30] Certainly one might say the same for the study of literature and art and those who produce such. Freud issues the same warning as Jung regarding studies that focus exclusively on intellect when he observes: "We remain on the surface so long as we treat only of memories and ideas. The only valuable things in psychic life are, rather, the emotions. All psychic forces are significant only through their aptitude to arouse emotions."[31] The opportunity for a fuller understanding of Emerson, therefore, has been subverted in most critical approaches by an emphasis on intellectual argumentation and interpretations that are exclusively grounded in analytical reasoning. Ironically, it is precisely the unreasonable, spontaneous, mystical, and emotional element in romantic art that constitutes an essential aspect of its gift to humankind. As Whitman asserts unabashedly in "Song of Myself," "Do I contradict myself? / Very well then I contradict myself, / (I am large, I contain multitudes)." And Melville says of Shakespeare, ". . . it is those deep far-away things in him; those occasional flashings-forth of the intuitive truth in him, those short, quick probings at the very axis of reality:—these are the things that make Shakespeare, Shakespeare."[32] Not surprisingly, Melville "instinctively" sensed this mystical depth in Emerson, as he notes in a letter to his cousin. "Now, there is something about every man elevated above mediocrity, which is, for the most part, instinctively perceptible. This I see," he says, "in Mr. Emerson. And, frankly, for the sake of argument, let us call him a fool:—then I had rather be a fool than a wise man.—I love all men who *dive*."[33] Norman O. Brown sees this element of the mystical and unreasonable in art as essential, and he paraphrases Freud in his statement that "art provides relief from the pressures of reason."[34] Wallace Stevens, who was himself influenced by Emerson, appears to make the same point when he represents poetic beauty as, "the imagination pressing back against the pressures of reality."[35]

A psychomythic approach to Emerson that takes into account his emotional, affective, mystical, and intuitional side provides unique insights. For Emerson, emotion, sentiment, and instincts are all directly related to the divine. They are integral to our understanding of ourselves and our world. He always recognized the necessary relationship between thought and passion in human experience and understanding. As he tells us in "The Poet" (1844), "it is not metres, but a metre-making argument, that makes a poem,—a thought so passionate and alive, that, like the spirit of a plant or animal, it has an architecture of its own, and adorns nature with a new thing."[36] For Emerson, thought without passion is arid and lifeless. It is passion that informs, more than anything else, his career as poet, philosopher, and reformer. Ironically, this element has seldom been recognized in his life and works.

Emerson's monumental reputation in his lifetime had more than a little to do with his enshrinement as an intellectual idol, and his literal disembodiment as a living being. The early biographies consistently depict him as a man of "elevation, purity" and "nobility of stature;" a creature whose spirit "had missed its way on the shining path to some greater and better sphere of being."[37] One asserts that even as a child he was "a spiritual looking boy,"[38] and yet another concludes that as an adult he "certainly seemed . . . hedged about with something of saintship" and perhaps due to this he "was a self-isolated thinker, and intellectually the creature of his religious moods."[39] Indeed, Wider observes that, following the publication of Oliver Wendell Holmes' influential biography in 1884, the "subordination of life to writing and writing to idealized life continued for the next two decades, and it arguably persisted so far into the twentieth century that its influence on Emerson studies remains palpably present today." She also observes: "For all the biographies of Emerson, there is a persistently static figure in their midst."[40] Generally, the emphasis throughout these biographies is upon the thinker and not the man. Even his private journals, when first published by his son, Edward Waldo, were expurgated of personal comments not in keeping with this established intellectual image.[41]

By the mid-twentieth century things had improved but little. F. O. Matthiessen, in his classic study, *American Renaissance* (1941), found the intellectual side of Emerson appealing while discounting the mystical element almost completely. Thus, he states, that "To-day [Emerson] has been overtaken by the paradox that 'The Over-Soul' proves generally unreadable; whereas, on the level of the Understanding, which he regarded as mere appearance, his tenacious perception has left us the best intellectual history that we have of his age."[42] Similarly, one of the most detailed and reliable Emerson biographies, Ralph Rusk's *The Life of Ralph Waldo Emerson* (1949), was received by critics, with some justification, as a load of learned lumber, wherein the man Emerson is lost somewhere amongst the five hundred or so pages of "facts" with which the reader is confronted. It tends to be, as various commentators have noted, "a useful tool of scholarship" rather than a life.[43] Occasionally there have been attempts to establish the existence of a real person behind the icon. Stuart P. Sherman in his *Americans* (1922), made a gallant effort in his chapter on Emerson, titled significantly, "The Emersonian Liberation," to reacquaint the reading public with the vitality and dynamism of the young New England rebel who did so much to set American minds and hearts afire. For Sherman, Emerson is something more than a disembodied idealist and "saint." As he says, "To know him is not merely knowledge. It is an experience; for he is a dynamic personality, addressing the will, the emotions, the imagination, no less than the intellect. His value escapes the merely intellectual appraiser."[44]

More recently, Gay Wilson Allen's *Waldo Emerson* (1982) is a deliberate effort to present something of "the intimate, personal life" of the subject.[45] Robert Richardson's *Emerson: The Mind on Fire* (1995), the best biography to date, began as an effort to present an intellectual history of the man, but the author soon found that "Emerson's intellectual odyssey turned out to be incomprehensible apart from his personal and social life."[46] Indeed, John McAleer's *Days of Encounter* (1984), and Carlos Baker's *Emerson Among the Eccentrics* (published posthumously in 1996), both make an effort to render Emerson's life largely through those personal relationships. However, the influence of such relationships, especially their emotional content, on Emerson's works and thoughts is largely undeveloped.

Lastly, there are many critics who find in Emerson a distressing "dualism" or "double-consciousness," that is seen as indicative of a schism between thought and feeling, the inner and outer worlds, the ideal and the real, the proponent of self-reliance and the social reformer. Stephen Whicher's *Freedom and Fate: An Inner Life of Ralph Waldo Emerson* (1953), perhaps the most influential study of Emerson in the twentieth century, was among the first of these. As Wider notes: "Whicher divides Emerson's life in two, sharply distinguishing between the affirming vision of the 1830s . . . and the cynicism bordering skepticism emerging in the 1840s. . . . As drawn by Whicher, the intellectual life shows an unbalanced dualism."[47] According to Whicher, it was the apparent failure of idealism that resulted in a withdrawal on the part of Emerson after 1838 as the "image of the hero scholar, leading mankind to the promised land, steadily gave way to the solitary observer, unregarded and unregarding of the multitude."[48] The ideal and the real, it seems, were simply not compatible, at least according to this construct of Emerson's life.

Whicher is not the first critic to be perplexed by this combination of the "Yankee" and the "mystic" in Emerson. Frederic Carpenter, in his *Emerson Handbook* (1953), outlines clearly the history of this attitude beginning with James Russell Lowell's *A Fable for Critics* (1848), which famously describes Emerson as "A Greek head on right Yankee shoulders, whose range / Has Olympus for one pole, for t'other the Exchange." The problem here, however, resides more with the critics than with Emerson. If one allows that Emerson could both think and feel at the same time, and that feeling is actually an essential element in the Emersonian thought process, the problem vanishes. Emerson's idealism, by his own admission, is "intuitive," and thus God-connected; he speaks for what he feels is right and suggests that other people should do the same.[49] His concern with reforming his society, which persisted throughout his lifetime, was simply an attempt to implement this idealism in the "real world," to put his "creed into his deed." Whicher, however, attempts to force feeling and thought into separate categories and, hence, insists that

Emerson did too. He claims that Emerson was an inexperienced idealist when he wrote *Nature* in 1836, and a realistic empiricist when he published the essay "Experience" in 1844. He also suggests that the period 1838–1844 was a crisis period for Emerson, a time when he "turns against himself" as his naive idealism came face-to-face with the hard facts of his life experience.[50] Ironically, the record of Emerson's life shows that at the very time Whicher claims that he was in the process of withdrawing from society and forgoing his ideal of reforming America, Emerson was actually publicly protesting the removal of the Cherokees from their homeland in the south to the trans-Mississippi (1838), and undertaking what would prove to be a major commitment to the antislavery movement. Indeed, Emerson's dedication to active social reform would endure through the Civil War in keeping with his emergence as a major moral force in American society.

The concept of "dualism" persists today in critics such as John Carlos Rowe and George Kateb, as well as others, who see in Emerson's idealistic efforts at social reform a deviation from his Transcendental idealism. Rowe claims that, "Emersonian transcendentalism and Emerson's political commitments from 1844 to1863 are fundamentally at odds with each other."[51] Which is to say, that Emerson is at odds with himself. Similarly, George Kateb sees Emerson's participation in reform movements as a "deviation" from his own doctrine of self-reliance.[52] Again, if one allows for the unity of thought and feeling in Emerson such "dualism" vanishes.[53] Emerson's social reform activities, like those of other Transcendentalists, were stimulated by his intuitive grasp of "higher laws" that reside within the unconscious of every person. His efforts to implement these ideals in his society were very much in keeping with his role as hero, redeemer, and reformer.[54]

Finally, at the other end of the spectrum, Emerson has been criticized, at least occasionally, for being overly emotional. Perhaps the harshest of these critics is Yvor Winters who believed that Emerson's idealism was based on frivolous emotional impulse and, therefore, "Emerson at the core is a fraud and sentimentalist."[55] More commonly, however, Emerson was accused of the opposite sin. In the inappropriately titled *Emerson the Mythmaker* (1954), J. Russell Reaver asserts that in his poetry Emerson, "reveals his most complete reliance on intellectual appeals; his poems in image and structure stimulate the mind primarily, not the emotions."[56]

The following chapters argue that Emerson was a passionate and dynamic artist, thinker, and reformer who was able, through accessing the content of his own unconscious, to shape from his personal experience, insights, and revelations of archetypal proportions and universal social import.[57] Because of this strong, archetypal strain, Emerson anticipates, to a surprising extent, many of the insights and beliefs of the psychomythic humanists who followed a century later. Using the theories provided by this school, it is possible to come to a much deeper understanding of Emerson's works and also to explore an aspect of the man long ignored by traditional criticism, namely, his affective, intuitive, and mythic side. The genesis of this study, as noted earlier, lies in an effort to reach some understanding as to how Emerson became Emerson, and to "get at" what lies at the core of his most essential writings. It all begins with his early transformation, which was something of a mystical experience. Not surprisingly, the works of his early maturity, 1836–1844, as David Robinson points out, are characterized by a certain "visionary ecstasy" that reflects that transformation.[58] Emerson experienced these visions, not merely as the result of a sustained intellectual endeavor, but through periods of extreme emotional crisis that preceded and made possible these early major works. They are the result of a discernable process of psychological and spiritual growth and maturation through which Emerson eventually came to know and to trust what Lawrence Buell calls, "the divinity of the self, the cornerstone of Transcendentalism."[59] The dynamic personality that evolved from this experience was fortified with both the insight and the passion that allowed this once obscure figure to fulfill the role of redeemer and reformer in an alienated and generally corrupt American society. This development enabled him to bring to that society the healing forces necessary to address the essential needs of his day, that is, to fire the "artillery of sympathy and emotion," and to "celebrate the spiritual powers in their infinite contrast to the mechanical powers & the mechanical philosophy of this time."[60]

In the study that follows, chapter 1 presents a brief and general discussion of the recurring need felt by individuals and societies to "re-center" reality in order to maintain vital and responsive patterns of human experience and thought that address the particular needs of the day. Looking back to the collapse of the Renaissance worldview under the weight of the New Science in the seventeenth century, and forward to the psychomythic humanism of the twentieth century, Emerson's Transcendental philosophy is viewed in a continuum that connects Neoplatonism and the modern world.

Chapter 2 develops many of the details of this general outline, and Emerson's role as a precursor of psychomythic humanism. This chapter also presents an overview of the relevant psychological and archetypal theories articulated by this group, as represented in their most seminal writings. Particular attention is paid to concepts such as time and history, economy and religion, and language and art.

Chapter 3 presents a detailed look at Emerson's inner and outer worlds for the period 1820–1844, a time of remarkable growth and development. It was during this period that Emerson experienced his greatest personal tragedies, including the deaths of his wife, Ellen, his brothers

Charles and Edward (who were also his closest friends) and, most painful
of all, his firstborn son, Waldo. But it was also the period that witnessed his
remarriage, the evolution of his Transcendental philosophy, and his initial
emergence as a prophet and reformer. Additionally, some of his most seminal writings, such as *Nature* (1836), *Essays, First Series* (1841), and *Essays, Second Series* (1844), would be published during this period.
Emerson's journals provide the venue where he first expressed his most important and profound insights. Here we see them in their raw form as the
immediate intellectual and emotional products of his life experience.
Through a detailed analysis of these journals, and other sources, it becomes
apparent that Emerson's life came to reflect the patterned form of the hero
archetype, which is the subject of Joseph Campbell's classic study. Through
tragedy and defeat, Emerson emerges in his society as a prophet and revolutionary, a reformer and redeemer who confronts the opposition of America's "terrible fathers" in an effort to build a better world. His journals
document the details of this experience and the elements of his thought that
would ultimately find expression in his published works.

Chapter 4 demonstrates the final transformation of Emerson's life
experience into his finished art as essays, lectures, addresses, and poems.
Here the topics of time, history, art, the Hero, and the Hermaphrodite are
examined from multiple perspectives that provide insights into some of
Emerson's most complex and revealing concepts. These concepts would,
in turn, provide the groundwork for his later social engagement with an
alienated and corrupt society.

Finally, chapter 5 describes and examines Emerson's emergence as
a major public figure in America. Fortified by the transcendent vision that
his earlier personal experience provided, and assured by the clarification
and articulation of that transcendence in his earlier writings, Emerson
now fully assumes the role of public oracle, reformer, and redeemer. His
message of humankind's essential divinity, dignity, and self-worth is
brought to bear on the corruption of contemporary institutions of education, religion, business, and government that served to deny this divinity and to diminish individual self-worth. These same institutions also
limited, or in some cases denied completely, the principles of freedom,
equality, and justice that Emerson maintained are the birthright of all
people. Nowhere was this corruption more apparent than in the heinous
institution of slavery. Ultimately, Emerson would wage, for two decades
of his public life, a hard-fought and finally successful crusade against this
evil. This struggle would touch every facet of his existence and influence
virtually all of his later writings and lectures. Several of the latter are
examined here for the first time.

Overall, this study will present an answer to the question posed earlier as to how a middle-class preacher of modest ability transformed him-

self into the nineteenth century's greatest prophet and reformer, the acknowledged genius of his age.[61] This journey will lead, ultimately, to the spiritual, mystical, and intellectual roots of Emersonian transcendence and the movement that he inspired, a movement that would have a profound effect on the transformation of American society in the nineteenth century. The reverberations of this movement continue to be felt today. While presenting an overview of Emerson's mature life and works, the style of this narrative will necessarily be circular as well as linear. (Emerson would call it a "spiral.") The reason for this is that Emerson's thought, while diverse, was also, ultimately, unified and harmonious. The experience of reality for him was holistic, with each element reflecting the other. As he says in his "American Scholar" address, "Nature is the opposite of the soul, answering to it part for part. One is seal, and one is print."[62] Because of this, the essential patterns or archetypes that inform his major writings appear again and again, throughout his journals first, and then in the works themselves. In speaking of them, therefore, we shall emulate this circularity ourselves. As a result, there will be an inevitable (but hopefully revealing) overlap between chapters 3 and 4.

I must also say something about terminology. One of the unique difficulties in a study such as this is that the terminology, as well as the psychological schema employed by Emerson and the psychomythic humanists, may appear to a contemporary reader to be overtly sexist. One example is Emerson's frequent use of the term "man" to represent all of humanity, a common practice in his day. There is also his tendency, shared by the psychomythic humanists who followed, to identify the conscious, the domain of reason and logic, as "masculine," while the unconscious, the domain of emotion and feeling, is identified as "feminine." Additionally, it may seem somewhat anomalous that, in an effort to establish psychological and cultural unity, all of these thinkers appear to bifurcate the psyche into masculine/feminine, conscious/unconscious polarities, thus seemingly contributing to the very oppositional thinking that they sought to defeat. Furthermore, in this division, masculine consciousness appears to be dominant and, therefore, preferred. In response to these legitimate concerns, I would first of all point out that whenever possible I have used gender neutral constructs. Nevertheless, it was often necessary for me to use the terminology employed by my sources for clarity and consistency. Furthermore, it should be noted that the terms "masculine" and "feminine" were used by the psychomythic humanists and Emerson primarily to represent specific psychological qualities that exist simultaneously in both sexes. Therefore, the terms should not be equated with the biological gender designations "male" and "female." Also, as we shall see in the chapters that follow, the "divided state" of the psyche was understood as a chronic and parlous condition by both Emerson and the psychomythic humanists. Their goal was to establish a unified psyche that combined both feminine and masculine, unconscious and conscious elements in a dynamic and healthy balance.

Finally, I have attempted to allow the principals here to speak for themselves, as much as possible. My reason for doing so is simple. When Robert Frost was once asked to explain the meaning of "Mending Wall," he replied, "What do you want me to do, say it again in different and less good words?"

CHAPTER 1

PSYCHOMYTHIC HUMANISM
Re-centering Reality

"The eye is the first circle."

—R. W. Emerson, "*Circles*"

With humanity emerging from the devastation of World War II and facing the challenges of a reality increasingly under the threat of nuclear annihilation, the second half of the twentieth century was a time of both hope and fear. During this period, as the fragments of Western civilization were gradually being reorganized into a new political world order, a number of important and diverse studies appeared that were strongly influenced by the psychological theories of Carl Jung and Sigmund Freud. These works tended to be intellectually eclectic, and far-reaching in scope. Drawing from a wide spectrum of psychological, mythological, philosophical, anthropological, historical, and aesthetic disciplines, these studies sought to present, in the context of vast social fragmentation, a unified and coherent vision of human experience on both an individual and social level. In essence, they sought to rediscover, in T. S. Eliot's words, "a still point in the turning world," a meaningful center of human identity. The key to this identity resided, for the most part, in the inner, unconscious realm of the human psyche. In their writings, these "psychomythic humanists" recapitulated, in remarkably similar ways, the unifying thrust of Emerson's mature Transcendentalism, which sought to answer a similar need in a similar fashion a century before. Among these studies are: Erich Neumann's *The Origins and History of Consciousness* (1949); Joseph Campbell's *The Hero with a Thousand Faces* (1949); Mircea Eliade's, *The Myth of the Eternal Return: or Cosmos and History* (1949); and Norman O. Brown's *Life Against Death* (1959), and *Love's Body* (1966). In the search for unity, all of these works basically attempt to identify and define those primal and universal patterns, commonly known as "archetypes," that manifest themselves in various aspects of human experience. In his study, Neumann invokes Jung's classic definition of the term as "the pictorial forms of the instincts," the means through which "the unconscious reveals itself to the conscious mind in images which, as in dreams and fantasies, initiate the process of conscious reaction and assimilation."[1] Brown offers a more casual definition. "Freud's myth of the rebellion of the sons against the father in the primal, prehistoric horde," he states, "is not a historical explanation of the origins, but a supra-historical archetype; eternally recurrent; a myth; an old, old story."[2]

These works also deal, in one way or another, with some version of what Jung called the "collective unconscious," which is the source of all archetypes. It is a psychological dynamic, below the level of consciousness, that is common to all human beings everywhere. Jung defines this concept as follows: "Just as the human body shows a common anatomy over and above all racial differences, so too, the psyche possesses a common substratum transcending all differences in culture and consciousness. I have called this substratum the collective unconscious."[3] In his "Foreword" to Neumann's study, Jung indicates clearly that it is a welcome extension of his own seminal work and that, "It begins where I, too, if I were granted a second lease of life, would start to gather up the *disjecta membra* of my own writings, to sift out all those 'beginnings without continuations' and knead them into a whole."[4] In essence, Neumann's work presents a comprehensive application of Jung's seminal theories to the development of individual as well as collective consciousness. This universal pattern of development is itself a major archetype.

While he does not cite either Jung or Freud, Eliade's study is also concerned with mythic, universal patterns, "what we have called 'archetypes and repetition,'" through which "archaic societies" seek to destroy "autonomous history" or the conscious progress of time.[5] It is primarily a study in anthropology and comparative religion, the implications of which have universal significance concerning humanity's effort to find its place in the cosmos.

Brown's *Life Against Death* is subtitled "The Psychoanalytic Meaning of History" and, like the others, has a very broad, even mythic sweep. While relying primarily on Freudian theory, Brown expands that theory to examine the historical evolution of human experience and to look towards its future. As he notes, his study is "concerned with reshaping psychoanalysis into a wider general theory of human nature, culture, and history, to be appropriated by the consciousness of mankind as a whole as a new stage in the historical process of man's coming to know himself."[6] Because of the broad dimensions of his study and its stated goal, it is not surprising that in his work Brown appropriates an important element of Jung's thought that is central to the present study, namely, the concept of the collective unconscious. Thus, he states, "the repressed unconscious which produces neuroses is not an individual unconscious but a collective one. Freud abstains from adopting Jung's term but says 'the content of the unconscious is collective anyhow.'"[7] Additionally, like the other theorists represented here, Brown also holds that individual human experience is similar to collective human experience, and that all people are in essence one in this regard. Thus, in Brown's view, the entire history of humankind is recapitulated, psychologically, in the life of a single individual. He quotes from Freud the fundamental thesis that in the few years of childhood, "we have to cover the enormous distance of development from primitive man of the Stone Age to civilized man today" or, to put it more technically, "ontogeny recapitulates phylogeny."[8] Brown's argument combines psychoanalysis, anthropology, and history. *Love's Body* is a highly creative continuation of the voyage begun in *Life Against Death*.

Joseph Campbell's classic work appropriates the insights of both Freud and Jung. *The Hero With a Thousand Faces* deals with a multitude of "Oriental and Occidental, modern, ancient, and primitive traditions" and materials, and, like the other works involved here, argues for the universality of human experience over time. As he notes: "Freud, Jung and their followers have demonstrated irrefutably that the logic, the heroes, and the deeds of myth survive into modern times."[9] These are manifested repeatedly in the diverse sources that Campbell utilizes in his study. However, diversity is not his subject, but just the opposite. "There are of course differences between the numerous mythologies and religions of mankind," Campbell observes, "but this is a book about the similarities."[10] In his study, Campbell describes a common, innate desire on the part of humanity, both individually and collectively, to periodically challenge the staid controls of the rationalistic conscious mind—the world of reason, law, and tradition that has become oppressive and dysfunctional—and to return to the instinctive, emotional wellsprings of psychic vitality that exist in the deep unconscious. This return is subsequently followed by a rebirth into the world of a "new Adam," a regenerated individual in whom head and heart, conscious and unconscious, are unified. For Campbell, this "monomythic" cycle of "separation, initiation, and return" appears both historically and mythically as the adventure of the hero and is a major archetype of individual psychological development. The hero becomes a rebel to the status quo, the established order of things, and manifests himself in historical time when the established world of reason and law, the current cultural paradigm, is no longer capable of satisfying the vital needs of humankind. "The familiar life horizon has been outgrown; the old concepts, ideals, and emotional patterns no longer fit; the time for the passing of a threshold is at hand."[11]

Appearing as they did in the mid-twentieth century, all of these works represent a concerted effort to respond to the critical needs of that time, a period of fragmentation, alienation, conflict, and anxiety. Following the devastation of two world wars, and now locked into a Cold War with two superpowers facing one another with enough nuclear weaponry to annihilate civilization itself, the world seemed to be poised on the edge of destruction. The times were out of joint; the old paradigm of meaning had failed; the center would not hold, and the world was threatening to spin out of control. Jung, who provided so much of the theory later utilized by the psychomythic humanists considered here, anticipated such a crisis at the end of World War I. Writing in 1918, he remarks on a new and pressing interest among intellectuals in understanding the human psyche. "This interest may be due," he suggests, "in no small measure to the profound shock which our consciousness sustained through the World War. The spectacle of this catastrophe threw man back upon himself by making him feel his complete impotence; it turned his gaze inwards, and, with everything rocking about him, he must needs seek something that guarantees him a hold."[12] Jung believed that the unconscious, the source of primal unity and a common human identity, held the key that could solve the problems of modernity.

Unfortunately, by mid-century, in the aftermath of yet another world war, the situation had only gotten worse. Humankind seemed even less capable of communicating with the inner self as consciousness continued to evolve and dominate. The inward gaze that Jung spoke of was difficult to achieve when any connection between the inner and outer worlds was generally ignored or even denied. All of these humanistic thinkers understood this. Writing thirty years after Jung, Joseph Campbell observed: "The problem of mankind today" is that "one does not know towards what one moves. One does not know by what one is propelled. The lines of communication between the conscious and unconscious zones of the human psyche have all been cut, and we have been split in two."[13] Formal religion, once the mainstay of human meaning, had become for Campbell what it was for Emerson, an empty shell. It had lost the element of spirit and mystery that is available only to the intuition and the imagination. Without these, religious worship was only a dusty and lifeless ritual. "The universal triumph of the secular state," Campbell insists, "has thrown all religious organizations into such a definitely secondary, and finally ineffectual, position that religious pantomime is hardly more today than a sanctimonious exercise for Sunday morning, whereas business ethics and patriotism stand for the remainder of the week. Such monkey holiness is not what the functioning world requires. . . ."[14]

Erich Neumann offered a similar perception of modern fragmentation whereby individuals no longer see themselves as part of the larger human family. "In the course of Western development," he states, "the essentially positive process of emancipating the ego and consciousness from the tyranny of the unconscious has become negative. It has gone far beyond the division of conscious and unconscious into two systems and has brought about a schism between them; and, just as differentiation and specialization have degenerated into overspecialization, so this development has gone beyond the formation of individual personality and given rise to an atomized individualism."[15] The result is acute alienation, paranoia, and a threatened descent into meaninglessness.

Eliade also saw the transpersonal or "transhistorical" element, which is an important aspect of the unconscious, as essential if one was to find significance and meaning in life. Indeed, its absence was one of the greatest failings of the time. "In our day," he writes in his chapter on the "Terrors of History," "when historical pressure no longer allows any escape, how can man tolerate the catastrophes and horrors of history—from collective deportations and massacres to atomic bombings—if beyond them he can glimpse no sign, no transhistorical meaning; if they are only the blind play of economic, social, or political forces?"[16]

Writing ten years after Eliade, Brown saw no improvement. In fact, the situation was dramatically worse. Jung's hoped-for inward gaze had been overridden by a conscious blindness. "When our eyes are opened," Brown writes, "and the fig leaf no longer conceals our nakedness, our present situation is experienced in its full concrete actuality as a tragic crisis. . . . Freud was right in positing a death instinct, and the development of weapons of destruction makes our present dilemma plain: we either come to terms with our unconscious instincts and drives—with life and with death—or else we surely die."[17] The times seemed perilous, indeed, and many undoubtedly wondered, "What rough beast, its hour come round at last" would finally precipitate the end of everything.[18] In response to this distressing fragmentation and pervasive alienation, psychomythic humanists sought to find unity within apparent diversity. Essentially, their goal was to recover humanity's common soul. This helps to explain the extremely eclectic nature of their writings, and also their consistent efforts to reopen lines of communication with the collective unconscious, the psychic inner self common to all humankind.

Placed in a larger historical context, the efforts of psychomythic humanism to bring harmony out of chaos can be seen as a natural response to a process of increasing fragmentation that dates back at least as far as the rise of the "New Science" in the late sixteenth and early seventeenth centuries. As psychologist Jeffrey C. Miller has recently noted, since "the scientific Revolution of Copernicus, Kepler, Galileo, and Newton, the Philosophical Revolution of Bacon and Descartes, and into the Industrial Revolution and the modern age, Western consciousness has moved seemingly single-mindedly towards what may be expressed in the Cartesian *cogito* [ergo sum]—'I think, therefore I am.'" The result of this development in

Western culture has been an inordinate and unnatural emphasis on consciousness at the expense of the affective, unconscious element of the psyche. Our "progress," it seems, has been dearly bought. As a result of constant ego development, notes Miller, modern humankind has suffered "a disunion with the undifferentiated consciousness that previously connected people; an amnesia regarding '*participation mystique*' with the natural world; a repudiation of the *anima mundi*, the soul of the world, that created the fabric of community, and a devaluation of unprovable and unscientific concepts like intuition, unknowing, fantasy, imagination, dreams, and emotions."[19] Clearly, the fragmentation and alienation that many experience today, as in the past, derives from an overemphasis on consciousness, the function of which is to divide, separate, and thus manage reality using a largely binary strategy. This function is especially pervasive in a world dominated by science and technology. As Miller goes on to observe, "The scientific attitude reflects the tendency in human consciousness to split and hold things in a dualistic, either/or way; we create mutually exclusive categories (such as mind/body, spirit/matter, fact/idea, subjective/objective, interior/exterior, self/other, etc.) and organize things by forcing them into one or the other." This inclination, Miller suggests, "profoundly affects how we view the world: we are immersed in the Cartesian assumption that all reality consists of an observing subject separated from the world outside."[20] As we shall see, Emerson was well aware of the deleterious effect of this tendency of consciousness to divide and fragment human experience during his own time. He once observed, "if the mind live only in particulars, and see only differences (wanting the power to see the whole—all in each), then the world addresses to this mind a question it cannot answer, and each new fact tears it in pieces, and it is vanquished by the distracting variety."[21] Laura Dassow Walls indicates in her comprehensive study of Emerson and antebellum science, that scientific, social, and economic developments in the first half of the nineteenth century led to a felt need for a "rock of principle [that] would hold against the corrosive river of mechanism, materialism, sensualism, [and] skepticism." She notes further "how urgently Emerson needed to erect and defend a center that would hold all together at a historical moment when everything seemed on the verge of flying apart."[22] Like the psychomythic humanists who would follow in his footsteps a century later, Emerson would spend his career responding to this need.

The deliberately empirical and largely binary approach to human experience is exacerbated by the tendency in the modern period to divide the study of humanity into specific disciplines which are, for the most part, mutually exclusive. Campbell refers to this as "overspecialization." While this approach has rendered a certain amount of insight and understanding, it has tended to further fragment human experience into potentially meaningless and contradictory particles. When one separates basic human activities and concerns into exclusive psychological, social, aesthetic, religious, scientific, economic, and historical categories, and then subdivides again and again within these categories, the ultimate unity of these important elements of human experience is lost. Emerson was acutely aware of the potentially pernicious effect of such a division. As he notes in the "American Scholar" address, in the face of such fragmentation it becomes necessary to "take the whole society to find the whole man. . . . [T]he individual to possess himself, must sometimes return from his own labor to embrace all the other laborers." Unfortunately, this is often nearly impossible to do because "the original unit, this fountain of power, has been so distributed to multitudes, has been so minutely subdivided and peddled out, that it spilled into drops, and cannot be gathered."[23] Functioning largely in the void of cold intellectualism and discrete, rational investigation, human experience tends to lose its humaneness. As Jung would observe, the continuing emphasis on consciousness and specialization, and the resulting loss of wholeness (and with it any notion of transcendent or universal meaning), has had a catastrophic effect on modern humanity. Reflecting on the generally distressing condition of modern, intellectual, and egocentric civilization in the first half of the twentieth century, he maintains that dreams often become nightmares when science is divorced from human empathy. He notes, for example, that "For ages man has dreamed of flying, and all we have got for it is saturation bombing!"[24] This ironic conversion of dream into nightmare where humanity is abused by its own creations resembles Thoreau's observation in *Walden*: "We don't ride the railroad. The railroad rides on us," and Emerson's warning to the young graduates of Harvard regarding the dangers of a "vulgar prosperity that retrogrades ever to barbarism."[25]

As we shall see more fully in chapter 2, while the eclectic nature of their writings implies a certain unity in the reality that humankind perceives, psychomythic humanists also tend to locate the source of such unity in the perceiver. Often this unifying element, the ultimate source of which is the unconscious, possesses a transcendent, religious quality, as it did for Emerson. Jeffrey Steele, for example, in speaking of both Jung and Emerson, asserts that "the unconscious or the Over-Soul are both myths—fictions created to orient individual being as the expression of a transcendent source." He goes on to assert that "Responding in similar ways to their respective senses of cultural crises, of decaying religious sensibility, both Emerson and Jung develop psychologies aimed at restoring faith." He explains further that "Like Jung, Emerson nourishes the vision of divinity buried in the heart of the psyche. He engages in psychological mythmaking, founded upon the development of depth psychology as substitute religion."[26] Indeed, the assertion that every person's being shares in a "collective unconscious," which is imbued with certain characteristic potentials,

energies, and desires common to all people, is not that far removed from
the religious notion that every person has a soul, a connecting link to the
eternal One. This soul is an immaterial and abstract entity that, despite its
incorporeality, is nevertheless "real." Because of its connection to divinity,
it has historically served as a key indicator of human dignity, self-worth,
and even immortality. At times, Jung suggests a specific correlation between the unconscious and the concept of the transcendent soul. "Bodies
die," he notes, "but can something invisible and incorporeal disappear?
What is more, life and psyche have existed for me before I could say 'I,' and
when this 'I' disappears as in sleep or unconsciousness, life and psyche still
go on, as our observation of other people and our own dreams inform us.
Why should the simple mind deny, in the face of such experiences, that the
'soul' lives in a realm beyond the body."[27]

Such quasi-religious statements clearly point to the "mystical quality" of the unconscious and have suggested to many Jungian scholars that
"the unconscious has a kind of divine quality, one that affects us in an
unexplainable and numinous way."[28] Since the unconscious is "collective," and transpersonal, it is the ultimate source of human connectedness, equality, and oneness with the world. For Emerson, this is the
essence of the "Over-Soul." He defines this important entity as, "that
Unity, that Over-Soul, within which every man's particular being is contained and made one with all other." It is our "common heart." As such,
it is the source of harmony and unity in life. "We live in succession," he
states, "in division, in parts, in particular. Meantime within man is the
soul of the whole; the wise silence; the universal beauty, to which every
part and particle is equally related; the eternal One." By accessing the
power of the Over-Soul (unconscious), the binary disjunction of subject-
object that Jeffrey Miller speaks of is overcome for both Emersonian
Transcendentalists and psychomythic humanists. "And this deep power
in which we exist, and whose beatitude is all accessible to us, is not only
self-sufficing and perfect in every hour, but the act of seeing, and the
thing seen, the seer and the spectacle, the subject and the object, are one.
We see the world piece by piece," says Emerson, "as the sun, the moon,
the animal, the tree; but the whole, of which these are the shining parts,
is the soul."[29] In chapter 5, we shall see that as a social reformer Emerson
understood this universal and divine force to be the power behind the
"self-evident" truth that "all men are created equal," as asserted in the
Declaration of Independence.

While the continued development of ego-consciousness (i.e., consciousness separated from the unconscious and dominated by rational
and logical functions) has become especially problematical in the modern
period, the felt need to displace the current cultural construct with something more satisfying is actually a largely cyclical phenomenon. It resembles the situation in Campbell's "monomyth" where the hero casts off the

strictures and beliefs of the ruling paradigm, which is failing, in order to begin the world anew. These moments come about historically because inevitably, all established systems of meaning atrophy and eventually fail to meet the emotional, spiritual, and political needs of the time. Such times require a new source of faith and meaning, one that satisfies the emotions as well as the intellect. At such critical moments, resistance to change on the part of the authority figures representing the status quo, "the fathers," inevitably precipitates revolutionary resistance and conflict.[30] One such period of dramatic cultural change was the Renaissance. Otto Rank observes that "in the Renaissance a new European personal consciousness arose that towered above religious and national boundaries and established a world reign of humanism that could vie with collective Christianity."[31] This new humanism often took the form of a revolt against the arid intellectualism of traditional scholastics and the methods of science as then known. For some, literature was seen as an alternative and superior source of knowledge of humankind and the world. As Thomas Kuhn points out, in the Renaissance: "The humanists themselves were often bitterly opposed to Aristotle, the scholastics, and the entire tradition of university learning. Their sources were the newly recovered literary classics, and like literary men in other ages, many of them rejected the scientific enterprise as a whole."[32] Renaissance thinkers also developed a strong interest in Plato and the mystical aspects of Neoplatonism as an alternative to the rationalistic philosophy of Aristotle.[33]

The psychomythic humanists of the twentieth century, like their Renaissance forbearers, also tended to ignore the formal limitations of traditional disciplines. Indeed, as noted earlier, they combine and recombine the interests of many fields in their effort to articulate a new, unified vision of humanity as possessing both intellect and feeling, reason and imagination, logic and intuition, body and soul. As was also the case in the Renaissance, this new view is consistently homocentric and humanistic. Humanity is to them what it was to Milton's God at creation: "The Master work, the end of all yet done."[34] Also like their Renaissance forbearers, their works have a distinctly mythic and highly creative literary quality that has the effect, whether intentional or not, of bridging the gap between art and science.[35] Finally, for most of them, as for Emerson, Neoplatonism was a significant influence.

The central position of humankind in the cosmos is clearly indicated in Erich Neumann's assertion that, "The integration of the personality is equivalent to an integration of the world. Just as an uncentered psyche which is dispersed in participations sees only a diffuse and chaotic world, so the world constellates itself in a hierarchical order about an integrated personality. The correspondence between one's view of the world and the formation of personality extends from the lowest level to the highest."[36] The integration that Neumann refers to here is that of the

conscious and the unconscious and the result is a satisfying balance and a
personal sense of harmony and well being. The resulting paradigm bears
a striking resemblance to the Ptolemaic system of the universe that was
popular throughout the Renaissance.[37] It is reflected in the "Elizabethan
worldview" that is described by E. M. W. Tillyard in his classic study by
that name. "The ordinary educated Elizabethan," he observes, "thought
of the universe as geocentric." While opinion varied on the precise constitution of the created universe (the number of concentric spheres that
composed it could be anywhere from nine to eleven), "no one doubted
that round a central earth revolved with differing motions spheres of di-
ameters ever increasing." These extended from the nearest, that of the
moon, to the farthest, that of the *primum mobile*.[38] This paradigm of
centrality imbued humanity in the Renaissance with a sense of cosmic importance that led, in turn, to great creativity. "Not only did Man, as man,
live with uncommon intensity at that time, but he was never removed
from his cosmic setting," according to Tillyard. This "cosmic setting" extended inward as well as outward. Agnes Heller describes as a "common
theme of the Renaissance, the theory of the parallelism of microcosm and
macrocosm." According to this theory: "If the whole of reality—the universe—is infinite and universal, then man (the microcosm) must also be
infinite and universal, and so—inseparably he must be capable of knowing the infinite and universal. And since experience shows that the body
is neither infinite nor universal, there must be in man 'something' of the
infinite and the universal. The mirror cannot differ from that which the
mirror reflects."[39] "It is the combination of these two facts," notes Tillyard, "that gives to Elizabethan humanism its great force."[40] A similar
process of cosmic re-centering would have a similar effect during the
American Renaissance.

As noted earlier, for the psychomythic humanists, the Renaissance
doctrine of the immortality of the soul became in the twentieth century
not only a religious belief, but also a psychological and philosophical concept. By loosening the repressive and stringent controls of intellectual ego-
consciousness, the primary function of which is to separate and limit, the
individual is able to establish a harmonious relationship with the expansive and unifying unconscious and, in this way, effectively transcend the
often distressing fragmentation of daily life. Perception becomes transparent, and one lives in an eternal present. Joseph Campbell explains the phenomenon. "The research for *physical* immortality proceeds from a
misunderstanding of the traditional teaching. On the contrary, the basic
problem is: to enlarge the pupil of the eye, so that *body* with its attendant
personality [ego] will no longer obstruct the view. Immortality is then experienced as a present fact: 'It is here! It is here!'"[41] The notion of centrality and the transcendent quality of the present is reflected throughout the

writings of the American Transcendentalists. It is clearly indicated, for example, in Thoreau's famous dictum that "God himself culminates in the present moment," and Emerson's assertion that "a true man belongs to no other time or place, but is the centre of things."[42] His most comprehensive treatment of this archetype is, of course, the classic essay, "Circles." The opening statement in this piece anticipates Campbell's behest to "enlarge the pupil of the eye" in order to overcome the limitations of mere ego-consciousness. "The eye is the first circle;" observes Emerson, "the horizon which it forms is the second; and throughout nature this primary figure is repeated without end."[43] Obviously, this enlarged perception places humans, individually and collectively, in the center of the cosmos, where Emerson and the psychomythic humanists believe we belong.

Even the Renaissance ideal of humankind's ultimate regeneration and return to a paradisial state of innocence and pleasure, represented frequently in the plastic arts and literature as the myth of Adam in the Garden, becomes for the psychomythic humanists the goal of both a psychological and spiritual redemption. Norman O. Brown insists that this innocence lies within the grasp of every individual in the deep unconscious, if that individual would but allow its influence. For Brown, the sense of primal and "original" sin must be denied and instead we should "cling to the position that Adam never really fell; that the children do not really inherit the sins of their fathers; [and] that the primal crime is an infantile fantasy, created out of nothing by the infantile ego in order to sequester by repression its own unmanageable vitality (id)."[44] In other words, "sin" is a construct of consciousness, employed to control the expansive unconscious. Releasing the unconscious and its divine force from this repression results in renewal, regeneration, and salvation. Emerson held a similar view. Barbara Packer has observed that, in such seminal works as *Nature* (1836), and the essays "Circles" (1841), and "Experience" (1844) Emerson "rejects the notion that what we call the Fall of Man has anything to do with sin or disobedience." She insists that, for Emerson, these notions are "a consequence of 'self-distrust,' the self's ignorance or denial of its own divinity."[45] Also, just as Brown asserts the need to return to the Garden, Emerson notes in his journals in 1839, that his goal as a lecturer is to become "Adam in the garden, I am to new name all the beasts in the field & all the gods in the Sky. I am to invite men drenched in time to recover themselves & come out of time, & taste their native immortal air."[46] For Emerson, timelessness is characteristic of the unfallen state, which can be recovered by reestablishing our connection with the Over-Soul / unconscious. Indeed, Emerson's grasp of the transcendent nature of the Over-Soul, leads him to insist, along with Eliade, that "there is no profane history; that all history is sacred; that the universe is represented in an atom, in a moment in time."[47]

Such comparisons suggest that there is a broad psychological, spiritual, and historical cycle at work here that unites Emerson, himself an enormously eclectic thinker, with these latter day psychomythic humanists, as well as their Neoplatonic and Renaissance forbearers in an historical and cultural continuum. This cycle involves a process of fragmentation of an old system (a construct of consciousness), followed by the establishment of a new system that offers a satisfying and necessary re-centering of reality. A brief historical overview of this process can help to clarify some aspects of our argument here.

Milton, who was one of Emerson's favorite writers and thinkers, attempted in his religious epic *Paradise Lost* (1667) to re-center the world of human experience and thought following the fragmentation that resulted from the influence of the New Science that arose in the first half of the seventeenth century. This development is reflected largely in the works of Copernicus (1473–1543), Galileo (1564–1642), Bacon (1561–1656), and Descartes (1596–1650).[48] Through the efforts of these four thinkers, as well as other lesser lights, the central harmony of the Elizabethan world picture that had prevailed throughout the Renaissance was fractured. The homocentric Ptolemaic system at the heart of this worldview gave way cataclysmically to a scientifically confirmed heliocentric system. Thoughtful people were shocked to discover humankind suddenly displaced from the center of all creation and now occupying, diminutively, the third planet from the newly central sun.[49] It is true that Copernicus had postulated a heliocentric system in his *De Revolutionibus Orbium Coelestium* [On the Revolutions of the Heavenly Spheres] decades earlier in 1543, but the treatise was complex, and only an elite group of specialists were capable of understanding its significance. Galileo, however, was able to confirm Copernicus' findings through the use of a telescope and published his results in 1610 in the dramatically titled, *Nuncius Sidereus* [Message from the Stars]. It now seemed, in this new age of discovery, that there was a "new America in the skys," and a new world to be contemplated as the old one died away.[50] Galileo's work had an immediate impact since it could be comprehended by the intelligentsia everywhere. As Thomas Kuhn notes, "The unique role of the telescope was providing generally accessible and nonmathematical documentation for the Copernican point of view."[51] The old system was now questionable, but traditionalists clung to it nevertheless. In reaction to the threat to stability posed by these new findings, Galileo was subsequently condemned to life imprisonment for "vehement suspicion of heresy," but the sentence was eventually commuted to house arrest.[52] Not surprisingly, the faith of the fathers was resistant to change. John Donne, the greatest of the English Metaphysical poets, expressed the disturbing consequences of this unanticipated development in his famous, "First Anniversary: An Anatomie of the World" (1610).

The new Philosophy calls all in doubt,
The Element of fire is quite put out;
The Sun is lost, and th'earth, and no man's wit
Can well direct him where to looke for it.
And freely men confesse that this world's spent,
When in the Planets, and the Firmament
They seeke so many new; they see that this
Is crumbled out againe to his Atomis.
'Tis all in peeces, all cohaerence gone;

                                                  (205–213)

Toward the end of the century, John Milton was to reassert the centrality of humankind and humankind's God. In *Paradise Lost* (1667), arguably the greatest epic in the English language, Milton returned to time *ab origne*, with Adam in his Garden in an as yet unfallen world. Though Milton well knew in 1667 that the Ptolemaic/Heliocentric controversy had long been settled in favor of the latter, he nevertheless employed the former for the creation scenes, and throughout his epic.[53] Centrality was simply more satisfying. What had been lost to science would be recovered by a symbolic act of creation in a work of art. Literature would salve the wounds inflicted by science in an effort to restore meaning to a badly fragmented world.

Milton's epic work would be virtually the last significant manifestation of the Renaissance worldview, and a more scientific solution to the problem of unifying the cosmos would come only a generation after the publication of his epic in the form of Isaac Newton's (1642–1727) remarkable *Principia Mathematica* (1687). This work, proclaiming the universal presence of gravity as the cohesive force that literally held the universe together, came as a welcome development to a culture hungry for certainty. Newton's famous "Laws of Motion" provided what might be called a scientifically accurate "poetry of reassurance" as darkness and uncertainty gave way to the Age of Enlightenment. The universal force of gravity became a metaphor for cosmic harmony that extended into every aspect of human existence, even religion. As Laura Dassow Walls reports: "One of Emerson's favorite authors, the Neoplatonist natural philosopher and clergyman Ralph Cudworth, had helped Newton develop the theological implications of his natural system. In *The True Intellectual System of the Universe*, Cudworth attempted to destroy atheism by showing that matter is nothing but a collection of passive, inert atoms, making mind the necessary creative force of the universe."[54] That mind now perceived unity everywhere. Kenneth Walter Cameron reports Emerson once commented that Cudworth's work "encouraged his self-reliance by pointing out in the works of old philosophers [mainly Neoplatonists] exact parallels to his own thoughts, and thereby convinced him that truth was accessible to him in the present as it had been to others in the past."[55] Vivian Hopkins also affirms Cudworth as an important source and notes that "the Neoplatonists . . . especially Plotinus, had a strong and decisive influence on Emerson's thought."[56] Later, we shall examine Cudworth's influence on Emerson's effort at psychological and spiritual cosmogony in greater detail.

John Locke's (1632–1704), *Essay Concerning Human Understanding* (1687) appeared as the philosophical and psychological help mate to Newton's science. It seemed to confirm the role of empirical reasoning as the only sure way to truth and certainty. Jean Jacques Rousseau (1712–1778) and Voltaire (1694–1778) would also contribute to an eighteenth century that would be characterized by a strong emphasis on reason and not traditional faith. Empiricism would dominate throughout the Enlightenment as rules, laws, and formal structures were observed everywhere—even in the arts (neoclassicism) and religion (Deism). Thus, Walls notes that "the new laws of science struck down the tyranny of the past and put man in an 'original' relation with the universe by showing that the creative mind, whether human or divine, was one and the same thing."[57] Basil Willey describes the results of these developments;

> [The] phase of religious thought with which the term "Deism" is often associated was rendered possible largely by the completeness with which the findings of seventeenth-century science, up to that date, could be made to fuse with the inherited religious certainties. Newton's Great Machine needed a Mechanic, and religion was prepared ahead with that which could serve this purpose. Everywhere what science had so far disclosed was nothing but "order, harmony, and beauty"; and finally the incomparable Newton had linked the infinitely great and the infinitely little in one inspired synthesis. The mighty maze [of the universe] was not without a plan, and Locke could declare with perfect candour that "the works of nature in every part of them sufficiently evidence a Deity."[58]

The new paradigm brought forth by the Enlightenment was harmonious and reassuring. It remained satisfactory throughout the eighteenth century. Eventually, however, a reaction would set in against the perceived aridity and tyranny of its relentless emphasis on reason, and a neoclassical aesthetic that insisted on imitation of the masters and following established "rules," rather than exercising original creativity.[59] The "God" of the Enlightenment eventually came to be seen as largely the product of thought, not feeling or spirit. Clearly, this once satisfying paradigm was wearing out. As a result, a "Romantic Revolution" emerged, beginning in the late eighteenth century in Europe. This new movement eventually spread to America in the first half of the nineteenth century.[60] Emerson, of course, would be an important player in this movement. Casting off Lockean empiricism and neoclassical restraints, romantics sought to revitalize the world, and to become, once again, like Adam in the Garden, beginning the world anew.[61] This Romantic Movement, and its philosophical/religious counterpart, Transcendentalism, provided the basis for a rebirth of literary life in America, aptly named the "American Renaissance" by F. O. Matthiessen in his classic study by that name. This movement sought, like the intellectual and cultural models discussed earlier, to re-center reality humanistically by casting off the staid restraints of an effete cultural ego-consciousness.[62]

Eventually, Romanticism and Transcendentalism would themselves give way in the second half of the nineteenth century to a process of fragmentation that began with the publication of Darwin's *Origin of Species* (1859). The impact of Darwin's work was appropriately compared by one turn-of-the-century historian to that of Copernicus and Galileo through which "the world was dethroned from its supposed central position in the universe."[63] This process was accelerated by other forces including rapid industrialization, and various economic, scientific, social, and cultural developments that would impact Western culture and consciousness generally. In the United States, the horrors of the Civil War (1861–1865) would substantially erode the humanistic idealism and optimism generally associated with the Romantic and Transcendental movements. By the end of the nineteenth century, Henry Adams offered a compelling expression of the results of this ongoing process of destabilization in his classic, *The Education of Henry Adams* (1908, 1918). In this quasi-spiritual autobiography, written appropriately by a man who was by profession a historian and by avocation a writer, the protagonist looks out upon a world lurching toward chaos. Scientific discoveries had revealed new worlds of force previously unknown. As the old paradigm fragmented, some scientists, reports Adams, seemed prepared for anything, "even for an indeterminable number of universes interfused," which for Adams amounted to "physics stark mad in metaphysics." The effects of such disturbing developments on modern consciousness were distressing. By the year 1905, Adams observes,

> Power seemed to have outgrown its servitude and to have asserted its freedom. The cylinder had exploded, and thrown great masses of stone and steam against the sky. The city had the air and movement of hysteria, and the citizens were crying, in every accent of anger and alarm, that the new forces must at any cost be brought under control. Prosperity never before imagined, power never yet wielded by man, speed never reached by anything but a meteor, had made the world irritable, nervous, querulous, unreasonable, and afraid.[64]

The Western world was once again lurching towards cataclysmic change.

The *Education* was Adams' effort to pull his own fragmented world
into shape, and this effort, not surprisingly, involved his own form of
mythmaking.[65] Its appearance virtually coincided with what is arguably
the most important scientific event of the twentieth century, the publication of Einstein's general theory of relativity. This theory finally and utterly destroyed the remnants of Newtonian physics and whatever image
of wholeness that formulation might still have offered. The impact of relativity was to further the fragmentation that was already well under way
at the turn of the century. It was a time of cultural ferment. E. L. Doctorow, in a recent essay on Einstein, observes that "Einstein came of age
at a moment not only in German culture but in world history—those
early years of the 20th century—that if I were a transcendentalist I might
consider as manifesting the activity of some sort of stirred-up world over-
soul."[66] This was most certainly the case. That "stirred-up" oversoul
would remain in a state of flux for some time to come.[67]

One of the overall effects of Einstein's discoveries was to render all
systems of knowing highly subjective, or "relative." As Einstein's biographer Ronald Clark notes regarding the impact of relativity: "Its epistemo-
logical implications are still hotly debated. Nevertheless, it is indisputable
that while the theory has enabled man to describe his position in the universe with greater accuracy, it has also thrown into higher relief the limitations of his own personal experiences." He then quotes Sir James Jeans'
statement that the theory of relativity ultimately suggests that any conventional concept of reality is necessarily, "private to single individuals or
to small colonies of individuals; it is a parochial method of measuring, and
so is not suited for nature as a whole. . . . Nothing in our experiences, or
experiments," says Jeans, "justifies us in extending either this or any
parochial scheme to the whole of nature, on the supposition that it represents any sort of objective reality."[68] Once again, cosmic harmony was
lost, and no man's wit could tell him where to look for it. The center did
not hold. Any "universal" system was now seen as merely parochial, pro-
visional, and subjective. What was perhaps most disturbing, was that this
breakdown was occurring at precisely the moment when science and technology were developing energies and powers that increased exponentially
the destructive capacity of humankind. In a world where traditional humanistic values no longer seemed relevant, Darwinian theory appeared to
fill the gap for many. Soon, survival of the fittest would manifest itself in
the form of gunboat diplomacy.

World War I (1914–1918), a catastrophe that Henry Adams is said
to have predicted, served to further convince many thoughtful people
that modern civilization certainly was, as T. S. Eliot called it in his famous poem by that name, a "Waste Land." In the 1920s in America, a
handful of "New Humanist" critics attempted to address this situation
while a group of young writers, known appropriately as the "Lost Gen-

eration," tried to find their way amid the rubble. Generally, the latter found all systems either irreparably broken, or deeply suspect. The New Humanists (critics such as Paul Elmer More and Irving Babbitt), on the other hand, "sought to reclaim the high ideals of pure culture purveyed by the old gentility," but with little success. They attempted to preserve the old, rather than create the new. It is perhaps revealing that notwithstanding their desire to reassert "old ideals," these critics were wary of Emerson, despite his status as an American icon, because he appeared far too revolutionary.[69]

Another World War would pass (1939–1945) before the appearance of the psychomythic humanists who provide the critical substratum for the present study. These writers would attempt to reestablish a humanistic center, largely through the concept of the collective unconscious, and its mode of expression, the archetype. As noted earlier, their major works appeared in the middle of the twentieth century, a time of Cold War and the constant threat of a nuclear conflict that threatened to bring the ultimate end of civilization. In response, they sought, like Emerson a century earlier, to re-center reality on humankind and thus bring harmony and meaning to a chaotic and threatening world. Also like Emerson, they attempted, both directly and indirectly, to restore faith to a faithless world, to rediscover a form of divinity or a spiritual dynamic within all individuals that could contribute to the preservation of the human race.[70] This effort was wrought not through creative literature per se but through their highly creative and eclectic studies of human experience, written so as to be understood by average, intelligent readers. These studies, as well as the earlier works of Jung and Freud, were occasionally appropriated by others as tools of literary and cultural criticism. Perhaps it was inevitable that, in the context of profound fragmentation, any effort to discover and assert unity, to re-center consciousness itself, necessarily involved an eclectic approach that embraced diverse elements of human experience in a comprehensive way. As suggested earlier, it is in this respect that the psychomythic humanists most resemble Emerson as well as other Transcendentalists and Romantics. The sixteen volumes of Emerson's journals, as well as the corpus of his published writings, clearly indicate that, more than any other major writer of his time, Emerson was deeply immersed in a broad range of disciplines that spanned a spectrum from the scientific, to the humanistic, to the mystic. Out of this chaos of intellectual ferment he was able to mold and articulate a truly comprehensive, coherent, and meaningful accounting of the human condition. This mystic, dynamic, and eclectic vision of humanity continues to attract readers today, both to Emerson and to the psychomythic humanists that he anticipated.[71]

The felt need for a unifying view of reality that led to psychomythic humanism would be experienced in a variety of ways from the decades of the 1950s, onward. In America, the 1950s, 1960s, and early 1970s were especially turbulent due to cataclysmic changes wrought through the Civil Rights Movement, the Women's Rights Movement, and the trauma and dissention caused by the Vietnam War and a president's perfidy. It was at this time that courses in "Archetypal Criticism," which utilized the insights of Jung, Freud, and the psychomythic humanists considered here, as well as others, began to appear in humanities departments in American colleges and universities. These courses were undoubtedly a response, at least in part, to the needs of the time. Such courses, where they dealt with American literature of the nineteenth century, were supported by a remarkable number of important critical works that were published in the 1950s and 1960s. All of these works, many of which are now considered classics in their own right, had one thing in common; they dealt in varying degrees with certain universal symbols, myths, and/or archetypes that were held to be characteristic of American writing in the period. As such, they provided a more or less unifying approach to both individual authors and movements, especially the American Romantic movement. Additionally, virtually all incorporated, or at least acknowledged, the influence of Jung and/or Freud in the development of their particular theses. The most notable among these are: Charles Feidelson, Jr., *Symbolism and American Literature* (1953), which holds that "the concept of symbolism" is a major unifying principle for nineteenth-century American Romantic writers. It "is not only a key to their situation, but a link between their literature and our own" (5). R. W. B. Lewis, *The American Adam: Innocence, Tragedy, and Tradition in the Nineteenth Century* (1955), references both Jung and Freud as the sources of major concepts developed in the work, which focuses on a major American archetype. Harry Levin, *The Power of Blackness: Hawthorne, Poe, Melville* (1958), references Jung and the collective unconscious. Leslie Fiedler, *Love and Death in the American Novel* (1960, 1966), acknowledges a substantial debt to both Jung and Freud. The author states: "I cannot imagine myself beginning the kind of investigation I have undertaken without the concepts of the conscious and unconscious, the Oedipus complex, the archetypes, etc."(14). Daniel Hoffman, *Form and Fable in American Fiction* (1961), deals with romance, folklore, and myths. Hoffman sees these as reflective of "the recurrence in our culture of certain basic patterns of experience" of the type proposed by "the followers of Jung" (x). Leo Marx, *The Machine in the Garden: Technology and the Pastoral Ideal in America* (1964), relies mainly on Freud, and also D. H. Lawrence in dealing with what Marx calls, "the American archetype of pastoral design" (26).[72] Finally, at the close of the 1960s, Joel Porte combined the insights of all of these "six major works of synthesis," as he calls them, to create a large and sweeping overview of the entire American Romantic movement, *The Romance in America: Studies in Cooper, Poe, Hawthorne, Melville, and James* (1969). The purpose of Porte's mega-synthesis was to show that all of these classic American writers "created, partially or completely, according to a theory of stylized art—

[that was] heavily dependent on the use of conventional, or archetypal, figures and on symbol, parable, dream, and fantasy—in order to explore large questions . . . about race, history, nature, human motivation, and art" (x). Porte's study was a major contribution to the comprehension of the American Romantic movement as a unified cultural phenomenon. However, like virtually all of his predecessors, his interest is almost exclusively in fiction, and, as a result, Emerson appears only on the margins of the study. Nevertheless, to read Emerson in the context of this larger movement, a movement aimed at reunifying the body and the soul of American society, is to rediscover and affirm his central role in defining the culture of his time. The psychomythic humanists considered here also provide a unique critical prism through which we might examine, for the first time, the personal and, at times, painful psychological and spiritual journey that transformed Emerson into the foremost spokesperson of his age.

One final note on the present status of the unconscious among students of the psyche: although philosophers and poets have been dealing with the unconscious in one form or another from the time of Plato, in the late 1970s and 1980s the concept of the unconscious, and psychoanalysis generally, began to fall out of favor. Clinical advancements in drug therapy, which suggested that many psychological conditions could have chemical or biological roots, the advent of Behaviorism, which generally ignored consideration of mental states, and dream research that suggested dreams were the products of random nerve signals sent out during REM sleep, all seemed to call into question the validity and value of psychoanalysis and the concept of the unconscious, collective, or otherwise. Recently, however, the unconscious has made something of a comeback, due in part to new developments in neuroscience. As psychologist Frank Tallis recently observed in his study, *Hidden Minds: A History of the Unconscious* (2002), "evolutionary theorists, neuroscientists, experimental psychologists, and those working in the field of artificial intelligence, have been forced to reconsider the concept of the unconscious." As a result of this turnabout, Tallis insists: "It is now almost impossible to construct a credible model of the mind without assuming that important functions will be performed outside of awareness."[73] This assertion appears to be confirmed in such recent studies as *The New Unconscious* (2005) where psychologist James Uleman observes that "Whatever historic frameworks have been used, thoughtful observers of human behavior have almost always found it necessary to distinguish between internal influences that are hidden and must be inferred (fate, temperament, soul, character) and those they believe are transparent, experienced directly, or open to inspection."[74] Correspondingly, the "new unconscious" is "still basically cognitive [and] firmly embedded in cognitive science." The difference is that "the new unconscious is much more concerned with affect motivation, and even control and metacognition, than was the old cognitive unconscious."[75] One might argue, given what follows in the present study, that the new unconscious is not *that* new after all. As Emerson and the psychomythic humanists consistently maintain, the unconscious is the source of the affections as well as dreams. The latter contain archetypes that are capable of providing insight and guidance that can help resolve the problems of daily life. Such guidance is not generally available to the logic-dominated conscious mind. Given this, it is interesting to note that, in a recent report on dream research, scientists using PET and fMRI technology to watch the dreaming brain have found that one of the most active areas during REM is the limbic system, which controls our emotions. Much less active is the prefrontal cortex, the part of the brain that is associated with logical thinking. The report further notes that another part of the brain that is active in REM sleep is the anterior cingulate cortex, the function of which is to detect discrepancies. In observing evidence of such brain activity during sleep, one researcher hypothesizes that this might possibly indicate how difficult life problems are sometimes resolved in dreams. "It's as if the brain surveys the internal milieu," he suggests, "and tries to figure out what it should be doing and whether our actions conflict with who we are."[76] Such hypothetical internal dialogue seems to echo Emerson's assertion that he "who looks with his own eyes will find that there is somebody within him that knows more than he does," and Jung's belief that "the unconscious could serve man as a unique guide."[77] Indeed, it is the findings of such empirical research that have led some psychologists like Tallis to conclude that "Many brain scan images—showing brightly lit areas of biological activity—are nothing less than snapshots of the unconscious at work." The result is that "the unconscious, only recently rejected as a historical curiosity, has made its way back to the heart of neuroscience."[78]

Additionally, while the unconscious may have been out of favor for a time with the neuroscientists, it has remained a firm fixture in the humanities. The writings of the four psychomythic humanists who form the core of the critical prism employed here—Neumann, Campbell, Brown, and Eliade—all remain in print fifty years and more since their original publication. The same is true for their mentors, Jung and Freud, after one hundred years and more. Apparently, the subjects that they treat, inward journeys in pursuit of timeless truths, are themselves timeless in nature.

A NOTE ON TERMINOLOGY

Throughout this study, several correlations will be made between the theoretical constructs developed by the psychomythic humanists and their predecessors, Jung and Freud, and Emerson's Transcendental/Romantic philosophy. Because the terminology used in both cases is not perfectly symmetrical, a brief clarification of equivalents is in order. We should also point out, as Jung does, that the psyche "is a thing . . . of infinite complexity."[79] Therefore, what follows is necessarily a simplification of complex concepts. However, in the course of our subsequent discussion, these concepts will be developed in greater depth.

Unconscious and Collective Unconscious

Although these terms have different definitions as distinguished by Jung, they are very often used synonymously by him and the psychomythic humanists who followed. Therefore, throughout this study the unconscious should always be understood as referring to the collective unconscious.

While often spoken of metaphorically as a sort of repository, as in the expression, "located in the collective unconscious," this entity is most properly understood as a psychological potentiality, activity, power, or energy that is present in all human beings, below the level of consciousness.[80] This transpersonal, universal entity is the source of symbolic pictures or archetypes that manifest themselves in dreams, art, myth, religious rituals, stories, tales, and literature of all types.[81] These archetypes are believed to reflect the collective experience of humanity and are therefore a source of knowledge that is innate and capable of providing guidance.[82] This knowledge is communicated primarily through dreams, intuition, and the active imagination.[83] The unconscious is also associated with the creative spirit, often represented mythologically as the Muse. Additionally, the collective unconscious is believed by many to contain the whole spiritual heritage of humankind's evolution and is therefore associated with divinity and religious insight.[84] The unconscious is also the source of the affective, emotional, and feeling function of the psyche, sometimes referred to by both Freud and Jung as "Eros."[85] It is this energy that connects human beings with one another, and it is sometimes seen as a reflection of the power of divine love in a teleological context.[86] The unconscious is also associated with the force of instinct that connects us with the natural world and its spirit, the *anima mundi*.[87] Finally, because of its association with nature, emotion, and creativity, the unconscious is often described as a feminine force. It is what Jung sometimes refers to as "the realm of the mothers."[88]

Conscious / Consciousness

The conscious is the seat of self-awareness (ego). It is responsible for our capacity to exercise logic, reason, and other cognitive functions.[89] Because of its orientation towards logic and reasoning, the conscious has often been defined as masculine in nature. It is the realm of the fathers.[90] The conscious serves as a guide during our waking hours as we deal with the issues of everyday life. However, ideally, the conscious should always function in a balanced relationship with the unconscious.[91] In this context, the unconscious is compensatory or complementary to consciousness. Indeed, psychological growth and health are only possible through an ongoing "conversation" between consciousness and the unconscious. Jung called this conversation the "transcendent function."[92] In the modern period, as in times of fragmentation in the past, the effort to achieve a balance between the two has largely meant an effort to recover the unconscious from the domination of the logical and rational conscious.[93]

Emerson's Terms for the Functions of the Unconscious and Conscious

The argument here, in part, is that Emerson's understanding of the structure and potentialities of the psyche is remarkably similar to that articulated by the psychomythic humanists and their predecessors, both ancient and modern. Additionally, it will be demonstrated that the pattern of Emerson's own psychological development and eventual evolution as a cultural hero, prophet, and seer, bears a striking resemblance to that of the archetypal hero described by Joseph Campbell. Emerson's terminology, however, differs somewhat from that of the psychomythic humanists, and varies depending upon his specific subject. While Emerson does occasionally use the term "unconscious," more frequently he uses the terms "the Reason" and "the Understanding" to represent the collective unconscious and the conscious aspects of the psyche, respectively. In a letter to his brother Edward in 1834, he offers the following succinct definitions. "Reason is the highest faculty of the soul—what we mean often by the soul itself; it never *reasons*, never proves, it simply perceives; it is vision." On the other hand, "the Understanding toils all the time, compares, contrives, adds, argues, nearsighted but strong-sighted, dwelling in the present the expedient the customary."[94] In *Nature*, Emerson describes the collective or transpersonal aspect of Reason. "Man is conscious of a universal soul within or behind his individual life," he notes. "This universal soul, he calls Reason."[95] Like the power of love, affection, or Eros of the collective unconscious, the Reason is also a source of unity in an otherwise fragmented and alienating world. Sometimes Emerson calls this universal force the "Over-Soul." Thus, he refers to "that Unity, that Over-Soul, within which every man's particular being is contained and made one with all other; that common heart."[96] It is this universal and unconscious quality of the Over-Soul that Emerson alludes to in his observation that "There is one mind common to all individual men."[97]

The power of the Over-Soul, or the Reason, like that of the collective unconscious, enables those who are open to it to reach a deeper wisdom by looking beyond the mere surface of things in order to grasp their symbolic meaning. This perception is intuitive. Thus, for Emerson, all things potentially "are symbols of the passage of the world into the soul of man, to suffer there a change, and reappear a new and higher fact."[98] The truth thus derived from the natural world possesses a divine quality because the world itself is "a projection of God in the unconscious."[99] One accesses this world soul, this *anima mundi*, through a process of introspection, initially, since for every individual "nature is the opposite of the soul, answering to it part for part. One is seal, and one is print. Its beauty is the beauty of his own mind. Its laws are the laws of his own mind."[100]

For Emerson, as for the psychomythic humanists, the insights of the unconscious, of the Reason or the Over-Soul, often express themselves through the active imagination, which he refers to as "a very high sort of seeing that does not come by study."[101] It is also the source of instinct, which for Emerson both derives from and connects us to nature and divinity. It is a divine and therefore infallible guide. "As the traveler who has lost his way, throws his reins on his horse's neck," he notes, "and trusts to the instinct of the animal to find his road, so must we do with the divine animal who carries us through this world."[102] The affective element of the unconscious, Eros (the god who brings harmony out of chaos), is also a source of moral guidance for Emerson. His Puritan ancestors called this force "religious affections," and their role, among other things, is to prompt virtuous conduct. This prompting is intuitive. As Emerson observes in his "Divinity School Address": "The sentiment of virtue is a reverence and delight in the presence of certain divine laws. . . . The intuition of the moral sentiment is an insight of the perfection of the laws of the soul. These laws execute themselves. They are out of time, out of space, and not subject to circumstance."[103]

For Emerson, the Over-Soul, the Reason, Eros, and Love represent a manifestation of the divine power that is the basis for all harmony and meaning in life. Unfortunately, most are oblivious to this potentiality because their consciousness dominates. As Emerson observes, "a large portion of ourselves lies within the limits of the unconscious" where, for many, it remains hidden.[104] The psychomythic humanists and Emerson believed that it was absolutely imperative, therefore, for individuals to open and maintain a conversation between the conscious and unconscious and access thereby this divine life force. This potentially redeeming power might then be brought to bear on the problems of individuals and the world that they face. As noted earlier, Jung called this process the "transcendent function," and it is central to his entire psychological schema.[105] As the following pages show, after going through a dramatic and transforming experience that brought him into union with this dynamic power, Emerson would spend his lifetime showing others the way to this divine life force.

CHAPTER 2

THE SPIRIT AND THE FLESH

We are amphibious creatures, weaponed
for two elements, having two sets of
faculties, the particular and the catholic.

—R. W. Emerson, *"Nominalist and Realist"*

Emerson saw human beings as "amphibious" creatures that
function in a reality that possesses both particular and universal dimensions. Consequently they have "two sets of faculties" that deal with this experience. This understanding
anticipates an important aspect of the theory that stands at the
center of the psychomythic humanists' thought, as outlined in chapter 1.
Strongly influenced by the insights of Jung and, to a lesser degree Freud,
this theory holds that the human psyche is a dialectic entity consisting of
two potentially antagonistic dimensions that are commonly referred to as
the unconscious and the conscious. The general character of these two is
dramatically different. This division resembles quite closely the distinction that Emerson makes between "the Reason" (unconscious) and "the
Understanding" (conscious), borrowing his terms, as many Romantics
and Transcendentalists did, from Kant via Coleridge.[1]

Between these two contending forces stands the ego. The function
of the ego is to balance the antagonistic dimensions of the psyche. In the
process of psychological development an imbalance in either direction
causes, in the individual, neuroses or psychoses. In collective society it
causes a sense of discontent that can, at times, lead to conflict, alienation,
and even revolution. Since the ego necessarily functions in the realm
of consciousness, it is inevitable that continued cultural development leads
away from the unconscious and into the world of light and reason. If
this development continues to an extreme, however, the individual eventually loses contact with her natural and instinctive roots, the wellsprings

of psychic vitality, and a harmful imbalance occurs. The symptom of this imbalance is that the world perceived by the conscious appears increasingly arid and lifeless. Very often this situation evokes the following patterned or "archetypal" response in the psyche. The ego retreats from the wasteland of consciousness, immerses itself in the vital springs of libidinal and spiritual energy in the deep unconscious, fights off the initial temptation to reside there continually, and returns, refreshed and made strong by its reconnection with the vitality of the unconscious. This new, balanced self is then prepared to reshape the face of his/her world according to a new and creative vision. When a balance between both polarities has been restored, the psyche is made whole again and a "new self" emerges.[2] This cyclic phenomenon of withdrawal-regeneration-rebirth occurs both in individuals and in societies. In the case of the latter, as noted in chapter 1, the result is a new cultural paradigm. Working through the psychological-archetypal theories of Norman O. Brown, Joseph Campbell, Erich Neumann, and Mircea Eliade, one finds this theme expressed repeatedly, albeit in different ways and with different emphases. However, they share a common matrix and thus reflect upon and enrich one another. What follows is an attempt to elucidate and synthesize this central concept and to suggest how Emerson anticipated this seminal archetype.

Norman O. Brown in *Life Against Death* (1959) presents a theory of human behavior that is based upon Freudian psychological theory but which also modifies and expands that theory considerably. His insights into the relationship between the body, sexuality, and the unconscious, as well as his understanding of the essentially revolutionary nature of art and artistic creativity, are both revealing and provocative. As we shall see, they are especially useful in reaching a deeper understanding of Emerson's view of art as the product of divine, erotic creativity, and the role of the poet as rebel and redeemer. According to Brown, every human being is possessed of a certain instinctual drive for sexual gratification or pleasure. When using the term "sexual," or "erotic," Brown always means a very general and unspecialized sense of emotional and sensual gratification, which is not limited to genital organization, that is, sexuality that primarily involves genital activity. Very simply, the goal of this instinctive drive, or "pleasure-principle," according to Brown, is happiness. This natural desire is very often thwarted by the demands of everyday existence, which are predominantly practical and pragmatic. This counterforce is the "reality-principle." Since the pleasure-principle and the reality-principle are located in the unconscious and conscious respectively, the friction between them must be mediated by the ego. As Brown explains, "man's desire for happiness is in conflict with the whole world. Reality imposes upon human beings the necessity of renunciation of pleasures; reality frustrates desire. The pleasure-principle is in conflict with the reality-principle, and this conflict is the cause of repression. Under the conditions of repression the essence of our being lies in the unconscious, and only in the unconscious does the pleasure-principle reign supreme."[3]

This conflict evidences itself in various ways. It might be seen as the struggle between business and pleasure, culture and nature, conscious and unconscious, or Death and Eros. Erik Erikson, for example, notes that the sometimes vitriolic dissent of youth is often related to their refusal to leave behind completely the ideal pleasures of childhood and to confront the trials of a harsh reality. Since their ideals of reform are based substantially upon a latent sense of childhood satisfaction, their protests, according to Erikson, display elements of both "prophesy" and "retrogression." "Youthful behavior," he states, "where it arouses ambivalent fascination, always appears to be both prophetic—that is, inspired by the vigor of a new age—and retrogressive insofar as it seems to insist on outworn simplicities and to display astonishing regressions. I am speaking, then, of the emotional charge of certain patterns of dissent, not of their political utility or detriment."[4]

Emerson anticipates this twentieth-century observation, and even its specific terminology, in a journal passage in 1834 wherein he considers the psychological and sociological significance of the child's passage into adulthood. Here, as with Erikson and Brown, the real world of the adult, the world of "consciousness," with its painful emphasis on necessity, logic, and survival, contrasts vividly with the "unconscious" and pleasure-oriented world of childhood. As noted earlier, Emerson here correlates the unconscious/conscious axis with the Transcendental Reason/Understanding.

> The age of puberty is a crisis in the life of the man worth studying. It is the passage from the Unconscious to the Conscious; . . . from faith to doubt; from maternal Reason to hard short-sighted Understanding; from Unity to disunion; the progressive influences of poetry, eloquence, love, regeneration, character, truth, sorrow, and of search for an Aim, & the contest for Property.[5]

In examining the nature of the struggle between these elements, Brown rejects the Freudian notion, inherent in his theory, that the reality-principle by its nature causes repression, since he feels that this statement "defines the problem rather than solves it."[6] After considering various possibilities, Brown suggests that, ultimately, it is humankind's desire to deny the fact of death that leads to an unnatural concentration of disembodied "spiritual" consciousness at the expense of the earthly unconscious, the source of instinct that connects us to the *animus mundi*, the world spirit. What humankind has lost sight of, in Brown's opinion, is the fact that we have a body. In fact, he says, "culture originates in the denial of life and the body."[7] As a result of this denial, civilized humanity is out of rapport with the natural environment to which we are connected through the body. We become painfully dissociated individuals for whom the gap between the me and the not me looms large. We enter into a struggle against death, a death that all other animals accept. This struggle, which cuts us off from the vital well-springs of libidinal energy in the unconscious, leads ironically to a death in life where all intimations of mortality are sublimated and made consciously ethereal. The ego of civilized humanity has in a sense become too conscious to die. Such an extreme emphasis on the conscious (referred to hereafter as "ego-consciousness") is extremely pernicious.

> This incapacity to die, ironically but inevitably, throws mankind out of the actuality of living, which for all normal animals is at the same time dying; the result is denial of life (repression). The incapacity to accept death turns the death instinct into its destructively human and distinctively morbid form. The distraction of human life to the war against death by the same inevitable irony, results in death's dominion over life. The war against death takes the form of a preoccupation with the past and the future, and the present tense, the tense of life, is lost—that present which Whitehead says, "holds within itself the complete sum of existence, backwards and forwards, the whole amplitude of time, which is eternity."[8]

As we shall see later, this concept of living life in the present and through the body will play a large part in Emerson's philosophy; indeed, it is a major theme for virtually all Transcendentalists and Romantics. In a journal entry in 1832, Emerson indicates his belief in immortality as a present fact. "Don't tell me to get ready to die," he scolds. "I know not what shall be. The only preparation I can make is by fulfilling my present duties. This is the everlasting life."[9] It is this principle that also underlies Whitman's later assertion in "Song of Myself" that

> There was never any more inception than there is now,
> Nor any more youth or age than there is now,
> And will never be any more perfection than there is now,
> Nor any more heaven or hell than there is now.
>
> (3:40–43)

This spontaneous sense of existence connects one, through the senses, to the here and the now, and to the life-sustaining processes of nature that are, in Emerson's view, a manifestation of the divine Over-Soul. The processes of nature are thus symbolic of eternal life. As Whitman observes, "The smallest sprout shows that there is really no death" (6:125). In a similar fashion, it also informs Thoreau's paean to the spiritual power of nature through-out *Walden*, especially in the "Spring" chapter where the greenness of the new grass and the bright warmth of the sun provide compelling proof of the ceaseless, ongoing life of the present. "There needs no stronger proof of im-mortality," Thoreau insists. "All things must live in such a light. O Death, where is thy sting? O Grave, where was thy victor then?"[10] For Romantics and Transcendentalists, the balanced unity of mind and body, conscious and unconscious, self and nature, is an essential element in reaching tran-scendence which, for them, was the firsthand experience of divinity.

Culture plays a very important role in the process of repression since, according to Brown, culture is a product of the collective con-sciousness. The aim of culture and civilization is obviously the control, and even repression, of the natural, instinctive unconscious. This function is accomplished largely through sublimation. As he notes: "The link be-tween psychoanalysis and the science of human culture is the concept of sublimation. If psychoanalysis is right, virtually the totality of what an-thropologists call culture consists of sublimations."[11] Through sublima-tion the unconscious promptings of the libido are repressed, transformed, and desexualized. As a direct result of this castration by culture, the un-conscious remains unsatisfied and unfulfilled. Consequently, "The fester-ing antagonism between man and culture remains,"[12] or, as Emerson puts it in his essay "Self-Reliance" (1841): "Society everywhere is in con-spiracy against the manhood of every one of its members."[13] In this case, "manhood" and "members" may constitute an intentional sexual pun. Emerson came to realize the importance of the relationship between the natural and spiritual worlds, and that the body was the connecting link between the two. He may have found this notion reflected in a work by one of his favorite Cambridge Platonists, Ralph Cudworth (1617–1688). In *The True Intellectual System of the Universe* (1678), Cudworth speaks of an unconscious force which he calls "that vital sympathy, by which our soul is united and tied fast, as it were with a knot, to the body." For Cudworth, this force "is a thing we have no direct consciousness of, but only its effects."[14] This insight became an important element in Emer-son's personal quest for transcendence. "To believe himself securely as God *in* nature," Joel Porte observes, "Emerson would have to learn to identify less ambiguously with his natural body and accept modalities of its experience as potential sources of transcendence; otherwise, the with-drawal of the divine afflatus would leave him nothing but a wilted veg-etable—a dying animal ashamed of its irrepressible urges and inexplicable needs." He also notes Emerson's realization that "the spirit was not *effi-cient* without the body. Elevation, he found was simply not possible unless it was rooted in 'sufficient bottom.'"[15]

According to Brown, Freud's incapacity to theoretically posit a solution to this problem rests in his determination to consider humankind dualistically as soul and body, with inevitable friction between the two. Brown, on the other hand, like Emerson, suggests that the relationship of these two entities is dialectical. Both participate in the normal and proper functioning of the individual psyche, and neither should acquire exclusive dominion. He states that, "The aim of psychoanalysis—still unfulfilled, and still only half conscious—is to return our souls to our bodies, to return ourselves to ourselves, and thus to overcome the human state of self-alienation."[16] Again, this is a major concern for virtually all Romantics, and one is reminded of Whitman's powerful psycho/sexual/spiritual passage in the fifth movement of "Song of Myself." Here the union of body and soul is described in terms of a sexual encounter that leads to a dynamic, even ecstatic, experience of unity and transcendence. Addressing "my soul, the other I am," the speaker relates the following.

> I mind how once we lay such a transparent morning,
> How you settled your head athwart my hips and gently turn'd
>   over upon me,
> And parted the shirt from my bosom-bone, and plunged your
>   tongue to my bare-stript heart,
> And reach'd till you felt my beard, and reach'd till you held
>   my feet.
>
> (5:85–90)

The result of this spontaneous union of body and soul is union with the world and all of humanity. As the speaker continues,

> Swiftly arose and spread around me the peace and knowledge
>   that pass all the argument of earth,
> And I know that the hand of God is the promise of my own,
> And I know that the spirit of God is the brother of my own,
> And that all the men ever born are also my brothers, and the
>   women my sisters and lovers,
> And that a kelson of the creation is love[.]
>
> (5:91–95)[17]

Brown goes on to indicate the larger aspects of the conflict between conscious and unconscious in humanity's relations with the world. One of the primary drives of Eros, the energy of the unconscious, is desire for union with the world, with the natural environment. Thus, Brown observes: "The aim of Eros is union with objects outside the self; . . . the abstract antinomy of Self and Other in love can be overcome if we return to the concrete reality of pleasure and to the fundamental definition of sexuality as the pleasurable activity of the body."[18] Ultimately, individuals are determined naturally to pursue this unity and harmony—which

was enjoyed in the infantile state before the conscious came to dominate—even in adulthood. Hence, Brown and Erikson would agree that,
symbolically, "childhood remains man's indestructible goal." Emerson
suggests this same attitude towards the ideal of childhood when he states
in his journal in 1834, "Blessed is the child; the Unconscious is ever the
act of God himself. Nobody can reflect upon his *unconscious* period or
any particular word or act in it, with regret or contempt. Bard or Hero
cannot look down upon the word or gesture of a child: it is as great as
they."[19] According to Brown, this ideal state must be reestablished on a
conscious level for the adult.

> If psychoanalysis must say that instincts, which at the level
> of animality are in a harmonious unity, are separated at the
> level of humanity and set into conflict with each other, and
> that mankind will not rest content until it is able to abolish
> these conflicts and restore harmony, but at the higher level of
> consciousness, then once again it appears that psychoanalysis
> *completes the romantic movement* and is understood only
> if interpreted in that light. . . . [T]he history of mankind con-
> sists in a departure from a condition of undifferentiated pri-
> mal unity with himself and with nature, an intermediate
> period in which man's powers are developed through differ-
> entiation and antagonism (alienation) with himself and with
> nature, and a final return to a unity on a higher level or har-
> mony [emphasis added].[20]

This desire for wholeness and unity with oneself and the outside world,
and its attendant frustrations, evidence themselves in several areas of
human thought and experience. The concept of time is one of the most
important. Brown tells us that the very idea of time is primarily part of a
defense mechanism that has as its end the control of instinctual behavior.
He refers to this factor as "isolation" and explains that "isolation is a
technique for protecting the ego from being overwhelmed by its own instinctual urges, and consists in fragmenting experience into separate
parts."[21] In so doing, the psyche establishes a "routine" that serves as a
protection against the uninhibited flow of instinctive behavior. The concept of time, however, is foreign to the unconscious, since "the instinctual
processes in the id [unconscious] are timeless, . . . only repressed life is in
time, and unrepressed life would be timeless or in eternity."[22] Consequently, a healthy human being, in whom conscious and unconscious
were balanced, would not be dominated and oppressed by time.

Ultimately, Brown suggests a cyclical view of history that equates its
movements with the conflicts between the conscious and the unconscious in
the individual. The ontogenetic thus becomes phylogenetic; the individual

is the microcosm and history is the macrocosm. In this way the movements or upheavals noted in human history, such as those described in chapter 1, are generally the result of "an irruption of fresh material from deeper strata of the unconscious made possible by a large-scale transformation in the structure of the projective system (the culture). The dynamic of history is the slow return of the repressed," that is, the return of the spontaneous, instinctive, affective element in human nature, the source of creativity, harmony, and progress.[23]

Another segment of human behavior directly affected by the conscious-unconscious conflicts of the human psyche is economics and also, as Brown views it, the parent of economics, religion. He feels that "religion is the middle term connecting psychoanalysis and society," and that any psychoanalysis of money must take into consideration the fact that "the money complex has the essential structure of religion." Brown goes on to state that money is a symbol of guilt and, hence, related to the death instinct. The concept is this: we have to work to earn money, and "Work is for most men a punishment and a scourge." (The necessity of work as a consequence of Adam's sin expresses this psychological truth: "By the sweat of your brow you shall earn your bread," [Genesis 3:19].) Because of this, money becomes a source of guilt. More money comes from more work which means more punishment, which, in turn, implies more sin. Thus, for Brown, "Money is condensed wealth; condensed wealth is condensed guilt."[24] American Romantics and Transcendentalists, generally, recognized very early the correlation between the pursuit of material wealth and the repression of the human spirit. Thoreau, of course, moved to Walden Pond to be close to nature and God, thereby reestablishing an essential linkage between the unconscious/instinctive/spiritual self and the natural world. In this way, he managed to escape the curse of Adam to which Brown refers. "It is not necessary that a man should earn his living by the sweat of his brow," Thoreau assures us, "unless he sweats easier than I do."[25] In this way he contrasts himself with the more ambitious and therefore guilt-ridden citizens of Concord who are "doing penance in a thousand remarkable ways" through their labors in "shops, and offices, and fields."[26] Emerson, of course, frequently condemned the gross materialism of his age, which he saw as the primary source of its alienation, corruption, and repressiveness. "Men have looked away from themselves and at things so long," he notes in "Self-Reliance" (1841), "that they have come to esteem the religious, learned, and civil institutions, as guards of property, and they deprecate assaults on these, because they feel them to be assaults on property."[27] The grossest example of this material and spiritual enervation and alienation for Emerson was slavery. Thoreau warns that the pursuit of wealth often results in self-alienation, as "when you are the slave-driver of yourself."[28]

Ironically, Brown contends that the very function of economics was traditionally to relieve humanity of this innate sense of indebtedness and guilt, that the gods existed "to make the debt payable." However, for modern humanity—from Martin Luther on—there is a "breakthrough from the unconscious of the truth that the burden of guilt is unpayable," at least in this form. As a result, humankind continues to pursue work as a form of self-punishment while the illusion of redemption is abandoned. The conscious dominates the unconscious; pleasure is eschewed as the devil's own and humanity trudges through life with a Promethean burden of guilt. A balance must be restored since "mankind will not cease from discontent and sickness until the antimony of economics and love, work and play, is overcome."[29] Historically, this relationship of goods with guilt might be seen as an aspect of America's "Puritan work ethic." As Edmund S. Morgan points out, "As the Puritan ethic induced a suspicion of merchants, it also induced, for different reasons, a suspicion of prosperity. Superficial readers of Max Weber have often leapt to the conclusion that Puritans viewed economic success as a sign of salvation. In fact, Puritans were always uncomfortable in the presence of prosperity."[30] Is there any wonder, then, why the most prosperous society would be the most discontent?

Finally, the invention of money only served to expedite the process of production and accumulation. Brown quotes Locke's observation that, "The desire of having more than men needed altered the intrinsic value of things, which depends only on their usefulness to the life of man." This, in turn, created a unique group of sufferers. Brown quotes Thoreau's description of "That seemingly wealthy, but most terribly impoverished class of all, who have accumulated dross, but know not how to use it, or get rid of it, and thus have forged their own golden or silver fetters."[31]

Expressions of Romantic and Transcendental opposition to this spirit-crushing busyness were sometimes seen by the general populace as evidence of laziness, or worse yet, stargazing. Whitman purposely thumbs his nose at society's obsessive work ethic as he "leans and loafs at [his] ease observing a spear of summer grass."[32] Contemporaries often saw Thoreau as a mere idler, indulging his boyish whimsy, during his stay at Walden Pond where he was a "self-appointed inspector of snow-storms."[33] For his part, Emerson was well aware of criticisms that his Transcendental philosophizing was, literally, a waste of time and energy. While in the process of defending himself against society's accusations in a journal entry in 1840, he associates the concept of economics with the idea of God in a way that is similar to Brown's. In the full passage from which the following statement is taken, Emerson answers at length anonymous criticism of his lifestyle and values. He explains that the "Essays," which he was preparing for publication at this time, are a "sort of apology to my country for my apparent idleness." But even in

this matter, he says, he does not feel compelled. As the following statement indicates, his attitude towards his financial status, and his society's
perverse emphasis on material productivity, is one of indifference. The
love of God transcends such material concerns and the guilt associated
with them.

> You think it is because I have an income which exempts me
> from your day-labor, that I waste (as you call it), my time in
> sungazing and stargazing. You do not know me. If my debts,
> as they threaten, should consume what money I have, I should
> live just as I do now: I should eat worse food & wear a
> coarser coat and should wonder in a potato patch instead of
> in the wood—but it is I & not my Twelve Hundred dollars a
> year, that love God.[34]

The final area of human activity that Brown considers in relation to
his theory concerns language and art. Primarily, Brown sees art as a powerful liberating element in humanity's battle against the domination of
consciousness and, ultimately, an important source of psychological liberation; "if man's destiny is to change reality until it conforms to the
pleasure- principle, and if man's fate is to fight for instinctual liberation,
then art appears, in the words of Rilke, as the Weltanschauung of the last
goal. Its contradiction of the reality-principle is its social function, as a
constant reinforcement of the struggle for instinctual liberation; its child-
ishness is to the professional critic a stumbling block, but to the artist its
glory."[35] Brown refers to art as "childish" because it denies the dominance of the reality-principle and seeks instead a condition of harmony,
unity, and pleasure that is associated with childhood. As Brown says elsewhere, "in the child the conscious and the unconscious are not yet separated." Emerson would agree. In *Nature* (1836) he observes that "The
lover of nature is he whose inward and outward senses are still truly adjusted to each other; who has retained the spirit of infancy even into the
era of manhood."[36] In his overall view of the function of art in relation to
the individual, Brown leans heavily upon Freud. "Art," he says, "like psychoanalysis itself, appears to be a way of making the unconscious conscious," which is in itself therapeutic since it makes possible a healthy
balance between the two. He notes further that Freud, at his seventieth
birthday celebration, disclaimed the title of "discoverer of the unconscious" saying that "the poets and philosophers before me discovered the
unconscious; what I discovered was the scientific method by which the
unconscious can be studied." For Brown and Freud, art liberates the
instincts and "provides relief from the pressures of reason."[37]

In his study, *The Unconscious Before Freud*, Lancelot Law Whyte
confirms the accuracy of Freud's observation regarding his theoretical

predecessors. He points out that Goethe, Schiller, and Schelling popular-
ized the concept of the unconscious. Also, the notion in its most basic
form was a common element in Romantic thinking generally. Whyte
summarizes this romantic vision succinctly. "The springs of human nature lie in the unconscious," he states, "for it links the individual with the
universal, or at least the organic. This is true, whether it is expressed
as the union of the soul with the divine, or as the realm which links
the movements of human awareness with the background of organic
processes within which they emerge."[38] This observation comports with
Brown's assertion that the concept of a spiritually dynamic unconscious
passed from Jacob Boehme (1575–1624), a seventeenth-century Christian
mystic, to William Blake, Novalis, Hegel, and Goethe. These latter, he asserts, "are the poets whom Freud credited with being the real discoverers
of the unconscious."[39] Gay Wilson Allen points out Emerson's familiarity with virtually all of these, especially Goethe and Boehme.[40] He also
describes an even earlier source of probable influence on Emerson, which
is that of the Neoplatonists and the Cambridge Platonists who, as will be
seen in chapters 3 and 4, Emerson read, admired, and frequently quoted
in his lectures and essays. In an early lecture titled "Art," for example,
Emerson quotes from Cudworth's *True Intellectual System of the Universe* (1678) Plato's statement that "those things which are said to be
done by Nature, are indeed done by Divine Art." Emerson adds that
"Art, universally, is the spirit creative," a statement that reflects the creative aspect of the unconscious. As Emerson states later in the same lecture: "The universal soul is the alone creator of the useful and the
beautiful."[41] In his journals, Emerson refers to Cudworth's *True Intellectual System*, the four volumes of which he owned, as "a magazine of quo-
tations of extraordinary ethical sentences, the shining summits of ancient
philosophy . . . wonderful revelations."[42] Indeed, there are so many
correspondences between Emerson's thought and Cudworth's presentation of long passages from Neoplatonists such as Proclus, Plotinus,
Imablichus, and others that Vivian Hopkins asserts "there is no question
of the fertilizing effect upon Emerson's thought of certain ideas which he
first discovered in Cudworth's monumental work."[43]

Other early thinkers who developed theories of the unconscious and
who were known to Emerson include A. A. Cooper, third Earl of Shaftesbury, Leibnitz, Lord Kames, Kant, Fichte, and Novalis. The last, notes
Allen, "almost epitomized Emerson's philosophy in his doctrine that in
man the conscious and unconscious reach a harmony." For Emerson,
Allen states, this harmony "was the ultimate goal for men to strive for."[44]

Brown also considers the importance of the third person, the audience, in the process whereby art liberates the instincts from repression. He
asserts that the audience must also be suffering from the same repressions
and frustrations as the artist. The audience identifies with the creative

artist and thus a subculture is formed in reaction to the rigid, oppressive norm. He maintains that, "In contrast with the repressive structure of the authoritarian group, the aim of the partnership between the artist and the audience is instinctual liberation." Because of this function, one might conclude that art, in a repressive society, is "subversive of civilization."[45] Considering further the relationship between art and civilization, Brown observes that very often the artist appears as a rebel. His function is thus somewhat the same as that of the mythic hero, who will be discussed at some length later. Brown quotes Rilke on this point. "The work of art is 'always in response to a present time,' but 'the times are resistance'; it is only from this tension between contemporary currents and the artist's untimely conception of life that there arises a series of small discharges which are the work of art."[46] The ideal artist, like Emerson's ideal poet, thus becomes rebel, savior, and hero who offers liberation and new faith to the repressed masses of civilization. Since the poet seeks to deliver humankind from the guilt of the Fall and to return to the paradise of childlike unity, thereby reuniting the spirit and the flesh, her function becomes in the fullest sense of the word, a religious one.

Emerson eventually came to view his own artistic function as poet, lecturer, and essayist, in this religious light. In a revealing journal entry in 1839, after having broken completely from his formal Unitarian religion, he states: "I look upon the Lecture room as the true church of today."[47] In his essay "The Poet" he tells us, "The poet is the sayer, the namer, and represents beauty. He is a sovereign, and stands on the centre. . . . He is the true and only doctor," and "The poets are . . . liberating gods."[48] Indeed, Lawrence Buell maintains that for Transcendentalists generally, "literary creation was not simply an amusement, or even a useful instrument, but a sacred act."[49]

Since Emerson achieved his fame through the use of spoken and written language, it is especially appropriate here to consider the relationship of Brown's psychological theory to language. Brown sees language as primarily associated with the sensual, libidinal instincts of the unconscious self. He notes that, "Jacob Boehme, speaks of the language of Adam—different from all languages as we know them—as the only natural language, the only language free from distortion and illusion, the language which man will recover when he recovers paradise. According to Boehme, Adam's language was an unclouded mirror of the senses, so that he calls this ideal language 'sensual speech.'"[50] Robert Richardson points out that Emerson was a close reader of Boehme and that what he found most attractive in his writings was his tangible account of spiritual experience, a combining of the spirit and the flesh, if you will. Boehme's *Aurora*, which Emerson was reading in the summer of 1835, tells of the writer's own "awakening to the sunrise of an eternity situated firmly in this world." Direct and convincing personal experience, says Richardson, "was what Emerson missed . . . at the divinity school" but what he found in Boehme.[51] Emerson also found the same earthy spirit in one of his earliest and most important spiritual guides, Aunt Mary Moody Emerson, whom Richardson describes as "an American Jakob Boehme."[52]

Ideally, everyone should possess naturally the type of speech that Boehme describes, but being the imperfect and neurotic creatures that we are, we must first confront a contrary force of conscious repression that seeks to remove the sensual element from language, an element at times considered a "disease" by the civilized. Brown discusses this unfortunate tendency and points out that, "Some of these linguistic analysts have had the project of getting rid of the disease in language by reducing language to purely operational terms." From the psychoanalytic point of view, he asserts, "a purely operational language would be language without a libidinal (erotic) component; and psychoanalysis would suggest that such a project is impossible because language, like man, has an erotic base, and also useless because man cannot be persuaded to operate (work) for operation's sake." Ultimately and ideally, all human beings should return to the natural and "essentially playful" aspect of language and in this way move closer to "their proper perfection as an animal species and [recover] the power of sensual speech."[53] This process, as noted above, was a primary concern of the Romantic artists. Emerson, for example, admired the rough language of "blacksmiths and teamsters [who] do not trip their speech; it is a shower of bullets." In contrast, "it is Cambridge men who correct themselves, and begin again at every half sentence . . . and refine too much." He found and admired the former type of "gutsy" language in Montaigne's writings, which present "the language of conversation transferred to a book." This sensual speech resembles Boehme's (and Brown's) Adam's talk. In this sense language is a living thing, imbued with the spirit of the natural world from whence language ultimately derives. "Cut these words," says Emerson, "and they would bleed; they are vascular and alive."[54] Correspondingly, Whitman is justly famous (or infamous) for his blunt assertion of the sensual role of the poet. For Whitman, words are literally the embodiment of life, a concept that is intimately expressed in his poem "So Long."

> Camerado, this is no book,
> Who touches this touches a man,
> (Is it night? Are we here together alone?)
> It is I you hold and who holds you,
> I spring from the pages into your arms . . .
>
> (53–57)

It is through the liberation of language and the senses that Brown feels the "resurrection of the body" will be accomplished. In this matter he addresses himself directly to the modern world, the immediate present. What modern humanity must learn is what primitive humanity knew instinctively, namely, that the life of humankind is the life of the body as well as the soul, or, as Emerson puts it, "in nature every body has a soul, but also, every soul has a body."[55] For both Emerson and Brown, humanity must literally come to its senses, in word and deed.

The romantic artist, whom Brown describes as the heroic liberator of the unconscious and the rebel who reestablishes a natural balance between the contending forces of the psyche, is also the subject of Joseph Campbell's mythic study, *The Hero with a Thousand Faces* (1949). Campbell's monomythic structure of the heroic quest constitutes an earlier confirmation of what Brown sees as the essence of the "romantic movement," whereby the individual returns to the realm of the unconscious, immerses herself in the renewing sources of life that are located there, and is then reborn into conscious reality as a new and balanced individual.[56] Campbell, like other psychomythic humanists, operates upon the assumption that basically myth is an externalized description of inner psychic processes and, therefore, any attempt to confront the one must also involve the other. In his study, Campbell distinguishes certain basic characteristics of behavior—archetypal elements—involved in the lives and adventures of mythic heroes from every corner of the world. Taken together, these elements form a consistently recurring pattern of behavior that Campbell refers to as the "monomyth." The basic form of the monomyth is tripartite. It consists of a separation, an initiation, and a return. Thus, "A hero ventures forth from the world of common day into a region of supernatural wonder: fabulous forces are there encountered and a decisive victory is won: the hero comes back from this mysterious adventure with the power to bestow boons on his fellow man."[57] Rendered in the psychoanalytic terms that we have been using, the "region of the supernatural wonder" is the unconscious.[58]

The emergence of the hero in time is always in response to a clearly defined need. This need appears in the macrocosm as the failure of present systems and institutions to meet the basic desires of humanity and in the individual, the microcosm, as a desire for personal fulfillment. Both of these occurred simultaneously in Emerson's early life, as well as Campbell's. Usually what has happened is that the society overall has become, in Brown's terms, too ego-conscious at the expense of the unconscious. The natural drives of the libido are—as Brown points out—sublimated, desexualized and rendered inadequate in meeting the needs of the individual, who requires a balanced combination of both. This situation resembles the cultural reality of the early nineteenth century in the Western world, where the values of the Enlightenment, with its emphasis upon reason, logic, empiricism, and in the realm of art, neoclassical imitation and moderation, were increasingly perceived as unsatisfactory and oppressive. This system would eventually give way to a "romantic revolution" both in Europe and in America, where Emerson would be one of its primary movers.[59] Campbell's description of the arid dominance of an outmoded consciousness captures succinctly the cultural reality of the early nineteenth century as Emerson and other Romantics perceived it. It also reflects the tense, war torn and threatening wasteland that was Campbell's mid-twentieth century world.

> Guided by the practical judgments of the kings and the instruction of the priests of the dice of divine revelation, the field of consciousness so contracts that the grand lines of the human comedy are lost in a welter of cross-purposes. Men's perspectives become flat, comprehending only the light-reflecting, tangible surfaces of existence. The vista into depth closes over. The significant form of the human agony is lost to view. Society lapses into mistake and disaster. The Little Ego has usurped the judgment seat of the Self.[60]

Consequently, as Campbell notes, the hero draws away from this ego-conscious reality and turns instead within. "The first step, detachment or withdrawal, consists in a radical transfer of emphasis from the external to the internal world . . . a retreat from the desperations of the wasteland to the peace of the everlasting realm that is within."[61] This immersion in the vital, erotic life forces of the unconscious eventually results in a type of rebirth, as the renewed individual returns to the conscious world as "hero." His function in the world now is to restore a workable psychic balance between the forces of the conscious and the unconscious, between culture and nature, or, in Transcendental terms, between the Understanding and the Reason. In order to do this, he shares with his society the treasures from beneath. Emerson saw the role of the hero in just this way. In his early lecture titled "Literature" (1839), he notes, "how large a portion of ourselves lies within the limits of the unconscious. . . . Whoever separates for us a truth from our unconscious reason, and makes it an object of consciousness, . . . must of course be to us a great man. We hail with gladness this new acquisition of ourselves. That man I must follow, for he has a part of me; and I follow him that I may acquire myself."[62] This is precisely the life-giving role that Emerson himself would play. The result of restoring a psychological and spiritual balance in society is the establishment of a new cultural paradigm (as Romanticism eventually displaced the rationalism of the Enlightenment). In a religious sense, the regenerated hero is able to scale the "'Wall of Paradise' which conceals God from human sight."[63] This return is to the paradise lost at the time of the Fall, which Brown asserts was a fall into consciousness, a consciousness that became alienated from its unconscious source. Emerson indicates a similar understanding of this phenomenon when he says in his 1844 essay "Experience": "It is very unhappy, but too late to be helped, the discovery we have made that we exist. That discovery is called the Fall of Man."[64]

Campbell emphasizes throughout his work that the primary foe that must be conquered or "annihilated" in order to carry on the process of rebirth is an overdeveloped ego-consciousness. In this respect, Campbell quotes J. C. Flugel to demonstrate that such ego-consciousness is generally associated with the "fathers" or "civilization" and the spirit, and that the repressed unconscious, as with Brown, is usually associated with the "mothers" or the natural world, the world of the flesh.

> "There exists," Professor Flugel observes, "a very general association on the one hand between the notion of mind, spirit, or soul, and the idea of the father or masculinity; and on the other hand between the notion of the body or of mother . . . and the idea of the mother or of the feminine principle. The repression of the emotions and feelings relating to the matter . . . has, in virtue of this association, produced a tendency to adopt an attitude of distrust, contempt, disgust or hostility towards the human body, the Earth, and the whole material Universe, with a corresponding tendency to exalt and overemphasize the spiritual elements, whether in man or in the general scheme of things."[65]

It is not surprising then that the world in which Campbell's hero appears is quite similar to the overcivilized and repressive society that Brown describes. It is one where a sense of sin derives from one's association with the natural forms of existence, the flesh. According to Campbell, what is necessary is a "more realistic view of the father, and therewith of the world. . . . But this requires an abandonment of the attachment to ego itself, and that is what is difficult."[66] With this diminution of what Campbell calls "ego" and what we have been calling ego-consciousness, comes a new, harmonious vision. No longer is reality divided between spirit and flesh, father and mother, conscious and unconscious—but rather one is able to see the unity of reality, as Whitman celebrates it in "Song of Myself," the happy fact of the spirit *in* the flesh. Indeed, God, the father, the spirit, is now seen as diffused throughout reality, as existing everywhere, as being part of everything. As Campbell notes, "Those who know, not only that the Everlasting lives in them, but that what they, and all things, really are *is* the Everlasting, dwell in the groves of the wish-fulfilling trees, drink the brew of immortality, and listen everywhere to the unheard music of eternal concord."[67] Again, this vision results primarily from the diminution of an oppressive ego-consciousness that stresses the differences between the me and the not me and that apprehends only the surface of things. Instead, one embraces the psychic forces of the unconscious that defy the limitations of time and space and manifest the unity of all things with the self. The result is that the hero possesses and, by her example offers, a kind of immortality or salvation to humankind.

For Campbell, this is the triumph of life over death. Emerson presents his own ecstatic version of this phenomenon in his famous "transparent eyeball" passage in *Nature*. The experience of transcending ego-consciousness and its limitations leads to a feeling of oneness with maternal nature, with the source of all life, with divinity itself. As Emerson puts it: "I am nothing; I see all; the currents of the Universal Being circulate through me; I am part or particle of God."[68] The process that results in this kind of renewal and rebirth is a cyclic one. Society must strive periodically to cast off old forms and values, to slough off the rigid and dusty dictates of the old law and return again to the unconscious, erotic, and creative sources of human vitality. Because of the cyclic nature of this process, the hero of one age could become the tyrant of the next. The son grows to be a father. "The golden age," says Campbell, "the reign of the world emperor, alternates, in the pulse of every moment of life, with the wasteland, the reign of the tyrant. The god who is the creator becomes the destroyer in the end."[69] Not surprisingly, revolutions often give rise to new dictators in an endless Hegelian cycle of thesis, antithesis, and synthesis.

The monomythic cycle of death-renewal-rebirth that the individual hero completes on a *microcosmic* scale, when applied to the revolutions of societies and cultures (the *macrocosm*), Campbell calls the "Cosmogonic Cycle"(literally "world building"). In this way, Campbell, like Brown, demonstrates his belief that the development of human societies mirrors the psychic experience of individuals. Because the hero's view of reality is not limited by the narrow horizons of ego-consciousness, and because she views the movements of reality in general as parts of a cyclic whole, a tragic view, which sees only the going down and not the coming up, only the death and not the rebirth, is obviated.

> The happy ending of the fairy tale, the myth, and the divine comedy of the soul, is to be read not as a contradiction, but as a transcendence of the universal tragedy of man. The objective world remains what it was, but, because of a shift of emphasis within the subject, is beheld as though transformed. Where formally life and death contended, now enduring being is made manifest—as indifferent to the accidents of time as water boiling in a pot is to the destiny of a bubble, or as the cosmos to the appearance and disappearance of a galaxy of stars.[70]

Romantics and Transcendentalists often saw this cycle as the basic and eternal rhythm of nature itself. Thoreau thus employs the progress of the seasons in *Walden* to emulate the cycle of birth-death-rebirth which, ultimately, testifies to his faith in immortality. For Thoreau, when life returns in the spring, "There needs no stronger proof of immortality."[71] Such spontaneous assertions of faith transcend the mere arguments of theological disputation. Indeed, because such refined and rational positions are by their very natures the staid products of logical, conscious minds, myth becomes the proper vehicle of communication for this vital truth. "Humor," Campbell asserts, "is the touchstone of the truly mythological as distinct from the more literal-minded and sentimental theological mood. The gods are icons and not ends in themselves. Their entertaining myths transport the mind and spirit, not *up to*, but *past* them, into the yonder void; from which perspective the more heavily freighted theological dogmas then appear to have been only pedagogical lures."[72] Ultimately, for Campbell, the myth of the hero is the story of cyclic renewal and rebirth, told in a timeless form and the form itself illustrates the validity of that concept. Like Thoreau, Emerson employs myth in the same liberating way, both in his personal life and in his writings. As Jeffrey Steele observes, for Emerson, "the unconscious energies embodied in myth entail what Kenneth Burke calls a 'machinery of transcendence'—literary forms which define a habitation for creative power." He further notes, "in Emerson's work we find a literary self-consciousness dedicated to re-grounding thought in the hidden energy of the unconscious."[73] We shall examine some specific examples of this "re-grounding" later.

As many biographers have noted, Emerson's rejection of the status quo would be constant throughout most of his adult life. Joel Porte's study *Representative Man* emphasizes an ongoing "*process* of self-creation and self-discovery" in Emerson whereby he was constantly "working his way indefatigably to that land's end which was always just disappearing over the horizon of his thought."[74] Also, for many biographers, this archetypal journey of discovery began, in part, with Emerson's rejection of his own father, who was also a prominent figure in the then new Unitarian movement in the early nineteenth century. Thus, he was a symbolic cultural father as well as an actual father to Emerson, and this is important to note. In abandoning the Unitarian ministry in 1832, Emerson was symbolically rebelling against all "fathers." A number of critics have suggested this. Evelyn Barish, in her appropriately titled *Emerson: The Roots of Prophesy* (1989), emphasizes how the death of Emerson's father when he was less than eight years old led to feelings of abandonment and anger and she maintains, "In assessing Emerson's willingness to lead the rebellion against—or rather the withdrawal from—the religion of his forefathers, these formative experiences are relevant."[75] Carolyn Porter, in her study *Seeing and Being* (1981), refers to Emerson's disappointment with the major literary figures that he met in England during his tour in 1832–1833, especially Coleridge and Wordsworth who were by then elderly. She notes that, by the end of this trip, as Emerson returned to Boston in 1833, "he had asserted his independence not only of the authority embodied in his father's church, but also of that enshrined in the reigning literary figures of the mother country. Emerson's reiterated rejection of the past," she contends, "can be quite easily read as an oedipal revolt."[76] Emerson's rebelliousness would eventually extend to any and all who threatened to impede the development of his authentic self. As he courageously asserts in "Self-Reliance," while consciously echoing the words of another rebellious hero, Jesus Christ, "The doctrine of hatred must be preached as the counteraction of the doctrine of love when that pules and whines. I shun father and mother and wife and brother, when my genius calls me."[77] This personal rebellion is only one of many factors that would impact Emerson's emergence as poet, hero, and reformer in his society.

Mircea Eliade in *The Myth of the Eternal Return, or Cosmos and History* (1949) offers an anthropological study of certain manifestations of the psychic process outlined here as it appears in certain rituals and rites of renewal performed by various archaic and primitive societies. Eliade demonstrates that, through the repetition of periodic rituals of renewal associated with an archetypal and cyclical view of cosmic time, archaic humanity attempts to destroy "profane" time and thus regenerate itself and its environment. In discussing several examples of this phenomenon, Eliade concludes that ultimately, one is "confronted with the infinite repetition of the same phenomenon, . . . creation-destruction-new creation."[78] This tripartite process is, of course, yet another archetypal recapitulation of what Brown refers to generally as the "romantic movement," and Campbell as the "monomythic" journey of the hero. In each case there is a separation or death, a period of regeneration and renewal and, finally, a new creation or (re)birth.

The reason that such rituals and attitudes have existed and still do exist, according to Eliade, is to repair the damage of the "Fall." The Fall, on a psychological level, as we have already seen, is the sense of guilt one feels in leaving behind the comfort and ideality of the unindividuated unconscious state that dominates in early childhood and precedes the evolution of consciousness. It would seem clear then that the rituals and rites discussed by Eliade have as their aim not only the destruction of profane time, but also the regeneration of humankind and society. Such primal regeneration requires a return to the wellsprings of psychic vitality—the unconscious—and the reestablishment of a new, satisfying, and ideal balance between the conscious and the unconscious.[79] The Fall is, indeed, a fall into consciousness; the cycle is the cycle of rebirth. As Eliade notes: "The need these societies also feel for a periodic regeneration is a proof that they too cannot perpetually maintain their position in what we have just called the paradise of archetypes, and that their memory is capable (though doubtless far less intensely than that of a modern man) of revealing the irreversibility of events, that is, of recording history. Thus, among these primitive peoples too, the existence of man in the cosmos is regarded as a fall." Eliade, like Brown, observes that it is imperative that time be periodically abolished because it is by its nature a means of fragmenting experience, making it ephemeral and ultimately destructive. Also, like Campbell, Eliade concludes that the isolation of any historical moment must necessarily make that moment tragic. As he states, "the historical moment despite the possibilities of escape it offers contemporaries, can never, in its entirety, be anything but tragic, pathetic, unjust, chaotic, as any moment that heralds the final catastrophe must be."[80] Emerson expresses this same idea in his journal in 1838 where he states: "It is strange how painful is the actual world, the painful kingdom of time & place. There dwells care & canker & fear. With thought, with the ideal is immortal hilarity, the rose of joy. All the muses sing: but with names & persons, & today's interests, is grief."[81] This condition, however, can be overcome. Thoreau's "Artist of Kouroo," described in the "Conclusion" of *Walden*, is able to transcend the cankers of time by focusing on his own creativity and the achievement of the artistic ideal.[82] As he concentrated on fashioning the perfect staff, "His singleness of purpose and resolution, and his elevated piety, endowed him without his knowledge, with perennial youth." As a result, "Time kept out of his way, and only sighed at a distance because he could not overcome him."[83] Through the process of artistic creation, the individual engages the unconscious. As a result, a psychological balance is established that imbues the present moment with eternality.

Because Eliade's main concern is with examining the ways in which various cultural groups deal with the problem of time and history, he notes something that appears curious to him but perhaps not to us, something which is an adjunct to the process of temporal regeneration: "namely, that a periodic regeneration of time presupposes, in more or less explicit form—and especially in the historical civilizations—a new Creation, that is, a repetition of a cosmogonic act. And this conception of a periodic creation, that is, of the cyclical regeneration of time, poses the problem of the abolition of 'history,' the problem which is our prime concern in this essay."[84] Eliade observes that the ceremonies and rituals associated with this concern actually celebrate a purifying process that results in a "rebirth." Thus, "Every New Year is a resumption of time from the beginning, that is a repetition of the cosmogony." Eliade's ultimate conclusion is that these rituals, which mimic participation in the archetypal cyclic process, constitute an attempt to impose meaning upon reality, to give it an enduring and transcendent significance, to celebrate the "mythical moment of the passage from chaos to cosmos." Such a view is ratified in Campbell's contention that "myth is the secret opening through which the inexhaustible energies of the cosmos pour into human cultural manifestation."[85] While this is undoubtedly the case, both statements leave largely unexplained the question of why a process of destruction and recreation need be the archetypal pattern that is imposed. Why does the imposition of meaning require destruction? In the context of the present study, it seems clear that this process of destruction and regeneration is necessary in order to complete the psychological exercise that must be fulfilled if one's sense of time is to be abolished. This involves, of course, the reestablishment of a balance between the contending forces of the conscious and the unconscious. As Brown has pointed out, "a healthy human being in whom Ego and Id were unified, would not live in time." However, humankind's continuous existence in a cultural environment that is of necessity consciously oriented inevitably results in an imbalance in that direction. Consequently, this ego-conscious existence must be symbolically destroyed, periodically, in order that humankind, individually and collectively, might be renewed. This renewal is projected cosmogonically as the recreation of the cosmos. It is undoubtedly with this very point in mind that Thoreau relates in *Walden* the story of the Mucclasse Indians who, every year, destroy their old possessions and replace them in a ritual of renewal. Thoreau anticipates Eliade's findings when he observes that "The customs of some savage nations might, perchance, be profitably imitated by us, for they at least go through the semblance of casting their slough annually; they have the idea of the thing, whether they have the reality or not."[86] Clearly, for Romantics and Transcendentalists, the regeneration of time will always presuppose a new creation—will always entail some type of symbolic, cosmogonic act by individuals. As Emerson asserts in 1836: "The man is the creator of his world."[87] For him, as for the psychomythic humanists whom he so clearly prefigures, a unified reality must necessarily be homocentric and self-generated. This is the ultimate and most primal act of self-reliance.

In *The Origins and History of Consciousness* (1949), Erich Neumann presents a theory of psychological genesis and development that is not only compatible with what has been said up to this point, but expands considerably upon it. Like Brown and Campbell, Neumann presents a dualistic view of human psychological development in which the conscious mind of the individual stands in a dialectical relationship with the equally important unconscious. Also like these thinkers, Neumann associates civilization, culture, time, and "masculine" rationality with the conscious, while nature, emotion, eternality, and "feminine" sensuality are associated with the unconscious. It should be noted here that Neumann considers consciousness itself to be "masculine" and the unconscious to be "feminine," regardless of a person's gender. He states, "one thing, paradoxical though it may seem, can be established at once as a basic law: even in a woman, consciousness has a masculine character. The correlation 'consciousness—light—day' and 'unconsciousness—darkness—night' holds true regardless of sex, and is not altered by the fact that the spirit-instinct polarity is organized on a different basis in men and women. Consciousness, as such, is masculine even in women, just as the unconscious is feminine in men."[88] This concept, too, was familiar to the Romantics and Transcendentalists alike. Margaret Fuller, for example, proclaims in *Woman in the Nineteenth Century* that, while "the especial genius of woman [is] . . . intuitive in function, spiritual in tendency," it is also true that "male and female represent two sides of the great radical dualism." As a result, "They are perpetually passing into one another. Fluid hardens to solid, solid rushes to fluid. There is no wholly masculine man, no purely feminine woman."[89] Emerson also anticipates these twentieth-century psychological insights and asserts the co-existence of both gender qualities in single individuals when he observes that "the finest people marry the two sexes in their own person."[90]

According to Neumann, the conscious self evolves from the unindividuated unconscious state that holds the seeds of the developing personality. Initially, the emergence of consciousness is a traumatic rupture and at first the opposing psychic forces, the unconscious and conscious, battle for supremacy. Eventually, and ideally, through a process which Neumann appropriately calls "centroversion," the two forces balance each other and a unified personality results. As with Brown and Campbell, Neumann insists that the microcosmic development of the psyche in the individual is identical to the macrocosmic evolution of human culture out of the primitive state. Also, like Campbell, he suggests that all cosmogonic myths reiterate the story of the rise of consciousness from the unindividuated unconscious state, which is symbolically depicted as bringing light out of darkness. Thus, for Neumann also, the phylogenetic and the ontogenetic are analogous. There is, however, a significant difference between Neumann's view of this phenomenon and that of Campbell and Brown. Essentially it is a matter of emphasis. For Neumann, the greatest danger to healthy psychological development lies in the soul-devouring magnetism of the Terrible Mother, the dark unconscious. While Campbell and Brown emphasize the necessity of periodically immersing the conscious in the revivifying energies of the unconscious, thus effecting a renewal and a rebirth, Neumann insists that more often the goal of consciousness is to slip the grasp of the Terrible Mother entirely and push ever onward in conscious development. In this sense, Campbell's and Brown's view of psychological development, reinforced by Eliade, is cyclical, while Neumann's is essentially linear. This predisposition on Neumann's part, however, is not exclusive and does not prevent him from discussing at some length those instances wherein the human psyche does experience a renewing process involving disintegration and rebirth. Perhaps most importantly, Neumann offers us the opportunity to view our own study of the process of psychic renewal in the larger context of the history of humanity's psychological development.

Neumann is very clear in indicating that his discussion of the history of consciousness will be based essentially upon his rendering of archetypal elements of myth that he feels are psychic in origin. He states: "It is the task of this book to show that a series of archetypes is a main constituent of mythology, that they stand in an organic relation to one another, and that their stadial succession determines the growth of consciousness. In the course of its ontogenetic development, the individual ego consciousness has to pass through the same archetypal stages which determined the evolution of consciousness in the life of humanity."[91] In a lecture titled "The Method of Nature," delivered in 1841, Emerson suggests his own version of this psychological concept when he says, "The history of the genesis or the old mythology repeats itself in the experience of every child. He too is a demon or god thrown into a particular chaos, where he strives ever to lead things from disorder into order."[92]

According to Neumann, in the beginning there is wholeness that is self-contained and unconscious. This state is usually symbolically represented by the womb, or the uroboros—the serpent that swallows itself, the all in the all, an image of perfect unity. With the rise of consciousness, this initial state of wholeness is divided. The uroboros gives rise to individual masculine and feminine entities, the World Parents, which are symbolic of the now separate conscious and unconscious. After this initial rupture, the differentiated masculine and feminine components give rise to a son, the ego, whom Neumann, like Campbell, associates with the mythic hero. As he states: "Once the Uroboros has divided into a pair of opposites, namely, the World Parents, and the 'son' has placed himself between them, thereby establishing his masculinity, the first stage of his emancipation is successfully accomplished. The ego, standing in the center between the World Parents, has challenged both sides of the uroboros, and by this hostile act has ranged both upper and lower principles against him." At this stage, the hero must contend with both of these powerful forces and establish a balance between them. Because this is primarily a conscious function, "the hero is always a light-bringer and emissary of the light."[93] His descent into the region of the unconscious, mythically represented as a journey to the underworld, or a night sea journey, provides the setting for combat with the Terrible Mother, the dragon. His capacity to defeat these forces and return to the world of light provides him, in part, with his unusual gifts and powers, the powers, which enable him, as Campbell points out, to grant boons to mankind. Here again Brown's "romantic movement," and Campbell's "monomythic" structure, are replicated. The descent into darkness and a consequent ascension, sometimes hard-fought, is also a common mythic pattern in American Romantic writing, as indicated in such studies as Harry Levin's, *The Power of Blackness*, and Leslie Fiedler's *Love and Death in the American Novel*.[94]

Neumann chooses to give particular emphasis to the culture-bringing aspect of the heroic adventure because of his determination to maintain the principle that continuous and ongoing development of consciousness is the best and proper direction of human social and psychological advancement. For him, the danger of lapsing into the unconscious and instinctive state is a constant. He observes that "One has no need to desire to remain unconscious; one is primarily unconscious and can at most conquer the original situation in which man drowses in the world, drowses in the unconscious, contained in the infinite like a fish in the environing sea. The ascent towards consciousness is the 'unnatural' thing in nature."[95]

This predisposition on the part of Neumann does not prevent him from noting further, albeit with less emphasis, that the ego hero must also contend with the negative forces of consciousness, which are represented as the Terrible Fathers. Ultimately, he too recognizes the necessary unity of the cycle. He states: "As Barlach says, the hero has to 'awaken the sleeping images of the future which can and must come forth from the night, in order to give the world a new and better face.' This necessarily makes him a breaker of the old law. He is the enemy of the old ruling system, of the old cultural values and the existing court of conscience, and so he necessarily comes into conflict with the fathers and their spokesman, the personal father."[96]

After completing his regeneration, and upon his return to the world of light, the hero finds himself in opposition to the old "system." "This spiritual system," Neumann contends, "appears as the binding force of the old law, the old religion, the old morality, the old order; as conscience, convention, tradition, or any other spiritual phenomenon that seizes hold of the son and obstructs his progress into the future."[97] This conflict of the emerging hero with the "fathers," who collectively constitute the establishment, is also a familiar theme with American Romantics and Transcendentalists. As we shall see, the conflict often has both personal and transpersonal qualities, and the hero's triumph is frequently presented as a type of rebirth. Emerson's conflict, as suggested earlier, was with his own father, William, and the surrogate fathers and authority figures who succeeded him. Another famous rebel, Frederick Douglass, presents a compelling version of this archetype in his autobiography, *Narrative of the Life of Frederick Douglass, An American Slave, Written by Himself* (1845). Douglass describes his descent into darkness as it occurred through his early experience with the slave breaker, Covey, who is a particularly vicious representation of the Terrible Father. The scene is rendered by Douglass in terms that suggest a mythic transformation.

> If at any one time of my life more than another, I was made to drink the bitterest dregs of slavery, that time was during the first six months of my stay with Mr. Covey. We were worked in all weathers. It was never too hot or too cold; it could never rain, blow, hail or snow, too hard for us to work in the field. Work, work, work, was scarcely more the order of the day than of the night. The longest days were too short for him, and the shortest of nights too long for him. I was somewhat unmanageable when I first went there, but a few months of this discipline tamed me. Mr. Covey succeeded in breaking me. I was broken in body, soul, and spirit. My natural elasticity was crushed, my intellect languished, the disposition to read departed, the cheerful spark that lingered about my eye died; the dark night of slavery closed in upon me; and behold a man transformed into a brute![98]

Douglass eventually emerges from this darkness, and is reborn as the heroic antislave. However, prior to his rebirth and his epic confrontation with Covey, Douglass escapes to the woods where he meets up with a shaman-like advisor, Sandy Jenkins. It is Jenkins who tells him that he must confront Covey, but "before I went, I must go with him to another part of the woods, where there was a certain *root*, which, if I were to take some of it with me, carrying it *always on my right side*, would render it impossible for Mr. Covey, or any other white man, to whip me."[99] This root serves as a symbolic connecting link, one that reaches down to Douglass's own deeply internal, unconscious power, his inner depth, what Neumann calls, "the fruitful center, the point of renewal and rebirth," which is the source of personal strength and, ultimately, self-reliance. It is this internal strength that makes possible Douglass's ultimate triumph over his oppressor, the "Terrible Father," Covey. In his titanic struggle with Covey, the young rebel triumphs both physically and spiritually. The hero's reflection on his victory emphasizes the element of rebirth.

> The battle with Mr. Covey was the turning-point in my career as a slave. It rekindled the few expiring embers of freedom, and revived within me a sense of my own manhood. It recalled the departed self-confidence, and inspired me again with a determination to be free. The gratification afforded by the triumph was a full compensation for whatever else might follow, even death itself. He only can understand the deep satisfaction

which I experienced, who has himself repelled by force the bloody arm of slavery. I felt as I never felt before. *It was a glorious resurrection, from the tomb of slavery, to the heaven of freedom.* My long-crushed spirit rose, cowardice departed, bold defiance took its place; and I now resolved that, however long I might remain a slave in form, the day had passed forever when I could be a slave in fact. (emphasis added)[100]

As we shall see in chapter 5, Emerson himself was uniquely touched by Douglass's example of heroic resistance, and it would reinforce his own determination to engage in direct and sometimes violent confrontations with the forces of evil and repression in his society.

Although it is obvious that Neumann recognizes the critical importance of the "rebel" aspect of the heroic function, the preference here for a more even-handed consideration of the importance of both conscious and unconscious factors in the rebirth process should be clarified. It can also be shown that Neumann's own thesis supports this approach. His insistence upon the primacy of the struggle of consciousness against the forces of the unconscious stems from his tendency to consider hero myths and creation myths as essentially analogous. However, while the primary struggle of the creation myth is between a young and feeble ego and a yet powerful and dangerous unconscious, and, hence, there is some real danger of regression, the same is not true for the hero myths. In a hero myth, as Campbell points out, the emphasis is upon *regeneration*, not simply generation. Consequently, the mature ego is far from feeble. The descent into the underworld, the immersion in the unconscious and incorporation of its powers in a potentially beneficent and helpful mother, and the consequent return of the hero to the world of light where she then battles the forces of the father, all seem to indicate that the hero is not fleeing the forces of the unconscious. Indeed, when adequately balanced, these forces are the source of her strength. Also, this regeneration and the new view of reality that the hero acquires brings him directly into opposition with the established collective consciousness, which Neumann himself refers to as "culture."[101] As Eliade shows, a state of timelessness, the destruction of profane history, a sense of rapport with one's natural environment, and a feeling of wholeness and emotional gratification and fulfillment, are all conditions that can only result from reconnecting with the unconscious. Ultimately then, while Neumann stresses the negative nature of the unconscious, as he himself indicates, "two father and two mother figures have to be borne in mind," one good, one evil.[102] When in balance, their faces are benevolent; when either is dominant it is deathly and chthonic. Indeed, this concept seems to be a truth as old as the mythic gods themselves. Walter Otto notes that the archetypal representative of the erotic unconscious, Dionysus, was seen as both the benevolent God of fertility and the gruesome God of Hades. "Today . . . one . . . asks how Dionysus, who was originally, after all, nothing but a fertility god, could have made his way into a festival of the dead."[103] While Otto was apparently never able to solve this problem satisfactorily, using the psychomythic concepts employed here, the answer seems clear. When the unconscious acts as a renewing force and is properly balanced, it is benevolent. When it comes to dominate, it is malevolent. Thus, as Otto notes, "the fullness of life and the violence of death are equally terrible in Dionysus."[104] The same could be said for Apollonian consciousness. Ultimately, however, both Neumann and Campbell agree that "Every culture-hero has achieved a synthesis between consciousness and the creative unconscious. He has found within himself the fruitful center, the point of renewal and rebirth which, in the New Year fertility festival, is identified with the creative divinity, and upon which the continued existence of the world depends."[105] The world depends upon such periodic renewal because "rationalization, abstraction, and de-emotionalization" are all qualities of consciousness, or civilization, or the Understanding, which are potentially dangerous if not balanced by the unconscious since "emotions and affects are bound up with the lowest reaches of the psyche, those closest to the instincts."[106] Neumann refers to this vital element as "libido charge." This concept helps to explain why Emerson placed such strong emphasis on the vital, and revitalizing, power of "instinct." In "Self-Reliance," he describes it as "at once the essence of genius, of virtue, and of life."[107]

While Neumann quietly recognizes that imbalance on the conscious side is always a possibility, he feels that this situation is unique to the modern era. "It is only now," he insists, "in the present crisis of modern man, whose over accentuation of the conscious, cortical side of himself has led to excessive repression and dissociation of the unconscious, that it has become necessary for him to 'link back' with the medullary region, [i. e., the unconscious]."[108] Neumann is more than acute in describing the overall characteristics of a society suffering from an overemphasis on consciousness. Such a society is preeminently a logical or, literally, an enlightened one—dominated by excessive reason. The energy of the collective libido is all but nil and, "thus, stripped of projection, the world becomes objective, a scientific construction of the mind. In contrast to the original unconsciousness and the illusory world corresponding to it, this objective world is now viewed as the only reality." This is the sere world of Newtonian laws and Lockean empiricism that Emerson faced as a young man at Harvard, a world of "common sense" that he would spend a lifetime battling.[109] It was also the world that Neumann experienced in the mid-twentieth century. When consciousness dominates, one is faced with a society that has lost its capacity to feel and dream due to its repression of emotion and imagination and its desire to preserve an increasingly oppressive economic, social, political, and one might add military, status quo. The result is deadness, or what Brown has called a "death in life." Neumann observes that "Where this [emotion] is lacking, there is only deadness: dead knowledge, dead facts, meaningless data, disconnected lifeless details, and dead relationships."[110] In this situation, institutions and value systems ossify. They lose their vitality and effectiveness. Religion is reduced to a dull formality, and, collectively, the system assumes the deadly aspect of the Terrible Father who opposes the vital hero and his life-renewing vision. The dominant characteristic of such an establishment is necessarily sterility since, "any authoritarian fixation of the cannon leads to sterility of consciousness."[111] This was certainly the case in 1836 when Emerson published his first major work, *Nature*. He opens this famous piece with a searing indictment of a backwards-looking culture of death. "Our age is retrospective," he complains. "It builds the sepulchres of the fathers. It writes biographies, histories, and criticism. The foregoing generations beheld God and nature face-to-face; we, through their eyes. Why should not we also enjoy an original relation to the universe? Why should not we have a poetry and a philosophy of insight and not of tradition, and a religion by revelation to us, and not the history of theirs?" For Emerson, the antidote to this musty, masculine sterility is found in nature, and our connecting link to nature, the unconscious. His imagery is strikingly feminine, fluid, and organic as "bosoms,' "floods," and streaming life are contrasted with "dry bones."

> Embosomed for a season in nature, whose floods of life stream around and through us, and invite us by the powers they supply, to action proportioned to nature, why should we grope among the dry bones of the past, or put the living generation into masquerade out of its faded wardrobe? The sun shines to-day also. There is more wool and flax in the fields. There are new lands, new men, new thoughts. Let us demand our own works and laws and worship.[112]

Neumann, like Brown, sees the artist as the primary agent of change and the harbinger of the new world to modern humankind. In this respect the artist becomes the hero and communicates her message through the use of appropriate archetypes. Neumann quotes from Jung's essay "On the Relation of Analytical Psychology to Poetry" in making his point.

> In this lies the social significance of art: it labors without cease to educate the spirit of the age, bringing to birth those forms in which the age is most lacking. Recoiling from the discontents of the present, the yearning of the artist reaches back to that primordial image in the unconscious which is best fitted

to compensate the insufficiency and one-sidedness of the spirit of the age. The artist seizes this image, and in the work of raising it from deepest unconsciousness and bringing it nearer to consciousness, he transforms its shape until it can be accepted by his contemporaries according to their capacities.[113]

It is primarily through the articulation of the appropriate image or symbol that the artist accomplishes this. By its very nature the symbol combines the inner and outer, the sensual and the spiritual. As Neumann notes, "The psychic world of images is a synthesis of experiences of the inner and outer world, as any symbol will show." The primary symbol of this unity is the circle, or mandala. "Structural wholeness," as Neumann notes, "with the self as center of the psyche, is symbolized by the mandala, by the circle with a center, and by the hermaphroditic uroboros."[114] As we shall later observe, Emerson made extensive use of all of these symbols in his effort to re-center American culture.

Finally, and ultimately, the individual's view of reality is a reflection of herself, or as Emerson puts it in his essay "Experience," "As I am, so I see; use what language we will, we can never say anything but what we are."[115] The imposition of order upon chaos, one of the primary goals of archaic humanity according to Eliade, results first from one's own ability to balance the conscious and the unconscious and, thus, to be reborn, to be whole. As was seen in chapter 1, for Neumann a "whole" person perceives a unified reality because "The integration of the personality is equivalent to an integration of the world."[116]

In chapter 3 we will examine the specific personal experiences and traumas of Emerson's life that led him to a process of psychological and spiritual development which resembles strikingly the journey of the hero/artist as described here, synthetically, by these four psychomythic humanists. As a result of this process of development, Emerson would emerge in the late 1830s as a radical redeemer and reformer, beloved by some but generally reviled by the fathers of his society, whose authority he directly challenged. His activities and private journal writings reflect his own personal experience, but in his published writings and his public discourse this personal experience would eventually be rendered in universal, archetypal terms.

CHAPTER 3

"GOD'S CHILD"
Emerson In His Journals
1820–1836

"All great thoughts come from the heart."

—R. W. Emerson, *The Fugitive Slave Law*

 An overview of Emerson's development from the young, ambitious, Harvard undergraduate in the 1820s, to the mature, sensitive, and seer-like artist of the *Essays, Second Series* (1844), reveals a profound change. Nowhere is this change more visible than in Emerson's attitude towards the value and function of the affective dynamic of the psyche. While the young Emerson boldly asserts in 1820 that one should "Trust not the Passions; they are blind guides," the mature Emerson of 1838 insists that it is necessary to "Trust your emotion" in order to find meaning and direction in life.[1] The process that led Emerson to this position, and through which he came to understand and trust his own emotional promptings, feelings, and intuitions, is complex and intriguing. This transformation, as reflected in the thirty-six hundred pages of journal entries inscribed during this period, closely resembles, from the psychomythic view, the "romantic movement" described in chapter 2. Although only a basic outline of this process as it evolved in Emerson's life can be presented in the following pages, an examination of his journals, letters, sermons, and other evidence from the period clearly reveals the existence of a dynamic, affective side of Emerson heretofore little noted by critics and biographers. What follows is a description of Emerson's dramatic personal transformation.

Before we begin our journey, it is necessary to say something about the journals that serve as the basis for this part of our study. The sixteen-volume "Harvard Edition" (1960–1982) differs greatly from the previous "standard edition" of the journals. This earlier work, completed in 1914 and edited largely by Emerson's son, Edward Waldo, reflects the standards of the "genteel tradition" of American letters that was then very much in vogue. Thus, it was deliberately and selectively expurgated of personal comments and reflections not in keeping with the established image of Emerson as an exemplary, nineteenth-century gentleman. While these journals did, no doubt, enhance the general understanding of Emerson, they did not allow the reader to make the acquaintance of the complex, passionate, and at times conflicted private man who exists behind the public voice. The Harvard edition, however, in the words of chief editor William Gilman, presents Emerson's journals, "pretty much in the form in which he wrote them," thus allowing us a unique opportunity to glimpse Emerson's inner mind and to witness his dynamic psychological, spiritual, and intellectual development as it actually occurred.[2]

1820–1832

The Emerson that appears throughout the earliest journals is predominately and typically a confident, ambitious, and intelligent young Harvard man, looking out into a world in which he hopes someday to prosper. Except for occasional moments of youthful self-doubt, the young Ralph Waldo Emerson might best be described as a man of conventional faith; faith in his rationalistic Unitarian religion, faith in the manifest destiny of his homeland, and faith in himself. Life's experiences would eventually shatter this innocent optimism, but early on, Emerson was a man in seeming rapport with himself and his world, a dutiful son following in the footsteps of the "fathers," both literal and symbolic.

Emerson began keeping a regular journal on January 25, 1820, in the middle of his junior year at Harvard when he was barely seventeen years old. Although the avowed purpose of this journal, in Emerson's words, was to fulfill "all the various purposes and utility real or imaginary which are usually comprehended under the comprehensive title Common Place Book," among which would be "a record of new thoughts (when they occur)," he quite often made personal comments which he assumed, at least initially, would always be private.[3] He notes at the outset, "With a serious expectation of burning this book I am committing to it more of what I may by and by think childish sentiment than I should care to venture upon vagabond sheets which Somebody else may light upon. (Mr. Somebody, will it please your impertinence to be conscience-struck!)."[4] Except for a few such personal comments, however, the dominant tone of these early journals is best described as self-consciously scholarly. They suggest a deliberate attempt to be serious and profound, which undoubtedly reflects the author's youthful ambition. Primarily, however, Emerson displays a considerable amount of confidence, if not facility, in confronting the ideas and philosophies that were presented to every young

Harvard undergraduate of the time. The names of Pope, Stewart, Newton, Scott, Milton, Locke, and Plato, among others, appear frequently. Generally, Emerson displays a consistent optimism and an unswerving faith in the social institutions of the day. He believes, by and large, that everything that is, is right. In an entry dated December 1820, for example, he proclaims confidently,

> The human soul, the world, the universe are labouring on to their magnificent consummation. We are not fashioned thus marvelously for nought. The straining conceptions of man, the monuments of his reason & the whole furniture of his faculties is adapted to mightier views of things than the mightiest he has yet beheld. Roll on then thou stupendous Universe in sublime incomprehensible solitude, in an unbeheld but sure path. The finger of God is pointing out your way.[5]

Like the enlightened eighteenth-century rationalists he so admires, Emerson believes at this time that the conscious aspect of man, his "reason," (here used in the conventional sense) will bring him to his ultimate fulfillment. Indeed, he cautions his fellow mortals, and himself, to "Trust not the Passions; they are blind guides. They act, by the confessed experience of all the world, by the observation within reach of a child's attention, contrary to Reason."[6] Even God is best perceived through the increased cultivation of the intellect, and Emerson asserts that "the readiest means of cultivating proper dispositions toward the Deity . . . [are] . . . conversation & reading."[7] All concepts of religion must, as Emerson's conservative Unitarianism largely held, be logical and rational since, "Infinite Wisdom established the foundations of knowledge in the Mind so that twice two could never make any thing else than four. As soon as this can be otherwise, our faith is loosened and science abolished."[8]

Emerson evinces this same kind of logical optimism when considering the ultimate destiny of his young nation. Blessed with the gifts of "Christianity, and a civilization more deeply engrafted in the mind . . . than ever it has before been. . . . This country is daily rising to a higher comparative importance & attracting the eyes of the rest of the world to the development of its embryo greatness."[9] From young Emerson's perspective, the nation is walking hand in hand with God towards a great and divinely ordained destiny.

Throughout this early period, the youthful Emerson consistently asserts his belief in the propriety of the ever-advancing dominance of logic and common sense. The term the "Age of Reason," he felt, can be applied "with . . . perfect propriety to this latter day when there is such an immense diffusion of knowledge."[10] He even goes so far as to assert that philosophers and scientists, as well as theologians, have established the basic truths of Christianity. As he notes, "I apprehend that Christianity is indebted to those who have established the grounds on which it rests; to Clarke, Butler, and Paley; to Sherlock, and to the incomparable Newton."[11] The problem of evil, which will shortly become a troublesome matter, at this time is explained, with a certain Calvinistic propriety, simply as evidence of God's demanding love. "[T]here is no longer any doubt of the Divine Benevolence arising from the existence of evil. Evil is the rough and strong foundation of human Virtue; weaning man away from the seductive dangers of vicious transient destructive pleasures to a hold and security of Paradise where they are perpetual and perfect."[12]

Despite this early overriding self confidence, certain intimations of skepticism begin to appear in Emerson's mind concerning the validity of accepted philosophies in answering the problems of life. The rationalistic equation, it seems, may hold a hidden flaw. Perhaps it is just such an obscure and foreboding feeling that leads the young nineteen-year-old Emerson to point out, in an entry dated November 30, 1822, that the optimistic philosophy which has thus far dominated his thinking is as yet an untested one. The firsthand experience of misery might yield a different perspective.

> Happiness lies at our door. Misery is further away. Until I know by bitter personal experience that the world is the accursed seat of all misfortunes, and as long as I find it a garden of delights—I am bound to adore the Beneficent Author of my life. The young, the healthy, & the prosperous,—we will make haste to thank God for his goodness, before the evil days come and the years draw nigh when thou shalt say I have no pleasure in them. No representations of foreign misery can liquidate your debt to Heaven. You must join the choral hymn to which the Universe resounds in the ear of Faith, and I think, of Philosophy.[13]

The intimation of change recorded here proved prescient. The ensuing ten years of the young scholar's life brought forth some rather astonishing developments. Emerson graduated from Harvard, in the middle of his class, in August 1821 and began teaching in his older brother William's school for young ladies. He continued this existence for a time but was somewhat less than satisfied with the possibilities it held for an ambitious youth still eager to make his mark in the world. Consequently, in February 1825, Emerson applied and was accepted into Harvard's Divinity College, thus following in the footsteps of his forefathers. After four years of conscientious but ultimately average performance, he was ordained as a Unitarian minister and accepted the position of junior pastor at the Second Church in Boston in 1829.[14]

Later that same year Emerson married the young and beautiful Ellen Tucker and settled into a comfortable existence as preacher, pastor, and husband. This nearly idyllic existence proved to be brief. In February 1831, Ellen died of consumption. This event precipitated the greatest crisis, both emotional and intellectual, of the young minister's life. By February 1832, Emerson began to consider leaving the ministry and on September 11, 1833, he submitted a formal letter of resignation. Seldom does a life evince such a dramatic and profound change of course. By resigning his position in the prominent Second Church, Emerson began casting his lines free of all that had held him bound to the world of his father(s). For the next year, he wandered in a spiritual and philosophical wilderness from which he would eventually emerge with a dramatically new vision of himself and his world. In the journals, one is able to trace the pattern of these remarkable developments.

At the end of the period 1822–1832, Emerson's worldview, a construct that rested largely on the traditional values and attitudes that he absorbed at Harvard, collapsed dramatically. The tragic death of Ellen, as we shall see, revealed to Emerson that his traditional faith, for the most part the product of his academic training, was a frail tissue. It could not withstand the battering of the "thousand natural shocks that flesh is heir to," and so a new vision had to be found, a new paradigm of meaning that would be equal to the task. The events of this period thus depict the execution and completion of the first aspect of what was referred to in chapter 2 as the "romantic movement." Eventually discovering the emotional, spiritual, and intellectual bankruptcy of the institutions and values with which he was raised, Emerson decided to abandon these former beliefs and set out bravely in search of a new and vital truth, one that he would eventually find within himself. Of course, none of this happens in a single instant, and certain developments are of more importance than others in precipitating this dramatic turn of events. Looking at the journal entries for this period, one notes a gradually accelerating sense of doubt, a growing feeling of dissatisfaction with the emptiness of reason and logic, and an increasing sense that something vital was lacking in his life experience.

As early as December 1822, Emerson gives evidence of a growing uncertainty in dealing with a subject that not long before presented no real difficulties, namely, the problem of evil. One journal entry finds him, after winding along a somewhat serpentine path of logical argument, entwined in a rather knotty problem. "And some plan will be developed, in which the good of *Evil*, will be made plain, on the general scale, that cannot be explained on the particular. It was with a vague idea of this kind, that I started, and fear that I have involved myself in a bold speculation. My results can be only detrimental to myself as they shall never be exhibited to bewilder others if I find they terminate in darkness."[15] Although Emerson is still determined to castigate the "lurid fires of malignant & infernal passions," his attitude toward the function and value of "reasoning," as he previously employed the term, slowly begins to change.[16] By April 1824, before starting his "professional studies" for the ministry, he begins to become aware of his own inclination towards the "imagination" and this leads him to object to the "Reasoning Machines" who attempt to remove completely the emotional element from religious experience. This development coincides, interestingly enough, with the personal confession that his talents have not yet been equal to his ambitions in life. The same passage also hints at Emerson's intuition that the search for the ultimate truth will, indeed, be an inward journey where he will be guided by his own "moral imagination."[17]

> I cannot dissemble that my abilities are below my ambition. . . . I have or had a strong imagination & consequently a keen relish for the beauties of poetry. The exercise which the practice of composition gives to this faculty is the cause of my immoderate fondness for writing, which has swelled these pages to a voluminous extent. My reasoning faculty is proportionately weak, nor can I ever hope to write a Butler's Analogy or an Essay of Hume. Nor is it strange that with this confession I should choose theology, which is from everlasting to everlasting "debatable Ground." For, the highest species of reasoning upon divine subjects is rather the fruit of a sort of moral imagination, than of the "Reasoning Machines" such as Locke & Clarke, & David Hume.[18]

Emerson later confides in his journal that, while his life ambitions have not yet been realized, his newly found vocation might offer him that opportunity. As he writes, "in Divinity I hope to thrive."[19]

As suggested in the passage above, it becomes increasingly clear in examining Emerson's journal entries for this early period that their movement draws steadily away from the arid concerns of rational consciousness towards the realm of the unconscious, the realm of emotion, imagination, and the senses. This latter element is not surprising in light of the fact, as noted by Neumann in chapter 2, that the "emotions and affects are bound up with the lowest reaches of the psyche, those closest to the instincts." The more Emerson moves in the direction of emotional gratification, imagination, and rapport with the natural world, the further he removes himself from the main stream of Unitarian orthodoxy. Because "rationalization, abstraction, and de-emotionalization," are the dominant qualities of consciousness, the individual who would, in Brown's words, liberate the instincts and provide "relief from the pressures of reason" must first overcome the repressive conscious structures of the prevailing cultural paradigm.[20] Not surprisingly, therefore, the more Emerson becomes attuned to his affective, imaginative, and poetic side, the less orthodox his thinking becomes. This leads, in turn, to a growing desire to act on these powerful feelings. And with this, the inchoate "liberating poet" begins to emerge. Also in these formative years, Emerson at times yearned for a more powerful affective, creative energy, one that would burn with true poetic intensity. "Even those feelings," he confesses, "which are counted noble & generous, take in me the taint of frailty. For my strong propensity to friendship, instead of working out its manly ends, degenerates to a fondness for particular casts of features perchance not unlike the doting of old King James. Stateliness & silence hang very like Mokannah's suspicious silver veil, only concealing what is best not shewn. What is called a warm heart, I have not."[21] While Emerson would express such emotional frustration from time to time later in his life, during this early period he did not yet have the compensating satisfaction that his art and later social reform efforts would eventually afford him both as a stimulant and as an outlet for passionate expression. His overflowing love of humanity would find expression, ultimately, in the marvelous essays, poems, and addresses that manifest his irrepressible desire to "Give all to Love" in an effort to redeem his world.

By 1825, Emerson was willing to assert that "Reason" cannot stand alone and must always be accompanied by sentiment. Not surprisingly, the illustration he uses to make his point possesses the same sexual polarity that Neumann attributes to the conscious and unconscious. "Altho' Reason makes merriment out of the tears of Nature," Emerson writes, "our praise of the Reason is always enhanced by the knowledge of its connexion with sentiment (It else wants the completeness of its nature. It is man without wife)."[22] While Emerson, in April 1826, could still assert the dominant importance of "facts" over "fictions, whether of the theorist or the poet," this attitude was clearly changing.[23] Also, a concern with the passage of time and the growing proximity of death begins to appear. As Brown and Eliade show, such a concern suggests that the unconscious, with its quality of timelessness, has not yet asserted a mature and thus compensating influence. Also, of course, Emerson lived at a time when medical science was virtually nonexistent and, much more so than today, death could come from accident or disease at any moment to anyone. Even youthfulness was no guarantee of enduring health. On March 27, 1826, at age twenty-two, Emerson records the following: "My years are passing away. Infirmities are already stealing on me that may be the deadly enemies that are to dissolve me to dirt and little is yet done to establish my consideration among my contemporaries & less to get a memory when I am gone."[24] Perhaps in response to such intimations of mortality, Emerson's movement away from objective standards and values towards the subjective, intuitive, and time-less would continue to accelerate for the next three years as he grew closer to the resources of his own inner self. To use his metaphor from the later essay, "Circles," during this period he gains velocity in orbits of increas-ing radius around the traditional centers of faith and orthodoxy. Eventu-ally, after building up sufficient speed, he will spin off into deep outer space, there to establish a new galaxy, a new ontogenetic and therefore homocentric cosmos.

By May 1826, Emerson, now in the midst of his formal divinity studies, clearly evidences a growing tendency towards independent think-ing based upon "feeling" and "instinct," and the "affections of the soul" (all expressions of the power of the unconscious), rather than purely log-ical argumentation.

> I please myself with contemplating & nourishing my own independence—the invincibility of thought; with imagining a firmness of purpose, or if that be not philosophically tenable, a fixedness of opinion which optimism is the growth of the Deity's laws indeed but over which even Omnipotence has no control. The conspiring universe cannot make me feel wrong to be right without altering the Constitution of my nature. Tho' I am prone to love & second this independence there are many things in mere speculation I dare not say and the last page affords an instance of the limits thus set by mind to its daring. This seems to me an evidence from my instincts of God's existence.[25]

On the "last page," which he references here, Emerson had written, "I feel that the affections of the soul are sublimer than the faculties of the intellect. I *feel* immortal."[26]

On October 10, 1826, Emerson was approbated to preach by the Unitarian church. Health problems, probably related to incipient tuber-culosis, led him to journey south at this time in an effort to recover.[27] Dur-ing this journey, the young preacher would continue his religious ruminations. In one journal entry, Emerson speculates upon the possibil-ity that moral knowledge is always intuitive, a seminal notion that would later become a cornerstone of his Transcendentalism. "But moral science is bestowed on all. We are born to it. It is the sun in heaven, by whose light we must walk. The rich & the poor, the wise & the foolish, bond & free, all partake of this universal beam and are guided by it at their own choice into evil or good, into the broad or the narrow way."[28] It is useful to note at this point the nuanced but perceptible difference in the very tex-ture and structure of Emerson's developing prose style. His journal entries show that his expression is becoming more metaphorical, imaginative, and cosmic, as the light of moral science becomes the "universal beam" of inner enlightenment. The creative element in Emerson's psyche is obviously now beginning to act upon the new possibilities that reality offers for recreation. As he moves away from the formal language of logic, a new world of spontaneous, playful imagery emerges. The process is similar to that experienced by Eliade's primitive who periodically "recreates" his cosmic environment in a symbolic fashion. Emerson would later describe the basis for this symbolic act in *Nature* (1836) where he says that, "The beauty of nature reforms itself in the mind, and not for barren contemplation, but for new creation."[29] The drift away from the rigid constraints of conventional scholarship, and toward the creative processes of nature and art, is also suggested in the increasing volume of poetry that Emerson commits to his journal during this period. In one poem we find a revealing description of a certain young man who wishes to turn away from his books and return to nature and its "heady wantonness."

> And tossing boughs combined their cadences
> The sweet & solemn melody they made
> Enticed him oft in heady wantonness
> To scoff at knowledge, mock the forms of life
> Cast off his years & be a boy again.[30]

Such an expression of sentiment anticipates Brown's statement that "mankind is that species of animal which has the immortal project of recovering its own childhood."[31] Clearly, at this point, Emerson has taken the initial, albeit tentative, steps in that direction.

Late in 1827, after returning to Cambridge, Emerson made an entry in his journal concerning the fact that "My days are made up of the irregular succession of a very few different tones of feeling."[32] This, perhaps, is not unusual in itself but directly above this passage is a notation which the journal's editors observe is "in a cramped hand and squeezed in between the preceding and following paragraphs." It says simply, "I ought to appraise the reader that I am a bachelor & to the best of my belief have never been in love."[33] This statement was probably written after Emerson's first meeting with Ellen Tucker at Christmas time, 1827. She was then sixteen years old. He was twenty-four.[34] Apparently the young minister and would-be poet was instantly smitten by the beautiful and intelligent Miss Tucker, and the feeling was reciprocated. A year later, on December 17, 1828, they became engaged. Shortly thereafter one finds, following an outline of a sermon on "the office of a Christian minister," a statement that reflects a new and important element in the life of Ralph Waldo Emerson. It reads simply, "Oh Ellen, I do dearly love you."[35] By falling in love with Ellen Tucker, Emerson, probably for the first time in his young adult life, felt the free and full influence of his emotional, affective side. It is a spark that would soon give rise to a bonfire.[36] Interestingly, it is this very image that Emerson would later use in his essay "Love" (1841) to describe this powerful and efficacious force.

> For it is a fire that kindling its first embers in the narrow
> nook of a private bosom, caught from a wandering spark out
> of another heart, glows and enlarges until it warms and beams
> upon multitudes of men and women, upon the universal heart
> of all, and so lights up the whole world and all nature with its
> generous flames.[37]

It is important to note here the movement from the one to the many, from the particular to the universal, since it not only indicates the biographical pattern of Emerson's actual experience, but it is also germane to his philosophic vision. In Emerson's published works, the particular "facts" of his own experience would provide the medium through which he experienced and later expressed the universal, the divine. Indeed, the editors of the journals state, "what seems remote, abstract, or impersonal in the essays will often turn out to be rooted in immediate experience and an active sense of life and persons in the journals."[38] For Emerson, facts in themselves, like individual lives when seen in isolation, are ephemeral, mutable, and mortal. It is humankind's failure to locate them in a universal pattern of being and becoming that eventually results in tragedy, as Campbell and Eliade affirm in discussing the destructive aspect of "profane time," noted earlier. Emerson's writings present an effort to reverse this tendency by placing experience in a timeless, cosmic context, "the universal heart of all."

Emerson married Ellen Tucker on September 30, 1829. Following this event, his theological and philosophical speculations become increasingly unorthodox. This is not surprising. Richard Lebeaux observes, using an Eriksonian model, that "while identity confusion may inhibit intimacy, intimacy itself may provide a 'gradual clarification' of identity[,] and . . . Emerson's relationship with Ellen Tucker served to re-inforce the process of identity development that would soon remove him completely from the orthodoxy of Unitarianism."[39] In fact, Emerson's journal comments show a consistent tendency to assert the importance and validity of an intuitive grasp of Christian truth and the immediate presence of God. This was at a time when Unitarianism was moving in the opposite direction, establishing the divinity of the historical Christ on the basis of his miracles and other empirical "evidence" derived through textual study and analysis.[40] An entry dated January 4, 1830 largely rejects this position. "It will not do to dogmatize. Nothing is more untrue to nature. The meanest scholar in Christian practice may often instruct the greatest doctor both in faith & practice. I have no shame in saying I lean to this

opinion but am not sure—I do not affect or pretend to instruct—o no—
it is God working in you that instructs both you & me."[41]

In a journal entry in August 1830, Emerson addresses religious for-
malists whose faith revolves around tedious arguments regarding doctrine and dogma. "Alii disputent, ego mirabor [Let others wrangle, I will
wonder], said Augustin. It shall be my speech to the Calvinist & the Unitarian."[42] By December 1830, he was prepared to simply state: "All
things are full of God." Finally he asserts, "my own mind is the direct
revelation which I have from God."[43] The implications of this dramatic
insight would soon be made manifest.

On February 8, 1831, after weeks of progressive debilitation, Ellen
Tucker Emerson died of "consumption," the plague of tuberculosis that
claimed multitudes throughout the nineteenth century. With this tragic
event, Ralph Waldo sustained what was probably the most severe emotional trauma of his life.[44] His first journal entry, just days after the event,
reflects his agony as well as the conventional theological context through
which he attempts to find solace.

> Five days are wasted since Ellen went to heaven to see,
> to know, to worship, to love, to intercede. God be merciful
> to me a sinner & repair this miserable debility in which her
> death has left my soul. Two nights since, I have again heard
> her breathing, seen her dying. O willingly, my wife, I would
> lie down in your tomb. But I have no deserts like yours,
> no such purity, or singleness of heart. Pray for me Ellen &
> raise the friend you so truly loved, to be what you thought
> him. . . . Not for the world would I have left you here alone;
> stay by me & lead me upward. Reunite us, o thou Father of
> our Spirits.[45]

Two days later, Emerson attempted a less conventional response. He
inscribed the first of several pages of poetry, all of which concern the fact
of Ellen's death, the overwhelming sense of loss that he feels, and also a
rather painful request for assurance that her spirit yet survives. The
experiment is revealing.

> Dost thou not hear me Ellen
> Is thy ear deaf to me
> Is thy radiant eye
> Dark that it cannot see
>
> In yonder ground thy limbs are laid
> Under the snow
> And earth has no spot so dear above
> As that below

And there I know the heart is still
And the eye is shut & the ear is dull

But the spirit that dwelt in mine
The spirit wherein mine dwelt
The soul of Ellen the thought divine
From God, that came—for all that felt

Does it not know me now
Does it not share my thought
Is it prisoned from Waldo's prayer
Is its glowing love forgot[46]

Rather than projecting a conventional heavenly setting, the major emphasis of the poem is on the immediate physical being of Ellen, the ear that does not hear, the eye that does not see, and the limbs that are now "laid / Under the snow." The poem associates Emerson's physical love for Ellen with the experience of divinity, "The soul of Ellen the thought divine / From God," thus suggesting the concept of the "spirit made flesh" that other Romantics, like Whitman, would later embrace so thoroughly. Emerson at this time, however, is unable to finally locate the fact of Ellen's death in a comprehensible pattern of life events. It remains for him largely a singular, temporal, and, consequently, tragic event. Also, his emotional attachment to Ellen has not yet been fully universalized into a loving union with the world. The probable reason for this is that the world at the moment offers no apparent avenues for such a rapprochement. Reality everywhere, especially the Unitarian church he serves, is dominated by the traditions and institutions of the "fathers," those largely unemotional and intellectual guardians of society who preside over this "Age of Reason." In order to establish a satisfying relationship with the world at large, it will be necessary for Emerson to break away completely from these obdurate encumbrances and to create the world anew. He must bring together intellect and emotion, reason and intuition, thought and feeling, conscious and unconscious, in a psychological paradigm that allows the free interplay of these polar elements. No longer must thinking and feeling be separate functions. In light of this, it seems highly likely, as Emerson's journal editors and other scholars have long suspected, that "The evidence in these journals . . . suggests that [Ellen's] death played a large part in his rejection of orthodox Christianity."[47]

Following the death of Ellen, Emerson continued his pastoral duties but with increasing uneasiness and a deepening depression. His growing dissatisfaction with his Unitarian faith became more and more centered upon its lack of emotional content and spiritual vitality. His comments relating to this problem leave little doubt that the emotional and spiritual void created by Ellen's death could not be filled by his formal religion as it was then constituted. Neither could the heavily freighted theological dogma, upon which that religion was based, offer a satisfactory explanation for such an event. Because Unitarianism had lost its "libido charge," and was predominantly a rational, ego-conscious entity, it could offer only, in Erich Neumann's words, "deadness; dead knowledge, dead facts, meaningless data, disconnected, lifeless details, and dead relationships," all of which was but cold comfort to a sensitive individual suffering through the loss of the first real love of his life.[48] The unconscious aspect of Emerson's psyche, experienced through the emotions and instincts, began to emerge in the later 1820s, and this process was accelerated dramatically by his loving relationship with Ellen. Deprived of that major source of psychological fulfillment and satisfaction, Emerson's continuing relationship with what he later refers to as "the icehouse of Unitarianism" became all but impossible. He now began an active search for a philosophy and a faith that would satisfy the whole person, both head and heart. Only such a philosophy could reunify his body and his soul, his spirit and his flesh, and thus effect his physical and spiritual rebirth. The critical role of Ellen's death in precipitating this process of rebirth has been noted by several of Emerson's contemporary biographers.[49] Emerson's profound depression (some refer to it as a nervous breakdown) following the death of Ellen produced in him tremendous emotional energy, a veritable psychic storm that unsettled everything in his life. This energy, like all psychic energy, could ultimately result in the catastrophic dissolution of the individual, or it could serve as the necessary resource for a complete reinvention of the man and his world. For Emerson, it would be the latter.[50] Through the experience of this tragic loss, Emerson opened himself fully, for the first time, to the inner voice of his own unconscious. The resulting conversation would constitute the beginning of his personal experience of the "transcendent function" from which would flow his psychological, spiritual, and intellectual rebirth.

With the death of Ellen, Emerson moved toward the first step in what Campbell has described as the "monomythic movement" of the hero. It consists in "detachment or withdrawal . . . a radical transfer of emphasis from the external to the internal world." Thus, Emerson frequently reminded himself at this critical time that he should "Trust to that prompting within" while he continued to battle with his sense of loss.[51] An entry dated April 4, 1831 notes, "The days go by, griefs, & simpers, & sloth & disappointments. The dead do not return, & sometimes we are negligent of their image. Not of yours Ellen—I know too well who is gone from me."[52] Later he quotes from Coleridge's "Wallenstein" the significant lines,

> The oracle within him that which *lives*
> He must invoke & question—not dead books
> Not ordinances, not mouldrotted papers[53]

Clearly, the vitality and emotional gratification that the bereaved Emerson sought was not to be found in merely intellectual pursuits, particularly when those pursuits are centered on "dead books," "ordinances," and "mouldrotted papers," the soon-to-be discarded debris of Unitarianism. By June 1831, he inscribed the following comment in his journal indicating his readiness to leave behind the formal arguments of rigid religious persuasions in favor of a more "natural" and satisfying feeling of rapport with the divine. "I suppose," he writes, "it is not wise, not being natural, to belong to any religious party. In the bible you are not directed to be a Unitarian or a Calvinist or an Episcopalian. . . . I am God's child." In July he notes; "Suicidal is this distrust of reason; this fear to think; this doctrine that 'tis pious to believe on others' words, impious to trust entirely to yourself. . . . To reflect is to receive truth immediately from God without any medium. That is living faith. To take on trust certain facts is a dead faith—inoperative." As this passage suggests, by this time Emerson's concept of "reason" itself was changing. It is no longer strictly the logical, rational, faculty of the mind, but concerns more the intuitive apprehension of truth received "immediately from God." What was formally understood by the term "reason" is now referred to by Emerson as "the Understanding," and is used that way in the entry that follows the above. "Calvinism stands, fear I, by pride & ignorance & Unitarianism as a sect, stands by the opposition of Calvinism. It is cold & cheerless, the mere creature of the understanding."[54]

In a letter to his younger brother Edward in May 1834, Emerson makes this distinction explicit and in the process, he indicates the sources for this new, Transcendental terminology. "Now that I have used the words," he says, "let me ask you to draw the distinction of Milton Coleridge & the Germans between Reason & Understanding. . . . Reason is the highest faculty of the soul—what we mean often by the soul itself; it never *reasons*, never proves, it simply perceives; it is vision." On the other hand, "the Understanding toils all the time, compares, contrives, adds, argues, nearsighted but strong-sighted, dwelling in the present the expedient the customary."[55] As noted earlier, this critical distinction, a hallmark of Emerson's Transcendentalism, parallels the distinction made by the psychomythic humanists between the conscious (Understanding) and the unconscious (Reason).[56] Emerson's further elaboration of the qualities of the two makes this correlation even more compelling. "Reason," he says,

> is potentially perfect in every man—Understanding in different degrees of strength. The thoughts of youth, & "first thoughts," are the revelations of Reason. The love of the beautiful & of Goodness as the highest beauty the belief in the absolute & universal superiority of the Right & the True [.] But understanding [,] that wrinkled calculator [,] the steward of our house to whom is committed the support of our animal

life[,] contradicts evermore these affirmations of Reason &
points at Custom & Interest & persuades one man that the
declarations of Reason are false & another that they are at
least impracticable.[57]

As he continued to be drawn away from the realm of arid intellectualism, Emerson became more and more concerned with the natural
world. A part of him was now attracted to it in a way that he had not experienced before. This is not surprising since, as Brown points out, "The
aim of Eros (the unconscious) is union with objects outside of the self."
Perhaps for this reason, we find Emerson making the following entry in
December 1831. "So love of nature. The soul & the body of things are
harmonized, therefore, the deeper one knoweth the soul, the more intense
is the love of outward nature in him."[58]

Eventually, as Emerson grew closer to the rhythms of nature, he became more aware of his own emotions and instincts as connecting links
with divinity, Eros, the eternal One, with the unconscious. To become
one with nature is to become one with oneself since, as he would later indicate in his seminal work, *Nature* (1836), "Strictly speaking . . . all that
is separate from us, all which Philosophy distinguishes as the NOT ME,
that is both nature and art, all other men *and my own body*, must be
ranked under this name, Nature" [emphasis mine]. He would later add:
"The world proceeds from the same spirit as the body of man. It is a re-
moter and inferior incarnation of God, a projection of God in the unconscious." Therefore, "We are as much strangers in nature, as we are aliens
from God" and, by implication, aliens from ourselves.[59]

The natural world would eventually become for Emerson a symbolic manifestation of the divinity within, "a mirror image of the soul."
The intrinsic unity of the symbol itself also reflects the ideal harmony of
the conscious and the unconscious. Otto Rank, in one of his most significant essays, "Art and Artists," suggests as much when he insists that all
art is inherently symbolic because it gives concrete expression to what
one intuitively feels, and that art itself originates with the religious impulse, or humanity's "idea of the soul." "Compared with the idea of the
soul," he insists, "or its primitive predecessors, even the abstractest form
of art is concrete," and therefore, "religion has always drawn art along in
its wake from the earliest times to the present day."[60] Eventually, this
would be the case for Emerson also; however, first it would be necessary
for him to free himself, finally, from the restrictions of society's dead institutions and to establish a new source of faith, a personal religion. But
the death of Ellen continued to haunt him. He had fallen into the habit of
taking daily walks to Roxbury to visit her tomb. On March 29, 1832,
during one of these visits, he records in his journal, "I visited Ellen's tomb
& opened the coffin."[61] At this point, Ellen had been dead for a year and
two months. Biographers have speculated as to Emerson's psychological

motivation in opening the coffin, and his journal contains no discussion of the act. It seems clear, however, that the burden of his loss still lay heavily upon him at this time. It remained difficult for him to accept the finality of Ellen's death. Also, as of yet, he had no meaningful context in which to place this traumatic loss that would satisfy him both emotionally and intellectually and thus provide closure.[62]

By February 1832, suffering in both body and mind, Emerson's former confidence, faith, and optimism in established forms had all but entirely melted away. He became convinced that he must now, "Settle everything anew."[63] On June 2, 1832, he sent a letter to the Second Church, where he had been serving quite successfully as minister, requesting a change in the communion service. Apparently, he still had some slight hope of breathing new vitality and life into his church and himself, and to make both more responsive to the immediate needs of the time. This hope was tentative at best, however, and Emerson undoubtedly felt a sense of personal crisis. He records on this day:

> June 2, 1832. Cold cold. Thermometer Says
>
> Temperate
> Yet a week of moral excitement.
> It is years & nations that guide my pen.
> I have sometimes thought that in order to be a good minister
> it was necessary to leave the ministry. The profession is anti-
> quated. In an altered age we worship in the dead forms of
> our forefathers. Were not a Socratic paganism better than an
> effete superannuated Christianity?
> Does not every shade of thought have its own
> tone so that wooden voices denote wooden minds?
> Whatever there is of Authority in religion is that
> which the mind does not animate[64]

The "Socratic paganism" to which Emerson refers comes increasingly to mean a teleologic sense of God in nature, or perhaps one might more correctly say, God in humankind as part and parcel of nature. The awakening sense of emotional energy or religious vitality that led Emerson to feel now that he was "God's child" also made him aware of the beneficent energy of God at work in the world around him. The panharmonic wood gods of the ancients were but an earlier manifestation of this same energy. Emerson's ability to respond to and appreciate these symbolic epiphanies is yet another indication of the growing influence of his unconscious religious instincts. Later in June, he retired to the White Mountains in New Hampshire. Here, at this time of deepening personal crisis, he felt a closeness with nature that he contrasts, as would be his habit, with the pedantical, mechanical world of sterile ego-consciousness. Emerson was now prepared to "undress himself" in an almost Whitmanesque embrace of nature.

> The good of going into the mountains is that life is re-considered; it is far from the slavery of your own modes of living. . . . He who believes in the woodloving muses must woo them here. And he who believes in the reality of his soul will therein find inspiration & muses & God & will come out here to undress himself of pedantry & judge right-eous judgment & worship the First Cause [.][65]

On July 15, 1832, Emerson made his final decision to resign his pastorate, rejecting the enervated rituals of a dead and lifeless church.

> The hour of decision. . . . I know very well that is a bad sign in a man to be too conscientious, & stick at gnats. The most des-perate scoundrels have been the over refiners. Without ac-commodation society is impracticable. But this ordinance is esteemed the most sacred of religious institutions & I cannot go habitually to an institution which they esteem holiest with indifference & dislike[.][66]

Emerson's resignation was voted upon and reluctantly accepted. Carlos Baker points out that "A clear majority among his parishioners were dis-inclined to let him go."[67] Clearly, the desire for separation was based en-tirely on Emerson's unhappiness with himself, with the church, and with his ministerial role, and not any dissatisfaction on the part of his congre-gation. Still suffering from ill health that was undoubtedly related in part to his profound depression, Ralph Waldo decided to set sail for Europe in the hopes of effecting both a physical recovery and a spiritual rebirth.[68] Appropriately enough, it was on Christmas day, 1832, that he cleared for Malta aboard the *Jasper*.

1832–1836

The four-year period from the resignation of his pastorate in 1832, to the publication of his first major work, *Nature,* in 1836, was a time of dra-matic transformation for Emerson. It represents the middle stage of Campbell's "monomyth," which involves the descent into darkness. Dur-ing this time, Emerson turned away from the perceived wasteland of con-ventional religious and social norms and values and began looking more deeply within himself for a new and satisfying philosophy. During this in-ward journey of discovery, he would probe the deepest, previously un-fathomed reaches of his own unconscious. Eventually, he would discover that this mysterious and long-repressed "other self" possessed the very

power of healing that he so desperately needed. Indeed, it would prove to
be a dynamic and life-changing manifestation of what Emerson considered
to be divinity itself. This dramatic source of strength and insight would ultimately inform his greatest writings. They are the by-products of this
journey. For Emerson, as for others, the unconscious is a source and not a
destination.[69] As Alan Hodder observes, during this period Emerson's
journals contain many passages that reflect the "themes of death and resurrection—of Ellen, of Christ, of Emerson himself." But he goes on to
note perceptively that "the power and enthusiasm of Emerson's revelation
of the god within have prompted many scholars to search for some decisive event, some mystical or creative breakthrough that could explain it.
The journals of the period give no evidence for such an event, however—
only death and darkness. Yet, here, ironically, is where Emerson felt the
impulse of new life. This darkness, and nothing else, was the source of revelation."[70] Clearly, this was a continuation of Emerson's dark night of the
soul, a time of profound sadness, uncertainty, and pain through which he
was able, finally, to discard the residue of orthodoxy that had inhibited his
regeneration. At the nadir of his internal journey, Emerson reached the
shores of primal darkness—that vast and boundless source from which all
life flows, finally, into the light. This time of pain was, therefore, also a
time of hope. The sere ashes of his former life would become fertile once
again and give rise to the birth of a new self. This newborn poet and
prophet would have little in common with the broken New England minister who had abandoned his paternal home in search of a new world and
a new self. His painful journey would lead, finally, to that fruitful center
of transcendence that would fortify him and precipitate his rebirth. From
these dark depths, Emerson eventually ascended again into the light,
regenerated, renewed and possessed of "the knowledge that passeth all
understanding." This process, however, would take time.

Significantly, throughout this dark period, Emerson continued to
move still closer to nature, that sensual object of life to which, as we have
seen, the instincts are naturally drawn. Not surprisingly, he would consistently attribute sensual, feminine characteristics to nature, at times equat-
ing it with his lost wife, as well as with divinity. In this way, he anticipates
a later time when he would refer to nature confidently as "my other self."
Throughout this period, Emerson remained very much involved with the
task of recreating himself, of unifying body and soul, flesh and spirit, unconscious and conscious. It was a time of personal healing and growth, the
necessary antecedent to his rebirth into the world.

Early in the process of personal discovery, Emerson indicates his
pressing desire to know himself and to look more deeply within. After
his arrival in Europe, in a passage dated February 10, 1833, he notes,
"Perhaps it is a pernicious mistake yet rightly seen I believe it is sound
philosophy, that wherever we go, whatever we do, self is the sole subject
we study & learn. Montaigne said, himself was all he knew. Myself is

much more than I know, & yet I know nothing else."[71] During this time, Emerson continued to develop an increasing sensitivity towards the natural world around him, something that is notably lacking in the early journals. In many instances, such as in the poem below, he associates the natural environment with the memory of his late wife, Ellen.

> Of any woman that is now alive
> Hath such a soul, such divine influence
> Such resurrection of the happy past
> As is to me when I behold the morn
> Ope in such low moist roadside, & beneath
> Peep the blue violates out of the black loam
> Pathetic silent poets that sing to me
> Thy elegy, sweet singer, sainted wife[.][72]

Eventually these two concepts, loving wife and an emotionally charged and living cosmic environment, will blend completely in Emerson. For a true man, he would later write, "the Universe is his bride."[73]

During his tour of Europe, Emerson recorded many thoughts about religion and religious sentiment. Perhaps, because of the grandeur and beauty of the ornate churches and cathedrals that he visited there, he became more certain his rejection of "dry, lifeless, unsightly . . . dogmas" in favor of the "beauty of the truths to which they are related."[74] His comments upon the physical beauties of the European churches that he visited strongly suggest a yearning for sensual gratification and religious sentiment that certainly would seem out of place for the average New England son of John Calvin. They undoubtedly affirm Rank's statement that "religion has always drawn art along in its wake."

> I hope they will carve & paint & inscribe the walls of our churches in New England before this century, which will probably see many grand granite piles erected there, is closed[.]
>
> . . . .
>
> Have the men of America never entered these European churches that they build such mean edifices at home?
>
> . . . .
>
> I love St. Peter's Church. It grieves me that after a few days I shall see it no more. It has a peculiar smell from the quantity of incense burned in it. The music that is heard in it is always good & the eye is always charmed. It is an ornament of the earth. It is not grand, it is so rich & pleasing; it should rather be called the sublime of the beautiful[.][75]

The kind of sensual pleasure and sublimity that Emerson sought in religion corresponds closely to that which he came to find in the realm of nature. It is not surprising, therefore, that in a journal entry recorded after his return home he should associate the two in a simple, symbolic way. "Fine walk this P.M. in the woods with C," he notes, "beautiful Gothic arches yes & cathedral windows as of stained glass formed by the interlaced branches against the grey & gold of the western sky. We came to a little pond in the bosom of the hills, with echoing shores."[76]

It is interesting to note that in 1842, some years after making his journal entries on European churches, Emerson had cause to reflect upon the unexpected conversion of a young female acquaintance of his, Abby Larkin Adams, the daughter of his friend Abel Adams, to the Roman Catholic faith. His comment seems to recall this earlier experience. Although most of her "decorous" Unitarian associates were somewhat shocked by the event, Emerson's sympathetic reaction indicates clearly his positive, understanding attitude toward the Roman Catholic Church's sensual, humanistic, and emotionally gratifying qualities. His only warning is that these rites and rituals not be embraced for their "surface" value only. He says of the event, "If the offices of the Church attract her, if its beautiful forms & humane spirit draw her, if St Augustine & St Bernard, Jesu & Madonna, Cathedral, Music & Masses, then go, for thy dear heart's sake, but do not go out of this icehouse of Unitarianism all external, into an icehouse again of externals."[77] Emerson's trip to Europe obviously had tempted him with the sensual attraction of the Roman Church. To a man awash with unmet emotional and spiritual needs, the sensual/spiritual appeal of St. Peter's was undoubtedly strong. It touched Emerson profoundly, and he felt its pull. However, he was not about to trade one dominant father for another, even one this attractive. For the time, he would continue as his own soul/sole believer.[78]

Slowly but determinedly, Emerson continued the exploration of the inner self which had been up to this point "much more" than he knew. Although he was not yet prepared to articulate for the world the nature of the discoveries he was making, he was no doubt already looking forward to the time when he would, as an entry in September 1833 clearly indicates: "But the men of Europe will say, Expound; let us hear. What is it that is to convince the faithful & at the same time the philosopher? Let us hear this new thing."[79]

When the time would finally arrive for "this new thing" to be expounded, Emerson was determined that it would be through a language closely associated with nature. This new language would be organic, sensual, and symbolic; it would be what Brown calls "the language of Adam." As Emerson notes in his journal:

There is not a passion in the human soul, perhaps not a shade of thought but has its emblem in nature.

Let a man under the influence of a strong passion go into the fields & see how readily every thought clothes itself with a material garment. Is it not an illustration to us of the manner in which every spirit clothes itself with a body?

Nature is a language & every new fact that we learn is a new word.[80]

In a later entry, Emerson expresses the idea that these symbols are liquid and volatile and should properly change with the times. "Language clothes nature as the air clothes the earth," he observes, "taking the exact form & pressure of every object. Only words that are new fit exactly the thing, those that are old like old scoriae that have been long exposed to the air & sunshine, have lost the sharpness of their mold & fit loosely."[81] This theory of evolving symbols corresponds to and reflects Emerson's later philosophical belief that "the speculations of one age do not fit another," an idea most clearly stated in his 1844 essay, "Circles." It is also eloquently expressed in his "American Scholar" address (1837), as will be seen in chapter 4.

By the time of his return from Europe, Emerson was well on his way towards establishing the kind of internal balance and harmony that had been so painfully lacking in the dark times immediately following Ellen's death.[82] He was also slowly coming to recognize his ambition to communicate to the world his newfound faith. A comment, recorded on September 5, 1833, just before the start of his voyage home, suggests that Emerson's seminal book, *Nature* (1836), was already begun. "I like my book about nature," he notes, "& wish I knew where & how I ought to live. God will show me."[83]

Perhaps anticipating more clearly his future role as poet, prophet, oracle, and, finally, social reformer, Emerson now began to look upon his once private journals as "my Savings Bank. I grow richer because I have somewhere to deposit my earnings." The principle use he would make of this capital would be to ransom the impoverished souls of his fellow Americans. The basis of his formal writings would be the private, spontaneous, eclectic entries of his journal, written when his mind was largely free from the logical constraints of formal composition. The lecture platform would become "the new pulpit of the age." Emerson now clearly understood the path that lay before him. In April 1834, at the beginning of what would be a lengthy, and at times tumultuous career, he asserted confidently, "The whole secret of the teacher's force lies in the conviction that men are convertible. And they are. They want awakening."[84]

During the period immediately following his return from Europe in October 1833 Emerson lectured on a variety of subjects, ranging from

"The Uses of Natural History" to the lives of such prominent religious rebels as Martin Luther, John Milton, and George Fox.[85] He also preached on occasion, something which he would continue to do until 1839. The beauties of the natural environment remained a source of refreshment, renewal, and wonder to Emerson and their vitality stood in vivid contrast to the arid, mechanical functioning of everyday conscious existence. In the following entry, he describes a walk in the beautiful cemetery at Mt. Auburn.

> Went yesterday to Cambridge & spent most of the day at Mount Auburn, got my luncheon at Fresh Pond & went back again to the woods. After much wandering & seeing many things, four snakes gliding up & down a hollow for no purpose that I could see—not to eat, not for love, but only gliding; then a whole bed of Hepatica triloba, cousins of the Anemone all blue & beautiful but constrained by niggard Nature to wear their last year's faded jacket of leaves; then a black capped titmouse who came upon a tree & would know his name, sang a *chick a dee dee*; then a far off tree full of clamorous birds, I know not what, but you might hear them half a mile. I forsook the tombs & found a sunny hollow where the east wind could not blow & lay down against the side of a tree to most happy beholdings. At last I opened my eyes & let what would pass through them into the soul. I saw no more my relation how near & petty to Cambridge or Boston, I heeded no more what minute or hour our Massachusetts clocks might indicate— I saw only the noble earth on which I was born, with the great Star which warms & enlightens it.[86]

The passage is epiphanic. The symbolic suggestiveness of the dark "noble earth on which I was born," and the sun, the "great Star" which "enlightens it" gives some indication of the reason why Emerson now found the natural environment a tremendous source of pleasure and peace. The uninhibited immersion in the senses relaxes the grip of consciousness and allows for the free expression of the energy of the unconscious. Here mother earth and father sky, Ghea and Ouranos, body and soul, enjoy a pristine harmony and union. It is an ideal and timeless state that transcends the ephemera of Emerson's daily life and the tragic details that depressed him so. He is now prepared to forsake "the tombs," emblems of death and sterility, and to substitute eternity. Emerson is not now concerned with "Massachusetts clocks" or the other demands of the world of arid consciousness. As Brown maintains, because "the instinctual processes in the id [unconscious] are timeless . . . only repressed life is in time. . . . A healthy human being, in whom ego and id, [conscious and unconscious], were unified would not live in time."[87] His journals indicate that this was now increasingly the case for Emerson. In epiphanic and quietly ecstatic moments, like that at the Auburn cemetery, Emerson frequently experienced this very transcendence, an emanation of the divine. In a later entry in December 1834, he describes this emerging psychic equipoise, now using his new Transcendental terms for the unconscious and conscious, the "Reason" and the "Understanding." "Today, riding to East Sudbury, I pleased myself with the beauties & terrors of the snow; the oak-leaf hurrying over the banks is fit ornament. Nature in the woods is very companionable. There, my Reason & my Understanding are sufficient company for each other."[88] It would be difficult to stress too strongly the importance of this concept of nature to Emerson's developing mind. It is seminal to his intellectual, spiritual, and psychological evolution. As the psychomythic humanists put it, there are two basic facts that humankind initially confronts as concomitant to existence. The first is the fact of one's own existence, and the second is the existence of the natural world outside the self. Emerson would express this succinctly in his "American Scholar" address (1837) where he says; "The first in time and the first in importance of the influences upon the mind is that of nature."[89] In order to be mentally healthy, the individual must establish a harmonious relationship with both nature and self as a part of nature. The unconscious provides the individual's link with that outside world. The world will flow through her fingertips or stay at arm's length depending upon her capacity and willingness to love it, and consequently, to love her own existence. The individual is simultaneously an observer of nature and a part of it. If the emotional, sensuous, erotic, and instinctive energies of the unconscious are repressed through an act of excessive ego-conscious control, the individual becomes dissociated from nature and, hence, at odds with herself. Instead of the "other me," the natural world (which includes human society) becomes the "not me." The consistent repression of the unconscious and the body through which it acts results, as Brown points out, in a death in life. Young Ralph Waldo had already experienced the "dead forms" of the inoperative cultural institutions offered him by his ego-conscious, rational, and "enlightened" society. In gravitating towards nature, which symbolizes and reflects the instinctual and emotional wellsprings of psychic vitality within, he sought to reestablish a vital harmony and balance so sorely lacking at this point. As a result, increasingly throughout this period Emerson turns to his senses, to his body, to Eros, in order to experience the world anew.[90] It is this new sensual and emotional grasp of reality that is later to inform his literary art, which he would describe as a mixture of the human mind with nature. For Emerson, "A work of art, is an abstract or epitome of the world. It is the result of an expression of nature in miniature."[91]

Similarly, Emerson's theory of language is predicated on the proposition that "Words are signs of natural facts" and "Particular natural facts are signs of particular spiritual facts."[92] The assertion that all things are a combination of both matter and spirit, that is, that they are perceived by both the senses and the intellect, is in itself a paradigm of the unified unconscious and conscious. One is thus able to express in words, through the use of conscious intellect, that which one emotionally "feels." Ideally, all language becomes, by Rank's definition, de facto, symbolic.

By March 1835, Emerson's growing inner faith and psychological harmony are sufficient to the point that, for the first time, he is able to accept the death of Ellen as a natural and inevitable thing. The passage is in stark contrast to the bitter outpourings of grief noted earlier. Clearly, something more than time has effected this dramatic change.

> In talking weeks ago with M [ary]. M [oody]. E [merson]. I was ready to say that a severest truth would forbid me to say that I ever had made a sacrifice. That which we are, in healthy times seems so great that nothing can be taken from us that seems much. I loved Ellen, & love her with an affection that would ask nothing but its indulgence to make me blessed. Yet when she was taken from me, the air was still sweet, the sun was not taken down from my firmament & however sore was that particular loss, I still felt that it was particular, that the Universe remained to us both.[93]

As Emerson's faith in the validity and authority of his own intuitional promptings and inner depths increased, he became more inclined to sharpen his criticism of the present age. He came to feel that in this "age of Propriety, . . . elegance is . . . superadded . . . cleanness is . . . painting and gilding." It is a superficial age that sees only the flat surfaces of things, (as Brown has already noted, consciousness is "the surface of ourselves"). While the youthful Emerson considered the "practicality" of the age one of its greatest attributes, the now reborn Emerson feels that "those who are styled Practical men are not awake, for they do not exercise the reason." It is this distressing lack of "Reason," or connectedness with the unconscious, that is responsible for the deathly aridity of the present social moment since, "Every fact studied by the Understanding is not only solitary but desart. But if the iron lids of Reason's eye can be once raised, the fact is classified immediately & seen to be related to our nursery reading & our profoundest Science."[94]

As Emerson gradually established a viable psychic equipoise between his unconscious and conscious, or, to use his Transcendental terms, his Reason and his Understanding, he began to develop some of his most seminal concepts. His attitude towards history, the external record of the passage of time, for example, changed dramatically. While the youthful Emerson felt that history was useful because it supplied concrete facts that might be put to practical employment in making present-day decisions, the mature Emerson came to see history as much more personal, and, at times, mythic and archetypal. For him, the history of one person was now understood to be the history of all people. Thus, he states in his journal: "I read the history of all men in myself." The present moment encompasses all time. He later explains further that "all history is to be written from man, is all to be explained from individual history or must remain words."[95] This insistence upon the archetypal significance of individual human experience as the central paradigm of history is simply another aspect of the overall sense of harmony and unity that Emerson increasingly felt and which characterizes his now re-centered and humanisticly self-centered way of seeing. This attitude would also further define the heroic role that Emerson was beginning to play with more certitude in his society. As Campbell points out, after "dying to the world" the hero "comes back as one reborn, made great and filled with creative power."[96]

Emerson's life throughout this critical period was not devoid of pain and suffering, nor was it devoid of happier experience. The death of Emerson's brothers, Edward in October 1834, and Charles in May 1836, both from consumption, saddened him considerably. In reflecting on Edward's death in his journal he states soberly: "So falls one pile more of hope for this life. I see I am bereaved of a part of myself."[97] He had been particularly close with Charles. Shortly after his death, Emerson wrote the following to Harriet Martineau, the controversial British reformer whom he and Charles had both befriended and defended during her recent visit to the United States.[98]

> I cannot tell you how much I miss him[.] I depended on him so much. . . . But I cannot find with the best thought that I can give it that I can attain to any thing beyond simple passion in relation to such events as this. Faith will become mere wonder and sad amazement. I can gather no hint from this terrible experience respecting my own duties[.] I grope in greater darkness & with less heed.[99]

Despite the somber tone of this statement, these sad events did not cause the kind of deep despair and lingering depression such as followed the death of Ellen. Ultimately, Emerson refused to relinquish his optimistic philosophy and the feeling of wholeness and unity that came increasingly to dominate his thinking. He survived these storms intact. Thus, he would go on to assert in his letter to Martineau: "But we can not stand still and Hope is behind all the changes even the last. We shall soon know all."[100]

External events came less and less to act as catalytic forces in shaping Emerson's mind. Rather it seems just the opposite, that his mind would now characterize, interpret, and ultimately comprehend those external events. Indeed, he became increasingly convinced that it was possible to "build your own world." Virtually every experience can now be accounted for, and Emerson seems confident that his theory of "compensation" is correct and that in the universe all things, ultimately, come full circle. Tragedy results from a limited vision. Tragedy can only occur in what Eliade calls "profane time," and Emerson has now found the key that will allow him to accommodate and even transcend the painful limitations of the ephemeral world. The influence of this new philosophy would extend even into the intimate details of his private life, which is where, after all, it originated. Emerson remarried in 1835. Notice of this event appears as the following simple journal entry.

14 September 1835, I was married to Lydia Jackson.[101]

Several critics have noted a significant difference in tone between Emerson's first marriage and his second. And there is his own statement in a letter to his brother William announcing his engagement with "a very different feeling from that with which I entered my first connection. This is a sober joy."[102] This comment has led some to question the emotional content of the marriage. Robert Richardson observes, for example, that "we have to estimate the real affection and affinity of the two of them across the stone walls of traditional New England reserve" but this was obviously not the case with his marriage to Ellen.[103] Given our discussion here, however, it is entirely likely that Emerson, having initiated an ongoing dialogue between the affective and intellectual aspects of his inner self, "the Reason" (unconscious), and "the Understanding" (conscious), which resulted in a dynamic balance between the two, was now prepared to enter into a union that supported this evolving harmony. Indeed, he tells Lidian (as he would later call her) nearly exactly that in a letter dated January 24, 1835, wherein he first proposed marriage. "I obey my highest impulses," he asserts, "in declaring to you the feeling of deep and tender respect with which you have inspired me. I am rejoiced in my Reason as well as in my Understanding by finding an earnest and noble mind whose presence quickens in mine all that is good and shames and repels from me my own weakness. Can I resist the impulse to beseech you to love me?" Recognizing that their relationship had developed over a short period of time (mere months likely), Waldo acknowledges that "the strict limits of the intercourse I have enjoyed, have certainly not permitted the manifestation of that tenderness which is the first sentiment in the common kindness between man and woman. But I am not less in love," he insists, "after a new and higher way. I have immense desire that you should love me, and that I might live with you always."[104] The now thirty-two-year-old ex-minister has clearly been deeply moved, in both heart and mind. In September, Waldo and Lidian were married and established their residence in Concord, Emerson's ancestral home. In the next few years, Emerson would occasionally record in his journals observations about the "new and higher" form of marriage alluded to in his letter to Lidian. In a journal entry in April 1838, less than two years after the commencement of his second marriage, he recorded the following commentary on the typical course of married life. The "youth & maiden" proceed "from exchanging glances . . . [to] . . . acts of courtesy & gallantry, then to fiery passion, then to plighting troth & to marriage. Immediately they begin to discover incongruities, defects." This leads to some transitory disappointment and friction but, after a period of adjustment, "At last they discover that all that at first drew them together was wholly caduceus," that is, existing merely on the surface level of consciousness. What the couple eventually comes to realize, however, is that "the unsuspected & wholly unconscious growth of principles from year to year is the real marriage foreseen & prepared from the first but wholly above consciousness."[105] This same concept appears at the conclusion of the poem, "Give All to Love," where the speaker maintains that personal romantic love is only a stepping-stone to cosmic love, "Heartily know, / When half-gods go, / The gods arrive."[106] This higher level of love, the level of Eros, is at once both emotional and spiritual, which undoubtedly explains Emerson's later observation that "Love is temporary & ends with marriage." This comment, taken out of context by some critics, sounds negative, indeed, but Emerson's further elaboration clarifies his point. "Passion" is merely transitory while real love, which has a spiritual as well as a physical dimension, is enduring and, therefore, far superior. Cupid gives way to Eros, and through the body and its attendant personality the individual connects with divinity. Thus, it follows for Emerson that "Marriage is the perfection which love aimed at, ignorant of what is sought. Marriage is a good known only to the parties. A relation perfect understanding, aid, contentment, possession of themselves & of the world—which dwarfs love to green fruit."[107] Emerson's marriage to Lydia Jackson would last for almost fifty years, until his death. In that time they faced many trials and tribulations, and endured many hardships together, including the births of four children and the death of one. The latter event, especially, would test the emotional and spiritual resources of both. Ultimately, however, Lidian never failed to meet these challenges, as her children and others have testified.[108] Throughout her long marriage to America's most notable poet-prophet, it was clear, as Lawrence Buell puts it, that "she was no ordinary being."[109]

Around this time, Emerson returned to speculations about the nature of sin, and spiritual wholeness. As noted by Eliade earlier, "the existence of man in the cosmos is generally regarded as a fall."[110] This is because the rise of ego-consciousness fractures that primal sense of unity that is characteristic of the unconscious state. Erik Erikson, in his *Child-hood and Society*, refers to this phenomenon as intrinsic to the psycholog-ical development of the individual. He points out that "even under the most favorable circumstances this stage seems to introduce into psychic life (and become prototypical for) a sense of inner division and universal nostalgia for a paradise forfeited. It is against this powerful combination of a sense of having been deprived, of having been divided, and of having been abandoned—that basic trust must maintain itself throughout life."[111] Individuals can rectify this situation by maintaining a balance between these contending forces, thus capturing again, on a conscious level, an ap-proximation of primal unity and wholeness. When this happens, the feel-ing of imperfection and sinfulness is largely lost. Consequently, we find Emerson asserting in 1836 something quite different from his earlier, youthful and brooding speculations on sin. These dark ruminations are now, like his initial grief at the death of Ellen, apparently nearly forgotten. He boldly asserts that, "Some young people suffer from speculations as Original Sin, Origin of Evil, Predestination &c. I was never sick of those mumps or measles or whooping coughs."[112] For Emerson, God is now within, made manifest as Reason, the vital force of the "eternal One," the unconscious and to be one with God is to be in harmony with oneself.

> Our compound nature differences us from God, but our Rea-son is not to be distinguished from the divine Essence. We have yet designed no words to designate the attributes of God which can adequately stand for the Universality & perfection of our own intuitions. To call the Reason "ours" or "human," seems an impertinence, so absolute & unconfined it is. The best we can say of God, we mean the mind as it is known to us.[113]

By age thirty-two, Emerson had become sufficiently aware of his own inner psychological processes so as to define in a few words that which it has been the purpose of the past several pages to explain.

> Man is conscious of a twofold nature which manifests itself in perpetual contradiction. Our English philosophers to denote this duality, distinguish the Reason and the Understanding. Reason is the superior principle. Its attributes are Eternity & Intuition. We belong to it, not it to us. Human individuality is an upstart just now added to this Eternal Beatitude.[114]

Like Campbell's mythic hero, Emerson has discovered now that the "Everlasting" lives in him and consequently, he "dwell[s] in the groves of the wish-fulfilling trees, drink[s] the brew of immortality, and listen[s] everywhere to the unheard music of eternal concord."[115] It is this inner harmony that made possible the ultimate resolution of the good/evil axis, along with other polarities of human perception, that he expresses in his poem "Brahma," a work in which he also manifests his own internalization of godhead.

> If the red slayer think he slays,
>   Or if the slain think he is slain,
> They know not well the subtle ways
>   I keep, and pass, and turn again.
>
> Far or forgot to me is near;
>   Shadow and sunlight are the same;
> The vanished gods to me appear;
>   And one to me are shame and fame.
>
> They reckon ill who leave me out;
>   When me they fly, I am the wings';
> I am the doubter and the doubt,
>   I am the hymn the Brahmin sings.
>
> The strong gods pine for my abode,
>   And pine in vain the sacred Seven,
> But thou, meek lover of the good!
>   Find me, and turn thy back on heaven.

While this provocative, oracular poem has often baffled critics, in the light of our discussion here certain aspects become reasonably clear. By unifying the previously divided polarities of the psyche, conscious and unconscious, Understanding and Reason, Emerson is able to transcend the perception of opposites that frustrates those in a divided state. The clash of life/death, good/evil, light/dark, doubt/certainty, and heaven/hell, and all other painful manifestations of the uncentered, unbalanced psyche, has given way to a transcendent perception of wholeness. Emerson, in such ecstatic moments, is truly "part and particle of God." It is through the unifying power of the Over-Soul (unconscious), that the binary disjunction of subject-object is overcome. As Emerson states in his essay on the Over-Soul, "this deep power in which we exist, and whose beatitude is all accessible to us, is not only self-sufficing and perfect in every hour, but *the act of seeing, and the thing seen, the seer and the spectacle, the subject and the object, are one.*"[116] Thus, David Porter says of "Brahma" and other such poems of transcendence, that they are not "distilled philosophy" but instead, "transformings of a persistent inner imperative that lodged below the level of Emerson's conscious aim."[117] Such a view certainly comports with our interpretation here.

1836–1844

During the period distinguished by the publication of *Nature* in September 1836 and *Essays, Second Series* in October 1844, Emerson's intellectual, spiritual, emotional, and artistic development reached a fulfillment that is reflected in his remarkable productivity. During this time he created most of the essays, addresses, and poems for which he is primarily remembered today. On the domestic scene, his marriage to Lidian would be a source of comfort and continuing fulfillment. Four children were born to them during this period. Three would survive to adulthood and provide both satisfaction and support to their often-doting father.[118] It is clear that by this time Emerson had found the answer to the question he first asked himself in 1833 concerning "where and how" he ought to live. While it was a satisfying life, it was far from a tranquil one. Emerson's Transcendental philosophy emphasizes the importance and validity of humankind's instinctive, intuitive, and emotional promptings. It encourages the individual to listen carefully to the voice within, and, if after reflection it appears to be the right and necessary thing to do, to follow that voice even if it runs counter to the accepted wisdom of the age.[119] Perhaps not surprisingly, this revolutionary philosophy eventually led Emerson into a head-on collision with the "fathers" of American society. Partially as a result of this confrontation, he came more and more to assume the active role of the mythic hero, whom Neumann describes as "a breaker of the old law . . . the enemy of the old ruling system, of the cultural values and the existing court of conscience."[120] It is primarily in this role that Emerson would establish his enduring fame. It was at this time that he began to engage his society in an effort to reform and redeem it. Ultimately, this would prove to be the beginning of the new "Great Awakening" that he once glimpsed as a young man. It is an enterprise that would occupy the balance of his life.

Of course, it is not possible to burn constantly with a hard, gem-like flame (to use Walter Pater's phrase), and during this period Emerson continued to have moments of self-doubt. At such times, especially following the loss of his two brothers, he felt frustrated with his own inability to achieve a greater intimacy with others in his life, as the following passage, inscribed in May 1837, indicates.

> Sad is this continual postponement of life. I refuse sympathy & intimacy with people as if in view of some better sympathy & intimacy to come. But whence & when? I am already thirtyfour years old. Already my friends & fellow workers are dying from me. Scarcely can I say that I see any men or women approaching me; I am too old to regard fashion; too old to expect patronage of any greater or more powerful. Let

me suck the sweetness of those affections & consuetudes that
grow near me,—that the Divine Providence offers me.[121]

He also exhibits a growing sense that his desire to serve his society as an
"oracle" and reformer was an obligation that was yet to be met.

> You think that because you have spoken nothing when others
> spoke and have given no opinion on the time, upon Wilhelm
> Meister, upon Abolition, upon Harvard College, that your
> verdict is still expected with curiosity as a reserved wisdom.
> Far otherwise; it is known that you have no opinion: You are
> measured by your silence & found wanting. You have no or-
> acle to utter, & your fellowmen have learned you cannot help
> them; for oracles speak.[122]

The function of the hero, of course, is to address society's ills in an effort
to bring about reform and redemption. Despite his self-accusation that he
had yet to fully engage his society, or perhaps because of it, within a year
of penning this passage Emerson would deliver his first antislavery address, publish an open letter to the president of the United States bitterly
criticizing him and his administration for mistreatment of the Cherokee
Indians, and publicly castigate the Harvard College establishment for its
failure to educate in his "American Scholar" address. He would soon follow this with an attack upon the genteel corruption of the Unitarian
Church itself in what was probably the most controversial presentation
of his life, his "Divinity School Address." Indeed, the "oracle" would
speak, and speak in thunder.[123] The consequences of these bold acts of
rebellion set the course for the balance of his life.

This descent into the turmoil, tribulation, and dynamic cultural flux
of antebellum American society was no easy thing for the gentle re-
former/poet. And yet, despite moments of doubt and anxiety when he
clearly would have preferred to put off the robe of reformer and to "let
this cup pass," Emerson continued to develop an emotional and spiritual
resiliency that fortified him for the role that he was destined to play. Additionally, having opened himself to the influence and energies of his unconscious, inner self, he began to see the expression of its content in his
writings as a satisfying compensation for the pain that he was at times
forced to endure.

> The advantage of the Napoleon temperament, impassive, unim-
> pressible by others, is a signal convenience over the other tender
> one which every aunt and every gossiping girl can daunt &
> tether. This weakness be sure is merely cutaneous, & the suf-
> ferer gets his revenge by the sharpened observation that belongs

to such sympathetic fibre. As even in college I was already content to be "screwed" in the recitation room, if, on my return, I
could accurately paint the fact in my youthful Journal.[124]

During this time of increasing social involvement, a development that
testifies to the growing strength of the "sympathetic fiber" within him,
Emerson became more certain of himself and, ultimately, more self-
reliant in his personal as well as his social relationships. Consequently,
in February 1838, he recorded in his journal a demand that he be accepted for what he was. The heroic equipoise between conscious and unconscious, thought and feeling, the Understanding and the Reason, that
Emerson had now achieved, is reflected in a dramatically increased level
of self-reliance, a quality that he came to see as the sine qua non of all
personal as well as social development. As Jung points out, this balancing
of the psyche's polarities, which he called the "transcendent function,"
becomes "a way of attaining liberation by one's own efforts and of finding the courage to be oneself."[125] That Emerson had achieved this state
by the late 1830s is reflected in the following journal passage.

> You must love me as I am. Do not tell me how much I should
> love you. I am content. I find my satisfactions in a calm con-
> siderate reverence measured by the virtues which provoke it.
> So love me as I am. When I am virtuous, love me; when I am
> vicious, hate me; when I am lukewarm, neither good nor bad,
> care not for me. But do not by your sorrow or your affection
> solicit me to be somewhat else than I by nature am.[126]

This statement may have been addressed to Margaret Fuller, destined to be his Transcendental cohort, whose relationship with Emerson
began in July 1836.[127] As their friendship grew more intimate, Fuller
sometimes chided Emerson for his purported failure to express his emotions more openly. In her journal for 1842, for example, Fuller, who
was at Emerson's home for a three-week visit at the time, complains
that his "life is in the intellect not the affections."[128] What Fuller may
have been witnessing was simply Emerson's effort to keep their relationship on an appropriately Platonic level while Margaret felt the need
for something more. Robert Richardson says of the two, "If Emerson
guarded his heart with her, it was because he had to. He loved her, and
he knew he loved her. More than any other person—except possibly
Ellen—Margaret Fuller got through to Emerson's emotional life."[129]
Whatever the case, it is clear that Emerson was sufficiently content with
the status of his affective side by this time to withstand the criticism of
others on this score, even those close to him. His relationship with Lidian was undoubtedly a help. As indicated earlier, his marriage to her

was founded on both personal and transcendent love and, despite whatever criticisms Fuller or her younger friend and fellow Emerson admirer, Caroline Sturgis, might offer, his psychological equilibrium was by now firmly established.[130] Within four years this stability would be sorely tested through personal tragedy.

It is at this time that Emerson's theory of organic language, which had been developing for some years, became increasingly refined. This is yet another indication of his continuing psychological, spiritual, and intellectual evolution. In journal entries that would eventually appear in various lectures, addresses, and essays, he consistently associates words with objects in nature and insists upon their organic, symbolic, and emotive quality. They came to represent for him the ideal combination of spirit and matter, fact and sentiment, or in our terms, conscious and unconscious elements. He states in an entry dated May 8, 1837:

> Years are well spent in the country in country labors, in towns, in the insight into trades & manufacturers, in intimate intercourse with many men & women, in science, in art, to the one end of mastering in all their facts a language by which to illustrate & speak out our emotions & perceptions. . . . My garden is my dictionary.[131]

If, as Brown maintains, the ideal language is Adam's, then Emerson's garden here becomes his own Garden of Eden.

In an entry recorded later in 1837, he associates language with the processes of life and as such divorces it from the arid realm of philological scholarship. For Emerson, all true language comes from God and is a reflection of this divine source. "So lies all the life I have lived as my dictionary from which to extract the word which I want to dress the new perception of this moment. This is the way to learn Grammar. God never meant that we should learn Language by Colleges or Books."[132] Still later, in 1840, he contrasts the vitality of the earthy language of the streets with the dusty sobriety of the *North American Review*. In Emerson's view, language is a living thing, literally and figuratively.

> The language of the streets is always strong. What can describe the folly & emptiness of scolding like the word *jawing*? I feel too the force of the double negative, though clean contrary to our grammar rules. And I confess to some pleasure from the stinging rhetoric of a rattling oath in the mouth of truckmen & teamsters. How laconic & brisk it is by the side of a page of the North American Review. Cut these words & they would bleed; they are vascular & alive; they walk & run.[133]

It was natural for Emerson to equate words with experience, with facts, and also with emotions, affections, and flesh. As noted earlier, he came to see words, as Whitman would, as symbols that reflect, among other things, the union of body and soul. As an artist who worked exclusively with such materials, much of Emerson's emotional and psychological satisfaction was undoubtedly derived from the artistic, creative process. His art was a way of "making the unconscious conscious," as Brown would say. It was a way of balancing the psyche, of enacting Jung's "transcendent function," of carrying on a conversation between the conscious and the unconscious. Emerson's vision of the natural world as a harmonious and symbolic entity, consisting of matter and spirit, is a reflection of his own internal, psychological equilibrium. Thus, in striving to maintain the unity of the conscious and unconscious through his art, Emerson moves in a direction similar to that outlined by Brown. Namely, he would return to the natural and "essentially playful" aspect of words in order to emulate the language of Adam and, hence, "recover the power of sensual speech."[134] This inclination, no doubt, helps to explain his later enthusiasm for, and support of, Walt Whitman. It is this kind of redeeming and unconventional exuberance that Emerson hoped to communicate in his lectures. The lecture, he felt, was essentially a new and largely underdeveloped art form that, when done right, was capable of reflecting the power of the sublime.

> Why should we write dramas, & epics, & sonnets, & novels in two volumes? Why not write as variously as we dress & think? A lecture is a new literature, which leaves aside all tradition, time, place, circumstance, & addresses an assembly as mere human beings,—no more—It has never yet been done well. It is an organ of sublime power, a panharmonicon for variety of note.[135]

Emerson sought to reshape the art of lecturing into an effective piece of sublime "artillery" which might be fired in the name of sympathy and affection. Like all creative artists, he was very much aware of the difficulties involved in developing a form adequate to the message. As Lawrence Buell points out, for Emerson, "literary creation was not simply an amusement, or even a useful instrument, but a sacred act."[136] This "sacred act" is the subject of the following comment by Emerson on his frustrations and past failures, and his determination to continue his campaign, nevertheless, in an effort to communicate "extacy," emotional fire, and ultimately the experience of the divine.

> These lectures give me little pleasure, I have not done what I hoped when I said, I will try it once more. I have not once

transcended the coldest selfpossession. I said I will agitate others, being agitated myself. I dared to hope for extacy & eloquence. A new theatre, a new art, I said, is mine. Let us see if philosophy, if ethics, if chiromancy, if the discovery of the divine in the house & the barn, in all works & all plays cannot make the cheek blush, the lip quiver, & the tear start. I will not waste myself. On the strength of Things I will be borne, and try if Folly, Custom, & Convention, & Phlegm cannot be made to hear our sharp artillery. Alas! alas! I have not the recollection of one strong moment. A cold mechanical preparation for a delivery as decorous,—fine things, pretty things, wise things,—but no arrows, no axes, no nectar, no growling, no transpiercing, no loving, no enchantment—.[137]

Emerson's use of the term "artillery" to describe his lecture hints at a new element of militancy associated with his evolving role as oracle, prophet, and redeemer. It puts one in mind of his previous reference to the "Napoleon temperament," aspects of which he clearly admired. (As Emerson undoubtedly knew, one of Napoleon's special strengths was his training and skill in the use of artillery.) In assuming the character of the cultural hero, Emerson wished to "fire the artillery . . . of sympathy & emotion" in an effort to redeem his "mechanical" society. As he well knew, sympathy, emotion, imagination, dream, and other life-sustaining functions of the unconscious, could provide the libido ballast necessary to revitalize and redeem his society, just as he himself was restored and reborn through the same agency following the death of Ellen.[138] As the hero/redeemer, the oracle of a new age, Emerson obviously sensed that he would be engaged in ongoing conflict with the repressive powers of what he called, "the establishment." Such heroes, notes Campbell, "are eloquent, not of the present, disintegrating society and psyche, but of the unquenched source through which society is reborn. The hero," he says, "had died as a modern man; but as eternal man—perfected, unspecific, universal man—he has been reborn." Following his rebirth, Campbell states, the goal of the hero is "to return then to us, transfigured, and [to] teach the lesson he has learned of life renewed."[139] This would clearly be the case for Emerson. Unfortunately, such heroism is more easily accomplished in myth than in the hodiernal world where the sharp elbows of time and space often intrude. Emerson was frequently frustrated that he had not sufficient time to make each lecture the liberating and moving instrument he hoped it would be. At one point he complains that could he "spend sixty hours on each" rather than "twenty-one" he should "hate [himself] less" and could better help his "friend" who is, obviously, humankind.[140] It is no doubt the unique but inevitable curse of every great artist that such friction should exist between a timeless cosmic vision and the stubborn limitations of time, place, publisher, lecture hall, or railroad timetable.

Increasingly, Emerson's insistence upon the necessity of recovering, as it were, the emotional and spiritual vitality of the unconscious, led him to an extended criticism of the "practical" society he once so admired. He came to feel that there was little of the heroic in American life, despite its presumed noble destiny. In May 1837 he states: "Yes, it is true there are no men. Men hang upon things. They are overcrowed by their own creation. A man is not able to subdue the world. He is a Greek grammar. He is a money machine. He is an appendage to a great fortune, or to a legislative majority or to the Massachusetts Revised Statutes or to some barking & bellowing Institution, Association, or Church."[141] By this time, in his own personal life, Emerson had reached a balance between the practical affairs of the world, matters of the Understanding, and the dynamic, instinctual, and spiritual realm of the Reason. Correspondingly, his concept of "Culture," which he increasingly sought to define for America, came to consist of a balanced society comprising both the sensual and the spiritual, rather than simply an ornate superficiality of manners and decorum that seemed to him to be prevalent at the moment. "Culture in the high sense does not consist in polishing or varnishing," he notes, "but in so presenting the attributes of Nature that the slumbering attributes of man may burst their iron sleep & rush full grown into day. The Heart in a cultivated nature is the emotion of delight which is awakened by any manifestation of goodness."[142] The question of the moment was, where is the "emotion of delight" in American culture? Where is the goodness?

On August 31, 1837, Emerson delivered his famous Phi Beta Kappa address, "The American Scholar," at Harvard. In the address he vigorously attacked the general lifelessness of the academic community at his alma mater and other such institutions in America. It was a bold opening shot that resonated with his youthful audience. Not surprisingly, at this time Emerson's journals reveal an increasing concern with the concept of heroism.[143] The publication of *Nature* in September of the previous year had established his reputation as an unorthodox thinker, but the Harvard address was Emerson's first major step in directly challenging the fathers of society and fulfilling his self-defined role as "oracle." At the time he wrote the address, according to Richardson, Emerson was in a "rebellious, challenging mood."[144] Allen maintains that many of the authorities on hand for the occasion left feeling that the man from Concord had succeeded in sowing discord, and that there was little doubt that he knew it.[145] Sensing that his time had come, Emerson recognized that the road he was called to travel would be, at times, a very difficult one. In October 1837, he recorded in his journal,

The Heroic cannot be common nor the common the heroic. Yet we have the weakness to expect the sympathy of people in those actions whose very excellence is that they outrun all sympathy & appeal to a tardy justice. If you would serve your brother because it is fit for *you* to serve him, do not take back your words or falter in your purpose & discountenance your brother, when you find that prudent people do not commend you. Be still true to your own act.[146]

Later, in November, he observed,

They do not know yet what their importunity hinders you from being. Resist their windy requests; give leave to Great Nature to unbind, fold after fold, the tough integuments in which your secret character lies, & let it open its proud flower & fruitage to the day, and when they see what costly and hitherto unknown blessing they had well nigh defrauded the world, they will thank you for denying their prayer & will say, we have used you as a handy tool, Now we worship you as a Redeemer.[147]

Armed with a growing confidence in his ability and obligation to address the egregious failings of American society, and convinced that it was his calling to do so, Emerson became increasingly aware that further confrontation with the established authorities was inevitable.[148] Four months before delivering what was destined to be his most controversial public presentation, the "Divinity School Address" (July 15, 1838), he made the following entry. "There must be a Revolution. Let the revolution come & let One come breathing free into the earth to walk by hope alone. It were a new World & perhaps the Ideal would seem possible."[149] There could be no doubt as to the grounds upon which this war was to be fought. Emerson, now acutely affective, attuned to his senses, and vitally responsive to the divine spirit stirring within, was determined to infuse a new breath of spiritual life and sublimity into the dry theology of his youth and the sickly soul of his society. The fathers, the leaders of society's established institutions, were equally determined that the infernal passions that were at the heart of the young heretic's vision would not take precedence over sober intellect in what Emerson himself once referred to admiringly as "this Age of Reason."

In a journal passage in June 1838, Emerson reminded himself that it was necessary to "Forget the past" and to "Trust your emotion." As for the established religious institutions around him, he says simply, "They call it Christianity, I call it Consciousness."[150] In his address to the Divinity School, he basically declared the Unitarian church a dead institution.

Not surprisingly, this brought a maelstrom of criticism.[151] Among his chief critics was Andrews Norton, who was called by some the "Unitarian Pope." Regarded as the "dean" of the Divinity School, he mounted the most blistering attack on this brash and perfidious rebel. Just weeks after the address, in the pages of the *Boston Daily Advertiser*, Norton accused Emerson of nothing less than denying Christianity itself. He would later repeat the charge in an address to the Harvard alumni appropriately titled "The Latest Form of Infidelity."[152] As a student, Emerson had thought of Norton as a "tyrant," and was certainly aware that he had been an important colleague of his own father in the early formative years of Unitarianism.[153] This compounding of authority would serve to make Norton a compelling and appropriate symbol of the "Terrible Father" who seeks to foil the hero's effort at liberation. Indeed, Mary Kupiec Cayton notes that in the aftermath of the Divinity School Address "Emerson found himself for the first time explicitly aligned with the party of innovation . . . against the entrenched conservative elite of Massachusetts." His position at this time, she states, was that "Religion was respected . . . not because it was conducive to religious sentiments, but because an inscrutable tyrant had commanded."[154] Emerson was now challenging that tyranny openly. The crossing of the threshold was at hand; there could be no turning back.

The criticism of Norton and others was bitter and, undoubtedly, hurtful. Indeed, Convers Francis recorded in his journal at the time that Boston conservatives had come "to abhor and abominate R. W. Emerson as a sort of mad dog."[155] Nevertheless, such opposition only served to further convince Emerson of the righteousness of his cause. On October 19 he wrote,

> It is a poor-spirited age. The great army of cowards who bellow & bully from their bed chamber windows have no confidence in truth or God. Truth will not maintain itself, they fancy, unless they bolster it up & whip & stone the assailants; and the religion of God, the being of God, they seem to think dependent on what we say of it. The feminine vehemence with which the A [ndrews]. N [orton]. of the *Daily Advertiser* beseeches the dear people to whip that naughty heretic is the natural feeling in the mind whose religion is external.[156]

In contrast to this "external" practice of religion, Emerson came even more to insist upon the value and importance of his own intuitions, whimsical as they may seem to his erudite critics who were more concerned with philosophical sources and proofs than the stirring of God within. In an entry appropriately dated July 4, 1839, he paraphrases Christ's challenge to his Apostles (Luke 14:26–27) to maintain an absolute faith, regardless of the demands others might make. This journal entry would later become a famous moment in "Self-Reliance."

> The doctrine of hatred must be preached as the counteraction of the doctrine of love when that pules & whines. I hate father & mother & wife & brother when my muse calls me & I say to these relatives that if they wish my love they must respect my hatred. I would write on the lintels of the doorpost, *Whim*.[157]

In this passage, Emerson indicates unequivocally the liberating nature of those passionate forces that well up from the deep unconscious and surge into the world of light. This erotic influx of unbounded psychic energy, which Neumann calls "libido ballast," inevitably overwhelms the repressive and normally dominant control of Apollonian ego-consciousness, which is a necessary first step in any revolution.[158] As Emerson would later note in "Man the Reformer" (1841), "every man should be open to ecstasy or a divine illumination, and his daily walk elevated by intercourse with the spiritual world."[159] Relieved momentarily of the arbitrary limitations imposed by the logically oriented conscious self, the individual is able to perceive reality as a collage of symbols, images, and concepts, which may be combined and recombined in a limitless kaleidoscope of possibilities. In other words, for the reformer reality can be re-formed to accord with an ideal vision. To the Emersonian poet / prophet, or, by extension, any truly inspired person, the elements of reality are "lifted from the ground and [are] afloat before the eye. He unfixes the land and the sea, makes them revolve around the axis of his primary thought and disposes them anew." For him, "the walls of time and space" crumble, and thinking itself becomes a "rage."[160] During these ecstatic moments, all objects acquire a certain symbolic significance that frees them from the confines of conventional perception and imbues them with qualities and properties never before recognized or considered. The world and society might thus be "re-created" a thousand times in the mind of the poet / reformer, but always the kinetic energy, the "rage" for such cosmogony, is supplied from below. Because of this, as Emerson notes, the "use of symbols has a certain power of emancipation and exhilaration for all men."[161] The poet, who employs such symbols as both the sign and substance of spirit, becomes a "liberating God." It is this transcendent "passion" that "rebuilds the world" and "makes all things alive and significant."[162]

Because the erotic and sensual unconscious seeks a natural bond with the outside world, as a sensitive person comes into contact with nature the passions resonate in a vital correspondence. In the woods the individual becomes, like Dionysus, a "fine madman." Freed from the restraints of conventional laws and norms, he becomes "a new man, with new perceptions." Like Emerson himself in the journal passage above, he is freed even from the ties of family and friends, church and state. "He does not longer appertain to his family and society . . . *he* is a person; *he* is a soul."[163]

By this time, Emerson recognized that those staid guardians of formal logic and social conservatism who dominated the cultural milieu of nineteenth-century America would inevitably consider any overt appeal to the intuitive rather than the rational faculties as pure madness. Nevertheless, he was perfectly willing to exacerbate that feeling by insisting repeatedly that his own intuitions or "whims" were considerably more important than the dictates of an uninspired, mechanical rationality. It is for this reason that virtually all visionaries have been labeled mad at one time or another by their pedestrian contemporaries and opponents. Emerson was determined to serve his muse, not conventional logic, and he glories in the recognition that his "renewed" vision "abolishes time and space," even though, as he well knew, "to speak with levity of these limits is, in the world, the sign of insanity."[164]

In an entry dated October 18, 1839, Emerson inscribed a detailed account of what he hoped to accomplish in his personal crusade to redeem his countrymen. In this *"whim"* passage, he demonstrates clearly the interrelated nature of his concerns with language, emotion, God, timelessness, and cosmic optimism, as well as his continuing opposition to the dead, "mechanical philosophy" of the age. As the psychomythic humanists would later maintain, they are each and all manifestations of that vital energy within, the unconscious, and in this their true unity lies. In the passage, Emerson contemplates a new series of lectures where he will heroically engage, once again, his emotional "artillery" in the battle for the minds and hearts of his age.

> What shall be the substance of my shrift? Adam in the garden, I am to new name all the beasts in the field & all the gods in the Sky. I am to invite men drenched in time to recover themselves & come out of time, & taste their native immortal air. I am to fire with what skill I can the artillery of sympathy & emotion. I am to indicate constantly, though all unworthy, the Ideal and Holy Life, the life within life,—the Forgotten good, the Unknown Cause in which we sprawl & sin. I am to try the magic of sincerity, that luxury permitted only to kings & poets. I am to celebrate the spiritual powers in their infinite contrast to the mechanical powers & the mechanical philosophy of this time. I am to console the brave sufferers under evils whose end they cannot see by appeals to the great optimism self-affirmed in all bosoms.[165]

Here, Emerson clearly envisions himself as the ideal Transcendental hero, a prophet, oracle, and reformer who will translate the revelations of his own interior odyssey into a liberating and renewing vision for his age.

One of the most interesting aspects of Emerson's development throughout this period is his marked propensity to describe humanity as simultaneously both male and female, to emphasize the feminine aspect of nature, and, finally, to assert the necessity of merging the qualities of both sexes. These sexual terms, for Emerson, appear as metaphors that reflect the psychological polarity of the conscious and unconscious. By employing them in this way, Emerson, who had himself by now achieved a dynamic balance of the two, indicates the validity of his own dictum, "As I am, so I see." As early as May 1837, he makes the following entry concerning his concept of humanity's psychological bisexuality. "I behold; I bask in beauty; I await; I wonder; Where is my Godhead now? This is the Male & Female principle in Nature. One man, male & female created he him. Hard as it is to describe God, it is harder to describe the Individual."[166] Edgar Wind, in his masterful, *Pagan Mysteries in the Renaissance*, quotes the biblical passage (Genesis 1:27) that Emerson echoes here: "So God created man in his own image, in the image of God created he him; male and female created he them." He then notes that "Philo and Origen inferred from this passage—and their authority ranked high with Renaissance Platonists—that the first and original man was androgynous; that the division into male and female belonged to a lower state of creation; and that, when all created things return to their maker, the unfolded and divided state of man will be re-enfolded in the divine essence."[167] It is likely that Emerson was familiar with this concept.[168]

In chapter 1, Erich Neumann's explanation of the psychological significance of the division of the sexes as it is rendered in various myths was noted and discussed. In the passage below, from *Love's Body*, Brown points out the element of opposition that this division implies. It is this polarization that Emerson artistically and personally sought always to overcome.

> The prototype of all opposition or contrariety is sex. The prototype of the division into two sexes is the separation of earth and sky, Mother Earth and Father Sky, the primal parents. The primal one body that was divided among the brothers was parental and bisexual—the two become one flesh—the parents in coitus; in psychological jargon, the "combined object."[169]

Emerson's effort to establish a new, unified and balanced psyche would inform, to a large extent, his theory of symbols. This theory would incorporate and unify gender values, and, as noted earlier, thereby symbolically reestablish the primal unity of Adam and Eve before the Fall. Here once again, Emerson anticipates the psychomythic humanists in his quest for oneness. Brown states:

> To make ourselves a new consciousness, an erotic sense of reality, is to become conscious of symbolism. Symbolism is mind making connections (correspondences) rather than distinctions (separations). Symbolism makes conscious interconnections and unions that were unconscious and repressed. Freud says, symbolism is on the track of a former identity, a lost unity; the lost continent, Atlantis, underneath the sea of life in which we live enisled; or perhaps even our union with the sea (Thalassa); oceanic consciousness; the unity of the whole cosmos as one living creature, as Plato said in the *Timaeus*.[170]

Emerson suggests a similar kind of primal unity in an entry dated November 21, 1840. In this passage, he comments on the concept of marriage and insists, as he did earlier, that the union of ephemeral lovers and family members is but a shadowy symbol of a far greater, divine, transcendent unity to which these will ultimately give way. Once again, he employs the myth of the garden in making his point.

> The Eden of God is naked & grand: Cold & desolate it seems to you whilst you cower over this nursery fire. But one to one, married & chained through the eternity of Ages, is frightful beyond the binding of dead & living together, & is no more conceivable to the soul than the permanence of our little platoon of gossips, Uncles, Aunts, & cousins. No, Heaven is the marriage of all souls.[171]

As with his earlier comments on the institution, some critics see this statement by Emerson as simply disparaging marriage. However, when viewed in connection with his earlier statements regarding the ideal, transcendent nature of marriage as a model of universal union, it reveals a deeper meaning. What Emerson is criticizing here is the outworn notion of "one to one," male-female marriage, which is fragmentary, limited, and, therefore, stultifying. It is the product of the same limited Understanding, or ego-consciousness, that divides reality into opposing binary units of time and space, positive and negative, me and not me. Also, because it was paternalistic and hierarchical, it served as the basis for the subordination of married women in Emerson's time, depriving them of the freedom necessary to develop as individuals. It is this sterile and repressive consciousness that builds the sepulchers of the fathers in *Nature*. By contrast, true marriage is expansive and life-sustaining for both partners. Its dynamic is centrifugal rather than centripetal. Furthering this notion is the fact that a short time later, Emerson enters into his journal an account of a dream, the significance of which is suggested by the passage above.

> A droll dream last night, whereat I ghastly laughed. A congregation assembled, like some of our late Conventions, to debate the Institution of Marriage; & grave & alarming objections stated on all hands to the usage; when one speaker at last rose & began to reply to the arguments, but suddenly extended his hand & turned on the audience the spout of an engine which was copiously supplied from within the wall with water & whisking it vigorously about, up, down, right & left, he drove all the company in crowds hither & thither & out of the house. Whilst I stood watching astonished & amused at the malice & the vigor of the orator, I saw the spout lengthened by a supply of hose behind, & the man suddenly brought it round a corner & drenched me as I gazed. I woke up relieved to find myself quite dry, and well convinced that the Institution of Marriage was safe for tonight.[172]

One need not be an expert dream analyst to comprehend the symbolic significance of this dream, especially in light of our previous discussion. The immersion of the audience in a spermatic shower, a universal application of the marriage act as it were, exactly reflects Emerson's emerging desire to find oneness with nature and the world, to see "Heaven as the marriage of all souls," and also to communicate this message of the primal unity of humankind to all men and women. The fact that he himself is subjected to a "drenching" by an unnamed "other" that responds to those who voice objections to the institution suggests, literally, the submersion of his own consciousness in an ocean of oneness. In the "waking world" of everyday reality, of course, the "practical" traditions and limitations of marriage appear to endure in society. Therefore, there are two Emersons in the dream, the sprayer and the sprayed, the world's lover and Lidian's husband. Emerson's continuing urge for cosmic unity, a unity symbolized by the ideal of divine marriage, noted earlier, is expressed in a comment that immediately follows his dream. "And why," he asks, "as I have written elsewhere, not be Universalists or lovers of the Whole World?"[173] This theme continues to appear frequently in the ensuing journals, and in an entry from August 1841, noted earlier, he says that, for the man with a "strong mind," "The Universe is his bride."[174] Such passages suggest his continuing focus on the importance of the power of the unconscious, expressed in this case as Eros, in maintaining the unity of humankind. Marriage, the fusion of male and female, man and woman, spirit and flesh, is the symbol of that spiritual and sexual harmony.[175]

Not long after recording these thoughts on marriage, Emerson had the opportunity to reiterate these ideas in a discussion with Margaret Fuller, who was at his home for another extended visit. Later, she recorded the following summary of that conversation in her journal.

> This golden afternoon I walked with Waldo to the hemlocks. There we sat down and stayed till near sunset. He read me verses.—*Dichtung und Wahrheit* [poetry and truth] is certainly the name for his life for he does not care for facts, except so far as the immortal essence can be distilled from them.
>
> .   .   .   .
>
> We got to talking, as we almost always do, on Man and Woman, and Marriage.—W. took his usual ground. Love is only phenomenal, a contrivance of nature, in her circular motion. Man, in proportion as he is completely unfolded is man and woman by turns. The soul knows nothing of marriage, in the sense of a permanent union between two personal existences. . . . There is but one love, that for the Soul of all Souls, let it put on what cunning disguises it will. . . .[176]

The harmony and ideal unity that Emerson envisioned would come through his "marriage to the universe" should not be seen as disembodied and ethereal. Indeed, the senses would necessarily remain key in reaching this ideal. In an entry of August 1842, he explains, "No matter whether thy work be fine or coarse, planting corn or writing songs, so only it be faithful work, done to thine own eye & approbation, then it shall earn a reward to the senses as well as to the thought. For in nature every body has a soul, & every soul a body."[177] Jung explains this same concept as follows.

> If we can reconcile ourselves to the mysterious truth that the spirit is the life of the body seen from within, and the body the outward manifestation of the life of the spirit—the two being really one—then we can understand why the striving to transcend the present level of the unconscious must give the body its due, and why recognition of the body cannot tolerate a philosophy that denies it in the name of the spirit.[178]

It had become habitual for Emerson, by this time, to describe the dual aspects of the psyche using gender symbolically. "Always there is this Woman as well as this Man in the mind; Affection as well as Intellect."[179] For him, the artist ideally combines these aspects of the psyche both in himself and in his art, and there can be no doubt that he saw himself in exactly this light. In August 1843, under the journal heading "Man-Woman," he notes: "It is true that when a man writes poetry, he appears to assume the high feminine part of his nature. We clothe the poet therefore in robes & garlands, which are proper to woman. The Muse is feminine. But action is male." Ultimately, Emerson concluded that, "The finest people marry the two sexes in their own person. Hermaphrodite is then the symbol of the finished soul. It was agreed that in every act should appear the married pair: the two elements should mix in every act."[180] On a symbolic level, of course, as Neumann points out, the merging of the masculine and the feminine is equivalent to the balancing of the psyche, conscious (masculine) and unconscious (feminine). This symbolic and literal presence of the psychological qualities of both sexes in one individual is a manifestation of the sense of wholeness that Emerson actively pursued as a person and which he sought to achieve as an artist. The hermaphroditic balance is an ideal that all individuals know initially in childhood. Indeed, this undoubtedly explains why, in Brown's words, quoted earlier, "childhood remains man's indestructible goal." Erich Neumann offers a similar explanation.[181] By this point in his life, the early 1840s, Emerson had developed the psychological unity and energy that lies at the very heart of his vision, his theory of literary art, and his perceived mission as a cultural seer, oracle, and prophet / redeemer for America. By opening an internal gateway to the compensating power of the unconscious, he achieved a dynamic balance between intellect and emotion that enhanced both tremendously.

The crucial test of this new, balanced centeredness came with what was undoubtedly one of the most sorrowful events of Emerson's entire life, the death of his five-year-old son, Waldo, from scarletina on January 27, 1842. Emerson's relationship with his firstborn child was one of unrestrained love and joy. From the time of Waldo's birth, Emerson's journals and letters are riddled with observations of the child; how he is growing, what he does, the way he looks, generally the things that any affectionate, loving, and proud father would note. Richardson says of this special relationship, "the child touched something deep inside Emerson. There is in some of his comments a defenseless, prayerful nakedness that had not been seen since the days of Ellen."[182] In a typical letter to Lidian, Emerson indicates this very attitude. "Here sits Waldo beside me on the cricket," he says, "with mamma's best crimson decanter-stand in his hand experimenting on the powers of a cracked pitcher handle to scratch & remove crimson pigment." He then reports on the youngster's progress in nursery school and assures the perhaps anxious mother that their beloved son, "seems to be in good health, & has just now been singing much in the admired style of his papa as heard by you only on several occasions." The very next day he would write again to tell Lidian, with obvious pride, of the child's progress in mastering the content of a children's book. "Waldo trots & falls & reperuses every day his small quarto on manners," he says, and he "names in it the 'bow wow' the 'poor putty' the 'tar' (moon) the 'beedy beedy' & the 'Moo moo' as he turns severally to those admirable works of art."[183] The unexpected death of this beloved child was a severe shock to Emerson, and one that sorely tried the underlying wholeness and optimism of his philosophy. The possibility of such a crisis was not entirely unanticipated by him, as the following journal statement, entered in 1838, indicates. The viability of the attitude described here was yet to be tested.

> I told J[ones]. V[ery]. that I had never suffered, & that I could scarce bring myself to feel a concern for the safety & life of my nearest friends that would satisfy them: that I saw clearly that if my wife, my child, my mother, should be taken from me, I should still remain whole with the same capacity of cheap enjoyment from all things. I should not grieve enough, although I love them. But could I make them feel what I feel—the boundless resources of the soul,—remaining entire when particular threads of relation are snapped,—I should then dismiss forever the little remains of uneasiness I have in regard to them.[184]

The sense of spiritual tranquility and equilibrium described here would now be severely tried. Emerson recorded the death of his son, his first-born child, in a brief entry on a single journal page dated January 28, 1842. "Yesterday night at 15 minutes after eight my little Waldo ended his life."[185] The four pages following are blank. Emerson was literally left speechless by the event. The next entry, dated January 30, expresses his overwhelming sense of loss.

> What he looked upon is better, what he looked not upon is insignificant. The morning of Friday I woke at 3 oclock, & every cock in every barnyard was shrilling with the most unnecessary noise. The sun went up the morning sky with all his light, but the landscape was dishonored by this loss. For this boy in whose remembrance I have both slept & awaked so oft, decorated for me the morning star, & the evening cloud, how much more all the particular of daily economy; for he had touched with his lively curiosity every trivial fact & circumstance in the household.[186]

Emerson understandably continued in this mood for some time, on occasion mournfully admitting that, "Sorrow makes us all children again [,] destroys all differences of intellect[.] The wisest knows nothing." By

May, however, one finds the following entry that suggests the persistent stirrings of his enduring optimism.

> Stick to thy affirming how faint & feeble soever. A poet is an affirmer. Such loud & manifold denial as certain chemists, astronomers & geologists make imposes on me & all & we think they will do wonders. Years pass & they are still exposing errors & some quiet body has done in a corner the deed which they must worship.

Later in May, Emerson records in his journal that in reading Charles Newcomb's romantic tale, "The Two Dolons," while comfortably ensconced in a natural setting, he felt a sense of compensation and faith in the universe once again. (Newcomb was a friend of the family and Emerson had solicited the manuscript for publication in *The Dial* which he was editing at this time.) "Let it be his praise," he writes, "that when I carried his MS story to the woods, & read it in the armchair of the upturned root of a pinetree I felt for the first time since Waldo's death some efficient faith again in the repairs of the Universe, some independency of natural relations whilst spiritual affinities can be so perfect & compensating."[187] Finally, by July 1843, Emerson was able to consider the event as a single element in an eternal circle of events. In Eliade's phrase, Emerson was able now to transcend the tragic nature of "profane time." Indeed, his emotional and spiritual resilience once again evinces itself in the assertion that all tragedy, ultimately, is transitory. Some of this rumination he would later incorporate into one of his most significant essays, "Experience" (1844).

> . . . life itself is an interim & a transition; this, O Indur, is my one & twenty thousandth form, and already I feel the old Life sprouting underneath into the twenty thousand & first, and I know well that he builds no new world but by tearing down the old for materials. Thy sickness, they say, & thy puny habit require that thou shouldst do thus or thus, & avoid so and so. But know, Beloved, that thy life & being is a flitting circumstance, a tent for a night, & do thou sick or well finish that stint—thou art sick but shall not be sicker, and thou & the Universe which holds thee dear, o small boy, will be all the better.[188]

The psychological process through which Emerson was eventually able to accept the death of his son is a replication of that which he experienced following the death of Ellen eleven years earlier. However, the trauma here is considerably less, at least in duration, and Emerson's success in dealing with this tragic blow is a tribute to the stability of his psychic equilibrium and the enduring faith that it energized. A basic outline of this process is evident in his moving poem "Threnody," which the journals indicate he began working on shortly after his son's death. The movement of the poem is from the particular fact of young Waldo's physical death to the universal significance of his continued spiritual existence. This apotheosis is accomplished not through an arbitrary assertion of a dogmatic religious faith in a life hereafter, but rather through an assured emotional grasp of the feeling, already articulated in *Nature*, that "Nothing divine dies," and that "All good is eternally reproductive."[189] Psychologically, what this requires is a transference of emphasis from the conscious mind's concrete grasp of a "factual," and consequently mutable and tragic reality, to the unconscious, with its intuitive grasp of a timeless, fluid, and symbolic reality that denies the finality of death.

Like so many of Emerson's poems, there are two voices in dialogue in "Threnody." Psychologically, the two voices represent the conscious and unconscious, or, to use Emerson's terms, the Understanding and the Reason. The poem opens with a description of the abundant vitality that animates the natural world.[190]

> The South-wind brings
> Life, sunshine and desire
> And on every mount and meadow
> Breathes aromatic fire;

However, the first speaker of the poem is unable to appreciate the beauty of the landscape because he mourns for "The darling who shall not return." Following a moving description of happy events and circumstances that relate to the boy's living existence, is the painfully blunt statement, "But the deep-eyed boy is gone." This sad fact, in turn, colors the speaker's entire perception of nature and he wonders aloud if "Perchance not he but Nature ailed, / The world and not the infant failed." This speculation extends also to human institutions and values and, as with the death of Ellen, this mortal event brings "the old order into doubt." However, whereas in the period following Ellen's death this critical doubt precipitated Emerson's break with these institutions and values, at this time that baggage has, for the most part, already been disposed of. Now he has only to remind himself of the greater truth which, as he had already discovered, lies within, beyond mere dogma and doctrine. Thus, the "deep heart," the second voice in the poem, at this point recalls to him:

> But thou, my votary, weepest thou?
> I gave thee sight—where is it now?
> I taught thy heart beyond the reach
> Of ritual, bible, or of speech;

It is this voice that reaffirms the existence of a vital spirit that animates all reality, a sense of eternal becoming that denies the momentary fact of death since death is not a terminus, but merely "Pours finite into infinite." It is consciousness that perceives reality as static and fixed—a straight line instead of a circle—and, hence, in this limited dimension death is final, absolute, and tragic. It is exactly such short-sighted vision that this voice warns against when asking, "Wilt thou freeze love's tidal flow, / Whose streams through Nature circling go?" To "freeze" the erotic stream of life is to deny life itself. This image of freezing also recalls Emerson's previous criticism of the "icehouse of Unitarianism" following the death of Ellen. There is a dynamic unity in life which must be recognized, "And many-seeming life is one,—/ Wilt thou transfix and make it none?" The first speaker is further reminded that heaven itself was not made "stark and cold," a fixed and lifeless entity, but rather it is "a nest of bending reeds, / Flowing grass and scented weeds." The association of "heaven" with images drawn from nature further suggests Emerson's continuing association of nature with the spirit of divinity.[191] Finally, just as Emerson came more and more to connect the image of Ellen with this eternal, regenerative and divine spirit of nature, here the same correlation is suggested with Waldo. Ultimately, his apotheosis is made possible by placing his existence in the context of a transpersonal, universal, and cyclic process of eternal being and becoming. Thus, while "House and tenant go to ground," they are "Lost in God" but are ultimately "in Godhead found." The poem, therefore, is a type of ritual that pushes through the profane experience of death to the sacred cosmic life cycle. This idea would be incorporated later in the complex, powerful, and ultimately life-affirming, essay "Experience" in the collection, *Essays, Second Series*, published in October 1844.

Emerson's psychological, spiritual, and intellectual development in the period 1820–1844 was dramatic, dynamic, and extraordinary. During this time he embarked upon a sometimes-painful inward journey of discovery from which he eventually emerged as a man transformed. The once sedate and thoroughly conventional minister to the Second Church evolved into one of America's most extraordinary poets, prophets, and seers. Emerson became, to use his own words, "a newborn bard of the Holy Ghost" who, blessed with a vision of a better world, set out to reform and redeem America.[192] These years were a watershed that would provide both the substance and the vehicle that would serve him in this effort. This crusade occupied the balance of what would turn out to be a long and distinguished career as America's most reviled and revered prophet and reformer. Having now traced the personal side of this spiritual and psychological development, aided by the unique insights of the psychomythic humanists, chapter 4 will examine Emerson's published works for the dynamic period, 1836–1844. It is in these early addresses, lectures, poems, and essays that he would initially enact his role as America's cultural hero and redeemer by raising his own individual experience, as recorded in his journals, to the level of the universal and archetypal.

CHAPTER 4

"THE DEVIL'S CHILD"
Emerson's Early Public Voice
1836–1844

"Nothing can bring you peace but yourself."

—Emerson, "*Self-Reliance*"

 Over the years, Emerson has frequently been accused by critics of producing a corpus of writings that are characterized by such a high degree of abstraction and subjectivity that they are largely incomprehensible to many readers. Thus, George Woodbury, an early biographer, refers to Emerson as "a self-isolated thinker, and intellectually the creature of his religious moods," while F. O. Matthiessen declares "The Over-Soul" and other such philosophical essays to be "generally unreadable."[1] The purpose of the present chapter is to demonstrate that Emerson's writings rest very firmly on the foundations of his own life experience and that they are, in fact, very much the distilled products of that experience. The abstract quality that many readers have perceived is simply the result of Emerson's effort to raise his experience to the level of the universal. His justification for doing so is predicated on his notion that, "to believe that what is true for you in your private heart, is true for all men—, . . . is genius."[2] In order to make this demonstration, it will be necessary to go over some of the same ground that we covered in chapter 3. The difference is that here we shall examine specifically how Emerson's personal experience, as reflected in his private journals (primarily), was translated into the public utterances (essays and lectures, primarily) upon which so much of his literary reputation rests. In this chapter, as in the last, certain key archetypes shall guide our discussion.

Emerson's rejection of the sterile authoritarian fixation of what he once proudly called "this Age of Reason," and his continued insistence upon the validity of his own intuitions as a source of truth and guidance, resulted in a personal, spiritual palingenesis, or rebirth. It was through this experience, as seen in chapter 3, that he was able to reach a high level of self-reliance, which he saw as reliance on God. After completing a deep and sometimes painful inward journey, Emerson became finely attuned to the emanations of godhead swirling through the cosmos and through himself. This sensation of direct participation in divinity provided him with a new and dynamic energy and, like the prophets of old, being "agitated," he now wished "to agitate others."[3] He exhorted his fellow Americans, whom he saw as people "drenched in time," to undertake their own journeys of discovery. He was confident that such personal introspection would ultimately have a redeeming effect on the entire society.[4] The first volume of the essays that would establish his career as one of America's foremost interpreters appeared in March 1841. Blessed with an ecstatic vision of sublime truth, Emerson would declare, in major statements like "The Over-Soul," that rather than cold Lockean logic, "The soul is the perceiver and revealer of truth," and that true revelation is "the emotion of the sublime." Such revelation is not to be found in dusty, dogmatic documents, but presents itself instead as "an influx of the Divine mind into our mind." This dramatic influx, in turn, brings unity, harmony, and wholeness by establishing a dramatic equilibrium between the conscious and unconscious, the Understanding and the Reason, or more simply, head and heart. As would be the case throughout the balance of his long career, in "The Over-Soul" Emerson articulates as universal truth the insights that he derived from his personal experience with suffering and loss. This now public voice is decidedly oracular, and Transcendental. Addressing an audience that at times feared the world was spinning towards what one scholar calls "atomized incoherence," Emerson offered the assurance that "within man is the soul of the whole; the wise silence, the universal beauty, to which every part and particle is equally related; the eternal *One*."[5] Having lived through his own traumatic and highly emotional transformation, one that brought him into personal contact with the "God within," Emerson was convinced that, in the fullest sense of the phrase, he was now "God's child." He could therefore speak, literally, with divine authority. Unlike the journals, where his voice is many times uncertain, tenuous, and angst-ridden, the public voice of Emerson is mature, self-confident, and increasingly seer-like. He soon came to realize, however, that many of his contemporaries saw his unorthodoxy in a different light, as the following dialogue from his classic essay "Self-Reliance" (1841) indicates. "On my saying What have I to do with the sacredness of traditions, if I live wholly from within? my friend suggested,— 'But these impulses may be from below, not from above.' I replied 'They do not seem to me to be such; but if I am the Devil's child, I will live then from the Devil.'" For Emerson, "sacredness" was now a matter of internal disposition and personal perception. He believed that it was so for everyone, and, in the face of opposition, he insists, "Nothing is at last sacred but the integrity of your own mind."[6] This significant inversion of perspective is not only indicative of the increasingly bold and self-assured nature of Emerson's spiritual independence, but it also informs, to a large extent, his growing understanding of the nature of the role he was destined to play in his society. He came to realize, following his controversial addresses at Harvard College (1837) and the Divinity School (1838), that opposition to the fathers was painful but necessary because, "Heroism works in contradiction to the voice of mankind, and in contradiction, for a time, to the voice of the great and the good."[7] As bitter as these early experiences were, the elements of contradiction and conflict would become even more pronounced in Emerson's later battle against America's most entrenched and heinous evil, the institution of slavery.

The development of Emerson's early public voice in the period 1836–1844 is considered here in light of several themes or topics that came to stand more and more at the matrix of his poetic vision and which, as we have seen, would be of primary concern to the psychomythic humanists. These came to represent the seminal components of his Transcendental philosophy of personal wholeness and liberation. They are Self-Reliance and Heroism, Freedom, Time and History, and Art. Although there is necessarily considerable overlap among these thematic categories due to Emerson's unified worldview, they are nevertheless sufficiently well distinguished to allow individual examination.

SELF-RELIANCE AND HEROISM

The theme of self-reliant heroism is probably the single most important element in the entire corpus of Emerson's public works. As Lawrence Buell has observed, it is "the best single key to his thought and influence."[8] Emerson believed self-reliance to be the sine qua non of a meaningful life because it provides us with the courage to be ourselves and to act in the world in accordance with the truth that we perceive. Indeed, because of this, as he declared to the young men at Harvard College: "In self-trust, all the virtues are comprehended."[9] Having freed himself personally from the grasp of an arid rationalism, and the cultural tyranny that it abets, Emerson turned to others in the hope of providing them with the opportunity to experience this liberation for themselves. In these seminal early works, Emerson translates his deeply felt emotional experiences, which were recorded initially in his journals, into a refined public utterance. As a result, these experiences are, to a certain extent, depersonalized—a fact, as noted earlier, that has led many critics to assume that they are works of the head and not the heart, mere representations of abstract philosophical concepts. As demonstrated in chapter 3, nothing could be further from the truth. Emerson himself consistently maintained that a personal, human quality is always necessary to the integrity of any intellectual expression. Indeed, he insisted that the value and validity of all thought lies in its relation to actual living experience, or, like poorly written history, it "must remain words."[10] His own works were no exception. Generally, his practice was to expand the context of his experience to archetypal, universal proportions, that is, to present his own experience raised to "the highest point of view." His affirmation of the validity of this practice is found in "Self-Reliance."

> To believe your own thought, to believe that what is true for you in your private heart, is true for all men,—that is genius. Speak your latent conviction and it shall be the universal sense; for the inmost in due time becomes the outmost,—and our first thought is rendered back to us by the trumpets of the Last Judgment.[11]

This view clearly reflects Emerson's commitment to the notion of a "collective unconscious" that is common to all humankind and that serves as the ultimate source of all essential truth. As Buell puts it, Emerson felt that "we are entitled to trust our deepest convictions of what is true and right insofar as every person's inmost identity is a transpersonal universal."[12] The essential thrust of Emerson's Transcendental vision is to move from the particular "facts" of experience to the universal, symbolic truth inherent in them, truths that are ultimately reached through intuition and active imagination. The latter he defined as "a very high sort of seeing."[13] This attitude is pervasive in the early essays. Through this practice, Emerson affirms his own concept of universal "genius." He is confident that what is true for him in his private heart is true for all because its ultimate source is the divinity that exists within all. This attitude is key to his unique, oracular style. As one critic has noted, "Emerson persuades us that his first person is universal" and therefore his public works always possess an "exemplary voice."[14]

The concept of self-reliance and heroism operates in Emerson's public works in two distinct ways. Primarily, and most significantly, Emerson enacts the role of hero himself, while encouraging others to do the same. Consistently in his early writings he urges, coaxes, prods, and exhorts others to rid themselves of their petty concerns for the trivia of profane time by accessing the universal, transcendent power that is within. He encourages them to put aside the gross materialism of the day, and to immerse themselves in the sacred and vivifying waters of the deep unconscious, to dream dreams, to return to the maternal other, to Eros, to nature, and to thus experience life renewed. This internal baptism, this reconnection with the divinity that resides within, is the first step in personal redemption. Emerson's desire to cast off the staid restraints of the conventional and to reestablish a harmonious and unified balance between the conscious and the unconscious, places him squarely in the role of Campbell's archetypal hero-redeemer. However, like most hero-redeemers, Emerson soon confronted the strong and sustained opposition of the "fathers" of his society. In the face of this hostility, a deeply sensitive Emerson would make his most moving statements on the sometimes lonely and self-sacrificial nature of the person he refers to as "hero." Self-reliance, he soon discovered, has its price.

Emerson's heroic perspective came to inform his vision of life. Since it was not a philosophy as such, but rather a way of seeing, it acted like a prism through which all experience was filtered. His own light metaphor, from his essay "The Transcendentalist," illustrates the concept. "The light," he says, "is always identical in its composition, but it falls on a great variety of objects, and by so falling is first revealed to us, not in its own form, for it is formless, but in theirs." This formless light, or heroic vision, is similar to the "thought-transcending truth" that Campbell describes as "emptiness, since it surpasses speech."[15] The mythic hero views and comprehends the phenomenal world from her higher point of view. She is a visionary of the first order.

It is in *Nature* (1836), his first major work, that Emerson initially and forcefully urges his readers to cast off the staid strictures of ego-consciousness and to "enjoy an original relation to the universe." He further challenges them to behold "God and nature face-to-face" rather than indirectly in the dead forms of their forefathers. Those dead forms, the legacy of the fathers, represent the obstacle that the hero must overcome. The confrontational quality of his opening lines is compelling and clear.

> Our age is retrospective. It builds the sepulchers of the fathers. It writes biographies, histories, and criticism. The foregoing generations beheld God and nature face to face; we, through their eyes. Why should not we also enjoy an original relation to the universe? Why should not we have a poetry and philosophy of insight and not of tradition, and a religion by revelation to us, and not the history of theirs?[16]

Emerson, at this point, believed that *he* had beheld God "face to face," in the natural forms through which divinity is made manifest in the world. From this, he derives the authority to announce his own "revelation," one that is available to all who possess the courage to seek it.

Joel Porte points out the similarity between Emerson's statement above and Christ's angry words to the lawyers in Luke 11:47–48, "Woe unto you! for ye build the sepulchers of the prophets, and your fathers killed them. Truly ye bear witness that ye allow the deeds of your fathers: for they indeed killed them, and ye build their sepulchers." Porte goes on to note that "Emerson . . . has collapsed his text by leaving out the prophets altogether, or at least insinuating that that is what his age does—building the sepulchers of the fathers and ignoring the prophets, those with direct knowledge of God."[17] The prophet in this case would be Emerson himself, the voice of the newest age and the oldest divinity, a new Christ at work in a still fallen world. Indeed, Porte goes on to suggest that Emerson's "assimilation of his own voice to that of Christ suggests that the opening paragraph of *Nature* is laced with more anger than we are normally willing to hear."[18]

Emerson's words also echo a later New Testament passage, Christ's famous condemnation of the hypocrisy of the Scribes and Pharisees where he tells them: "Ye are like unto whitened sepulchers, which indeed appear beautiful outward, but within are full of dead men's bones, and of all uncleanness" (Luke 23:27). Both of these readings stress deadness, which, as noted earlier, is exactly the quality that prevails when an age loses its emotional and spiritual vitality, its "libido charge." Where these are lacking, as Neumann observes, reality consists primarily of "lifeless details and dead relationships."[19] In addressing this central problem of American society and culture, Emerson gradually assumes the role of the new prophet, hero, and oracle of his age. Wesley Mott, whose seminal study of Emerson's ministerial career traces the evolution of his Transcendentalism from its Unitarian roots, places him in just such a role. He observes that "the transition from Unitarianism to Transcendentalism is . . . nowhere better illustrated than in Emerson's movement from speaking *about* Jesus to speaking *as* Jesus."[20] Emerson sometimes expressed this attitude explicitly. For example, Ellis Gray Loring, a Boston lawyer, abolitionist, and longtime friend of Emerson, describes a conversation that he had with him on the topic of divinity just months before Emerson delivered his famous, and infamous, "Divinity School Address." In his journal, Loring notes "After considerable conversation, I discovered that our point of divergence was this. He does not believe, or rather positively *dis*believes in any thing out of himself. He carries idealism to the extreme. Consequently if there is a God, he is God. God and he are one—and, again, the external universe is only a form of him; a manifestation which only exists from and for him."[21]

Emerson believed that the old lifeless formalities must finally give way to inspiration and creative vitality. In psychological terms, he was actually insisting that others return to their own unconscious, erotic, and spirit-filled selves to which the world of nature both corresponds and responds. This feminine "other self" is the source of both personal and social vitality, and, hence, as Neumann notes, "The task of the hero is to free, through her, the living relation to the 'you,' to the world at large."[22] In a religious sense, this fecund power of the unconscious, of Eros, of nature and the body, is represented as the cosmic power and influence of God. Campbell says of it: "This is the power known to science as energy, to Melanesians as manna, to the Sioux Indians as *wakonda*, the Hindus as *shakti*, and the Christians as the power of God. Its manifestation in the psyche is termed, by the psychoanalysts, *libido*. And its manifestation in the cosmos is the structure and flux of the universe itself."[23] The body is thus simultaneously erotic and mystical when it functions as a conduit of this power. In the Christian tradition, this truth is reflected in the words of Christ, addressed to his disciples. "Let me solemnly assure you, if you do not eat the flesh of the Son of Man and drink his blood, you have no life in you" (John 6:53). This statement, and the ritual gesture of eating bread and drinking wine that was used to symbolize it at the Last Supper, became the source of the sacrament of the Eucharist, the celebration of which involves a symbolic meal that repeats the original ritual. For Roman Catholics and some other Christian denominations, through the principle of "transubstantiation," the bread and wine are literally transformed into the sacramental body and blood of Christ, which is then consumed by the priest and communicants. As noted in chapter 3, Emerson's resignation from the Second Church was based upon his rejection of this ritual, which became a symbol of religious formalism that he now found offensive.[24] For Emerson, this symbolic act had lost its emotional/spiritual charge (Neumann would say its "libido charge") and become "dead." His comments in this regard, uttered in his farewell sermon, "The Lord's Supper" (September 9, 1832), are plain to the point of bluntness. "That form out of which the life and suitableness have departed," he declared, is "as worthless . . . as the dead leaves that are falling around us."[25]

For Emerson, the alternative to such superannuated and dead rituals lies in the living divinity found in nature, which now must be reclaimed. New, living leaves eventually displace dead ones. By uniting with this spontaneous divinity, which is the vitalizing power of Eros, the Over-Soul, the unconscious, humanity might once again assume a central position in a unified and harmonious reality. As Emerson states of nature: "A virtuous man is in unison with her works, and makes the central figure of the visible sphere." A person thus in unison with nature and God is necessarily in unison with herself since under the general heading of things belonging to "nature" Emerson includes "my own body." The result of such an ideal harmony for the self-reliant hero is that all of reality comes to reflect the unity of her own psyche because, as noted in chapter 2, "The integration of the personality is equivalent to an integration of the world." Emerson expresses this central idea succinctly enough later in *Nature* when he says simply, "what we are, . . . we see." It is in light of this realization that he invites his reader to "Build, therefore, your own world." In this way, the hero effectively resolves humankind's primal psychic conflict, that "opposition between ego and body" which is, in Neumann's words, "an original condition" of the overly civilized person.[26] Emerson recognized that the primary deficiency of his age was its lack of emotional and spiritual content in public life, its collective denial of the body (the source of emotion, instinct, and the experience of divinity), and a corresponding overabundance of arid rationality and repressive common sense, usually in the service of material productivity. Because of this, the "man of genius," the redeeming hero, is one who is able to establish a balance between these two and then both represent and communicate that balance to the masses. "He must draw from the infinite Reason, on one side; and he must penetrate into the heart and sense of the crowd, on the other."[27] Additionally, Emerson assures his readers that the world can be reformed and renewed if we all would "Let our affection flow out to our fellows."[28] Thus, the "soul of reform" for Emerson was a "reliance on the sentiment of man, which will work best the more it is trusted."[29] He felt this confidence himself, and he assures his audience in "The American Scholar" that "if the single man plant himself indomitably on his instincts, and there abide, the huge world will come round to him."[30] Goodness and love will eventually triumph.

Through the regeneration of individuals, society itself will eventually be reformed, or so Emerson initially hoped. The regenerated or "renewed" person is able to experience, first hand, both the world and the life-giving spirit that animates it. Emerson describes this personal ecstasy in the famous "transparent eye-ball" passage in *Nature*. "Standing on the bare ground,—my head bathed by the blithe air, and uplifted into infinite space,—all mean egotism vanishes. I become a transparent eye-ball. I am nothing. I see all. The currents of the Universal Being circulate through me; I am part or particle of God."[31] Tony Tanner, in speaking of this and similar passages expressing spontaneous ecstasy, suggests that Emerson's emphasis on seeing and centrality is significant throughout his works. Further, he notes that, "In this kind of visual relationship between the eye and the world, the eye stands completely passive and unselective while the surrounding world flows into it." The diminution of the ego, Tanner maintains, is the key to this unifying process because once "relieved of the active will and conscious thought, Emerson could feel himself reabsorbed into the flowing continuum of unselfconscious nature," an insight that affirms Neumann's paradigm of the ideal, balanced psyche.[32]

Richard Poirier makes a similar point when he says of the "transparent eyeball" episode, "There is plenty of evidence in the passage of Emerson trying to transport us from the society of 'joint stock companies'—where the landscape belongs to Miller, Locke, and Manning, who own its farms—to the world of Emerson's imagination, where such ownership is relinquished so that the self may be possessed by and come into possession of the cosmos."[33] Such liberation from "mean egotism" results in Emerson's feeling of personal renewal since, as Neumann contends, it is, "Ego consciousness . . . [that] introduces suffering, toil, trouble, evil, sickness, and death, into man's life."[34] Counterbalancing such pernicious ego-consciousness with the libido ballast of the unconscious mitigates this painful situation and ameliorates the suffering associated with the human condition. After experiencing the renewing power of the divinity within first hand, Emerson notes in *Nature*, "no man fears age, misfortune or death, . . . for he is transported out of the district of change."[35] Finally, one might also observe that by "standing on the bare ground" with his "head bathed by the blithe air," Emerson metaphorically connects the heavens and the earth, the spirit and the flesh. It is this dynamic equipoise that both symbolizes and enables his ecstatic transcendence as well as his heroic stature.

The sense of divine love, Eros, and the raw energy, and vision that it gives rise to, is drawn from the deep unconscious and floods into the hero, filling him with a sense of eternal vitality unbounded by the limits of time. As Emerson asserts, "love . . . has already made death impossible, and affirms itself no mortal, but a native of the deeps of absolute and inextinguishable being."[36] This energy, in turn, provides the basis for heroic activity in the world, and represents another aspect of the dynamic potential derived from such energizing harmony. As Neumann points out, "Every culture-hero has achieved a synthesis between consciousness and the creative unconscious." Because the hero has been renewed by returning to the source of all psychic energy, he possesses the power to create. "These images, ideas, values, and potentialities of the treasure hidden in the unconscious are brought to birth and realized by the hero in his various guises," Neumann explains. These guises include "savior and man of action, seer and sage, founder and artist, inventor and discoverer, scientist and leader."[37] For the heroic personality, the world is plastic and can become what you wish it to be. Thus, the social reformer and idealist envisions a better world, and then applies herself to bring it into actual existence. As Thoreau states in *Walden*: "If you have built castles in the air your work need not be lost; that is where they should be. Now put the foundations under them."[38] Such idealism demands a unified perception of reality through both the senses and the spirit; it requires the equal participation of both the conscious and the unconscious. Imagination is vital to the creative process. A flat, ego-conscious perception of reality, by comparison, is superficial and ultimately sterile. It fails to comprehend and to connect with the vital flow of energy inherent in all things and, as a result, sees the world as inflexible, obdurate, and impervious to change.

The procreative aspect of the hero appears most obviously in Emerson's favorite embodiment of her, the poet. In his earliest published work, *Nature* (1836), the poet is specifically described as a "hero," a gifted individual who recognizes and connects with the vital flux of reality and draws energy from it. The poet does not deny the existence of the material world. On the contrary, she revels in it, at the same time insisting upon its spiritual vitality. She comprehends both the phenomenal surface as well as the noumenal energy that underlies it. The true poet for Emerson stands in the center of things. He both commands and shapes his world as he, like the mythic poet, Orpheus, "unfixes the land and the sea, makes them revolve around the axis of his primary thought, and disposes them anew. Possessed himself by a heroic passion, he uses matter as symbols of it. The sensual man conforms thoughts to things; the poet conforms things to his thoughts."[39] Emerson employs the persona of the "Orphic poet" at the conclusion of *Nature* to present "some traditions of man and nature." These truths, he states, "have always been in the world, and perhaps reappear to every bard." As such, they "may be both history and prophesy." Among them is the assertion that "'A man is a god in ruins.'" Fortunately, by accessing the god within, here manifested as the power of "Instinct," mankind can recover this original divinity. "'He perceives that if his law is still paramount, if still he have elemental power, 'if his word is sterling yet in nature,' it is not conscious power, it is not inferior but superior to his will. It is Instinct.' Thus my Orphic poet spoke."[40]

Several critics have commented on Emerson's affirmation of the "mystical" quality of reality as suggested in such passages. Unfortunately, for some at least, this quality implies a disembodiment of thought and feeling. Sherman Paul, for example, in his classic study, *Emerson's Angle of Vision*, notes that "Emerson felt called upon to raise the vertical axis, to give the universe its spiritual dimension, to reinstate its mystery and wonder by giving scope to the mythic, symbolic, and religious components of human experience" which is certainly true. But Paul then goes on to assert that, "the vertical was the inner and spiritual and 'put nature under foot' by making nature serve the moral needs of man."[41] Given our discussion here, it would be more accurate to suggest that nature, as a manifestation and reflection of the vital unconscious, was both the object *and* the source of Emerson's spiritual vitality, and not something to be "put under foot." Paul's "vertical axis" then, would have to be seen as possessing depth as well as height, since it *descends* to the spirit in the deep unconscious before *ascending* to the conscious articulation of faith and worldly action. It is this vertical axis, reaching from the firm earth to the blithe air, that Emerson describes in his "transparent eyeball" passage. Albert Gelpi comes closer to the mark when he observes that, for Emerson, "the more deeply the poet plunges into nature; and the more surely he unriddles the secret of the Self, the more securely he touches the Truth that holds the frame of creation together."[42] It is this essential inner truth, in Emerson's view, that has the potential to provide every individual with cosmogonic power.

Campbell points out that part of the hero's sense of personal and cosmic immortality is her understanding that "All things are in process, rising and returning."[43] Emerson expresses this same notion in

"Compensation," another essay from the 1841 collection, where he insists "Man's life is a progress, and not a station."[44] The monomythic cycle of birth-death-rebirth is a constantly revolving one. As Emerson states in "Brahma," "If the red slayer thinks he slays, / Or if the slain think he is slain, / They know not well the subtle ways / I keep, and pass, and turn again." It is only when a person becomes trapped in her own sense of time and place that immortality is lost. Such stasis must be constantly resisted by appealing to one's own sense of wonder and delight, and by remaining open to the flow of vital, creative energy from the divine source within. It is this energy that constantly revitalizes and reshapes the world about. It is the power of nature and nature's god. In "Circles," one of the most provocative essays of the 1841 volume, Emerson points out that once an individual has been touched by this spirit "All that we reckoned settled shakes and rattles; and literatures, cities, climates, religions, leave their foundations and dance before our eyes."[45] In this same essay, while seeking to avoid the possibility that others would embrace his particular truth second hand rather than exploring their own inner realms, Emerson insists that his attitude is based upon his personal "whims" (a word of vital significance to him). "But lest I should mislead any when I have my own head and obey my whims, let me remind the reader that I am only an experimenter. Do not set the least value on what I do, or the least discredit on what I do not, as if I pretended to settle anything as true or false. I unsettle all things."[46] It is, of course, exactly this perception of flux and fluidity that is the ultimate source of freedom. Life must always be seen as a continuous "experiment" that never solidifies into inflexible laws. Like children, we are always learning as we go. The only valid laws are the truths that we intuit. Emerson's poet, the subject of one of the most famous of the *Essays, Second Series* (1844), by remaining attuned to these vital affections, reminds us of the powers that we possess within as every day we begin the world anew. He touches us with "a wand," says Emerson, "which makes us dance and run about happily, like children."[47]

Somewhat paradoxically, the consistency of this flux is the basis for harmony, and the hero is aware of this. Campbell quotes Heraclitus to clarify the concept. "The unlike is joined together, and from differences results the most beautiful harmony, and all things take place by strife."[48] Because of this, one of the most important functions of Emerson's poet-hero is the constant affirmation of the primal unity of all reality. Here again, the spiritual aspect of the unconscious appears as the power of God. There is a teleological unity in the world that the poet / hero perceives. Because of this, the poet fulfills the function of the priest by reconnecting humankind to Godhead.[49] "For it is dislocation and detachment from the life of God that makes things ugly, the poet, who re-attaches things to nature and the Whole,—re-attaching even artificial things and violations of nature, to nature, by a deeper insight,—disposes very easily of the most disagreeable facts."[50] Among those "disagreeable facts," as Emerson learned

from his own experience, are all those natural ills and emotional dyspep-
sias that are experienced by a painfully alienated ego.[51]

As Emerson himself gradually assumed the role of liberating hero and
oracle, it became increasingly clear that he was on a collision course with
the "fathers" of nineteenth-century America, the tyrannical guardians of
its institutions, the stalwart pillars of American society. He would eventually refer to them simply as "the Establishment" while their opposition
was, appropriately, "the Movement."[52] It has already been noted that in
"Self-Reliance," Emerson acknowledges that he might very well appear to
be the "Devil's child" to the more conservative elements in his society. Nevertheless, he felt compelled to continue his crusade, whatever the costs.[53]
Like his admired Milton, he could not praise a fugitive and cloistered
virtue, and he understood that "God will not have his work made manifest by cowards."[54] The hero must descend into the dusty lists of life to do
battle with the evil of the time. He was now utterly convinced, as he told
the newly ordained ministers in his "Divinity School Address" (1838), that
"Wherever a man comes, there comes revolution," and that "The old is for
slaves." In that address, he also attacked as "a decaying church and a wasting unbelief" institutional religion in America at the time.[55] The reason for
this deadly malaise, in Emerson's view, was that religious institutions had
suffered the loss of their emotional and spiritual dynamic as a result of an
increasing emphasis on intellectually conceived "doctrine" rather than the
unconscious and spontaneous power of love. "There is no doctrine of the
Reason," Emerson warned, "which will bear to be taught by the Understanding." If true faith is to be restored, it must come from within. True
faith arrives through feeling. "A true conversion, a true Christ, is now, as
always, to be made by the reception of beautiful sentiments." Preachers can
restore faith only by personal inspiration, and each must become "a new-
born bard of the Holy Ghost," rather than a mere "retained attorney,"
defending the outworn doctrines of the past.[56]

The counterattack following Emerson's address at the Divinity
School (which Porte refers to as a "bombshell"[57]) was bitter and severe.
Perhaps because of this, afterwards, in both his journals and his public
works, Emerson frequently discussed the nature and the qualities of the
self-reliant hero. In these ruminations, he consistently stresses the solitary
nature of the rebel who is alienated by a bitter and unbelieving society.
Mary Cayton notes that during this somber period in the late 1830s
"Emerson reflected on the meaning of his . . . forceful expulsion from the
ranks of the reigning social order, his own fall from society's graces into
the sad knowledge of conflict and isolation."[58] He now faced a public
test of his private strength. Not surprisingly, the works that grow out of
this period reflect an especially strong personal element. For example, in
"The Conservative," a lecture delivered in December 1841, Emerson displays a solitary determination, combined with a hint of defensiveness.

It will never make any difference to a hero what the laws are. His greatness will shine and accomplish itself unto the end, whether they second him or not. . . . Whatsoever streams of power and commodity flow to me, shall of me acquire healing virtue, and become fountains of safety. Cannot I too descend a Redeemer into nature? Whosoever hereafter shall name my name, shall not record a malefactor, but a benefactor in the earth.[59]

These personal and heroic sentiments would receive their fullest treatment in "Self-Reliance," which appeared three years after the confrontational address at the Divinity School. In this classic essay, the voice of the hero rings clearly and defiantly as Emerson encourages his reader to "Trust thyself" since "every heart vibrates to that iron string." In taking such a daring position, the prophetic Emerson is willing to accept that in the eyes of his sometimes strident critics he may indeed be the "Devil's child." So be it; he will live by the devil, if needs be and he will do what he must do. He deliberately challenges the conservatives of the age, who admire consistency and conformity, with his contention that "with consistency a great soul has simply nothing to do." He felt no obligation to believe as his father had believed, or even as he himself had once believed. The hero transcends the binary world of opposites: life—death, up—down, yes—no, right—wrong. His consistency is based on a personal intuition of a unified and transcendent truth. It is only in the limited realm of Understanding that a pernicious binary construct holds sway, and a fear of contradiction leads to a petty concern for consistency at all cost. For Emerson, "A foolish consistency is the hobgoblin of little minds, adored by little statesmen and philosophers and divines."[60] The hero possesses a wisdom that derives from the unconscious, the realm of the "eternal One." "We will denote this primary wisdom as Intuition," says Emerson, "whilst all later teachings are tuition. In that deep force, the last fact behind which analyses cannot go, all things find their common origin." A hero, who is in touch with this original and dynamic force, inevitably sees most long-established formularies as outworn, oppressive, and misleading. Hence, Emerson warns, undoubtedly with contemporary critics like Andrews Norton in mind, "if . . . a man claims to know and speak of God, and carries you backward to the phraseology of some old mouldered nation in another country, in another world, believe him not." Like all mythic heroes, Emerson has found God on his own and is now prepared to "stun and admonish the intruding rabble of men and books and institutions, by a simple declaration of divine fact, [that] God is here within." The obligation of the hero, as Campbell maintains, is to carry this liberating message forth and to redeem the world from the tyranny of the fathers. Emerson does precisely this throughout this powerful Jeremiad. He ends with an exhortation and a warning. "Nothing can bring you peace but yourself. Nothing can bring you peace but the triumph of principles."[61] Such a principled existence, however, does not come without a cost.

In a later essay, "Character" (1844), Emerson describes the hostile reception often afforded "divine persons" who would reject the status quo and who dare to challenge the rule of the current "divine persons," which has now become a tyranny. He maintains that such oracles "are usually received with ill-will, because they are new, and because they set a bound to the exaggeration that has been made of the personality of the last divine person."[62] However, despite this hostility, the hero must continue the struggle, regardless. Thus, Emerson asserts in "Heroism" (1841), his most comprehensive statement on the subject, "Self-trust is the essence of heroism. It is the state of the soul at war, and its ultimate objects are the last defiance of falsehood and wrong, and the power to bear all that can be inflicted by evil agents." This sense of silent suffering, of determined perseverance, marks Emerson's essential understanding of the nature of the true hero. It is the role that he himself was destined to play. The following couplet from his poem "Heroism," which precedes his essay, offers an interesting and often neglected insight into the heart and mind of this sensitive "Devil's child." It appears that at this early point Emerson has already learned from his sometimes bitter experience that, "The hero is not fed on sweets, / Daily his own heart he eats."[63]

FREEDOM

To modify the message of John the Evangelist somewhat, for Emerson, the hero is the person who proclaims, "Ye shall know the truth, and the truth is that you *are* free." This freedom originates in liberation from the dominance of the Understanding, or ego-consciousness, which, as noted, locks individuals rigidly into time and place while insisting upon their sinful imperfection and consequent mortality. It busies itself with the trivia of daily life and dull routine while the eternal cosmos whirls around unregarded. The freedom that the balanced psyche offers resembles the freedom of childhood, that idyllic and innocent time when, as Brown remarks, "the conscious and the unconscious are not yet separated."[64] It is also a freedom that allows an uninhibited, spontaneous, and erotic enjoyment of the natural world. The spirit within resonates with the spirit without as the "inward and outward senses" harmonize. The result is "perpetual youth." It is this youthful freedom that is the subject of the following statement from *Nature*.

> To speak truly, few adult persons can see nature. Most persons do not see the sun. At least they have a very superficial seeing. The sun illuminates only the eye of man, but shines

into the eye and heart of the child. The lover of nature is he whose inward and outward senses are truly adjusted to each other; who has retained the . . . spirit of infancy even into the era of manhood. In the woods too, a man casts off his years, as the snake his slough, and at what period soever of life, is always a child. In the woods, is perpetual youth.[65]

"The woods," or nature in general, became for Emerson synonymous with his own feminine self, which, in "The American Scholar," he refers to as "the other me."[66] He sometimes renders this regenerative phenomenon in biblical metaphors where childhood and infancy are associated with humankind's lost paradise, and the rise of ego-consciousness is synonymous with the "Fall of Man."[67] Emerson identifies the psychological significance of this mythic event in the essay "Experience" in which he states: "It is very unhappy, but too late to be helped, the discovery we have made that we exist. That discovery is called the Fall of Man."[68] Mankind's freedom, represented here as freedom from "original sin," is therefore contingent upon redemption from morbid self-consciousness.[69] It is this egocentric stagnation that Brown refers to when he insists that ego-consciousness is intrinsically death-oriented. The rise of consciousness itself is equated with eating from the "tree of the knowledge of good and evil," which precipitates a descent into the world of opposites where time and mortality are facts of life. This primal act thus inevitably leads humankind to the realization that we "shalt surely die" (Genesis 2:17). With the loss of psychic balance, people lose the capacity to recognize the eternal beauty and harmony of the world around them; their vision grows distorted. It becomes limited to the ephemeral and transitory, the mere mutable surfaces of things. In light of this unfortunate development, as Emerson asserts in Nature, "The problem of restoring to the world original and eternal beauty" must be "solved by the redemption of the soul."[70] The hero-messiah offers this salvation, and the freedom it brings, by reestablishing a viable psychic balance reminiscent of that which obtains in childhood. "Amen I say to you, whoever does not accept the kingdom of God as a little child will not enter into it" (Luke 18:7). Hence, for Emerson, speaking in Nature through the voice of his "Orphic poet," "Infancy is the perpetual Messiah, which comes into the arms of fallen men, and pleads with them to return to paradise."[71] The diminution of ego-consciousness, of arid rationalism, results in humankind's liberation from the primal curse of sin and death. What Emerson once said of himself in his private journal, he now applies to humanity in general. The statement appears in "Spiritual Laws."

> Our young people are diseased with the theological problems of original sin, origin of evil, predestination, and the like.

These never presented a practical difficulty to any man,—
never darkened across any man's road who did not go out of
his way to seek them. These are the soul's mumps and measles
and whooping-coughs, and those who have not caught them
cannot describe their health or prescribe the cure. A simple
mind will not know these enemies.[72]

Psychologically, sin is a state of self-alienation and the person who is in
harmony with herself knows it not. Salvation lies in being true to one's
self, and in the spontaneous living of life rather than the somber contemplation and complication of it. The conscious must always be balanced by the influence of the instinctive unconscious if harmony is to be
preserved. Purely intellectual efforts at restoration, ironically, only
worsen the problem. "The moment the doctrine of . . . immortality is
separately taught," Emerson warns in "The Over-Soul," "man is already
fallen."[73] Formal religions, historical institutions that are, for the most
part, the products of sober thought and applied doctrine divorced from
religious sentiment, can do little to relieve humankind's suffering, as
Emerson learned following the death of Ellen nine years earlier. "The
faith that stands on authority is not faith. The reliance on authority measures the decline of religion, the withdrawal of the soul."[74] Once liberated from this sterile and authoritarian rationalism, humanity is also
liberated from the narrow confines of these dusty institutions, which are
merely its extensions. Experience taught Emerson that institutional
Christianity had become stagnant and ossified, isolated in a moment of
time, and hence, nonvital. It had, ironically, lost touch with God, or in
Campbell's words, "that continuous miracle of vivication which wells
within all things."[75] In "The Divinity School Address" (1838), Emerson
explained to the young ministers that,

> Historical Christianity has fallen into the error that corrupts all
> attempts to communicate religion. . . . It has dwelt, it dwells,
> with noxious exaggeration, about the *person* of Jesus. The soul
> knows no persons. It invites every man to expand to the full
> circle of the universe, and will have no preferences but those of
> spontaneous love. . . . The manner in which his name is sur-
> rounded with expressions, which were once sallies of admira-
> tion and love, but are now petrified into official titles, kills all
> generous sympathy and liking.[76]

The result is entrapment in a frozen moment of the past, incarceration in
the tomb. The ministers of religion, Andrews Norton and his crowd, now
speak "as if God were dead."[77] In such cases only a spiritual revolution
could free the individual from this deadly confinement.

The same is true for those civil institutions of government that seek to uphold a rigid and antiquated system of values, traditions and laws and thus deny true liberty. Such institutions are also supported by the tyrannical "fathers" in order to protect property and insure the continued dominance of an increasingly corrupt and moribund status quo. When Emerson eventually threw himself into his personal campaign against slavery in August 1844, it was in response to his government's patent denial of the divinity and self-worth of *all* humanity. In response, he insisted that there was a "higher law" than the Constitution that took precedence in such matters. For Emerson, the only laws that *must* be followed are the laws that are ratified by one's own soul. As early as *Nature* (1836), he had insisted that "The intuition of the moral sentiment is an insight of the perfection of the laws of the soul. These laws execute themselves. They are out of time, out of space, and not subject to circumstance. Thus; in the soul of man there is a justice whose retributions are instant and entire." If there is a conflict between the individual and the state, the dictates of civil institutions must always be subordinated to the voice that ultimately speaks in the heart of every citizen. Civil laws will always be secondary to moral laws. Truth, says Emerson, "is an intuition. It cannot be received at second hand."[78] Indeed, he reminded those who would reform American society that, "Obedience to . . . genius is the only liberating influence."[79] Despite the enormous pressures of a society whose primary operational ethic is that of a "joint-stock company" and whose overriding concern is for "conformity," individuals must maintain the value and primacy of their own personal integrity because "Nothing is at last sacred but the integrity of your own mind." Those who would be free must actively assert their freedom, when necessary, from outmoded, conventional beliefs. Society, however, is naturally conservative. It is resistant to change and worships conformity. It must therefore follow that, "Whoso would be a man must be a nonconformist."[80] To some this may appear to be a formula for anarchy. However, it must be born in mind that Emerson, like most reformers then and now, believed absolutely in the essential goodness of humankind. He was convinced that if every rightly informed citizen acted in accordance with his/her conscience, society would not go far astray. On the contrary, evil results when individuals abdicate their responsibility and choose instead to "go along to get along," usually to preserve social order and their own material comfort, even when this means supporting a morally flawed status quo. For Emerson, the most compelling example of this abdication was America's continuing toleration of the heinous institution of slavery, but his concern also extended to all marginalized groups, including Native Americans and women.

This assertion of the freedom and primacy of the individual applies to the arts as well as political and social institutions. As Brown indicates, art is the primary mode of society's instinctual liberation. It "struggles against repressive reason," and "in this sense [is] subversive of civilization."[81] Therefore, it is imperative that the art form and style employed be appropriate to the needs of the moment. However, art can also become the tool of a tyrant, if institutionalized. Emerson describes this very process in "The American Scholar." "The poet chanting," he says, "was felt to be a divine man. Henceforth the chant is divine also. The writer was a just and wise spirit. Henceforward it is settled, the book is perfect; as love of the hero corrupts into worship of his statue. Instantly, the book becomes noxious. The guide is a tyrant. We sought a brother, and lo, a governor." In order to avoid this situation, Emerson insists that "Each age . . . must write its own books." The proper use of such books, he contends, is "nothing but to inspire." Such influence insures the freedom and growth of the individual, which is the ultimate good because "The one thing in the world of value, is, the active soul,—the soul, free, sovereign, active." Not surprisingly, Emerson objected strongly to nineteenth-century America's continuing fixation upon the neoclassical poetic mode, so popular in England a century before. He describes "the style of Pope, of Johnson, of Gibbon" as "cold and pedantic," and he warns, "We have listened too long to the courtly muses of Europe."[82] America needs an indigenous, exuberant, and democratic, poet-priest, inspired by the vitality of the ambient gods and the nation's revolutionary heritage. Although the underlying message of the poet-hero is always one of primal unity, equality, and freedom, that message must be constantly uttered anew; "For the experience of each new age requires a new confession."[83]

For Emerson, who sought "to unsettle all things," stasis is always the enemy of freedom. This can be seen in his consistent opposition to the dominant political and cultural institutions of antebellum America. They represent the spectrum of oppressive social forces, that Emerson refers to as "the Establishment." By their very nature, these powers stand opposed to the spontaneous manifestations of the instinctive unconscious. Since their primary function is the orderly and collective control of human nature (through the maintenance of established canons and traditional standards of conduct and thought), they are, in large part, responsible for what Brown refers to as the "festering antagonism between man and society." This antagonism occurs when institutions lose their "libido charge" and with it the ability and the willingness to change. While most institutions initially come into existence in response to some clearly defined need, over time they inevitably become impotent, arid, and outmoded, and, like the "old clothes" Emerson's friend Thomas Carlyle had described in *Sartor Resartus* (1833–34), they need to be changed. "The reality which the ego thus constructs and perceives," says Brown, "is culture; and culture . . . has the essential quality of being a 'substitute-gratification,' a pale imitation of past pleasure substituting for present pleasure, and thus essentially desexualized." Hence, in this sense, "Culture originates in the denial of life and body."[84] Emerson recognized this problem early on. In his lecture "The Conservative" (1841) he sees it, quite correctly, as yet another aspect of the eternal war between the Understanding and the Reason, or, in psychological terms, the conscious and unconscious. What is true for the microcosm, the individual, is also true for the macrocosm, the society. "Such an irreconcilable antagonism . . . must have a correspondent depth of seat in the human constitution," he notes. "It is the opposition of Past and Future, of Memory and Hope, of the Understanding and the Reason. It is the primal antagonism, the appearance in trifles of the two poles of nature." These are the same polarities that, in Emerson's eyes, constitute the natural political divisions of the country; that is, "the party of Conservatism and that of Innovation" who "have disputed the possession of the world ever since it was made." These are primal forces, characteristic of the psyche itself. Conservatism is the social expression of a reactionary and sterile consciousness and as such it is prepared "to defend . . . the actual state of things, good and bad." The party of Innovation, on the other hand, is radical, stemming from the very roots of humanity, disrespectful of the status quo, visionary, liberal, idealistic, and eager to establish "the best possible state of things."[85] It is this latter group that Emerson primarily denotes by the term "Transcendentalist" in the lecture by that name. Historically, this group was consistently identified with Emerson's own thought and feeling, but in this lecture, delivered in Boston in 1841, he is critical of their failure, thus far, to make themselves felt as a force in American society. As Emerson makes clear in his presentation, their major failing, ironically, is that they have atrophied. Their idealism has become desexualized and effete and reflects a sort of disembodied spiritualism that is never translated into action in the world. They lack the gutsy "libido charge" that energizes and fortifies the hero. These young Transcendentalists thus possess only a passive virtue and have not yet engaged the world to do battle with the tyrannical fathers who jealously defend "the actual state of things," including, for example, the institution of slavery. Consequently, as the poet-hero who seeks to redeem a corrupt and oppressive society, Emerson exhorts these young men (primarily) to active engagement with the world.[86] They must be heroic. Transcendentalists, as youthful idealists, have an obligation to "unsettle all things" and build a new and better world. So far the obligation has not been met.[87] If the youth of the nation are lethargic, and refuse to strike for freedom and reform, what can be expected of adult authority? If gold will rust, what will iron do? The strong prophetic voice Emerson assumes here is clearly, once again, that of Jeremiah.

> The good, the illuminated, sit apart from the rest, censuring
> their dullness and vices, as if they thought that, by sitting very
> grand in their chairs, the very brokers, attorneys, and congress-
> men would see the error of their ways, and flock to them. But
> the good and the wise must learn to act, and carry salvation to
> the combatants and the demagogues in the dusty arena below.[88]

"Salvation" can only come through a revolutionary confrontation with
the Establishment. In order for this to happen, would-be revolutionaries
must be empowered by opening their hearts to the transforming energy of
the unconscious, the power of which courses through nature and humankind. By reconnecting with this vital force they will acquire both the
energy and the insight necessary to assert their freedom, to cast off the
past, and to "re-make" the world according to a new vision. Emerson
makes this idea explicit in "Man the Reformer" (1841) through the use
of a compelling organic metaphor. "What is a man born for but to be a
Reformer, a Re-maker of what man has made; a renouncer of lies; a re-
storer of truth and good, imitating that great Nature which embosoms us
all, and which sleeps no moment on an old past, but every hour repairs
herself, yielding us every morning a new day, and with every pulsation a
new life?"[89] Ironically, even those who presently deem themselves reformers and activists have become somewhat rigid and structured as a result, in part at least, of forming associations and societies. Like all
institutions, these organizations tend to stifle both feeling and creativity
in the name of party unity. They have become trapped in their own limited and dogmatic positions and, hence, in Emerson's view, are in danger
of becoming largely nonvital, ineffective, and irrelevant. They, like the
young Transcendentalists from whom Emerson expected so much, have
lost contact with the vital spirit of life. "Each 'Cause,' as it is called,—say
Abolition, Temperance, say Calvinism, or Unitarianism,—becomes
speedily a little shop, where the article, let it have been at first never so
subtle and ethereal, is now made up into portable and convenient cakes,
and retailed in small quantities to suit purchasers. You make very free use
of these words 'great and holy,' but few things appear to them such."[90]
Emerson's conspicuous use here of mercantile terminology makes the
irony especially pungent. The reformers have "set up shop" and thus become part of society's "joint-stock company." Also, these liberal, idealistic, would-be reformers, may have the proper spiritual inclination, but in
the arena of the "real world" the pragmatists, the materialists, and the
conservatives outdo them. Emerson's understanding of this unfortunate
situation would lead him to note in a later essay, "Politics," (1844) that
in the contest between the liberal and conservative parties in America,
"one has the best cause, and the other contains the best men."[91] In order
to correct this situation, he suggests in "New England Reformers" (1844)

that the idealists should become more holistic in their approach to reform, and avoid the fragmentation that comes from a conscious fixation
on one particular wrong. He warns against making "a sally against evil
by some single improvement, without supporting it by a total regeneration. Do not be so vain of your one objection," he tells them. "Do you
think there is only one?"[92] The true hero-reformer offers a new world,
not merely a fragment of one. Individuals must work towards a comprehensive culture of reform.

As seen in chapter 3, Emerson came to envision himself more and
more as a definer of true culture for America. Culture in this "high sense"
is not merely "polishing or varnishing," but is broadly revolutionary and
consists of an ideal combination of the Reason and the Understanding, or,
in psychoanalytic terms, unconscious and conscious qualities.[93] Culture in
this sense becomes the product of individual personal experience and,
hence, is properly termed "self-culture."[94] Through the practice of individual self-culture, Emerson believed, the entire society could be freed from
the stagnation of the past and thus transformed and renewed. This concept
would emerge as a central element of the Transcendental movement. In
contrast to the present superficial and materialistic norm that "ends in a
headache," the new appearance of true culture is liberating.[95] It puts one
into contact with the vital, universal energies and potentialities of the unconscious that empower the individual to transcend the limitations of a
morally enervated material existence. Emerson gives an early hint of the intrinsic qualities of this new cultural ideal in *Nature* (1836) when he says,
speaking of the reality of the senses and the reality of the spirit, "Culture in-
verts the vulgar views of nature, and brings the mind to call that apparent,
which it uses to call real, and that real, which it uses to call visionary."[96]

With the realization of this new culture, people will be freed from a
limited ego-conscious grasp of the mechanical surface of things that leads
to an increasingly gross materialism, a truly "vulgar prosperity." They
will become infused with the power of love, of Eros, of the divinity
within, which makes true reform possible since "only Love, only an Idea,
is against property as we hold it," and, therefore, "only Love can abolish
slavery."[97] Ideally, "Man thinking," as he notes in "The American
Scholar," will become the "world's heart" and "will resist the vulgar
prosperity that retrogrades ever to barbarism by preserving and communicating heroic sentiments."[98] This entire enterprise of revitalization, the
recombination of unconscious and conscious, Reason and Understanding, feeling and thought, is for Emerson subsumed under the general
heading of "true culture." This true culture imparts life and spirit and as
such it is not a prison but a paradise. It connects one to the vital spirit of
nature, as suggested in the root meaning of the word culture itself, "to
cultivate, to till," that is, to make living things grow, expand, and develop
to their full potential. It also opens one to the divine truth that inspires

and makes one free. As such, it is revolutionary. Emerson sought to pro-
claim this message of liberation throughout American society in the hope
of initiating a new "great awakening."

> Men such as they are, very naturally seek money or power;
> and power because it is as good as money,—the "spoils," and
> so called, "of office." And why not? for they aspire to the
> highest, and this, in their sleep-walking, they dream is highest.
> Wake them, and they shall quit the false good and leap to the
> true, and leave governments to clerks and desks. This revolu-
> tion is to be wrought by the gradual domestication of the idea
> of Culture.[99]

Like the prophets of the past, Emerson believed that all people, in their
heart of hearts, wish to be redeemed: "We desire to be made great, we desire to be touched with that fire which shall command this ice to steam,
and make our existence a benefit."[100] The image of converting "ice to
steam" is a wonderful symbolic representation of the spiritual change
that Emerson envisions. That change is from a sterile, deathly cold to a
vital heat: from stasis to volatility: from solid, to liquid, to gas: from rigid
form to flowing formlessness. "Fire" connotes the transforming powers
of the unconscious that precipitate such a dramatic change. Thus, "fire"
suggests passion and ardor, as well as enthusiasm, fervor, and zeal. Emerson's correlation of these physical terms and processes with the psychological and spiritual transformation they are used to represent is surely
not accidental. As Laura Dassow Walls indicates, "Emerson's new natural theology pointed to dynamic processes of nature as evidence of an
inflowing and overarching spirit or intelligence, a force which precipitated itself as matter according to laws that governed simultaneously the
physical and moral worlds."[101] It is this "new natural theology" that underlies Emerson's confidence that progressive change is inevitable because
it is commanded by both natural and moral law. It is the dictate of nature
and nature's god that life is never inert but instead characterized by constant change. Nowhere should the political and cultural implications of
this fact be more clearly demonstrated than in freedom-loving America, a
democratic nation, a child of revolution that is still in its infancy. A revolutionary society constantly looks to the future and its limitless possibilities. As Emerson asserts in his lecture "The Young American" (1844):
"It seems so easy for America to inspire and express the most expansive
and humane spirit; new-born, free, healthful, strong, the land of the la-
borer, of the democrat, of the philanthropist, of the believer, of the saint,
she should speak for the human race. America is the country of the
Future. . . . It has no past."[102] Emerson's ultimate goal as a reformer was
to make this ideal vision of America a reality.

TIME AND HISTORY

Our discussion of self-reliance, heroism, and freedom has already shown that one of the essential functions of the hero is the liberation of humankind from the ravages of time and the tyranny of the past. As was seen in chapter 3, this process of liberation was enacted in Emerson's own life by returning the conscious mind to a state of harmonious balance with the creative, instinctive self, the divine energy of the Over-Soul, Eros, the unconscious. As a result, the self-reliant person "lives with nature in the present, above time."[103]

Earlier, in *Nature* (1836), Emerson described his perception of the ongoing, fluxional, cyclic harmony of all reality, a harmony that also defies the fragmentation of conventional concepts of time and space. He asserts that, "Time and Space relations vanish as laws are known."[104] These "laws," as noted earlier, have both physical and moral dimensions, and they reflect, simultaneously, the harmony of the cosmos and the mind of the perceiver. For Emerson, reality came to represent a balanced and dynamic combination of matter and spirit that resembles the human psyche prior to the rise of consciousness and the consequent perception of space and time distinctions. Neumann describes this "unindividuated" condition.

> Originally, there were no abstract spatial components; . . . Gradually, with the growth of consciousness, things and places were organized into an abstract system and differentiated from one another; but originally thing and place belonged together in a continuum and were fluidly related to an ever-changing ego. In this inchoate state there was no distinction between I and You. . . . Everything participated in everything else, lived in the same undivided and overlapping state in the world of the unconscious as in the world of dreams.[105]

This harmonious state can be replicated in the mature psyche by bringing the conscious into a balanced relationship with the dynamic energies of the unconscious. The "laws" of the unconscious, rather than limiting perception, reveal a timeless progression of eternal life, the "life ever after" that is associated with divinity. Emerson asserts that it is only through an intuitive grasp of these eternal laws that individuals comprehend and experience true immortality. Where this is lacking, morbidity and "faithlessness" result, as he notes in his "Lecture on the Times" (1841).

> Faithless, faithless, we fancy that with the dust we depart and are not; and do not know that the law and the perception of the law are at last one; that only as much as the law enters us, becomes us, we are living men,—immortal with the immortality of

this law. Underneath all these appearances, lies that which is, that which lives, that which causes. This ever renewing generation of appearances rests on a reality, and a reality that is alive.[106]

For Emerson, this "continuous miracle of vivication which wells within all things," as Campbell describes it, is synonymous with godhead, or, with godhead as it manifests itself in individuals, that is, the soul.[107] As he indicates in "The Over-Soul,"

> The soul circumscribes all things. As I have said, it contradicts all experience. In like manner it abolishes time and space. The influence of the senses has in most men overpowered the mind to that degree that the walls of time and space have come to look real and insurmountable; and to speak with levity of these limits is, in the world, the sign of insanity. Yet time and space are but inverse measures of the force of the soul.[108]

Emerson expresses this same idea in a slightly different fashion in "Self-Reliance." "Whenever a mind is simple, and receives a divine wisdom," he states, "old things pass away,—means, teachers, texts, temples fall; it lives now, and absorbs past and future into the present hour."[109] If the balanced individual thus lives in a continuous present, then, one might ask, what is the significance or value of recorded history? For Emerson, history rightly considered simply describes the archetypal, transpersonal aspect of human experience that is common to all humankind. As he states in his essay "History," "If the whole of history is in one man, it is all to be explained from individual experience. There is a relation between the hours of our life and the centuries of time." Because of this, "there is properly no History, only Biography," and the individual is "the compend of time."[110] This attitude towards the temporal aspect of human experience is clearly "archetypal" in the sense that Neumann, Eliade, Campbell, and Brown understood the term. Emerson considers history in essentially the same light as Neumann does myth. Neumann contends, "a series of archetypes is a main constituent of mythology, . . . In the course of its ontogenetic development, the individual ego-consciousness has to pass through the same archetypal stages which determined the evolution of consciousness in the life of humanity." For Neumann, the "collective human background" is thus a "transpersonal reality."[111] Emerson expresses a similar concept when he says simply; "There is one mind common to all individual men."[112] This commonality derives from the fact that all human beings participate in the "Over-Soul, within which every man's particular being is contained and made one with all other."[113] It necessarily follows then that the basic patterns of human experience are the same, regardless of place or time. Consequently, for Emerson, history must be approached as a collective reflection of individual human experience. "Civil and natural history, the history of art and of literature, must be explained from individual history, or must remain words. There is nothing but is related to us, nothing that does not interest us,—kingdom, college, tree, horse, or iron shoe,—the roots of all things are in man."[114] Emerson thus abolishes "profane space" by positioning humankind "in the center of things," the navel of the world, and constellating reality around this human center. He abolishes "profane time" by asserting the primal, cyclical, and archetypal nature of virtually all human history and the unity of humanity throughout time. Eliade considers that this attitude is characteristic of the "mystic," or the "religious man," terms that are certainly applicable to Emerson in the continuing evolution of his function as redeeming hero, prophet, and oracle. "Like the mystic," explains Eliade, "like the religious man in general, the primitive lives in a continual present. And it is in this sense that the religious man may be said to be a 'primitive'; he . . . lives always in a temporal present."[115] For Emerson, the value of history lies in its revelation of the essential truths of human existence.[116] In this sense, for Emerson, as for the psychomythic humanists, history is never truly "past." By reconnecting with the unconscious, by accessing the powers of "the Reason," Emerson loosens the ego's deathly grasp of time and space limitations, the artificial constructs of "the Understanding." One person becomes every person, one moment is every moment; reality consists of a seamless, eternal flux with the individual as the central, enduring figure around which all things flow. "As I am, so I see," says Emerson, and the regenerate person lives in a world that is constantly new and renewed.[117] The energy of the unconscious, of Eros, is boundless, fertile, and regenerative. As Emerson states in his essay "Love" (1841), "no man ever forgot the visitations of that power to his heart and brain, which created all things new."[118] All might share in this re-creation if they would open themselves to it. Like an ancient prophet, Emerson approaches nineteenth-century America offering the gift of eternal life to "men drenched in time." He himself becomes Eliade's "archaic man" who "is free to be no longer what he was, free to annul his own history through periodic abolition of time and collective regeneration."[119] Clearly, at this midpoint in his life, Emerson has more fully assumed the role of redeemer, freeing all from the ravages of time and history by offering a vision of eternal renewal. Large and small, near and far, past and present are one.

> So I come to live in thoughts and act with energies which are immortal. Thus revering the soul, and learning, as the ancient said, that "its beauty is immense," man will come to see that the world is the perennial miracle which the soul worketh, and be less astonished at particular wonders; he will learn that there is no profane history; that all history is sacred; that the universe is represented in an atom, in a moment of time.[120]

ART

Having examined Emerson's role as a self-reliant hero-redeemer, and having also noted his affirmation of the archetypal nature of human experience as evidenced in history, it remains to say something of the modality through which he expressed these concepts. Such a discussion must necessarily include both what he has to say about art, and how he himself implemented his unique artistic theory.

In *Nature* (1836), Emerson's first published work of literary art, he offers the following definition of his effort. "A work of art is an abstract or epitome of the world. It is the result or expression of nature, in miniature."[121] Since for Emerson all of reality is symbolic,—"We are symbols and inhabit symbols,"—and since the symbol itself is an ideal combination of matter and spirit,—"Particular natural facts are symbols of particular spiritual facts,"—art becomes a way of expressing and enacting the unity of the conscious and unconscious, Understanding and Reason. This is a unity that he himself, and by implication all other true artists, has achieved.[122] The world is the macrocosm and the artist is the microcosm who, in turn, presents the world "in miniature" in the work of art. Emerson's organic sense of language is indicative of a unified sensibility that perceives a harmonious relationship between the inner and outer worlds, the me and the not me. As he goes on to observe: "Every appearance in nature corresponds to some state of the mind, and that state of the mind can only be described by presenting that natural appearance as its picture."[123] This is a concept that Neumann also expresses when he observes that, "The psychic world of images is a synthesis of experiences of the inner and outer world, as any symbol will show."[124] The combination of matter and mind, inherent in the symbol, corresponds to and reflects the original, harmonious psychic balance enjoyed by the child in whom the unconscious is not yet repressed and for whom, consequently, as Brown maintains, "language is first of all a mode of erotic expression."[125] This harmony, according to Emerson, characterizes "the infancy" of language itself, "As we go back in history, language becomes more picturesque, until its infancy, when it is all Poetry; or, all spiritual facts are represented by natural symbols."[126] Such a poetic theory requires a high level of sensory participation, testifying once again to the importance of the body in Emerson's philosophy and in his poetics. As David Porter points out, "Everywhere in Emerson's theoretical poetics . . . he insisted on the primacy of the senses. He understood in a crucial way that fidelity to sense was the difference between the formulaic blockage of the poetic imagination and its liberation."[127] Unfortunately, however, as a result of humanity's psychological development, both ontogenetic and phylogenetic, for most of us the conscious comes to dominate, and we gradually lose this capacity to respond to and employ symbolic language, the language of Adam. We are, in effect, expelled from the paradise of the unconscious. In short, we grow up. As Brown explains, language, originally sensual, "succumbs to the domination of the reality-principle, it follows, or perhaps we should say mirrors, the path taken by the human psyche."[128] Emerson expresses his version of this concept in *Nature*, using the religious metaphor of the Fall and corruption of man. "A man's power to connect his thought with its proper symbol, and so utter it," he says, "depends on the simplicity of his character, that is, upon his love of truth and his desire to communicate it without loss. The corruption of man is followed by the corruption of language."[129]

We eat of the fruit of "the tree of knowledge of good and evil" (i.e. suffer the rise of ego-consciousness) and, hence, are corrupted and expelled from the garden of unity into a fallen world of clashing opposites. Now out of rapport with nature, with our other self, with the potentialities of the unconscious, we can no longer utilize sensual, organic symbols. An arid and disembodied consciousness insists upon a logical, superficial functionalism and represses the erotic and the sensual. Because consciousness is naturally conservative it uses only words that it has received from the "fathers," words that have been sanctioned by tradition and codified. The symbols become dusty and dry, devoid of the erotic, fluid, emotional/ affective element of natural language that derives from firsthand sense experience. Language is reduced to "grammar," a set of "rules." "In due time," says Emerson, "the fraud is manifest, and words lose all power to stimulate the understanding or the affections."[130] The language of poetry gives way to the language of insurance policies and the saccharine clichés of political rhetoric. The goal in such cases is deception. Stripped of all feeling, words lose their power to communicate, to move the heart as well as the head. When this occurs, language, like the conscious mind that employs it, becomes rigid, ossified, and dead. Not unlike the worn out ritual of the Lord's Supper that helped push Emerson out of the church, a dying language gives little indication of its former emotional vitality and earthy, erotic origin. As Emerson observes in "The Poet," "The etymologist finds the deadest words to have been once a brilliant picture. Language is fossil poetry. As the limestone of the continent consists of infinite masses of the shells of animalcules, so language is made up of images or tropes, which now, in their secondary use, have long ceased to remind us of their poetic origin."[131] However, salvation can still be achieved by establishing a new harmony with God, (i.e., the divine spirit manifest in nature, Eros, the unconscious, the Over-Soul), which is expressed, once again, in the symbol. The use of symbolic language signifies a new and original relationship to the universe. The old and ossified is abandoned, and a new, organic language emerges as "wise men pierce this rotten diction and fasten words again to visible things; so that picturesque language is at once a commanding certificate that he who employs it, is a man in alliance with truth and

God."[132] This regeneration reflects a return to the lost paradise that is associated with childhood. Thus, as Brown observed, all art serves as "a constant reinforcement of the struggle for instinctual liberation." Its function is "to help us find our way back to sources of pleasure" that have been lost to the dominance of ego-consciousness. Art thus enables us to "regain the lost laughter of infancy."[133] This instinctual liberation results in regeneration, a new sense of life. Most importantly for the artist-hero that Emerson sought to be, as a result of this regeneration the individual acquires the power of heroic persuasion, the power of Orpheus. "At the call of a noble sentiment," Emerson states, "again the woods wave, the pines murmur, the river rolls and shines, and the cattle low upon the mountains, as he saw and heard them in his infancy. And with these forms the spells of persuasion, the keys of power are put into his hands."[134]

As the artist-hero turns to the world to create her art, the choice of symbols is virtually unlimited. But there is one configuration that has a special importance in Emerson's writing, and that is the circle. As noted earlier in discussing heroism and time, for Emerson the individual who succeeds in reconnecting with the Over-Soul, the "eternal One," perceives a unified reality of which she is the center. As for the psychomythic humanists, this "re-centering" process is essential if life is to regain meaning and coherence, especially during a time of acute cultural or personal breakdown. On the other hand, those in whom consciousness dominates, to the detriment of the God-connected unconscious, would perceive a spiritually fallen, un-centered, and fragmented world. A unified, homo-centric reality is clearly the ideal. As noted earlier, in his "Divinity School Address" Emerson maintained that the soul "invites every man to expand to the full circle of the universe, and will have no preferences but those of spontaneous love."[135] He opens his famous essay "Circles," with the statement: "The eye is the first circle; the horizon which it forms is the second; and throughout nature this primary figure is repeated without end."[136] The circle is the most perfect of all symbols for Emerson.[137] In its essence, it is representative of the human psyche in its original unindividuated, uroboric state, before the rise of consciousness. It is this original state of harmony that the hero seeks to recover and maintain on a conscious level by balancing the conscious and the unconscious, by enacting the "transcendent function." Emerson represents this renewed state by placing the "eye," or "I," in the center of the first circle. The original harmony associated with this condition is traditionally considered as symbolic of the energy of godhead, as Neumann points out.

> Circle, sphere, and round are all aspects of the Self-contained, which is without beginning and end; in its preworldly perfection it is prior to any process, eternal, for in its roundness there

is no before and no after, no time; and there is no above and no below, no space. All this can only come with the coming of light, of consciousness which is not yet present; now all is under sway of the unmanifest godhead whose symbol is the circle.[138]

When an ideal balance is achieved between the conscious and unconscious, this godhead is perceived as existing both within the individual and her world. The divinity in humankind resonates in harmony with the divinity manifest in nature; the soul responds to and participates in the divine unity of the Over-Soul. From a psychomythic point of view, it is the unconscious, Eros, seeking unity with objects outside of itself. The result is balance, symmetry, and wholeness. Emerson expresses the concept in *Nature*. "The eye is the best of artists. By the mutual action of its structure and of the laws of light, perspective is produced, which integrates every mass of objects, of what character soever, into a well colored and shaded globe, so that where the particular objects are mean and unaffecting, the landscape they compose is round and symmetrical."[139] The "mean and unaffecting" elements of reality are so precisely because they are fragmentary. Art offers humankind the opportunity to re-create the world as a new and harmonious whole.[140] This re-creation is in itself a reflection of the individual's own personal psychic and spiritual regeneration and wholeness. For Emerson, "Art is the need to create," and this continuous creation, and re-creation, is a sign of an uninterrupted flow of divine energy surging forth from the unrepressed unconscious, the realm of spirit, dream, and wonder.[141] Because of this, Transcendentalists generally viewed "the artist's vocation as profoundly religious."[142]

Imagination, another aspect of the energy of the unconscious that is essential to the creation of art, is also the key to a spiritual life that liberates one from the icehouse of ordinary perception. It reveals the dynamic flux of life in an otherwise static scene. "The quality of the imagination is to flow, and not freeze," says Emerson.[143] The conscious and unconscious elements in the psyche, when brought into harmony, possess a powerful charge. This erotic energy, as Neumann has already pointed out, is the creative force for virtually all human endeavor, not just the fine arts and religion. Thus, for Emerson, "Beauty must come back to the useful arts, and the distinction between the fine and the useful arts be forgotten." As he remarked in his original lecture on the topic, "The universal soul is the alone creator of the useful and the beautiful."[144]

The circle, like Heraclitus' flame, is energized, and it symbolizes the constancy of continual change. "All symbols are fluxional; all language is vehicular and transitive," and hence, "true art is never fixed, but always flowing."[145] As Campbell maintains, the artist-hero, the poet-prophet, becomes a conductor of the eternal currents, "the incarnation of God," and is "himself the navel of the world, the umbilical point through which the energies of eternity break into time."[146] For Emerson, as for the Neo-platonists, this vital flux is key to nature itself and the essence of a living and spiritually charged reality. It is the mystical force that imparts a symbolic quality to all natural objects.

> The method of nature; who could ever analyze it? That rushing stream will not stop to be observed. We can never surprise nature in a corner; never find the end of a thread; never tell where to set the first stone. . . . Its permanence is a perpetual inchoation. Every natural fact is an emanation, and that from which it emanates is an emanation also, and from every emanation is a new emanation.[147]

As Otto Rank observed earlier, religion always draws art along in its wake. For Emerson, art is the vehicle through which humanity returns to nature and divinity, since "nature appears to us one with art," or, perhaps more properly speaking, art is "nature passed through the alembic of man."[148] The artist senses and expresses nature's symbolic quality. "Thus in art, does nature work through the will of a man filled with the beauty of her first works."[149] Ideally, the experience of such art, both for the artist and the audience, returns humankind, at least for a time, to an original, uroboric-like state of unity, that ideal condition of being that is frequently associated with childhood. It is revealing, but not extraordinary, therefore, that Emerson should instinctively associate both of these symbolically with literary art in the following brief journal entry recorded in 1842. "A reading man or a child self-entertained," he observes, "is the serpent with its tail in the mouth."[150]

Despite some critical arguments to the contrary, it is clearly the case that Emerson deploys his symbolic theory of art in his own writings.[151] We have already noted in chapter 3 the steady evolution of his style from the staid and self-conscious intellectualism of the early journals, to the spontaneous lyricism of the later journals, to the self-assured, oracular style of the published works. It is this oracular style, for better or worse, that came to be associated with Transcendental expression. Eventually, Emerson would help to establish a magazine dedicated solely to Transcendental writing, the *DIAL*, where such expression was the rule.[152] The mythic and seer-like quality of Emerson's early public voice is evident in his subtle use of symbolic language, the significance of which we have already established.[153] However, it would be well at this point to consider the rather unique meaning of the terms "spiritual" and "sensual" as Emerson employs them, since they are often misunderstood by critics. This misunderstanding is no doubt responsible, in part at least, for some of the criticism of Emerson, noted in the prologue, that depicts him as a rather cold intellectual or a largely disembodied spirit. Most often, Emerson uses the term "spiritual" in reference to the workings of the unconscious where these workings evidence themselves as instinct, intuition, and affection. It thus has a Kantian connotation for him; it refers to the noumenal, essential, and dynamic underside of reality. The "soul" for him is always associated with divine cosmic energy, with the eternal power of godhead, and with creation. In Emerson's view, body and soul form a unified whole. "Soul" is thus more correctly representative of what Brown calls "Eros" and Neumann calls "libido" than the disembodied ethereal essence commonly associated with the term. As Emerson states, "within man is the soul of the whole; the wise silence; the universal beauty, to which every part and particle is equally related; the eternal One."[154]

The same is true for the term "sensual." Some critics appear to assume that when Emerson rejects the sensual he is rejecting the earthy, physical, and passionate foundation of life. The opposite is actually the case. According to Emerson, the sensual man is the unemotional, ego-conscious individual who lives in the arid world of "facts" (revealed to him by his senses) and whose grasp of reality is literally superficial. Because he lacks imagination and insight, his Understanding never penetrates the surface of things (recall that Brown describes the ego as "the surface of ourselves"). The term "sensual" thus refers to a kind of Lockean empiricism. It usually indicates a failure to perceive the vital flux inherent in all things. Thus, Emerson states in *Nature*, "The sensual man conforms thoughts to things . . . [and] . . . esteems nature as rooted and fast," rather than, "fluid."[155]

Finally, Emerson's constant employment of images based upon circles, fluid cycles, and spirals indicates the extent to which these forms dominate his entire mode of seeing and feeling. Besides the examples that appear most obviously in the essay "Circles," the form also appears in more oblique ways. For example, the very doctrine of "compensation" is itself a philosophical representation of a circular and cyclical view of a homogenous reality wherein every part has its counterpart and all elements flow into one another and thus serve to complete a "subtle chain of countless rings."[156] Perhaps the most exuberant and intense example of Emerson's employment of this symbolic mode is the opening of the "Divinity School Address."

> In this refulgent summer it has been a luxury to draw the breath of life. The grass grows, the buds burst, the meadow is spotted with fire and gold in the tint of flowers. The air is full of birds, and sweet with the breath of pine, the balm-of-Gilead, and the new hay. Night brings no gloom to the heart

with its welcome shade. Through the transparent darkness the
stars pour their almost spiritual rays. Man under them seems
a young child, and his huge globe a toy. The cool night bathes
the world as with a river, and prepares his eyes again for the
crimson dawn.[157]

Here, in one tightly woven statement, is a virtual compendium
of the metaphors and symbols that are absolutely germane to Emerson's
vision. Standing before an audience composed mainly of young ministers
dedicated to the perpetuation of what Emerson considered to be an
inflexible, inert, arid, and moribund religious institution, he defiantly
bodies forth the vibrant natural images of that eternal flux of energy,
growth, and fluid life, that were for him the symbols of true godhead.
Emblems such as "breath of life," "breath of pine," "fire," "heart," and
"new hay,"—and kinetic symbols such as "refulgent" (from the Latin,
shining brightly), "grass grows," and "buds burst," as well as fluid
images such as "pour," "draw," "bathes," and "river" all suggest flowing movement, growth, vitality, and regeneration. Expressions such as
"balm-of-Gilead," and "spiritual rays" carry an obvious spiritual connotation that serves to reinforce the latent suggestion that it is God's power,
the power of the Over-Soul, that is represented in this dramatic display of
cosmic energy. Even the term "luxury," in its archaic sense of "lust,"
serves to suggest the sensual-spiritual axis of life. Additionally, the fact
that the "Man" in his spontaneous response to the influx of these natural
symbols becomes "a young child," manifests Emerson's belief in the spiritual redemption that comes with a return to nature and the spontaneous
innocence of childhood. The state of childhood itself symbolizes paradise.
Also, the entire perspective of the passage gives the distinct impression
of concentricness, with humanity the centered perceiver. All things exist
for and minister to this central figure. The "huge globe" (another cir-
cle/sphere) itself becomes a "toy" and a plaything to the child-man who
is in a state of ideal rapport with his own unfallen existence and its divine
source. The concluding reference to the "cool night" and "dawn" suggests the cyclical movement from night to day, cool to warm, and darkness to light. Finally, the juxtaposition of "eyes" and "dawn" reminds
one of Emerson's statement in "Circles," noted earlier, that "The eye is
the first circle; the horizon which it forms is the second; and throughout
nature this primary figure is repeated without end."[158] The entire passage
is an extraordinary tour de force for the Emersonian artist-redeemer. It
is also a compelling example of Emerson's ability to enact in his own
writing his organic philosophy of composition.

Emerson hoped to redeem and re-center his society, to lead "men
drenched in time" to a higher vision of a world reflective of the divine energy that is the source of all life, all meaning, and all hope. Such a vision

of redemption, a return to paradise, to a Ptolemaic sense of centrality and wholeness, requires the psychological reunion of the conscious and unconscious, the Understanding and the Reason, shop-life with the life of the Over-Soul. This reunion, Emerson felt, could only be accomplished through enacting a revolution in American culture that would begin by opening oneself psychologically and spiritually to the other, repressed self, the inner soul, the deep unconscious. To the person who has achieved this ideal equipoise, "The world looks like a multiplication-table or a mathematical equation, which, turn it how you will, balances itself."[159] To Emerson, as artist, hero, oracle, and redeemer, the phenomenal world ceases to be a place riven by the contradictions of life and death, love and hate, pleasure and pain. These opposites are reconciled. Ironically, it is a "Devil's child" who leads the way to this paradise regained. Neumann describes this central archetype, this Neoplatonic ideal.

> The "Wall of Paradise," which conceals God from human sight, is described by Nicholas of Cusa as constituted of the "coincidence of opposites," its gate being guarded by "the highest spirit of reason, who bars the way until he has been overcome." The pairs of opposites (being and not being, life and death, beauty and ugliness, good and evil, and all other polarities that bind the faculties to hope and fear, and link the organs of action to deeds of defense and acquisition) are the clashing rocks (Symplegades) that crush the traveler, but between which the heroes always pass. This is a motif known throughout the world.[160]

As Emerson says in *Nature* when speaking of the realm of "Ideas," the "Olympus of gods," "no man touches these divine natures, without becoming, in some degree, himself divine. Like a new soul, they renew the body. We become physically nimble and lightsome; we tread on air; life is no longer irksome, and we think it will never be so. No man fears age or misfortune or death, in their serene company, for he is transported out of the district of change."[161] This is the gift of life and hope that Emerson, as oracle and seer, offers.

Perhaps because of the powerful and sometimes mystical quality of Emerson's writings in this early period, he has often been accused of remaining somewhat aloof from the everyday concerns of his society. His philosophy of personal transcendence is frequently seen as one that tends to minimize the issues and concerns of social life by constantly looking beyond them. From the comfort of his study in idyllic Concord, some critics insist, Emerson philosophized about reforming the world, but never actually descended into the dusty lists of life, there to do battle with actual evil. His virtue, it is asserted, was indeed a fugitive and cloistered one.[162] It is true, as we have seen, that in Emerson's early writings (1836–1844) there is a strong and even pervasive emphasis on personal renewal through the discovery of one's own inner divinity. But it is also true that even in these early works there is an assumption that such personal renewal will necessarily contribute to the reform of the entire society. Indeed, for Emerson, Transcendentalism was a philosophy of active reform, reform of individuals and reform of society. He expected a great deal from those who had been themselves transformed. As indicated earlier in our discussion of Heroism, the power within has the potential to reshape the world, and those who have it have an obligation to act on others. Emerson made this explicit on the threshold of his public ministry when he told the young scholars at Harvard, "Inaction is cowardice . . . there can be no scholar without the heroic mind. The preamble of thought, the transition through which it passes from the unconscious to the conscious, is action. Only so much do I know, as I have lived."[163] It is not enough, as he told an audience of young Transcendental idealists four years later, to "sit apart from the rest, censuring their dullness and vices. . . . The good and the wise must learn to act, and carry salvation to the combatants and demagogues in the dusty arena below."[164] He himself would do exactly this. In chapter 5, we shall trace the final stages of Emerson's evolving role as redeemer, oracle, and social reformer from 1844 to the virtual end of his creative and intellectual life.

CHAPTER 5

THE CALL TO SERVE
Re-centering America
1844–1871

> "What is a man born for, but to be a Reformer; a Re-
> maker of what man has made; a renouncer of lies; a re-
> storer of truth and good."
>
> —Emerson, *"Man the Reformer"*

The publication of *Essays, Second Series* in October 1844 marked the end of the first stage of Emerson's emergence as America's poetic oracle, seer, and redeemer. One of the most significant essays in this collection is a work that reflects both the triumphs and the tragedies endured by him in this prolific period. Titled simply, but tellingly, "Experience," it is a powerful, complex, and highly personal rumination on the vicissitudes and trials of life. It was stimulated, in part, by the tragic death of Emerson's firstborn child just two years earlier. The essay reveals both the strengths and the limitations of his Transcendental philosophy as he had articulated it up to this point.

The essay begins with the observation that we live in a world of illusions where "dream delivers us to dream." In spite of this disconcerting lack of certainty in our lives, we must live in this world as well as we can. "We live amid surfaces," observes Emerson, "and the true art of life is to skate well on them." As a means towards this end, he offers the reassurance that amid this "flux of moods" and scenes, we are intuitively aware that "there is that in us which changes not." This divine power within, described variously here as "Fortune, Minerva, Muse, Holy Ghost," provides guidance and a sense of direction in a belittered world. It is this divine genius that makes possible our individuality, which rests on "the capital virtue of self-trust."[1]

All of this is well and good and consonant with Emerson's philosophy as previously articulated. But in this particular rendering of it, a dissonant note is sounded that does not appear in the earlier works of this period. The answer to life's challenge as presented here does not fully satisfy. Merely skating gingerly on the surface of things is not, finally, an adequate answer to the complex question, "How shall I live in this world?" Something more is needed. Emerson himself seems to sense this deficiency. "I know better than to claim any completeness for my picture," he says. "I am a fragment, and this is a fragment of me." Indeed, there is an unusual tentativeness and uncertainty in this essay that undoubtedly derives from Emerson's own growing discomfort with the general badness of the present time in America. Despite his own efforts to encourage reform, the nation was clearly becoming more corrupt by the day. Materialism was rampant. People in public office were subservient to the power of government rather than the masters of it, and slavery, America's most egregious moral and social failing, was about to expand exponentially with the imminent annexation of Texas as a slave state. Meanwhile, the churches remained dumb as the corrupting influence of the slave power spread. It was now threatening to infect virtually every aspect of America's social and political life. Clearly, something more than a call to self-culture was required if social justice was to become a reality. What that something would eventually be is hinted at obliquely at the conclusion of the essay. "Never mind the ridicule," says Emerson, "never mind the defeat: up again old heart! . . . there is victory yet for all justice; and the true romance which the world exists to realize, will be the transformation of genius into practical power."[2] Bringing about this romantic transformation became the focus of Emerson's life for virtually all of his remaining years.

In the mid-twentieth century, the psychomythic humanists articulated a re-centered vision of humanity that emphasized the unifying potential of the collective unconscious in opposition to an excessive and debilitating emphasis on consciousness that then dominated Western culture. In the mid-nineteenth century, Emerson articulated a re-centered vision of humanity by emphasizing the unifying potential of the "Over-Soul," which he also called "our common heart." He hoped thereby to overcome a pervasive feeling of alienation and fragmentation that afflicted his society. His primary opposition resided in what he called simply, "the Establishment," by which he meant a complex of conservative property interests and the cultural and political institutions that protected them.[3] As noted earlier, Emerson saw such conservatism as one of the inherent polarities of human nature. In his early lecture, "The Conservative" (1841), he observes that the "irreconcilable antagonism" between conservatism and humanistic reform has a "correspondent depth of seat in the human constitution. It is the opposition of Past and Future, of Memory and Hope, of the Understanding and the Reason." Emerson respected the values of an authentic conservatism, as well as liberalism, and felt that "in a true man, both must combine." However, he also recognized that the reform of American society would involve him in an ongoing contest with this formidable giant. As a reformer, he learned first hand that it is the nature of conservatives to believe that "to change would be to deteriorate" and therefore they "suspect and stone the prophet."[4] But change is necessary if there is to be life. By the mid-1840s, it was clear to Emerson that the future of America was being held hostage to an increasingly reactionary conservative class that clung desperately to power and was prepared to resist the winds of change with tooth and nail. The old, expansive vision of the American Republic, which had begun so well with a declaration of equality and freedom, had hardened into a system that was increasingly dominated by tyrants whose main source of wealth derived from the "ownership" of human beings. Such transitions are common. "The hero of yesterday," observes Campbell, "becomes the tyrant of tomorrow." Hence, "the boon brought from the transcendent deep becomes quickly rationalized into nonentity, and the need becomes great for another hero to refresh the world."[5] Because Emerson's transformation revealed to him, as it had to Augustine, that "the nature of God [was] . . . a circle whose center was everywhere, and its circumference nowhere," it necessarily followed that all of humanity must be within this divine, cosmic circle.[6] Collectively, humankind partakes of that "Unity, that Over-Soul, within which every man's particular being is made one with all other."[7] Emerson believed that this was certainly a divine and "self-evident" truth, one that the Founding Fathers perceived and subsequently expressed so eloquently in the Declaration of Independence. Unfortunately, political compromise and material corruption postponed its fulfillment. The moral laws of the universe, however, could not be denied forever. A second Revolution, Emerson felt, was inevitable. In the decade of the 1840s, "The contest between the Future and the Past" was becoming heated as the abuses of the present became more intolerable.[8] In this titanic contest, the cultural hero had a critical role to play. The prophet must not only provide a vision to unify and justify the new world struggling to be born, but also he must play an active role in the birthing process.

In the final stage of the "cosmogonic cycle," as described by Joseph Campbell, the hero, after completing the formation of his character, emerges in human history. "The cosmogonic cycle is now to be carried forward," he explains, "not by the gods, who have become invisible, but by the heroes, . . . through whom human destiny is realized." In the process of world building, or rebuilding, the hero becomes the "source of revelations," and an example to others who must learn from him "in order to break through, in the same way as he, to the transcendent, redemptive experience."[9] Historical examples of such heroes for Campbell include Moses, Christ, and St. Thomas Aquinas. As noted in chapter 4, Emerson offers a multitude of insights into personal transcendence

throughout his early writings and lectures. Also, early in his career he ac-
quired something of a following among young intellectuals in New England. However, as he indicated in his lecture, "The Transcendentalist"
(1841), these young men had yet to make a mark in the world. So far,
they had not significantly engaged the major social ills of the time. Indeed, until the summer of 1844, Emerson's own engagement with his society had been largely in the role of the serene oracle and bard. The
numerous addresses, essays, and lectures produced up to this time indicate the new depths that he had reached and the new, heroic character he
had formed as a result of his intensive inward journey. The tone and content of these pieces reflect the sublime sense of personal harmony that em-
anated from within. Indeed, one contemporary described Emerson's
melodic lecture style as having "an impersonal character, as though a
spirit were speaking through him."[10] As we have seen, he was occasionally prompted to engage his society in a more confrontational way, as in
the "American Scholar" and "Divinity School" addresses, but these were
exceptional. For the most part, Emerson was content to focus on exhor-
tations to his fellow citizens to regenerate themselves personally by looking inward and connecting with the life-renewing, divine spirit that
dwells within. This, he believed, would be the first step leading eventually
to the renewal and redemption of the entire society. When that moment
comes, "A nation of men will for the first time exist, because each believes himself inspired by the Divine Soul which also inspires all men."[11]
His focus at this time remained largely on the individual, and he was not
interested in a more direct political engagement with his society. Emerson
was dedicated to preaching "the infinitude of the private man," and he
felt that meddling in political affairs would be a distraction and a deviation from his proper role as poet-reformer.[12] During this time, he tended,
for the most part, to be more focused on the inner world than the outer
world. Thus, after publishing his "Letter to President Van Buren" (1838),
pleading for the cause of the Cherokees, who were being forcibly displaced from their lands, he recorded the following in his journal.

> Yesterday went to V[an]. B[uren]. a letter hated of me. A de-
> liverance that does not deliver the soul. . . . [T]his stirring in
> the philanthropic mud, gives me no peace. . . . I fully sympa-
> thize, be sure, with the sentiment I write, but I accept it rather
> from my friends than dictate it. It is not my impulse to say it
> & therefore my genius deserts me, no muse befriends, no
> music of thought or of word accompanies. Bah![13]

This feeling of resistance to the call for a more tangible, political engagement would continue to haunt Emerson for some time, and, occasionally,
he would defend himself against those who expected more from him in

this regard. In 1841 he delivered his lecture, "Reforms," at the Masonic Temple in Boston to an audience populated with reformers of all types. Many were abolitionists who were hoping that he would soon actively join their cause. "Though I sympathize with your sentiment and abhor the crime you assail," he states, "I shall persist in wearing this robe, all loose and unbecoming as it is, of inaction, this wise passiveness until my hour comes when I can see how to act with truth as well as to refuse."[14] This attitude was a disappointment to those activists who already had recognized in Emerson a certain unorthodox and prophetic quality. (Even his refusal, "until my hour comes," was couched in Christ-like language).[15] One of them, Maria Chapman, in a draft article on Emerson written around this time, reflects this sense of disappointment. "His [Emerson's] character being rather contemplative than active, . . . he has been a philosophical speculator rather than a reformer. His wisdom has therefore made fools of some, & his naturalness [has] been the occasion of affectation in others. Hundreds of young persons have made him their excuse for avoiding the Anti Slavery battle & talking about the clear light."[16]

All of this, however, was about to change. Despite his reluctance to engage the problem directly, Emerson came to recognize by the summer of 1844 that the institution of slavery, by far the greatest moral blight on the American landscape, was not succumbing to the universal force of moral and spiritual regeneration that he sought to promote in American society. In fact, the opposite was true. The Slave Power was becoming aggressive. Resistance to abolitionists was growing as "the Establishment," the citadel of authority controlled by the corrupt and tyrannical "fathers," naturally sought to protect itself from the threat of change. As Neumann remarks, the "fathers" are "pillars of the institutions that embody the cultural canon."[17] Not surprisingly, everywhere from Boston to Charleston, institutions of church and state closed ranks against those who had the temerity to oppose the most heinous evil of the times.[18] Most distressingly, after winning its independence from Mexico in 1836, it now seemed certain that Texas would be annexed and enter the Union as a slave state, thus significantly enhancing the slave power's influence on the national government.[19] Emerson was not insensitive to these developments, and he felt that the annexation should be resisted "with tooth & nail."[20]

Emerson's initial reluctance to join the antislavery movement had many sources. As indicated earlier, as a proponent of self-reliance he was suspicious of organizations and institutions of all types because they tended to limit individual freedom in preference for a collective agenda. That agenda inevitably demanded a consensus among members. In other words, everyone was expected to toe the party line. Additionally, organized efforts at reform often turned into shop-keeping enterprises that degenerated into self-sustaining "businesses," the survival of which often outweighed the reform itself. It frequently happened, too, that the self-professed reformers associated with such enterprises were narrow-minded and self-serving. Another concern was that one-issue reform was a misstep in Emerson's view because true reform must always be holistic. Finally, Emerson felt that his true calling as prophet and oracle was not to be a "martyr" to a narrow cause. Instead he was to speak to the larger, universal and spiritual concerns that were rarely afforded recognition in the realm of reform politics. His conscience, however, remained restive. Thus, early in 1844 he states in his journal: "My Genius loudly calls me to stay where I am, even with the degradation of owning bankstock and seeing poor men suffer whilst the Universal Genius apprises me of this disgrace and beckons me to the martyr's & redeemer's office." Later he states: "I also feel the evil, for I am covetous and I do not prosecute the reform because I have another task nearer. I think substantial justice can be done. . . , yet I do not know how to attack it directly, & am assured that the directest attack which I can make on it is to lose no time fumbling and striking about in all directions, but to mind the work that is mine, and accept the facilities & openings which my constitution affords me."[21]

Ultimately however, in spite of these serious reservations, Emerson could no longer resist the call to action. The times were critical and, like it or not, his hour had come. Shortly after he recorded the passages above, the Concord Women's Antislavery Society (whose membership included his wife and mother) invited him to speak at a gathering in celebration of the tenth anniversary of the abolition of slavery in the British Empire. He accepted. A brash, young, Negro abolitionist named Frederick Douglass was to share the platform with him that day. This would prove to be an historic turning point in his career as a social reformer and America's would-be redeemer. The rebellious son, having been transformed by a profound and deeply personal experience of conflict and regeneration, would now do battle with the "fathers" more directly than ever before. It would prove to be a titanic contest that ultimately changed the face of American society. It would also prove to be the greatest challenge of Emerson's public life, leading him into sometimes violent protest, confrontation, civil disobedience, and, ultimately, to the Civil War. Such a development was inevitable. As Neumann points out, quoting Ernst Barlach, "the hero has to 'awaken the sleeping images of the future which can and must come forth from the night, in order to give the world a new and better face.'"[22]

Emerson's earlier confrontations with the "fathers," at Harvard College (1837) and the Divinity School (1838), were but a prologue to this new and major struggle. These earlier skirmishes, while personally significant, were largely local and parochial—affecting mainly the Harvard establishment and the Unitarian community. Emerson's antislavery crusade, and his general commitment to the concepts of freedom, equality, and social justice, by contrast, represent a substantial widening of the circle. They would affect the entire country and, perhaps more than anything else, contribute to his eventual enshrinement as an American icon, and "the conscience of the nation."[23]

Many critics have observed that after 1844 Emerson's works show a movement towards a more practical and even pragmatic response to the often thorny issues that arose in everyday life. None has been more discerning in this regard than David Robinson. In *Emerson and the Conduct of Life*, Robinson describes a movement from the "visionary ecstasy" of the early works, to "ethical engagement as a means of spiritual fulfillment," a movement that parallels the emergence of the hero into human history as described by Campbell.[24] In this paradigm, Emerson's desire to philosophically "unsettle all things" gradually led to a realization that "Unsettlement . . . demanded action as its appropriate counterpart." Robinson sees this expressed inchoately in "Experience" (1844) where Emerson comes to recognize, as noted earlier, that "the true romance which the world exists to realize, will be the transformation of genius into practical power."[25] As Otto Rank observes, this is always the role of the hero. The sociological significance of the "notion of genius," says Rank, is that it ultimately becomes, "a culture-factor of the highest value to the community since it takes over on earth the role of the divine hero."[26] Robinson maintains that Emerson's antislavery career did much to serve this end, and that all of his later writings reflect this practical, ethical concern, whether directly or indirectly.[27] As such, they "suggest the extent to which he had come to address political reform, daily experience, work, and community as the keys to his moral vision."[28]

One of the major factors in this dramatic evolution of Emerson's heroic character was the sheer passion that the slavery issue elicited from him. In chapter 3, we witnessed Emerson's dramatic inward journey, one that served to reconnect him with the affective, erotic resources of his own unconscious. This fusion with the divinity within freed him from the deathly grasp of an arid rationalism that had rendered his world a spiritual and emotional wasteland. It is this dynamic, affective side—the realm of divinity expressed as the transcendent Over-Soul—that would subsequently empower him in his lifelong struggle with the manifold corruptions of a fallen world. It is also worth noting that Emerson was persuaded to give his address by the women of Concord. Historically, the abolition movement, in the early years especially, was largely dependent on the efforts of women to keep it afloat.[29] Emerson was well aware of this, and in his 1855 address, "Woman," attributed it to the fact that women are more susceptible to the influence of emotion than men. "The starry crown of woman," he notes, "is the power of her affection and sentiment and the infinite enlargements to which they lead." Based on his own transformation, which was effected by the power of Eros, he understood that "these affections are . . . introductory to that which is sublime." Because affections derive from Eros, the God within, and God is the ultimate source of moral feeling and the concept of justice, women were naturally drawn to the cause of antislavery. Knowledge of the slaves' condition quickly led to sympathy and sympathy led to outrage. As Emerson notes, speaking of the movement, "It was easy to enlist woman in this; it was impossible not to enlist her."[30]

In preparing for his first major antislavery address, "Emancipation of the Negroes in the British West Indies," Emerson read extensively in the history of slavery and antislavery, especially in the West Indies. The searing accounts of cruelty and abuse that he found in works such as Thomas Clarkson's *The History of the Rise, Progress, and Accomplishment of the Abolition of the African Slave Trade by the British Parliament* (1808, 1839), aroused his passions to the level of fury, and catapulted him into a public role as an angry crusader, a role that would only grow over time. The highly emotional tone of the speech is exceptional and compelling.

> [I]f we saw the whip applied to old men, to tender women; and, undeniably, though I shrink to say so,—pregnant women set in the treadmill for refusing to work, when, not they, but the eternal law of animal nature refused to work;—if we saw men's backs flayed with cowhides, and "hot rum poured on, superinduced with brine or pickle, rubbed in with cornhusk, in the scorching heat of the sun;"—if we saw the runaways hunted with blood-hounds into swamps and hills, and in cases of passion, a planter throwing his negro into a copper of boiling cane-juice,—if we saw these things with eyes, we too should wince. They are not pleasant sights. The blood is moral: the blood is anti-slavery: it runs cold in the veins; the stomach rises with disgust, and curses slavery.[31]

Clearly, Emerson's normally serene, oracular style was displaced in this antislavery address by a voice that reflects the white heat of an outraged conscience. In addition to expressing his anger at the brutality of slavery, Emerson, like the prophet Jeremiah, is filled with a righteous wrath and indignation at America's ongoing and obscene sinfulness in allowing this evil to continue. He castigates the failed "fathers," particularly the political leaders of the Free States, for their failure to act in the face of an increasingly aggressive evil. "I am at a loss how to characterize the tameness and silence of the two senators and ten representatives of the State [of Massachusetts] at Washington," he complains, politicians who are "bullied into silence by southern gentlemen" and thus allow the crime to fester. Clearly, "there is a disastrous want of *men* from New England" he

taunts. This repressive age requires new, vigorous, and even heroic moral
and political leaders who are willing to use force, if necessary, in the name
of virtue. Emerson contends here that, "government exists to defend the
weak and the poor and the injured party" and clearly this was not being
done.[32] He undoubtedly still believed that Eros, "the power of Love," will
redeem the world, as he had stated only months earlier in "New England
Reformers," but it will take a decidedly tough love to do it.

As a further indication of this new toughness and growing militancy, Emerson goes on in his address to offer praise to those heroic revolutionaries among the slaves themselves who are willing to fight for
freedom and justice. He applauds "the arrival in the world of such men
as Toussaint and the Haytian heroes, and the leaders of their race in Bar-
badoes and Jamaica." The appearance of such courageous men testifies
to the enduring reality of a divine moral force in the universe and, hence,
"outweighs in good omen all the English and American humanity. The
anti-slavery of the whole world, is dust in the balance before this." Such
men show by their actions the power of the transpersonal, universal, divine spirit that dwells within all, regardless of race or gender, time or
place. It is the source of all goodness and truth, and also the force behind
them. "The might and the right are here," Emerson insists, "here is the
anti-slave: here is man: and if you have man, black or white is an insignificance."[33] The young Frederick Douglass would soon embody this
striking image of the heroic anti-slave in his own *Narrative*, published
just months later. The obvious militancy of Emerson's address demonstrates clearly his growing realization that, in Robinson's words, "An evil
that is invulnerable to compassion or moral appeal, . . . must of necessity
be confronted with power."[34]

One of the remarkable things about this address is that in it Emerson does not invoke any authority other than an intuitive sense of justice
in his condemnation of the horror and the moral wrongness of slavery.
Moral outrage at this gross injustice should come naturally to anyone
who has not hardened his heart. The "moral sentiment" rises from the
soul, and the soul is integral to the body. Hence, as Emerson notes, "the
blood is moral," and instinctively rises in disgust at this desecration of divine humanity, once it is made known. It is not necessary to quote chapter and verse from the Bible to condemn this wrong. In fact, such efforts
are counterproductive since they are the cold products of a rational consciousness and are easily countered by the heartless apologists for slavery
who quote chapter and verse in their own defense.[35] Additionally, slavery
was a long-established, legal, and lucrative commercial enterprise in
America, a central feature of what Emerson once referred to as America's
"vulgar prosperity that retrogrades ever to barbarism."[36] His goal, therefore, was to arouse in his audience the same moral disgust that he himself
so clearly feels by appealing to the divine sentiment of justice that exists

in all people. For Emerson, truth and justice never require an explanation or an argument. They are intuitively perceived and self-evident. The goal of the reformer is to encourage individuals who have become morally blind through habit and neglect to open themselves to the truth that lies in their own hearts. The Understanding must make room for the Reason to manifest its influence. The conscious must open a dialogue with the unconscious.

In contrast to his earlier emphasis on individualism and self-reliance, Emerson concludes this address with a reminder that differences between people and races are merely superficial. All human beings are part and particle of the same divinity, the same human family. Therefore, "the civility of no race can be perfect whilst another race is degraded. It is a doctrine alike of the oldest, and of the newest philosophy, that man is one, and that you cannot injure any member, without a sympathetic injury to all the members."[37] This commitment to a transpersonal, transracial view of human divinity made Emerson an implacable foe of racism and racial stereotyping. As one scholar has recently noted. Emerson's firm "commitment to the highest truth of all, . . . [the] 'infinitude of the private man,' of the God within," informs his argument against "racial determinism."[38]

Overall, Emerson's August 1 address was a dramatic performance: vivid, compelling, and passionate, and it had a decidedly emotional effect on all those who heard it. Emerson's ultimate goal as a lecturer, as indicated in chapter 3, was to "agitate others," being agitated himself. He wished to deliver lectures that were ablaze with the feelings that burned in his own heart, to use words that would "make the cheek blush, the lip quiver, & the tear start."[39] On this special occasion, he accomplished just that. In this dramatic and moving address, Emerson discovered, possibly for the first time, the considerable power of "heart talk." It is the kind of eloquence that flows when the vocal chords resonate with the heart strings, resulting in a dynamic melding of thought and feeling. It is what Emerson once described as the passionate eloquence of Orpheus. It would come to characterize virtually all of his verbal assaults on America's most heinous institution. The grotesque sin of slavery set Emerson afire like no other cause. George Curtis, a young man with Transcendental aspirations of his own, was deeply moved by the presentation and reported to a friend that, "It was not of that cold, clear, intellectual character that chills so many people, but full of ardent life." He then speculates tellingly that Emerson's "recent study of Anti Slavery has infused a fine enthusiasm into his spirit & the address was very eloquent." Margaret Fuller, who had earlier faulted Emerson for being less emotional than she would like, remarked in her journal that the address was "great heroic, calm, sweet, fair. . . . So beautifully spoken too! Better than he ever spoke before: it was true happiness to hear him; tears came to my eyes." Apparently many in the audience had a similar reaction. A later report in the antislavery paper, the *Herald of Freedom*, recorded that, as Emerson spoke, "our hearts swayed to and fro at his bidding, and tears found their way down the cheeks of sturdy men as well as of tender-hearted maidens."[40] The comments from witnesses to Emerson's address testify to the power of the feminine, affective side of his character, the original source and wellspring of his own spiritual regeneration. He became more convinced than ever, as he would later tell an audience of abolitionists, that "it is a law of our nature that great thoughts come from the heart."[41] What Campbell calls "the transcendent, redemptive experience" was here employed more powerfully than ever before by Emerson in a public performance designed to move the minds and the hearts of his audience. Not surprisingly, it is this feminine side of the hero that Neumann sees as the conduit to "the world at large."[42]

The values that informed Emerson's August 1 address would be the mainstay of his subsequent twenty-year campaign for social justice in America. Like the later psychomythic humanists, Emerson consistently projected a unified and harmonious vision of a reality that is re-centered on humanity and humanity's universal and potentially divine nature. He insisted that all Americans, regardless of race or gender, had an inalienable right to freedom, equality, and justice. He found a compelling expression of these rights in the Declaration of Independence, a document that virtually all American reformers before and since have embraced as a commanding and moving statement of essential American values and beliefs. Not surprisingly, because of its insistence on the "self-evident" nature of essential truths, truths that are literally heartfelt or intuitively perceived, the Declaration has been described as a "semi-Transcendental document."[43] Indeed, most, if not all Transcendental reformers, Emerson among them, saw the Declaration exactly this way.[44] In a later lecture titled, "Books," given during the Civil War, Emerson would describe this revolutionary document as "the greatest achievement of American literature," a political prose poem expressing the highest and finest human truths. He could offer no greater compliment.[45] For Emerson, literature was clearly the finest form of art, and the one to which he dedicated his life. His ideal hero is the poet-prophet whose works are a vital repository of transcendent truths that enlighten and give meaning and dignity to life. These truths emanate from the mind of God and, as seen in chapter 4, they are by their very nature liberating. As Emerson observes in his early lecture, "Art" (1836), "In poetry, every word is free, every word is necessary. Good poetry could not have been otherwise written than it is. The first time you hear it, it sounds rather as if copied out of some invisible tablet in the Eternal mind, . . . The feeling of all great poets has accorded with this."[46] As stated earlier, Brown contends that, because it is imaginative and visionary and appeals to the heart as well as to the mind, art is by its nature always liberating and therefore always revolutionary. "The function of art," he insists, "is to form a subversive group" that opposes the "authoritarian group" that dominates society.[47] For Emerson, the Declaration was such a work, written by revolutionaries who were the rebellious sons of their day, America's first political prose poets and "liberating gods." As Emerson would go on to remark in his 1864 lecture, "Books,"

> The shaft words of the preamble of the Declaration—"We hold these truths to be self-evident, that all men are created equal, endowed by their Creator with certain inalienable rights, among which are life, liberty, and the pursuit of happiness"—these words, little heeded at the time, deemed oratorical, lampooned by flippant rhetoricians in our day as "glittering generalities," have turned out to be the only immortal words, the fresh, matin song of the universe.[48]

In Emerson's view, these "immortal words" of the Declaration, emanating from the "Eternal mind" and dictated by the Reason, by Eros, by Love, provide the true and only basis for American democracy. This idea is not unique to Emerson and the Transcendentalists. In fact, the notion that certain universal and intuitively perceived moral truths provide the basis for all social compacts and political life reaches back at least to Aristotle. It appears as "concord" in the *Nicomachean Ethics*, a term that Richard Klonoski defines as "some sort of primordial agreement" which "serves as a foil against civil discord" and is akin to friendship. It is the basis for a just social order and, as such, "is at once moral *and* political."[49] Emerson, who had read Aristotle on ethics and politics, as well as friendship, clearly affirms this notion.[50] Closer to his own time, Immanuel Kant, whose philosophy more than any other would influence the evolution of Transcendentalism, argues for the efficacy of "moral laws" that are the product of "moral feeling." Kant held that the "standard of our moral judgment . . . [is] the subjective effect" that derives from an intuitive source that he describes as "reason," and which is present in all rational beings.[51]

Emerson's political vision, like the other essential values that informed his worldview, was largely the product of the inward journey, described in chapter 3, that brought him into contact with the collective unconscious, "the Divine Soul." As T. Gregory Garvey effectively argues: "Emerson sought to promote a mode of reform that was premised on the possibility of infusing all of society with the same kind of insight that the individual gains at moments of inspiration." As noted earlier, for Campbell, this is the primary role of the hero in history, i.e., to provide by his example, a "transcendent, redemptive experience."[52] Garvey refers to this as Emerson's "political spirit" and he maintains that Emerson's "highest aspiration for reform was to generate broad-based belief in a transcendent 'Spirit' that would be publicized by a prophetic spokesperson."[53] Obviously, one such "prophetic spokesperson" was Emerson himself. The truths that he learned through his own personal experience of transcendent regeneration would now be brought to bear directly on the worst evils of American society. Thus, as Garvey maintains, "Even though Emerson's analysis of transcendence is usually understood in relation to individual spiritual regeneration, he saw this underlying motivating force, whether he calls it Spirit, Nature, the Over-Soul, or just Soul, in both political and spiritual terms."[54]

Throughout the balance of the 1840s, Emerson would speak repeatedly on the slavery issue, in spite of occasional concerns that such exercises in social agitation were a diversion from his true vocation as philosopher-poet. He also took strong stands on many other related public issues, protesting the annexation of Texas in 1845, insisting on the right of abolitionist Wendell Phillips to speak on the topic of slavery in the Concord Lyceum when Concord's conservative town fathers strongly objected, very publicly boycotting the New Bedford Lyceum because of their racist membership policy, and enthusiastically endorsing the efforts of the Boston Vigilance Committee to defend fugitive slaves, with force if necessary.[55] At times, the lack of progress in overcoming the evil of slavery, as well as the associated evils of bigotry and racism, and the distressing materialism of American society depressed him. Nevertheless, he felt compelled to continue the struggle. "We must have society," he wrote in his journal, "provocation, a whip from the top. A scholar is a candle which the love & desire of men will light. Let it not lie in a dark box."[56]

Toward the end of the decade, Emerson traveled to England for a lecture tour (1847–48) and, while in Europe, witnessed the "Revolutions of 1848" firsthand.[57] He was impressed with this apparently spontaneous eruption of the spirit of liberty throughout the Continent, and he felt that a better day was dawning in the Western world. Subsequently, he returned to his country with renewed confidence that social amelioration was inevitable. Addressing yet another abolition rally at the invitation of William Lloyd Garrison, he expressed his belief that "the progress of the great universal human, and shall I not say, divine genius" was evident everywhere, and that slavery would soon give way to liberty and justice.[58] Very shortly, this sublime confidence would be sorely tested.

Virtually all of Emerson's later writings would be influenced by his evolving public role as oracle, prophet, and redeemer to his society. *Representative Men* was published in January 1850. This book, a series of seven essays on representative historical figures and their influence, evolved from Emerson's lyceum lecturing throughout the 1840s, the period that witnessed his new and growing engagement with immediate social problems. Not surprisingly, as David Robinson observes, the work "abounds with solid human living, and although its whole structure revolves around the moral judgments Emerson makes about his heroes, it remains one of his worldliest books." Emerson is clearly concerned in this major work with the role of practical ethics and, as Robinson goes on to note, "in no book is there a more ringing or repeated endorsement of the power of the moral sentiment than in *Representative Men*."[59] In his introductory essay, "Uses of Great Men," Emerson indicates that the heroes he presents are empowered by and reflect a divine moral force that exists in *all humankind*. As Campbell points out, the hero always represents and acts upon this power of God within. He illustrates this point by quoting one of Emerson's favorite sources, the *Bhagavad-Gita*. "The mighty hero of extraordinary powers . . . is each of us . . . the king within. [The god] Krishna declares: 'I am the Self, seated in the hearts of all creatures.'"[60] The ultimate gift of such great men is power, and with power comes liberation, equality, and justice. In this way, each heroic representative figure presented by Emerson, though imperfect, resembles in some respect the archetypal redeemer-reformer that he himself both envisions and exemplifies. "The search after the great is the dream of youth," he states, "and the most serious occupation of manhood." The power of such greatness is divine in origin and manifests itself, as Eliade suggests, in religion, myth, and history. Hence, Emerson observes, "Our religion is the love and cherishing of these patrons. The gods of fables are the shining moments of great men."[61] While it would seem that most great men of history have been men of worldly power who impose their iron wills on lesser humanity, Emerson, in keeping with the needs of the time and his own special role, as America's poet-prophet, indicates that the proper and ideal role of true heroes is always to be liberators. Thus, while they possess "Sword and staff, or talents sword-like or staff-like, [and] carry on the work of the world," that work is primarily and properly to encourage freedom. They accomplish this by asserting the reality of the divine power that lies deep within us all, and which is at once the source of our divinity as well as our equality. In speaking of such a hero, Emerson insists: "I find him greater, when he can abolish himself and all heroes, by letting in this element of reason, irrespective of persons, this subtle and irresistible upward force, in our thought, destroying individualism;—the power so great, that the potentate is nothing. Then he is a monarch who gives a constitution to his people, a pontiff, who preaches the equality of souls, and releases his servants from their barbarous homages; an emperor, who can spare his empire." Clearly, for Emerson, the truly great man, the ideal hero-redeemer, is essentially a harbinger of democracy, who asserts that "there are no common men. All men are at last of a size. . . . Heaven reserves an equal scope for every creature."[62]

Obviously, this democratic ideal had yet to be fully realized in America, especially in the slave-holding South. As Emerson would observe in a later antislavery speech, "in the Southern States, the tenure of land, and the local laws, with slavery, give the social system not a democratic, but an aristocratic complexion; and these states have shown every year a more hostile and aggressive temper" By contrast, "Democracy stand[s] . . . for the good of the many . . . of the poor . . . for the elevation of entire humanity."[63] This vision would remain at the center of Emerson's political philosophy throughout his campaign to redeem American society from the gross injustice of slavery, as well as all other forms of social injustice that deny the divinity, equality, and dignity of all people.

Not long after the publication of *Representative Men* in the fall of 1850, the United States Congress passed the Fugitive Slave Law. This development had a profound effect on Emerson. More than any other single event, it led him into an immediate and dramatic conflict with the corrupt political fathers of his morally decayed society. Prior to 1850, fugitive slaves who were fortunate enough to make their way to a Free State could be reasonably confident that they might live out the remainder of their lives there without being molested. The new law changed that by allowing agents from the South to enter any Free State in an effort to recover fugitives, no matter how long they had resided there, and regardless of various state laws designed to protect them. The law also made it a crime punishable by fine and imprisonment to aid a fugitive in any way.[64] The passage of this law appalled and infuriated abolitionists everywhere. It was also deeply resented by many who previously had no strong opinions on the slavery issue but saw the law as a blatant violation of states' rights and a distressing indication that the slave power now dominated the national government. Ultimately, it would be an endless source of conflict and controversy up until the Civil War.[65] It is somewhat ironic that it was passed as part of the "Compromise of 1850," an effort to preserve the Union in the face of growing sectional tension over the slavery issue. One of its key supporters was Massachusetts' most distinguished public figure, Senator Daniel Webster. Emerson attacked Webster relentlessly and bitterly in his two addresses on the Fugitive Slave Law (1851, 1854), by far the most acerbic and caustic public presentations that he would ever deliver. He had once admired the distinguished senator, who was arguably the most eloquent orator of his day, as an embodiment of American democracy. As recently as *Representative Men,* he had identified Webster as one of the "heroes of the day," undoubtedly because of his previous opposition to the extension of slavery.[66] Emerson apparently hoped that eventually Webster would use his considerable power more dramatically against the pro-slavery faction. At one point in his early journals, he observed that if Webster "had given himself to the cause of Abolition of Slavery in Congress, he would have been the darling of this continent, of all the youth, all the genius, all the virtue in America."[67] Unfortunately, this was not to be. Webster, rather than placing himself in the service of freedom and justice, instead became a perfidious "Terrible Father," rendered in his most tyrannical form. Similar to Emerson's previous adversary, Andrews Norton, Webster was mired in the past, and dedicated to the preservation of an effete status quo. Articulate and powerful, he presented a formidable opposition to the redeemer-hero. Emerson would attack him relentlessly as the epitome of the corrupting influence of America's growing materialism and the sterile and conservative ego-consciousness that supported it.

In his first speech on the subject, "Address to the Citizens of Concord on the Fugitive Slave Law," Emerson bitterly castigates this fallen idol and declares that "The fairest American fame ends in this filthy law. Mr. Webster cannot choose but regret his loss. . . . [T]hose to whom his name was once dear and honored, as the manly statesman to whom the choicest gifts of nature had been accorded, disown him."[68] Webster is bound to the past and cannot get beyond it. It is this past that must be destroyed so that, as Eliade maintains, "evils and sins [can be] eliminated."[69] Webster, though a hero to the defenders of the establishment, is a perversion of the true, revolutionary and liberating character of the nation he presumably serves. "In Massachusetts, in 1776," says Emerson, "he would have been a refugee. He praises Adams and Jefferson; but it is a past Adams and Jefferson that his mind can entertain. A present Adams and Jefferson, he would denounce."[70] Because he is a creature of the Understanding only, the servant and victim of a pragmatic rationalism, Webster lacks the power to exercise an intuitive judgment and is thus disconnected from the source of all true morality, the "moral sentiment," the God within. Consequently, when his blood should *rise* in disgust at the abomination of slavery (like Emerson's did), "All the drops of [Webster's] blood have eyes that look downward. It is neither praise nor blame to say that he has no moral perception, no moral sentiment, but, in that *region*, to use the phrase of the phrenologists, a hole in the head."[71] Such a tyrant could never speak authentically for freedom, and Emerson caustically observes: "The word liberty in the mouth of Mr. Webster, sounds like the word love in the mouth of a courtesan."[72]

Regarding the law that Mr. Webster helped bring into being, Emerson urged outright civil disobedience and demanded that members of his audience break the law "on the earliest occasion." He defends such resistance on the grounds that this "filthy" enactment of Congress is "contrary to the primal sentiment of duty," which he refers to as a "Higher Law." This Higher Law, of course, is a manifestation of that "subtle and irresistible upward force" that he described in *Representative Men*, and its ultimate source is the Divine Mind, the Reason, the Over-Soul, Eros, the collective unconscious. As Emerson further notes in his address: "All arts, customs, societies, books, and laws, are good as they foster and concur with this spiritual element." The moral dictates of this power are obvious to all those who are willing to open their hearts. The Revolutionary Founders themselves held that such truths were "self-evident," and so too, for Emerson it is obvious that "A man's right to liberty is as inalienable as his right to life." A fugitive slave has simply asserted this God-given right. Webster, on the other hand, the "Defender of the Constitution" and mere creature of the Understanding that he was, argued for the legitimacy of the Fugitive Slave Law on the basis of established legal tradition and practice. For Webster, the laws of the fathers, the dictates of the past, simply cannot be violated. Emerson was not persuaded. For him, the universal right to freedom is self-evident and compelling. "Against a principle like this," he asserts, "all the arguments of Mr. Webster are the spray of a child's squirt against a granite wall."[73] The petty arguments of the Understanding are no match for the compelling moral sentiments of the Reason.

Emerson goes on to expresses in his address his disappointment that "the Higher Law was reckoned a good joke in the courts," and he therefore "took pains to look into a few law-books" to research the matter. What he found confirmed his view "that it was a principle in law that immoral laws are void," and he cites several classical sources from Cicero, to Blackstone, to Jefferson to prove it.[74] His point is that, if immoral laws are void, and morality is necessarily a matter of personal judgment, then personal morality must always trump statutory law. Put another way, if the source of morality is conscience, and conscience is derived from "moral sentiment" that flows from divinity, then "Higher Law," which is the product of that moral sentiment (the product of Reason) must be considered superior to "lower law" (the product of Understanding). This concept has always been vital for those reformers who seek to justify the use of civil disobedience as an instrument of protest and social change. Thoreau used it to protest against the Mexican War and slavery. Gandhi employed it against the British in India and, more recently, Dr. Martin Luther King, Jr. invoked the concept to fight against the laws of segregation, laws that he deemed immoral. All three read and admired Emerson.[75]

While Emerson's notion of Higher Law has received relatively little scholarly attention as a serious legal concept, Greg Crane contends that intuitively perceived values have always played an important role in the pursuit of social justice and in the evolution of the American legal system. Frederick Douglass, who both inspired and enacted Emerson's notion of the heroic anti-slave, also relied on this principle.[76] According to Crane, Douglass's Higher Law argument, as presented in his *Narrative of Frederick Douglass, An American Slave* (1845), "begins with the faculty of moral cognition. This indwelling and universal faculty of moral perception," Crane asserts, "enables even an untutored child to intuit the wrongness of slavery." Such intuitions then move "from private moral inspiration to dialogue and action." This action, in turn, becomes part of a larger cultural movement that eventually results in changes to the legal structure, to the laws themselves. Historically, Crane argues, the results in the case of the antislavery movement can be seen in "the Thirteenth and Fourteen Amendments [which] provide a unitary context for the legal treatment of blacks and whites, and reimbue the defining documents of American government with the moral authority of the higher law tradition."[77] Emerson, as cultural hero-redeemer, eventually lived to see his vision of an improved Constitution become a reality, and, as the recognized "conscience of America," contributed a great deal to the cultural ferment that made it possible.[78]

Emerson continued his attack on the institution of slavery in a second "Fugitive Slave Law" address in March 1854. In this address, he continued, like the ideal, liberating hero he described in *Representative Men*, to exhort others to access the divinity within themselves and, armed with its power, to confront directly the evils of the times. His tone is both urgent and demanding. While transcendence is personally ennobling, Emerson continues to insist that idealism requires action in order to be efficacious. "Whilst the inconsistency of slavery with the principles on which the world is built guarantees its downfall," he observes, "I own that the patience it requires is almost too sublime for mortals and seems to demand of us more than mere hoping. And when one sees how fast the rot spreads,—it is growing serious,—I think that we demand of superior men that they shall be superior in this, that the mind and the virtue give their verdict in their day and accelerate so far the progress of civilization." Emerson's message here, learned through his own earlier, hard-fought battles with "the Establishment," the resisting fathers, is that virtuous people must believe in themselves and their own divine power before they can be of service to others. "Self-reliance," he states, "the height and perfection of man, is reliance on God."[79] However, this God is not the God of conventional Christianity, but the God that dwells within. The established churches are presently dominated by a narrow consciousness and they have been co-opted by the corrupt material powers of the world. Consequently, they have lost their spiritual charge and with it their moral authority. Ironically, they have actually now become the pillars that support a corrupt and degenerate status quo. Many ministers, for example, actually applauded the passage of the heinous Fugitive Slave Law.[80] This historical situation is not unique. Because churches are firmly established institutions, they are by nature conservative and resistant to change. They rest upon the dictates of a sterile ego-consciousness. As mere products of the Understanding, for the most part, they become disconnected from the primal sources of spiritual and emotional vitality within, the Reason, the Over-Soul. Brown describes an earlier historical instance where "Protestantism degenerated from Luther and Boehme" and "abandoned its religious function of criticizing the existing order and keeping alive the mystical hope of better things. In psycho-analytical terminology," he asserts, the church "lost contact with the unconscious."[81] When Eros, the God within, is thus abandoned, any abomination can be justified by the Understanding in defense of the status quo. Thus, Emerson complains bitterly in his journal about those perfidious ministers who support outrages like the Fugitive Slave Law and thus gladly "deduce kidnapping from their Bible." This moribund form of Christianity, he insists, has become "a religion of dead dogs."[82] As the archetypal hero of true virtue, Emerson seeks to renew the spirit of love by returning to its source. He tells his audience that, "to interpret Christ, it needs Christ in the heart. The teachings of the spirit can be apprehended only by the spirit that gave them forth. To make good the cause of Freedom, you must draw off from all these foolish trusts on others. You must be citadels and warriors, yourselves Declarations of Independence, the charter, the battle, and the victory." As seen in chapter 3, Emerson, in the first stage of his career as poet-reformer, sought to re-center reality and the cosmos around the individual in order to bring wholeness and meaning to an increasingly fragmented world. Thus, he maintains here: "It is the office of the moral nature to give sanity and right direction to the mind, to give centrality and unity."[83] The glue that would hold this new world together derives from the power of Love that lies within us all. Such an inward perspective places a new and significant emphasis on individual conscience. But, as Emerson indicates, individual conscience derives from contact with the eternal and universal spirit within. This primal individualism, therefore, is what makes social action possible. As a consequence of his own inward journey and the personal transformation that resulted, Emerson learned first hand that you must be a unit before you can experience unity. You must connect internally with that which bonds all of humanity, the power of love, Eros, the Over-Soul, God, the eternal One. Like Aristotle's "concord," such love is not only the glue that holds all of society together, but it is also the source of all social justice. It is something that can be felt before it is understood, and it begins with the individual's personal experience of the infinite. This is why Emerson insists on emphasizing the importance of self-reliance as the key to social reform. Social reform begins with individualism, but it does not end there. The Declaration of Independence is only efficacious as a social and political document if one is open to an intuitive affirmation of its statement of universal truth. Once this is felt and comprehended, the individual then becomes a "walking Declaration," and ultimately joins with others who also feel this truth and perceive the injustice that it illuminates. Emersonian self-reliance does not, therefore, remove the individual from society, as some critics maintain, but just the opposite. As Wesley Mott observes, "For Emerson . . . genuine individualism was not narcissism, monomania, or isolation. Indeed, it was the *answer* to these diseases of the self as well as the remedy for the 'existing evils' of institutional and social life."[84] In conformity with this view, it is not surprising to find Emerson, the icon of self-reliance, proclaiming in 1855, "But whilst I insist on the doctrine of the independence and the inspiration of the individual, I do not cripple but exalt the social action. . . . A wise man delights in the powers of many people."[85] Indeed, by this time the association that Emerson had formed with the abolitionist women in Concord more than a decade earlier had blossomed into a full-blown alliance with abolitionists everywhere. They now saw him as one of their own. Emerson touched many hearts in his campaign for social justice and was touched, in turn, by them. The resulting synergy was dynamic. Emerson's powerful, Transcendental idealism enhanced the motivation and enthusiasm of reformers and as a result, as Albert von Frank has noted, "in 1854 the antislavery revolution virtually fell into the hands of Emerson's followers."[86]

Emerson's lifelong, heroic campaign for the principles of freedom, equality, and justice has since resonated with audiences of all types. As Lawrence Buell observes, throughout his public career Emerson, "opened up the prospect of a much more profound sense of the nature, challenge, and promise of mental emancipation, whatever one's race, sex, or nation might be."[87] Indeed, Emerson's Transcendental arguments for human dignity and self-worth, based upon self-evident principles that derive from a divine source that dwells within all, provided a powerful stimulus for reform of all types. His notion of ever widening and all-inclusive circles of being, with divinity as the unifying center, provides a dynamic vision for any social reform agenda that is based on liberty, toleration, and equal rights. The goal of the reformer is to broaden the circle of society until all are included and no group or person remains, literally, marginalized.

Emerson's interests were diverse, as indicated in chapter 4. He wished to promote *universal* reform, and in his struggle against the corrupt and repressive fathers of American society, he would find a formidable resource in the power afforded by the "mothers," both literally and symbolically. Not surprisingly, in this period of masculine domination, the position of women was not that different from the position of slaves. As Margaret Fuller complained in *Woman in the Nineteenth Century* (1845), women were second-class citizens at best. For the most part, they were denied property rights, as well as educational and professional opportunities, and were not allowed to vote or to hold office.[88] Emerson sympathized with their plight, and recognized the extent to which women both symbolized and possessed the very power that was necessary to redeem America. As pointed out earlier, in his 1855 address "Woman" he observed that "the starry crown of woman is in the power of her affection and sentiment." For Emerson, "these affections are only introductory to that which is sublime."[89] Indeed, it is precisely this "sublime" power that is required to effect the redemption of American society. It is this power that Emerson sees at work in "the action of the age on the antagonism to slavery." Ironically, for many, even among the reformers themselves, the active participation of women in antislavery organizations was considered inappropriate and, therefore, controversial.[90] However, for Emerson, it was not only appropriate, but necessary. The desire for liberty is a natural instinct and, like American slaves, American women had been consistently denied freedom, equality, and social justice. They had been left outside the divine circle of human equality. But the movement towards liberty and justice is irrepressible. It reflects a universal and divine imperative. Hence, as Emerson states, "one truth leads in another by the hand; one right is an accession of strength to take more. And the times are marked by the new attitude of woman urging, by argument and association, her rights of all kinds, in short, to one half of the world: the right to education; to avenues of employment; to equal rights of property; to equal rights in marriage; to the exercise of the professions; to suffrage."[91] Despite some early reservations regarding the possibility that the full exercise of these rights might have a deleterious impact on the affective side of women, Emerson nevertheless supported them. "They have an unquestionable right to their own property. And, if the woman demands votes, offices, and political equality with men, . . . it must not be refused."[92] Emerson maintained this commitment to equality throughout his long public career. In 1869, he accepted the titular post of vice-president of the New England Women's Suffrage Association.[93]

Throughout the 1850s, Emerson continued his efforts at reforming and redeeming American society by promoting an intuitive morality. This effort would, due to the critical demands of the time, be focused primarily upon the issue of slavery. As David Robinson observes, during this period Emerson "had come to see antislavery as the fundamental contemporary manifestation of the eternal struggle of moral forces."[94] He saw these forces manifested, as he notes in his "Fugitive Slave Law Address," as "Will, or Duty, or Freedom" and he placed them in opposition to "the power of Fate, of Fortune, the laws of the world, the order of things."[95] It is this very opposition—the eternal friction of the Reason and the Understanding, unconscious and conscious, the Movement and the Establishment, liberal and conservative—that he had been dealing with since his own emergence from personal darkness. It would become the primary concern of what many consider to be his last major work, *Conduct of Life* (1860), a work that is in many ways indebted to his heroic crusade against slavery. Along the way, Emerson would continue to promote personal liberty as the sine qua non of a just society. In his 1855 "Lecture on Slavery," he demanded "to each man the largest liberty compatible with the liberty of every other man," and he reminded his audience that in a true democracy, "No citizen will go wrong who on every question leans to the side of general liberty." Such liberty, of course, facilitates self-reliance, but Emerson saw such individualism as only a necessary first step towards social reform. Unlike the liberty that derives from personal ecstasy that more or less predominated in his earlier writings, a fully engaged Emerson now promoted a movement that begins with personal inspiration but ends in collective action. "Men inspire each other," he tells his audience. "The affections are Muses. Hope is a muse, Love is, Despair is not, and selfishness drives away angels. It is so delicious to act with great masses to great aims," he asserts, especially "the summary or gradual abolition of slavery."[96] Of course, the opposition to "the enterprise of relieving this country of the pest of slavery" continued to come from those with a strong interest in maintaining the economic status quo, the conservative elite. "The Party of Property, of education, has resisted every progressive step. . . . With their eyes over their shoulders, they adore their ancestors. . . . [They] do not wish to touch the Constitution. They wish their age should be absolutely like the last." Such resistance to change is not only stultifying, but with the nation lurching towards civil war, it is tantamount to a death wish. "What means this desperate grasp on the past; if not that they find no principle, no hope, no future in their own mind?"[97] Eventually, the nation would cast off this intolerable tyranny in favor of a new vision, but this change would not come except with great sacrifice in a conflict of biblical proportions.

English Traits (1856), another major work of this turbulent decade, also reflects Emerson's continuing commitment to his role as liberator and spokesperson for the Divine Soul, for Eros, for the power of Love. While offering limited praise for British accomplishments, Emerson is just as often critical of their failings. As Phyllis Cole observes, England and the British Empire came to represent to Emerson "a society thoroughly imprisoned by 'laws of the world,' a society where the individual soul is impotent."[98] Despite a strong tradition of liberty dating back as far as the Magna Carta, British society is currently dominated by a conservative materialism that Emerson would later refer to as a "shop-keeping mentality." In his chapter on "Literature," he asserts that England possesses "a strong common sense, which is not easy to unseat or disturb" and which by its nature is stultifying and soul-deadening. The "English type" for Emerson is a walking incarnation of all that he came to despise in those dominated by the Understanding, a sterile and arid consciousness that addresses only the business end of life. "He is materialist, economical, mercantile."[99] Ultimately, as Robinson points out, in this work the English "embody the values against which Emerson the transcendentalist had to contend in his search for ways to shore up his fading visionary stance."[100] Robert Weisbuch confirms this insight when he observes that, in *English Traits*, Emerson's criticism of England's mercenary materialism reflects a concern with a similar development in America. Emerson "employs England," he observes, ". . . to reinvest America with its utopian promise at a time when the sense that the New World would be the scene for a revolution in consciousness has been threatened by the horrors of the slave trade and the hundred doubts of commercial development at home."[101]

Indeed, Emerson's "visionary stance" was repeatedly challenged in the balance of the decade as the slave power grew and antiabolition violence became ever more common. His foray into the realm of reform politics brought with it public criticism every bit as bitter as that which followed his address at the Divinity School years earlier. His first presentation on the Fugitive Slave Law was met with hisses, groans, and jeers, by a crowd of rowdy Harvard students when he gave the talk in Cambridge. Following that event, the *Boston Semi-Weekly Advertiser* added its criticism and cautioned that Emerson was a dangerous guide when it came to politics because his philosophical views are clothed in "misty jargon" and the man himself has "the acknowledged character of a perpetual doubter, or inquirer . . . [who] has been most anxious to lead his hearers to the habit of questioning authority of every description."[102] Indeed, Emerson's son Edward would later recall that, as a result of his growing prominence as an abolitionist, Emerson became "a marked man in Boston as belonging to the despised minority who held for honor and humanity rather than for smooth and easy prosperity of complicity in wrong."[103] Things were soon to get much worse.

Because of his voluble and, at times, vitriolic attacks on slavery and those who supported it, Charles Sumner, senator from Massachusetts and eventually a close Emerson ally, was attacked and nearly beaten to death on the floor of the United States Senate in the spring of 1856. His assailant was a southern representative from South Carolina, Preston Brooks, who was offended by Sumner's recent speech where he criticized supporters of the pro-slavery ruffians who were terrorizing free soil farmers in what had come to be known as "bleeding Kansas." Emerson was appalled by the brutal attack. He responded with a scathing address to his fellow citizens of Concord where he asserted bluntly, "I think we must get rid of slavery, or we must get rid of freedom."[104] Times were growing more violent by the day. When Kansas first erupted into open warfare between pro and antislavery forces, a development that had been set in motion by the passage of the notorious Kansas-Nebraska Act of 1854, Emerson contributed money to buy Sharpe's rifles for the freedom fighters. It was another sign of his growing militancy. He also later entertained one of the most famous antislavery partisans, John Brown, in his home when he came to Concord to raise money for his cause. The decade would end with John Brown's famous raid on the Federal Arsenal at Harper's Ferry, Virginia. Emerson publicly defended him after the raid, describing Brown as "the rarest of heroes, a pure idealist."[105] John

Brown's capture, trial, and subsequent execution in December 1859 laid the final groundwork for the Civil War, a conflict in which Emerson, not surprisingly, would come to "personify the Union's highest ideals."[106]

On the threshold of the war, in December 1860, Emerson published *Conduct of Life*, a work deeply indebted to his experience throughout the turbulent 1850s.[107] Robinson maintains that the work punctuates a development that began in the mid-1840s and which has been outlined here. It is a movement whereby the fully formed hero assumes his proper place in the world as the incarnated prophet-oracle who leads others to the same transcendent, redemptive experience. Robinson reports that at this point Emerson's faith, was "sustained by the access to power that the moral sense promises, a clear indication of the way ethics [had] come to replace ecstasy as Emerson's point of spiritual reference."[108] In the opening essay "Fate," Emerson observes that at this critical juncture in American history, "the question of the times resolved itself into a practical question of the conduct of life. How shall I live?" Living rightly and righteously has never been more important to American society as a whole and, "We are fired with the hope to reform men."[109] The force that is ranged against reform, as he had noted in his second Fugitive Slave Law address, is the power of "Fate, or, laws of the world," that is, things as they are. While this status quo seems fixed and obdurate, like the granite sepulchers of the fathers that are filled with corruption, it is nevertheless subject to change. "If we must accept Fate," says Emerson, "we are not less compelled to affirm liberty, the significance of the individual, the grandeur of duty, the power of character."[110] If "Fate" is the masculine product of a sterile ego-consciousness, or Understanding, it can be offset by the strength of the unconscious, the feminine force of Reason, the power of Eros, the love that emanates from the Divine Mind. Indeed, Emerson asserts that "History is the action and reaction" of these two polarities.[111] The winds of change are blowing; American society is in a dramatic and, at times painful, state of flux. As he envisioned in his "American Scholar" address so many years earlier, the time of revolution was fast approaching. As the bloody conflict in Kansas and the continued resistance to the Fugitive Slave Law suggest, the Establishment was now rocking on its foundations. Seer-like individuals such as Emerson, who are gifted with a feminine sensitivity and insight, are most aware of this fact.

> Certain ideas are in the air and the most impressionable brain
> will announce it first. . . . So women, as most susceptible, are
> the best index of the coming hour. So the great man, that is,
> the man most imbued with the spirit of the time, is the impressionable man. . . . His mind is righter than others because
> he yields to a current so feeble as can be felt only by a needle
> delicately poised.[112]

In the essay "Power" (which he posits as the counterforce to fate) Emerson expresses his faith that great good can even now be accomplished, regardless of the continued opposition of the status quo, strong as that opposition may appear. "There are men," he maintains, "who, by their sympathetic attractions, carry nations with them and lead the activity of the human race."[113] While frequently leadership is corrupt, and great men like Webster can prove perfidious, the general tendency of things is towards moral improvement because "we have a certain instinct, that where is great amount of life, though gross and peccant, it has its own checks and purifications, and will be found at last in harmony with moral laws." Emerson continued to maintain a strong faith in the democratic process, despite its many failings, because every person, even the most common, possesses a spark of divinity and divine insight that will eventually lead in the right direction. Thus, "whatever hard head Arkansas, Oregon or Utah sends, half orator, half assassin, to represent its wrath and cupidity at Washington," these will finally come round, and the natural forces at work "will bestow promptness, address and reason, at last, on our buffalo-hunter, and authority and majesty of manners." Because he believes that divinity resides even in the lowliest, a keystone of his democratic faith, Emerson had no doubt that, ultimately, "the instinct of the people is right."[114] One month before he published these words in *Conduct of Life*, Abraham Lincoln, a common man of the people, was elected President of the United States. Emerson was elated. The power of the spirit was made manifest at last. In his journal he observed, "the news of last Wednesday morning . . . was sublime, the pronunciation of the masses of America against Slavery.[115]

Because of his opposition to the further expansion of slavery, the most significant and controversial plank in the platform of the Republican Party, Lincoln was elected without receiving a single southern electoral vote.[116] The nation was moving inexorably towards a crisis, and many conservatives held the abolitionists responsible. It was now dangerous to attempt to hold an antislavery gathering anywhere. Wendell Phillips, the most eloquent of New England's abolition orators and a man Emerson admired, had taken to carrying a gun. He was surrounded by a bodyguard wherever he went. Despite the obvious dangers, however, when Phillips asked Emerson to join him at a Boston antislavery rally in January 1861, he felt bound to go. As expected, the gathering was infiltrated by antiabolition ruffians who, when Emerson attempted to speak, broke out in jeers, hisses, and catcalls. Soon a melee erupted, and the police eventually cleared the hall. Emerson never finished his speech, but he felt that his mere presence at the rally made a statement. As he later wrote in his journal: "If I were dumb, yet I would have gone & mowed & muttered or made signs."[117] By this time, Emerson was accustomed to opposition and was fully prepared to play his part regardless. As Neumann observes,

"Every culture-hero has achieved a synthesis between consciousness and the creative unconscious. He has found within himself the fruitful center, the point of renewal and rebirth which . . . is identified with the creative divinity, and upon which the continued existence of the world depends."[118] Emerson was determined that his effort to reform his society, to re-center it based on a vision of the divinity and equality of all persons, would go forward whatever the opposition. The nation was driving towards a crisis, but the times were electrified by the possibility of positive change. It was indeed, a revolutionary time, "when the old and the new stand side by side, and admit of being compared; when the energies of all men are searched by fear and by hope."[119] Now was the time when the voice of the prophet must be heard. The words that he wrote many years before regarding the duty of the poet-hero must have come back to him now with special poignancy. "Doubt not, O poet, but persist. Say, 'It is in me, and shall out.' Stand there, baulked and dumb, stuttering and stammering, hissed and hooted, stand and strive, until, at last, rage draw out of thee that *dream*-power, which every night shows thee is thine own."[120] Emerson's "dream" for America was one of democratic equality, freedom, and social justice.[121]

The situation on the national scene continued to degenerate rapidly throughout the "winter of secession," 1860–1861. Tensions were at the breaking point. The die had been cast, and ten years of growing mistrust and animosity exploded in a cannonade over the ramparts of Fort Sumter. On April 12, 1861, the Civil War commenced. Emerson was surprised but relieved that years of undeclared war were over, and that the project of ending slavery through the application of power could now begin in earnest. He had come to believe some time before that "For Slavery, extirpation is the only cure."[122] At the outset, the ostensible purpose of the war was simply to preserve the Union as it was, with slavery unmolested wherever it already existed. Emerson, however, was convinced that a greater power was at work, a "moral force," that was destined to bring about what Lincoln would call "a new birth of freedom" in America.[123] This rebirth would bring with it the long-delayed fulfillment of the promise made by the nation's first revolutionaries, namely, that "all men are created equal." What was needed now was for the redeemer-hero to provide the moral leadership and vision that would help to take America's people to this Promised Land.[124] "Where there is no vision," Emerson would observe in a lecture midway through the war, "the people perish."[125] Now widely recognized as America's foremost philosopher, oracle, and prophet, he was not about to let that happen. The power of the Over-Soul would make itself felt through him and the nation would experience a revolutionary re-centering. In Emerson's vision of a reborn America, equality, freedom, and justice would finally be guaranteed for everyone. All of humankind would stand together in the center of a divine and unified cosmos.

In July 1861, in an address to the students at Tufts College titled "Celebration of the Intellect," Emerson observed that the war must be properly understood as a revolutionary application of moral power against the obstinate limitations of fate, that is the corrupt state of things as they are. Thus, he observes, "The brute noise of the cannon has . . . a most poetic echo in these days, when it is an instrument of freedom and the primal sentiment of humanity." This "primal sentiment," of course, is yet another name for the "moral sentiment," the divinity within that is the ultimate guide in the conduct of life. It resides in the heart, not in the head. It is a source of wisdom and spiritual vitality that goes far beyond the limited range of mere Understanding. Unfortunately, up to this point in America, education has been of the Understanding only, and "knowledge, the divine oracle which it ought to have delivered, it has failed to deliver." As a result, "National calamities punish the want of knowledge." Colleges themselves bear much of the blame for this failure for, as Emerson warned at Harvard so many years earlier, they address only the head while repressing the soul, the source of the life-sustaining Divine Spirit in humankind. When this happens, "the college is suicidal; ceases to be a school; power oozes out of it just as fast as truth does; and instead of overawing the strong, and upholding the good, it is a hospital for decayed tutors, a musty shop of old books in Rotten Row."[126] The solution to this problem is to look within for wisdom and truth, for he "who looks with his own eyes will find that there is somebody within him that knows more than he does; that his education of the Understanding is not always wise." Intuition is a surer guide than traditional learning, especially in this time of crisis, and because of this those who would truly improve the world must "enthrone the Instinct. There, must be the perpetual rallying and self-recovery."[127] Emerson remained more convinced than ever that essential life-sustaining truth was available to all if they would but open themselves to it. For him, at this time of national crisis, when the very survival of the nation was at stake, that truth demanded not only the restoration of the Union, but also the perfection of the Republic by insuring the freedom and equality of all citizens. Only the promise of equal justice, an aspect of Aristotle's "concord," could heal the social fragmentation and discord that are the inevitable consequence of inequality, bigotry, and the dominance of material self-interest. The brotherhood and sisterhood of humankind in America, a nation "conceived in liberty and dedicated to the proposition that all men are created equal," as Lincoln would soon express it at Gettysburg, must become a reality at last. In the appropriately titled lecture "Moral Forces," delivered in the spring of 1862, Emerson articulates this grand vision of unity and love, the political dimension of the unifying and life-sustaining power of the Over-Soul, the eternal One, the unconscious, using his favorite symbol, the circle. Those who are willing to fight for what is eternally right and true become thereby part of a great "ring," a circle of "brotherhood."

> By the magic of a shout, and the unfurling of a flag, he who was alone, caring for nobody, and for whom none cared, is surprised with the delight of feeling himself one in the ring of a vast brotherhood, across the mountains, across the state border, from the Atlantic to the Pacific: that he and they all have one will, that this grand territory confided to them by the hand of God shall remain one, and shall remain for the benefit and not for the nuisance of mankind, for a country, and not for a slave-pen. This thought uplifts him: he has grown wise and elevated in a few hours more than in years before.[128]

Not every American, however, concurred with the content of this noble and unifying vision. Racial prejudices were strong, and many still insisted upon making a bitter and narrow-minded distinction between the "me" and the "not me." For such as these, the inferiors whom they deem "others" must forever remain outside the circle of true humanity. Sadly, many Northerners undoubtedly agreed with the southern planter's son who, early in the war, observed that, "It is insulting to the English common sense of race [to say that we] are battling for an abstract right common to all humanity. Every reflecting child will glance at the darkey who waits on him & laugh at the idea of such an 'abstract right.'"[129] Indeed, when Lincoln issued his Preliminary Emancipation Proclamation in September 1862 in which he declared his intention to free all slaves residing in states that remained in rebellion, it created a morale crisis in the Union armies.[130] Only a minority of Union soldiers at the time had any interest in fighting for the slaves' freedom. Many undoubtedly felt like the soldier from New York who insisted in a letter home that "we must first conquer & then its time enough to talk about the *damn'd niggers.*"[131]

Emerson, of course, had a different vision. In his lecture "Perpetual Forces" (November 18, 1862), delivered just two months after Lincoln's preliminary proclamation, he insisted that not only should slavery be abolished throughout a reconstructed nation, but that emancipated slaves should be accorded all of the rights of other citizens, including the right to vote, an extremely radical position at this time. Nevertheless, with the assured voice of the prophet, Emerson declared that in the new America that will inevitably emerge from the ashes of conflict, we must "Leave slavery out. Since nothing satisfies but justice, let us have that, and let us stifle our prejudices against common sense and humanity, and agree that every man shall have what he honestly earns, and, if he is a sane and innocent man, have an equal vote in the state, and a fair chance in society." This utterly simple and honest vision of justice and equality is the intuitive and compelling dictate of "our moral sentiment" for Emerson. In keeping with his redeemer role, he is indignant at the resistance to this ethical imperative. With its source deep in the wellsprings of our common and divine being, this "moral sentiment" can and must be America's infallible guide at this critical time. It is the source of all truth, the source of all life, and the source of all justice. Unfortunately, because the moral sentiment is, like the "higher law," an abstraction that is intuitively perceived, practical people who follow only their Understanding have little confidence in its reality. Speaking of this mystical, universal, and divine force, Emerson asserts,

> We are made of it, the world is built by it, things endure as they share it; all beauty, all health, all intelligence, exist by it; yet we shrink to speak it, or to range ourselves on its side. Nay, we presume strength of him or them who deny it. Cities go against it, the college goes against it, the courts snatch at any precedent, at any vicious form of law, to rule it out; legislatures listen with appetite to declamations against it, and vote it down. Every new assertor of the right surprises us, like a man joining the church, and we hardly dare believe he is in earnest.[132]

A prophet is rarely accepted in his own land, as Emerson well knew from his earlier struggles. Following his impassioned address, a conservative Albany newspaper complained that Emerson's lecture was merely "a re-hash of his Abolition sophistry" and noted pointedly that "When he argued in favor of forcible emancipation, a few old ladies and gentlemen applauded; but when he insisted that the negro should have 'an equal chance with the white man,' even they were indignantly silent."[133] But the prophet would not be silenced. Emerson realized from his earlier experience that the key to emancipation is self-emancipation, which, in turn, is the product of self-reliance, that is, reliance on the God within. A belief in oneself, confidence in the power of the divinity that resides in all, leads to a willingness to face opposition with courage and determination. The manifestation of such personal courage and heroic character becomes itself a compelling argument for equality. Undoubtedly with this thought in mind, when the Federal government finally and reluctantly allowed for the formation of the Union Army's first, regular Negro regiment, the Massachusetts Fifty-fourth, in January 1863, Emerson joined Frederick Douglass and others in raising funds and giving speeches to

encourage black enlistments. In his journal appears an outline for one
such speech. Its content is reminiscent of the "rise of the anti-slave" sentiment of his 1844 "Emancipation of the Negroes in the British West Indies" address. "If war means liberty to you," he asserts, "you should
enlist. . . . If you will not fight for your liberty, who will? If you will not
. . . the universe of men will say you are not worth fighting for. Go & be
slaves forever & you shall have our aid to make you such. You had rather
be slaves than freemen."[134] This stern exhortation, and others like it, apparently had the desired effect, and recruitment was a great success. The
Massachusetts Fifty-fourth would go on to win glory and respect in a
courageous though unsuccessful attack on Fort Wagner, South Carolina,
on July 18, 1863. In this attack the regiment suffered a staggering 42 per-
cent casualty rate. The following month Emerson observed in an address
at Waterville College that "War always exalts an age, speaks to slumbering virtue, makes of quiet, plain men unexpected heroes."[135] Undoubtedly he had the Fifty-fourth in mind.[136] The experience of this and other
Negro regiments demonstrated clearly the validity of Negro claims to
equality. As James McPherson notes, "the organization of black regiments marked the transformation of a war to preserve the Union into a
revolution to overthrow the old order."[137] Most certainly Emerson was
delighted to be an important instrument in this ongoing, moral rebirth of
American society. The corrupt "old order" was giving way, finally, to a
new and nobler vision of the nation, a nation whose fundamental vision
was gradually expanding to include the equality and dignity of all people.
The effects of this change could be felt even within the ranks of the Union
Army where the pro-emancipation position eventually became dominant.[138] With this transformation, the Union Army could be seen as
a truly revolutionary moral force, itself imbued with the divine power
of the spirit. For Emerson, Union soldiers now became true instruments
of change, embarked on a divine mission to redeem and reform the
character of the nation and instill within it a new faith. As he would observe after the war, "The armies mustered in the North were as much
missionaries to the mind of the country as they were carriers of material
force, and had the vast advantage of carrying whither they marched a
higher civilization."[139]

Emerson continued to actively support the Union cause and President Lincoln throughout the war, especially in the dark days of the winter
of 1863–1864.[140] Following major victories at Gettysburg and Vicksburg
in the summer of 1863, the Union Armies bogged down in what soon became a gruesome war of attrition. War weariness set in. In response, a
"Peace Party," led by "Copperheads," was formed in the North with the
aim of negotiating a cessation of hostilities and, eventually, a resumption
of the Union as it was, with slavery intact. For reformers, it was a dark

time, indeed. Even Lincoln's re-election was in serious doubt.[141] Emerson was appalled at these developments and in one of his most important, powerful, and prophetic addresses, "Fortune of the Republic," he exhorted Unionists to be true to their better selves and continue the fight, no matter how great the sacrifice, in order to insure the ultimate triumph of those universal and transcendent principles of freedom, equality, and justice. These immortal values reflect the divine power of the Over-Soul. They are the "self-evident truths" that are so eloquently expressed in the Declaration of Independence. "It is the young men of the land," Emerson urged, "who must save it: it is they to whom this wonderful hour, after so many weary ages, dawns, the Second Declaration of Independence, the proclaiming of liberty, land, justice, and a career for all men, and honest dealings with other nations." These values, Emerson prophetically insists, are of inestimable importance in this great contest that will determine the nation's and democracy's future. It is a heroic struggle for the minds and hearts, indeed, the very soul of the nation. "When men die for what they live for, and the mainspring that works daily urges them to hazard all, then the canon articulates its explosions with the voice of a man. Then the rifle seconds the canon, and the fowling-piece the rifle, and the women make cartridges and all shoot at one mark, and the better code of laws at last records the victory." The "artillery of sympathy and emotion" that Emerson had once deployed only metaphorically, was now an actual instrument of war, but still in the service of the same universal cause. It is true that the sacrifices demanded thus far in the war had been great, indeed, had been of biblical proportions. Literally hundreds of thousands of lives had already been lost in this costliest of all American wars, but Emerson insists that the gains are beyond valuation. "Slavery is broken, and, if we use our advantage, irretrievably. For such a gain,—to end once for all that pest of all free institutions,—one generation might well be sacrificed,—perhaps it will be,—that this continent be purged, and a new era of equal rights dawn on the universe. Who would not, if it could be made certain, that the new morning of universal liberty should rise on our race, by the perishing of one generation,—who would not consent to die."[142]

The tides of war eventually changed. In September, Atlanta fell to Sherman's army, and Northerners opted to follow Emerson's advice and stay the course. In November 1864, Lincoln was re-elected. Emerson wrote to a friend shortly after expressing "joy of the election," and noting, "Seldom in history was so much staked on a popular vote.—I suppose never in history."[143] Once again, "the instinct of the people," proved reliable. With Lincoln's re-election, the war was prosecuted to a successful conclusion and the nation began to experience the "rebirth of freedom" that the president promised. "Equal rights" and "universal liberty" remained the core elements of Emerson's prophetic vision of a truly unified America. His hope was that the nation's collective consciousness could now be re-centered on these universal values, which derive from the divinity that exists within all and impart dignity and meaning to every human life, regardless of race or gender.

Following the southern surrender and the tragic assassination of President Lincoln in April 1865, the process of reconstruction began. The Republic re-created itself largely through the establishment in law of those transcendent and revolutionary values that Emerson had prophetically preached throughout his lengthy career. Once disparaged as "glittering generalities," or the questionable and airy dictates of some mystical "Higher Law," the principles of freedom, equality, and social justice for all were now encoded in the American Constitution. The Thirteenth (1865), Fourteenth (1866), and Fifteenth (1870) Amendments solemnly promised liberty, equal protection, and voting rights to all adult males, regardless of race. In keeping with Emerson's belief that "one truth leads in another by the hand; one right is an accession of strength to take more," these measures, in turn, led to yet another social revolution in the form of the Women's Suffrage Movement and, eventually, the Civil Rights Movement of the twentieth century.[144] The struggle still continues, of course, as it must. As Emerson well knew, the perfect society must always be just beyond the horizon. His major contribution to the process is his compelling articulation of an ideal vision of America as a land of liberty and equality, and the fact that he urged the process of reform onward through exhortation and example. Emerson was willing to "put his creed into his deed" and in the process he inspired countless others to do the same. Like the prophet that he aspired to be, Emerson served as the reassuring voice that reminds those who seek to improve the world that, despite the apparent darkness of the moment, "This time, like all times, is a very good one, if we but know what to do with it."[145]

In looking back over the accomplishments of this dramatic period in 1871, it seemed clear to Emerson that a great victory had been won. The power of the unconscious, Eros, the Over-Soul, the Reason, had wrought a second revolution that truly changed the face of America. In one of his last public lectures, "Resources," this prophetic rebel paid tribute to the moral revolution to which he had dedicated his life. The corrupt establishment had been dis-established and the tyrannical "fathers" finally deposed. "We have seen slavery disappear like a painted scene in a theatre," he says. "We have seen the old oligarchs tumbled out of their powerful chairs into poverty, exile, and shame. We have seen those who were their victims, occupy their places, and dictate their fate. We have seen the most healthful revolution in the politics of the nation." And, finally, "the Constitution is not only amended, but construed in a new spirit."[146] That "new spirit" for Emerson was clearly the spirit of Eros,

Love, the eternal One, the same dynamic force that had transformed this quiet, middle-class minister into the prophet of his age. For Emerson, it was the ultimate source of love and brotherhood as well as the eternal mainspring of justice. It made him what Campbell calls "the supreme hero . . . who reopens the eye—so that through all the comings and goings, delights and agonies of the world panorama, the One Presence will be seen again."[147] As he prophesied in "The American Scholar" so many years before, when this force comes to animate the lives of all, "A new nation of men will for the first time exist, because each believes himself inspired by the Divine Soul which also inspires all men."[148] The hero's work was now, finally, complete.

EPILOGUE

EMERSON, WHOLENESS, AND THE SELF

Eros—October
I cannot tell rude listeners
Half the tell-tale South-wind said,—
'T would bring the blushes of yon maples
To a man and to a maid.

—Emerson, *Eros—October*

 In his classic study, *The Great Mother: An Analysis of an Archetype* (1955), Erich Neumann maintains that archetypes are a natural and important component of the human psyche. They are an essential part of life, and they have the power to "determine human behavior unconsciously but in accordance with laws." For Neumann, the "dynamic component of the unconscious has a compelling character for the individual who is directed by it, and it is always accompanied by a strong emotional element."[1] This was most certainly the case for Emerson whose mature, heroic personality was formed, in large part, by the archetypes that he experienced in exploring the content of his own unconscious, especially at times of emotional intensity and personal crisis. These archetypes of wholeness, circularity, uroboric harmony, of masculine and feminine junction, all had a healing effect for him. Because of the dynamic nature of his deeply imaginative and profoundly creative personality, at times his experience of these primal archetypes reached a state of ecstasy where he and divinity were one. In his own words, he became "part and particle of God." These intense and dramatic experiences were transforming. They led to Emerson's remarkable evolution from pedestrian minister of an orthodox faith, to prophetic poet, oracle, and, finally, reformer.

193

It was precisely Emerson's perception of harmony, unity, and the divinity within that was acutely lacking both in mid-nineteenth and mid-twentieth century America. By repeatedly manifesting these archetypes in his writings and lectures, Emerson was able to offer his society the same healing experience that he himself had undergone. Correspondingly, in the mid-twentieth century the psychomythic humanists considered here sought in their own diverse and eclectic works to draw the attention of their contemporaries to the archetypal images, concepts, and symbols of harmony, unity, and spiritual transcendence that could provide solace and healing to their badly fragmented and increasingly faithless world. Many influential literary critics would follow this lead as "archetypal criticism" became an important critical tool for many readers. Psychomythic humanism continues to find a significant audience today because, as Jung once pointed out, "We moderns are faced with the necessity of rediscovering the life of the spirit; we must experience it anew for ourselves."[2] For many, Emerson continues to be a great help in this process.

Ralph Waldo Emerson died quietly in his sleep in April 1882, just weeks short of his eightieth birthday. By this time, he was considered "a *national* treasure."[3] His popular poems, such as "Concord Hymn," appeared in schoolbooks throughout the land, while now classic essays like "Self-Reliance" found an appreciative audience in those who were eager to identify an authentic *American* voice in a still young and culturally insecure nation. But the majority of his writing, while well-respected, was seen, as a critic in the *Saturday Review* put it at the time, as "more easily reflected upon than described, more easily felt than reflected upon."[4] It's not a bad description. It suggests the very mystic and affective qualities that characterize Emerson's most significant and profound expressions. Indeed, it is this very quality that the philosopher William James chose to emphasize in his address celebrating the one-hundredth anniversary of Emerson's birth in 1903. James summarized the "creed from which Emerson's life followed" as one that connects the facts of everyday life with the eternal spirit that gives them meaning. "Through the individual fact" James states, "there ever shone for him the effulgence of the Universal Reason. The great Cosmic intellect terminates and houses itself in mortal man and passing hours. Each of us is an angle of its eternal vision, and the only way to be true to our maker is to be loyal to ourselves."[5] He later adds,

> For Emerson, the individual fact and moment were indeed suffused with absolute radiance, but it was upon a condition that saved the situation—they must be worthy specimens,—sincere, authentic, archetypal; they must have made connection with what he calls the Moral Sentiment, they must in some way act as symbolic mouthpieces of the Universe's meaning. To know just which thing does act in this way, and which thing fails to make the true connection, is the secret (somewhat incommuni-

cable, it must be confessed) of seership, and doubtless we must not expect of the seer too rigorous a consistency. Emerson himself was a real seer. He could perceive the full squalor of the individual fact, but he could also see the transfiguration.[6]

James himself would later have a substantial impact on Carl Jung, who, in turn, articulated remarkably similar insights. The line of influence from Emerson, to James, to Jung is an interesting and provocative one. Recently, scholars have provided many insights into Emerson's influence on James, both early and late. Emerson was adored by the philosopher's eccentric father, Henry James, Sr., and the two families were close. William's acquaintance with the bard was both personal and intellectual. As an infant, William's father asked for and received Emerson's blessing on the child. As he grew to maturity, Emerson became a constant presence, intellectually. Charles Mitchell indicates that James was intimately familiar with Emerson's writings. He "owned copies of all but a few of Emerson's published volumes . . . and his extensive marginalia indicates he read aggressively almost everything Emerson wrote, most of it more than once." The influence of this reading was considerable. Mitchell goes on to note that "James freely incorporated his reading of Emerson into his own work, and the intellectual encounter between these two men reveals the ways in which one strong, independent mind alternately is possessed by and repossesses another."[7] The influence of this reading is especially apparent in James's classic study, *Varieties of Religious Experience* (1902). In this work, as Lawrence Buell observes, "Emerson becomes one of James's focal exempla—and to a greater extent than a casual reader will grasp because Emersonian apercu often get silently woven into James's prose."[8] Gay Wilson Allen made a similar observation somewhat earlier, stating more explicitly that "Emerson was familiar with the theory that an 'unconscious' mind somehow influenced or even blindly directed consciousness. And this 'unconscious' mind was, as William James said in his conclusion to *Varieties of Religious Experience*, the doorway between 'the infinite self' and the 'absolute self . . . one with God and identical with the soul of the world.'"[9]

Undoubtedly, it was because of the connection between the two families, and also because of his high regard for the bard, that William was invited to speak at the Emerson Centennial in Concord in 1903. In preparation for the event, James reread virtually all of Emerson's works. He reported the result of this experience in a letter to his brother, Henry. "The reading of the divine Emerson," he states, "volume after volume, has done me a lot of good." What most impressed James at this time was "the incorruptible way in which [Emerson] followed his own vocation, of seeing such truths as the Universal Soul vouchsafed from day to day . . . and reporting them in the right literary form."[10] Emerson's concept of the "Universal Soul" obviously made a great impression on the philosopher, both early and late, and he came to see the existence of the "effulgence of the Universal Reason" or "the great Cosmic intellect," as indicated earlier, as the centerpiece of "the creed from which Emerson's life followed."

As noted in the prologue to this study, Carl Jung read Emerson first-hand and was impressed by what he found. But Jung also experienced Emerson indirectly through James's philosophical and psychological writings, which he admired. The two became personally acquainted when they met at a gathering at Clark University in Worcester, Massachusetts in 1909. Twenty-seven distinguished scholars were invited by the school's president, G. Stanley Hall, to celebrate Clark's twentieth anniversary. Because the gathering brought together James, Jung, and also Sigmund Freud, one scholar maintains that it "served to create a watershed for the spread of psychoanalysis in the continents of North America and Europe." During their time in Worcester, Jung and James met twice at Hall's home where they discussed "parapsychology."[11] While their personal acquaintance was brief, it was nevertheless significant. Jung eventually read widely in James's writings and once said of the philosopher that he was "indebted to him for his books" and the insights that they provided.[12] Indeed, Jung makes frequent references to James's writings throughout his own works. In a study of the influence of personal relationships on Jung's life and writings, Robert C. Smith notes that he "greatly admired" James, especially his belief in "the subjective character of human judgments." He also perceives a similarity in their views on religious experience and the transcendent. "Focusing on religious experience somewhat in the manner of William James," Smith observes, "Jung was one of the first 'scientific investigators' to posit a universal or archetypal stratum for religious experience."[13] Given this shared interest, it is not surprising that Jung on occasion defended James's Pragmatism against the charge that it was "profoundly unspiritual."[14] Such charges simply did not comport with his reading of *Varieties*, arguably James's most Emersonian work. It was here that Jung would find most clearly articulated the Emersonian concept of the ever expansive "Soul" or "Over-Soul" associated with the "subconscious self."[15] Perhaps it is this, as well as other insights regarding the transcendent element in human experience, that led Jung to conclude his wide-ranging essay on "Psychological Factors in Human Behaviour" with the following statement.

> In my survey, far too condensed I fear, I have left unmentioned many illustrious names. Yet there is one which I should not like to omit. It is that of William James, whose psychological vision and pragmatic philosophy have on more than one occasion been my guides. It was his far-ranging mind which made me realize that the horizons of human psychology widen into the immeasurable.[16]

And so it would seem that William James provides another significant connecting link between Emerson, Jung, and the psychomythic humanists of the twentieth century considered here. Because their theories, in turn, largely inform the view of Emerson developed in this study, it would seem that we have completed an Emersonian circle of our own. The father reflects the children, and the children the father.

Given their universal, archetypal qualities, it should not be surprising that Emerson's writings affected, and continue to affect, diverse readers in remarkably diverse ways. As one critic insists, it was the "perception of Emerson's indefiniteness" and "the uncategorizable nature of his writings—that enabled him to be made and remade by those who wished to shape and influence American culture and society during the last decades of the nineteenth century."[17] Such "remaking" would undoubtedly have pleased Emerson immensely because it indicates that each individual was encouraged by this seer to embark upon his/her own inward journey of discovery, just as he had done. The ideal result of such a journey is a personal transformation that provides the necessary foundation for individuality and self-reliance. This individuality, in turn, makes possible our connection to humanity and the world about. This Emersonian influence continues to this day, and it has taken many forms. Because of his relentless idealism and his personal commitment to social reform, it is not surprising that those seeking to promote equality in America and elsewhere in the world have frequently embraced Emerson. These include early feminists like Julia Ward Howe, who applauded his efforts on the behalf of women and all others who suffered oppression.[18] Also included are Moorfield Storey, an Emersonian idealist and early civil rights reformer who was destined to become the first President of the NAACP, and other civil rights leaders from Booker T. Washington, to W. E. B. Du Bois, to Martin Luther King, Jr., as well as Cuban revolutionary and poet, José Martí, all of whom found inspiration and insight in Emerson's words.[19] There are also poets from Edwin Arlington Robinson, to Robert Frost, to Wallace Stevens: mythic storytellers and critics like C. S. Lewis: philosophers from William James to Stanley Cavell: industrialists such as Henry Ford: artists and architects like Frank Lloyd Wright; composers such as Charles Ives: political leaders from Teddy Roosevelt to John F. Kennedy: even football coaches like Woody Hayes, and, of course, psychomythic humanists and students of myth such as Jung, Mircea Eliade, and Joseph Campbell, to name but a few who have been directly inspired by Emerson over the ages.

Ralph Waldo Emerson was able, and is still able, to influence such diverse minds not only because his own thinking was so eclectic and diverse, but also because he constantly provokes thoughtful people to explore their own inner regions in order to mine the treasures that are to be found there. It is such treasures as these that serve to bring meaning and harmony to what is all too often a threatening and fragmented world. In this sense, Emerson has been and continues to be, in the words of Lance Morrow, "The Bishop of our possibilities."[20]

NOTES

PROLOGUE

1. Hedge, "Reminisces of Emerson," 96.
2. Buell, *Emerson*, 13.
3. Gougeon, "Looking Backwards," 50; Buell, *Emerson*, 48.
4. Myerson, *Historical Guide*, 3.
5. The term comes from Henry Steele Commager's classic work, *The Era of Reform*.
6. Thoreau, *Walden*, 62.
7. Ibid., 25, 62, 4, 5.
8. Emerson, CW 1:53.
9. Ibid., 1:65.
10. Emerson, *AW* 20, "An Address on the Emancipation of the Negroes in the British West Indies" (1844).
11. Emerson, CW 2:29.
12. Emerson, CW 1:88.
13. Ibid., 1:7, *Nature* (1836).
14. Ibid., 1:77.
15. Miller, *The Transcendentalists*, 2.
16. Emerson, CW 1:43.
17. Ibid., 1:53, 65.
18. Emerson, *JMN* 4:357.
19. Emerson, CW 1:69.
20. *New Larousse Encyclopedia of Mythology*, 132.
21. Emerson, CW 9:210.
22. Ibid., 6:149.
23. Ibid., 1:62, American Scholar.
24. Ibid., 1:42, *Nature*; 3:5, 17, The Poet.
25. Carl Jung, who provided much of the theoretical foundation on which these others built, kept Emerson's writings on hand in his library and refers to Emerson's thought as well as his personality from time to

time in his published works. Sometimes the overlap in sources utilized by Emerson and Jung is especially notable. Thus, in his study *Psychology and Religion: West and East*, when speaking of the ancient use of the circle as a symbol of the Deity, Jung quotes Augustine's definition of God as "an intellectual figure whose centre is everywhere and the circumference is nowhere." He goes on to note: "A man as introverted and introspective as Emerson could hardly fail to touch the same idea and likewise quote St. Augustine." In his footnote, he references Emerson's essay, "Circles," which was apparently one of his favorites, and, as we shall see, a seminal statement of Emerson's philosophy (*Psychology and Religion*, 53). As noted in the epilogue here, Jung's initial interest in Emerson may very well derive from his friendship with and admiration for William James, whose writings are frequently cited in his works. James himself was strongly influenced by Emerson, a person whom he deeply admired.

Joseph Campbell was also an admirer of Emerson, as his most recent biographer attests. Stephen Larsen relates that while filming a lecture series late in life, Campbell became somewhat out of sorts. A companion attempted to calm him down a bit by talking about the death of his own father, who had recently passed away. In the process of doing so, he quoted something from Emerson about the death of a man's father. The response, as reported, was rather dramatic. "Joe [Campbell] just stopped in his tracks and said, 'Yes, Emerson is one of the few Americans who got it! He was a transcendentalist, and as my friend Durkheim said, 'myth can only be understood when one is transparent to the transcendent'. . . . He loved that little wordplay, that little connection with the Transcendentalists. The situation was resolved and we went on" (547).

Like these others, Mircea Eliade had a strong attraction to Emerson. His personal journals show that he not only read Emerson carefully, but also transcribed with fair frequency passages from Emerson, which, as he once declared, "fascinate me" (Eliade, *Journal V*, 29). Additionally, while Norman O. Brown does not cite Emerson specifically in his works, he certainly was familiar with American Transcendental writing, and he quotes Thoreau occasionally in *Life Against Death*, citing both *Walden* and the lesser-known *A Week on the Concord and Merrimack Rivers* (*Life*, 255, 308). Also, a fair number of critics have noted a distinct Emersonian quality in Brown's major works. Martin Green, for example, in his review of Brown's *Love's Body*, observes that the work is "a modern *Thus Spake Zarathrustra*," which places Brown in "a major line of 19th- and 20th-century prophets, Nietzsche, Carlyle, D. H. Lawrence, [and] oddest of all, Emerson." Green concludes his review with the statement that "Emerson would have understood Professor Brown, and so would Whitman" (Green, 23).

Other critics and biographers, like Gay Wilson Allen, have observed that "Emerson anticipated later psychologists of the unconscious (Freud) or the subconscious (Jung)" (Allen, *Waldo*, xi). A number of others have also made similar connections among Emerson, Jung, Freud, and Brown. For example, Gloria Young, in her essay, "'The Fountainhead of All Forms': Poetry and the Unconscious in Emerson and Howard Nemerov," states: "The purpose of this essay is to confirm that Emerson's ideas of the unconscious anticipate certain psychological, linguistic, and aesthetic theories of Carl Jung" (242). Albert Gelphi, in *The Tenth Muse: The Psyche of the American Poet*, observes that the source of Emerson's "images and ideas" is "very much like the Jungian Collective Unconscious or Objective Psyche" (80–81). Quentin Anderson in *The Imperial Self* attacks Emerson for his individualism which he contends is really just "imaginative desocialization." Carolyn Porter, in turn, interprets such desocialization as "that dangerous neurosis marking Emerson and Norman O. Brown alike—the imperial ego" (6). In her own study, *Seeing and Being*, as shall be seen later, Porter describes Emerson in Freudian terms, stating that "Emerson's reiterated rejection of the past . . . can be quite easily read as an Oedipal revolt" (58). Also, Martin Bickman, in *American Romantic Psychology: Emerson, Poe, Whitman, Dickinson, Melville*, states that, "This book is an approach to American Romanticism through Jungian psychology" (5), and Emerson is a key figure in his study. Finally, Jeffrey Steele, whose study, *The Representation of the Self in the American Renaissance*, "began as a study of Emerson and Jung," offers a detailed discussion of "both Emerson's and Jung's vision of the unconscious" which Steele maintains has a "quasi-theological value" for both (xi).

26. I would like to take this opportunity to express my gratitude to my colleague, Professor John Norcross, for guiding me, like Jason, through the labyrinth of modern psychological theory. For information on these and other approaches, see Norcross and Prochaska, *Systems of Psychotherapy: A Transtheoretical Analysis*.

27. For a complete and comprehensive listing of secondary studies of Emerson to the date of publication see, Joel Myerson and Robert Burkholder, *Emerson: An Annotated Secondary Bibliography*. For Emerson's original works, see Myerson, *Ralph Waldo Emerson: A Descriptive Bibliography*.

28. The exceptions here, in addition to those noted above, are: Barbara Packer, *Emerson's Fall* (1982); Eric Cheyfitz, *The Trans-Parent: Sexual Politics in the Language of Emerson* (1989); Richard Lebeaux, "Emerson's Young Adulthood: From Patienthood to Patiencehood," [*ESQ* 25 (4) 1979, 203–10]; and Evelyn Barish, *Emerson: The Roots of Prophesy* (1989). Among biographers, as noted, the exceptions include Gay Wilson Allen, *Waldo Emerson* (1982); and Robert Richardson, *Emerson: Mind on Fire* (1995). All of these studies, as we shall see, touch upon various psychological aspects of Emerson's life and work, but none exclusively or comprehensively.

29. Emerson, *AW* 77, The Fugitive Slave Law (1854).

30. Jung, *Psyche and Symbol*, 32.

31. Qtd. in Brown, *LIFE*, 7.

32. From "Hawthorne and His Mosses," a review in *The Literary World*. 17, August 24, 1850. Reprinted in Melville's *Moby Dick*, eds. Hayford and Parker.

33. Melville, *Correspondence*, 121. It is interesting to note that Jung, who was also an admirer of the Emerson who dives, considered *Moby-Dick*, "the greatest American novel," "Psychology and Literature," in *Modern Man*, 154.

34. Brown, *LIFE*, 63.

35. Stevens, *The Necessary Angel*, 37.

36. Emerson, *CW* 3:6.

37. Holmes, *Emerson*, 76.

38. Cabot, *A Memoir*, 384.

39. Woodbury, *Ralph Waldo Emerson*, 70, 157.

40. Wider, *Critical Reception*, 13.

41. Ralph Waldo Emerson, *Emerson's Journals*, vol. I., ed. Edward Waldo Emerson, (Boston: Houghton Mifflin Company, 1909), V. By this time Emerson's reputation had been so clearly typed by Cabot, Holmes, Woodberry and others that even his own son refers to him, in the introduction to the journals, as "Mr. Emerson." It is this attitude that largely informs the selection of materials for this first edition of the journals and as a result, rather than acquainting the reader in any way with Emerson the man, they do little more than fill in a bit of background of one of America's "intellectuals" of the nineteenth century.

42. Mattheissen, *American Renaissance*, 3.

43. Ralph Rusk, *The Life of Ralph Waldo Emerson* (New York: Columbia University Press, 1949). The editors of *Eight American Authors: A Review of Research and Criticism* (1963) refer to this study as "an authoritative work, designed for the student, and more likely to be consulted for information than read for pleasure" (55).

44. Sherman, *Americans*, 64.

45. Allen, *Waldo*, viii.

46. Richardson, *Mind*, xi.

47. Wider, *Critical Reception*, 34.

48. Whicher, *Freedom and Fate*, 76.

49. Albert von Frank provides a succinct expression of this Emersonian concept when he states that, "Self-trust (or self-reliance) is nothing other than an operative belief that the self has an innate capacity in the direction of truth, coupled with the courage to explore it, even at the cost of appearing ridiculous to the neighbors" ("Essays, First Series," 109).

50. Whicher, *Freedom and Fate*, 117.

51. Rowe, *At Emerson's Tomb*, 25.

52. Kateb, *Emerson and Self-Reliance*, 178.

53. G. William Barnard maintains that for psychologist/philosopher William James, "feelings" had a special function. "'Feelings' for James," he states, ". . . are not just emotive, but also cognitive—they are 'states of knowledge.'" (14). The same is true for Emerson, who, as noted in the epilogue here, had a substantial influence on James.

54. Interestingly, by employing a psychological approach, Jeffrey Steele finds Emerson consistently connected to his society. He observes: "Emerson does not treat myth allegorically, translating its lessons term by term into ideas; instead, he relates to it as a symbol of transformation, as a field of energy in which the interpreter can participate if he establishes the right connection. In this way, the detached observer, who eschews action in the world in favor of sterile contemplation, is replaced by the related communicant" ("Interpreting the Self," 97–98).

55. Qtd. in Wider, *Critical Reception*, 121.

56. Weaver, *Emerson Mythmaker*, 27.

57. Jeffrey Steele notes that, "Emerson . . . focuses both on the ideal and the process of attaining it. Thus, we have in Emerson's text not just the interpersonal voice of prophecy, but also the personal tone of spiritual aspiration" ("Interpreting the Self," 93).

58. Robinson, *Conduct*, 3.

59. Buell, *Emerson*, 16.

60. Emerson, *JMN* 7:270–71.

61. In his recent study, Lawrence Buell refers to the "canonization" of Emerson as "the first modern public intellectual" (*Emerson*, 9).

62. Emerson, *CW* 1:55.

CHAPTER 1: PSYCHOMYTHIC HUMANISM

1. Neumann, *CONSCIOUSNESS*, XV.
2. Brown, *LOVE* 3.
3. Jung, *Psyche and Symbol*, 308.
4. Neumann, *CONSCIOUSNESS*, XIII.
5. Eliade, *MYTH*, ix.
6. Brown, *LIFE*, xi.
7. Ibid., 13.
8. Ibid.
9. Campbell, *HERO*, 4.
10. Ibid., vii.
11. Ibid., 51.
12. Jung, *Two Essays on Analytical Psychology*, 5.
13. Campbell, *HERO*, 388.
14. Ibid., 389.
15. Neumann, *CONSCIOUSNESS*, 436.

16. Eliade, *HISTORY*, 151.

17. Brown, *LIFE*, x.

18. From William Butler Yeats, "The Second Coming."

19. Miller, *Transcendent Function*, 1–2.

20. Ibid., 125.

21. Qtd. in *Emerson the Essayist*, ed. Kenneth Walter Cameron, 2:417.

22. Walls, *Emerson's Life in Science*, 8, 7.

23. Emerson, *CW* 1:53.

24. Jung, *Psyche and Symbol*, 126.

25. The theme of intellect gone amok through its divorce from human values was popular among American Romantics. Hawthorne made it the subject of many stories including, most famously, "The Birthmark," and "Rappaccini's Daughter." The most famous European example is Mary Shelley's *Frankenstein, or the Modern Prometheus*.

26. Steele, *Representation*, 11, 16–17.

27. Jung, *Modern Man in Search of a Soul*, 184.

28. Miller, *Transcendent Function*, 13.

29. Emerson, *CW*, 2:160, The Over-Soul.

30. Students of Hegel will certainly note the familiarity of this concept.

31. Rank, *Myth*, 123.

32. Kuhn, *Copernican Revolution*, 127.

33. See Wind, *Pagan Mysteries in the Renaissance*.

34. Milton, *Paradise Lost* 7:505.

35. Frank Tallis, for example, speaks of Jung's "poetic, lyrical vocabulary," 78.

36. Neumann, *CONSCIOUSNESS*, 359.

37. Thomas Kuhn refers to the Ptolemaic system as "homocentric," *Copernican Revolution*, 80.

38. Tillyard, *Elizabethan World Picture*, 38.

39. Heller, *Renaissance Man*, 417.

40. Tillyard, *Elizabethan World Picture*, 67.

41. Campbell, *HERO*, 189.

42. Thoreau, *Walden* 66–67; Emerson, *CW* 2:35, Self-Reliance.

43. Emerson, *CW* 2:179.

44. Brown, *LIFE*, 270.

45. Packer, *Fall*, X.

46. Emerson, *JMN* 7:271.

47. Emerson, *CW* 2:175, The Over-Soul.

48. Willey, *Seventeenth-Century Background*, 103.

49. Angus Armitage describes the opposition of church authorities, both Catholic and Protestant, to the scientific discoveries of Copernicus because they were seen as a threat to faith (120). Frank Tallis observes that

with the loss of the Ptolemaic system, "The human race had been demoted. The human race no longer occupied a preeminent position in the cosmos. After Copernicus, the old medieval certainties (including an assumed existence of God) seemed less robust" (xii). Jung remarks on the vivid contrast between the medieval and the modern worldview. "How totally different did the world appear to medieval man! For him the earth was eternally fixed and at rest in the center of the universe, encircled by the course of a sun that solicitously bestowed its warmth. Men were all children of God under the loving care of the Most High, who prepared them for eternal blessedness; and all knew exactly what they should do and how they should conduct themselves in order to rise from a corruptible world to an incorruptible and joyous existence. Such a life no longer seems real to us, even in our dreams. Natural science has long ago torn this lovely veil to shreds," *Modern Man in Search of a Soul*, 204.

50. DeSantillana, *Crime of Galileo*, 5.

51. Kuhn, *Copernican Revolution*, 224. For an interesting and informed discussion of the impact of these seventeenth-century scientists on Emerson's thinking, see Walls, *Emerson's Life in Science*, 42 ff.

52. De Santillana, *Crime of Galileo*, 330.

53. Hughes, "Introduction," *Milton's Complete Poems*, 187.

54. Walls, *Emerson's Life in Science*, 43.

55. Cameron, *Emerson the Essayist*, 1:57.

56. Hopkins, "Emerson and Cudworth," 82.

57. Walls, *Emerson's Life in Science*, 43.

58. Willey, *Seventeenth-Century Background*, 276–77. For an informed discussion of the impact of the Enlightenment in America, see Henry Steele Commager, *The Empire of Reason: How Europe Imagined and America Realized the Enlightenment*. For more on the revolutionary nature of intellectual discovery in the Renaissance see, Giorgio De Santillana, *The Crime of Galileo*.

59. Alexander Pope, the greatest of the neoclassical poets, expressed this notion succinctly in his "Essay on Criticism" (1711).

> Learn hence for ancient rules a just esteem;
> To copy nature is to copy them.
> Part I, 139–40

> Those rules of old discovered, not devised,
> Are Nature still, but Nature methodized.
> Part II, 188–89

60. For an excellent discussion of this development see Joel Porte, *The Romance in America*.

61. For a detailed discussion of this important archetype in American writing, see R. W. B. Lewis, *The American Adam*.

62. It is interesting to note that Kantian philosophy was perceived by Romantics and Transcendentalists in the early nineteenth century as restoring the lost centrality of the Ptolemaic model. This "Copernican reversal" according to Madame de Staël, would place "the soul of man in the centre, and . . . make it, in every respect, like the sun, round which eternal objects trace their circle, and from which they borrow their light" (Qtd. in Walls, *Emerson's Life in Science*, 8).

63. Henry Smith Williams, *A History of Science*, 4:175.

64. Adams, *Education*, 382, 499. For more on Henry Adams and his times see Gougeon, "*The Education of Henry Adams.*"

65. See Gougeon, "Adams in the Garden."

66. Doctorow, "Seeing the Unseen," 42.

67. As noted earlier in the prologue, the centennial of Emerson's birth was celebrated in 1903, the epicenter of this period of flux. In light of this, it is not surprising that the anniversary was observed in ceremonies that were held in virtually every major city in America. A remarkable number of newspaper accounts indicate that at many of these gatherings Emerson was celebrated as a prophet, seer, and spiritual guide. Thus, an article in *The Daily Journal and Tribune*, Knoxville, TN, May 24, 1903, states that "This is the secret chiefly, of his [Emerson's] enormous spiritual influence—an influence ever-widening and deepening; it is that his message was prophetic. A call to the future, and that it proceeded from inward sources of great depth and insight." For more on the Emerson centennial see Gougeon, "Looking Backwards."

68. Clark, *Einstein*, 102–103.

69. Wider, *Critical Reception*, 89.

70. Martin Bickman touches upon the association between the American Romantics and some of the psychological theories considered here in *American Romantic Psychology: Emerson, Poe, Whitman, Dickinson, Melville*. He states there that, "This book is an approach to American Romanticism through Jungian psychology. Its wider implications, however, and the special character of its methodology will be missed if it is not read also as an approach to Jungian psychology through American Romanticism" (5). We shall speak more of this connection and Emerson in chapters 3 and 4.

71. Creative literature alone would not suffice in this effort, and for this reason Emerson tends to stand apart from his distinguished contemporaries in the range of his interests and the enormous impact that he had on his culture. Emerson was surrounded by artists of considerable genius, including Thoreau, Whitman, Hawthorne, Poe, Fuller, and Melville. But none of these rose to his level of intellectual and artistic accomplishment. (Thoreau probably comes the closest because he also possessed a wide-ranging intellectual curiosity and presents in the corpus of his writings a

multifaceted and comprehensive worldview.) Emerson's other contemporaries, while they are rightfully celebrated today as great literary figures,
were not considered cultural heroes, mystics, seers, prophets, philosophers, reformers, or spiritual guides, as Emerson was during his lifetime,
and later. Edna Dow Cheney, abolitionist, feminist, and writer, was not
the exception when, following Emerson's death in 1882, she memorialized him with the following words.

> As we look back over forty years, to the time when I can re-
> member Mr. Emerson as the strongest, most spiritual, and
> most intellectual influence in my life, and know what he was
> to me, and what he was to every hungry, earnest and true
> heart which came near him, I feel a sense of pity and respon-
> sibility to all young people who are growing up, who cannot
> know him as we knew him; who cannot hear that voice which
> penetrated so to the very portals of the soul; who cannot look
> into those eyes, which always seemed to look into infinity and
> eternity. (*Emerson in His Own Time*, 113)

Nor have the others drawn the kind of diverse intellectual attention—
religious, philosophical, scientific, social, cultural, mythic, linguistic, historical, political, to name but a few, to the extent that Emerson has.

72. Lawrence reflects Freud's strong influence in his *Psychoanalysis and the Unconscious* (1921), *Fantasia of the Unconscious* (1922), and
Studies in Classic American Literature (1923). Freud was also a strong influence in another important American critical text of this period, Simon
Lesser's, *Fiction and the Unconscious* (New York: Vintage Books, 1957).
In this work, Lesser offers a consideration of the function of literary art
in meeting the psychological need of the time which is primarily "to ally
the anxieties and guilt feelings our experience arouses" (46). The American authors he considers include Hawthorne, Melville, and Poe. Also,
while not an Americanist per se, another major voice in the field was
Northrop Frye whose *Anatomy of Criticism* (1957) was concerned with
"those parts of criticism that have to do with such words as 'myth,' 'symbol,' 'ritual,' and 'archetype'" (vii).

73. Tallis, *Hidden Minds*, xi.

74. Uleman, *The New Unconscious*, 4.

75. Ibid., 6.

76. "What Dreams are Made Of," *Newsweek*, August 9 (2004): 44.

77. Emerson, *LL* 2:246; Jung also insists that "the unconscious is
continually active, combining material in ways which serve the future. It
produces . . . subliminal combinations that are prospective" (qtd. in
Miller, 18).

78. Tallis, *Hidden Minds*, xiii.

79. Jung, "The Structure of the Psyche," in *The Portable Jung*, 23.

80. Jung, "On the Relation of Analytical Psychology to Poetry," in *The Portable Jung*, 319.

81. Jung "The Aims of Psychotherapy," in *Modern Man in Search of a Soul*, 72.

82. Miller, *The Transcendent Function*, 15, 13, 18.

83. Ibid., 22, 23.

84. Jung, "The Structure and Dynamics of the Psyche," in *The Portable Jung*, 45.

85. Neumann, *CONSCIOUSNESS*, 330.

86. Frank Tallis observes that, "Like Freud's psychoanalysis, Jung's analytical psychology has implications that extend well beyond psychotherapy. Indeed, Jung's framework resembles a complete metaphysical belief system," 76.

87. Neumann, *CONSCIOUSNESS*, 330.

88. Jung, "Psychology and Literature," in *Modern Man in Search of a Soul*, 170.

89. Neumann, *CONSCIOUSNESS*, 328; Jung, "Aion: Phenomenology of the Self," in *The Portable Jung*, 141 ff.

90. Neumann, *CONSCIOUSNESS*, 42.

91. Miller, *Transcendent Function*, 26.

92. Ibid., xi; Jung, "The Transcendent Function," *The Portable Jung*, 273–300.

93. Miller, *Transcendent Function*, 6.

94. Emerson, *L* 1:412–13.

95. Emerson, *CW* 1:18.

96. Emerson, *CW* 2:160, The Over-Soul.

97. Ibid., 2:3, History.

98. Emerson, *CW* 3:12, The Poet.

99. Emerson, *CW* 1:39, *Nature*.

100. Ibid., *CW* 1:55, The American Scholar.

101. Emerson, *CW* 3:15, The Poet.

102. Ibid.,16.

103. Emerson, *CW* 1:77, Divinity School Address.

104. Emerson, *EL* 2:56, Literature.

105. Miller, *Transcendent Function*, 7; Jung, *Memories, Dreams, Reflections*, 209.

CHAPTER 2: THE SPIRIT AND THE FLESH

1. See Boller, *American Transcendentalism*, 44–54.

2. Jung called this process the "transcendent function"; it results in a new consciousness. As Jeffrey Miller notes: "Jung asserts that the interaction between consciousness and unconscious yields something new

and different, something more than a mixture of or compromise between the two, a third thing that transforms consciousness" (29).

3. Brown, *LIFE*, 8.

4. Erikson, "Dissent," 154.

5. Emerson, *JMN* 4:348.

6. Brown, *LIFE*, ix.

7. Ibid., 297.

8. Ibid., 284.

9. Emerson, *JMN* 4:41.

10. Thoreau, *Walden*, 11.

11. Brown, *LIFE*, 138.

12. Ibid., 142.

13. Emerson, *CW* 2:29.

14. Qtd. in Whyte, *Unconscious Before Freud*, 89.

15. Porte, *Representative Man*, 295.

16. Brown, *LIFE*, 158.

17. For a discussion of the similarities between Emerson and Whitman on the importance of the body, see Gougeon, "Emerson, Whitman, and Eros."

18. Brown, *LIFE*, 45.

19. Emerson, *JMN* 4:309–10.

20. Brown, *LIFE*, 85–86.

21. Ibid., 276.

22. Ibid., 93.

23. Ibid., 230. It might be suggested at this point, particularly in view of material that we shall examine later, that the equation that Brown presents here could also be reversed. Since it is true that humankind seeks always to reestablish the pleasures of childhood, and that the source of these pleasures lies deep in the unconscious self, then it is the irruption of these pleasurable impulses into the world of light that actually precipitates the "large-scale trans-formation" of the culture, and not vice versa.

24. Brown, *LIFE*, 266.

25. Thoreau, *Walden*, 48.

26. Ibid., 2.

27. Emerson, *CW* 2:49.

28. Thoreau, *Walden*, 4.

29. Brown, *LIFE*, 271, 53.

30. Morgan, "Puritan Ethic," 185.

31. From *Walden* (10). Qtd. in Brown, *LIFE*, 255. For an excellent discussion of the obsessive concern with work and productivity in Emerson's and Thoreau's America, see William Gleason, "Re-creating *Walden*."

32. Whitman, "Song of Myself," 1:5.

33. Oliver Wendell Holmes expressed criticism of both Thoreau and Whitman in the notes he prepared for his 1884 biography of Emerson, the former for his boyish whimsy and the latter for his primitive earthiness, both qualities that Emerson admired. See Gougeon, "Holmes's Emerson," 109–11.

34. Emerson, *JMN* 7:405.

35. Brown, *LIFE*, 58.

36. Emerson, *CW* 1:8.

37. Brown, *LIFE*, 62, 63.

38. Whyte, *Unconscious*, 70.

39. Brown, *LIFE*, 311.

40. Gustaaf Van Cromphout argues convincingly that "Goethe was a major factor in Emerson's long experiment in self-definition," (9).

41. Emerson, *EL* 2:43, 44.

42. Emerson, *JMN* 9:265, Harding, *Emerson's Library*, 73.

43. "Emerson and Cudworth," 81. See also *Spires of Form*, 63 ff.

44. Allen, "Emerson and the Unconscious," 27.

45. Brown, *LIFE*, 63–64.

46. Ibid., 66.

47. Emerson, *JMN* 7:277.

48. Emerson, *CW* 3:6,7,18.

49. Buell, *Literary Transcendentalism*, 30.

50. Brown, *LIFE*, 72.

51. Richardson, *Mind*, 204.

52. Ibid., 23. Phyllis Cole makes a persuasive argument for the importance of Emerson's aunt in the development of his most essential Transcendental concepts in her, *Mary Moody Emerson and the Origins of Transcendentalism*.

53. Brown, *LIFE*, 71, 73.

54. *CW* 4:95, Montaigne.

55. Emerson, *JMN* 8:194.

56. Brown, *LIFE*, 86.

57. Campbell, *HERO*, 30.

58. See Brown, *LIFE*, 67.

59. See Boller, *American Transcendentalism*, 34–54; Sacks, *Understanding Emerson*, 8–9.

60. Campbell, *HERO*, 308.

61. Ibid., 17.

62. Emerson, *EL* 2:56, 57.

63. Campbell, *HERO* 89.

64. Emerson, *CW* 3:43. Jung notes that the "widening of consciousness" brings about "the necessity of saying goodbye to childlike unconsciousness." This necessity, he maintains, "is a psychic fact of such

importance that it constitutes one of the most essential symbolic teachings of the Christian religion. . . . The biblical fall of man presents the dawn of consciousness as a curse." "The Stages of Life," in *Portable Jung*, 4, 5.

65. Campbell, *HERO*, 113.

66. Ibid., 130.

67. Ibid., 167.

68. Emerson, *CW* 1:10. Sherman Paul reports that in the mystical philosophies of Boehme, Law, Swedenborg, and others, the eye is seen as "the mirror of deity" and symbolizes intuitive communication between the individual and the deity in various mystic charts. See *Emerson's Angle of Vision*, 71–102.

69. Campbell, *HERO*, 352.

70. Ibid., 28.

71. Thoreau, *Walden*, 211.

72. Campbell, *HERO*, 180.

73. Steele, *Interpreting*, 88.

74. Porte, *Representative*, xiii.

75. Barish, *The Roots*, 30.

76. Porter, *Seeing and Being*, 58.

77. Emerson, *CW* 2:30. Christ's words are reported in Luke 14:26: "If anyone comes to Me and does not hate his father and mother, wife and children, brothers and sisters, yes, and his own life also, he cannot be my disciple," and Matthew 10:37: "He who loves father or mother more than Me is not worthy of Me."

78. Eliade, *HISTORY*, 115.

79. Such rituals stand as good examples of Jung's "transcendent function" where the individual initiates a "conversation' between the conscious and the unconscious in order to balance the two. In Eliade's study it is enacted by an entire community.

80. Eliade, *HISTORY*, 75, 131.

81. Emerson, *JMN* 5:67.

82. Jeffrey Cramer indicates that Thoreau created this mythic fable himself. *Annotated Walden*, 317.

83. Thoreau, *Walden*, 218.

84. Eliade, *HISTORY*, 52–53.

85. Campbell, *HERO*, 3.

86. Thoreau, *Walden*, 46.

87. Emerson, *JMN* 5:172.

88. Neumann, *CONSCIOUSNESS*, 42.

89. Fuller, *Woman*, 68–69.

90. Emerson, *JMN* 8:380.

91. Neumann, *CONSCIOUSNESS*, xvi.

92. Emerson, *CW* 1:128.
93. Neumann, *CONSCIOUSNESS*, 152, 16.
94. Edgar Allan Poe presents several powerful renderings of this pattern. The most compelling and complete appears in *The Narrative of Arthur Gordon Pym* (1838), his only novel. It was also a favorite of Hawthorne, whose classic short story, "Young Goodman Brown" (1835) provides an excellent example. Melville's *Moby-Dick* (1851) is a powerful example of that author's confrontation with a "blackness, ten times black." Even the optimists among American writers of the time were subject to this phenomenon. As noted earlier, Thoreau offers a version of this journey in his descent into the darkness of winter that brings his doleful ruminations on death and dying in the chapter, "Former Inhabitants; and Winter Visitors." Whitman's most powerful rendering of this journey into night is his magnificent mythic poem, "The Sleepers." Finally, for Emerson, this dark journey is undertaken most notably in his essay, "Experience," (1844) and his poem "Threnody," both strongly influenced by the death of his young son, Waldo.
95. Neumann, *CONSCIOUSNESS*, 16.
96. Ibid., 174.
97. Ibid., 187.
98. Douglass, *An American Slave*, 45.
99. Ibid., 49.
100. Ibid., 50.
101. Neumann, *CONSCIOUSNESS*, 186.
102. Ibid., 176.
103. Otto, *Dionysus*, 117.
104. Ibid., 141.
105. Neumann, *CONSCIOUSNESS*, 212.
106. Ibid., 328, 330.
107. Emerson, *CW* 2:37.
108. Neumann, *CONSCIOUSNESS*, 331.
109. Henry Steele Commager describes the dominant thinkers of the Enlightenment in Europe and America as "Natural philosophers—what we call scientists—. . . . [who] worshiped at the altar of Newton: a passion for astronomy, mathematics, botany, geology, anthropology, chemistry, physics, and medicine seems to have been their common denominator." In America, Benjamin Franklin is the preeminent example (237).
110. Neumann, *CONSCIOUSNESS*, 341, 373.
111. Ibid., xix.
112. Emerson, *CW* 1:7.
113. Neumann, *CONSCIOUSNESS*, 376.
114. Ibid., 294, 417.
115. Emerson, *CW* 3:46.
116. Neumann, *CONSCIOUSNESS*, 359.

CHAPTER 3: "GOD'S CHILD"

1. Emerson, *JMN* 1:131; 7:25.
2. Ibid., 1:xxxvii.
3. Ibid., 1:3.
4. Ibid., 1:54–55.
5. Ibid., 1:46.
6. Ibid., 1:131.
7. Ibid., 1:313–14.
8. Ibid., 1:63.
9. Emerson, *JMN* 2:77.
10. Ibid., 2:17.
11. Ibid., 2:34.
12. Ibid., 2:57.
13. Ibid., 2:61.
14. Rusk, *Emerson*, 109, 136.
15. Emerson, *JMN* 2:66.
16. Ibid., 2:158.
17. It is a path towards which he was directed, at least in part, by William Ellery Channing, an early source of inspiration to virtually all who would later be known as Transcendentalists. David Robinson points out that in his early career "Emerson's moral sentiment . . . is extremely close to the 'divine monitor within us' which Channing urged as a guide to the soul's moral perfection" (*Apostle of Culture*, 53).
18. Emerson, *JMN* 2:238. Kenneth Sacks observes that the opinion that Emerson "did not think rigorously" was "widespread" among his early critics, 88.
19. Ibid., 2:239.
20. Neumann, *CONSCIOUSNESS*, 330.
21. Emerson, *JMN* 2:241.
22. Emerson, *JMN* 3:314.
23. Ibid., 3:19.
24. Ibid., 3:15.
25. Ibid., 3:26.
26. Emerson, *JMN* 3:25.
27. For a detailed discussion of Emerson's lifelong struggle with tuberculosis and other illnesses, see, Barish, *Emerson*, 177–97.
28. Emerson, *JMN* 3:58.
29. Emerson, *CW* 1:16.
30. Emerson, *JMN* 3:85.
31. Brown, *LIFE*, 84.
32. Emerson, *JMN* 3:99.
33. Ibid., 3:99.
34. Richardson, *Mind*, 84.

35. Emerson, *JMN* 3:153.

36. For Ellen's side of the romance, see *One First Love: The Letters of Ellen Louisa Tucker to Ralph Waldo Emerson.*

37. Emerson, *CW* 2:100. The notion of love expanding from a personal experience with another to "the universal heart of all" suggests the distinction between the personalized "Cupid" and the ancient, world-shaping god, "Eros." It also explains the meaning behind the concluding lines of Emerson's poem, "Give All to Love," "When half-gods go, / The gods arrive" (*W* 9:92).

38. Emerson, *JMN* 1:xxxxi. Another critic has suggested that Emerson's use of specific genres indicates a "division of labor" in his published writings. In this division, the essays were largely reserved for philosophical speculations arising out of actual experience, but raised to the highest point of view, that is, universal truth. Poetry and occasional addresses, however, like those dealing with the issue of slavery, reflect more emotional content related to, and growing out of the experience at hand and its immediate impact on individuals (Ellison, "Tears for Emerson," 149). Ironically, it is this very tendency to move from the particular to the universal in his essays that has led many critics, both early and late, to fault Emerson for projecting a seemingly disembodied Transcendental idealism that appears to have little or no connection to the real world (see Wider, *Critical Reception*, 121).

39. Lebeaux, "Emerson's Young Adulthood," 206.

40. For an excellent discussion of this phenomenon see, David Robinson, *The Unitarians and the Universalists.*

41. Emerson, *JMN* 3:171.

42. Ibid., 3:193.

43. Ibid., 3:216, 312.

44. Rusk, *Emerson*, 149.

45. Emerson, *JMN* 3:226–27.

46. Ibid., 3:228.

47. Emerson, *JMN* 3:xi. Evelyn Barish suggests, correctly I think, that "it seems probable that both the extremity of his grief after Ellen's death and his withdrawal from the ministry in 1832 were conditioned to a considerable extent by his special vulnerability to such loss" (230). Albert von Frank observes "The death of Ellen Tucker Emerson . . . at the age of nineteen looks in retrospect like the central episode in a drama of love and death in which it was Emerson's part simply—or not so simply—to understand. The conception he had of immortality, a main prop to his religious sense, did not quite carry him through this wrenching experience" (*Chronology*, 55).

48. Neumann, *CONSCIOUSNESS*, 373.

49. Robert Richardson's comment in this regard is telling. "Emerson was twenty-seven when Ellen died. Her loss and the simultaneous

spiritual crisis Emerson was undergoing constitute his second birth." He goes on to state that, "Before this time Emerson was a rationalist who was fascinated but not wholly convinced by the truth of idealism. After this time Emerson believed completely, implicitly, and viscerally in the reality and the primacy of the spirit, though he was always aware that the spirit can manifest itself only in the corporeal world" (*Mind*, 110). Lawrence Buell places a similar emphasis on the significance of Emerson's loss. "Their brief but intense relation had lifelong repercussions for [Emerson]," he insists. "In a way he could never have foreseen, loss and isolation helped set him loose and make possible his second birth" (*Emerson*, 14). Gay Wilson Allen also sees Emerson's emotional experience at this time as a major formative element in the development of his subsequent life and thought. He observes that this was "a period of rapid and profound spiritual and intellectual growth for Emerson" because Ellen Tucker "thawed his emotions and expanded his human sympathies." In turn, after she died, "his desperate struggle to find the means of living without her strengthened his reliance upon himself and liberated his mind from the stereotypes of his education and Church" (*Waldo*, 147). Finally, echoing the psychological theories employed here, Albert Gelpi maintains, "In Emerson's own development the death of Ellen . . . became one of the transformative and revelatory events of his life. Her spiritual conviction and exaltation in the face of death made her afterward to him an angel, his angel confirming the reality and primacy of spirit." He goes on to state: "Ellen became what Erich Neumann calls, in his detailed study of the feminine archetype, 'the transformative anima'" (87).

50. It is interesting to note that Carl Jung went through a similar process of breakdown followed by a rebirth. Frank Tallis reports that "After the trauma of breaking with Freud, [Jung] experienced a period of extreme mental instability. The mechanisms that hold the unconscious in check broke down, and the unconscious erupted into Jung's life. Instead of resisting this process, he let it take a natural course" (77). As for Emerson, Jung's experience would reshape both his life and his thought. As he himself states: "After the parting of the ways with Freud, a period of inner uncertainty began for me. It would be no exaggeration to call it a state of disorientation. I felt totally suspended in mid-air, for I had not yet found my own footing" (*Memories*, 77). Also like Emerson, Jung emerged from this chaos a new man possessing a new truth. "The years when I was pursuing my inner images," he later reflected, "were the most important in my life—in them everything essential was decided. It all began then; the later details are only supplements and clarifications of the material that burst forth from the unconscious, and at first swamped me. It was the *prima materia* for a lifetime's work" (*Memories*, 170, 199).

51. Emerson, *JMN* 3:244.

52. Ibid., 3:244.

53. Ibid., 3:251.

54. Ibid., 3:259, 279, 301.

55. Emerson, *L* 1:412–13. Emerson's inclusion of Milton, one of his favorites, with Coleridge and "the Germans," (Kant and Goethe) may seem a bit surprising at first until one recalls the Puritan character of the great bard, with his strong emphasis on the inner light. As Basil Willey points out, in *Paradise Lost*, "Milton argues that the moral sense, which is the law of God written upon the heart, is the final tribunal—superior even to Scripture itself" (77), something that Emerson no doubt felt especially comforting at this time.

56. Indeed, Jeffrey Steele makes this very connection when he notes, Emerson's "representations of 'Reason' . . . we would call the 'unconscious'" (*Interpreting*, 97). As Kenneth Sacks reports, Emerson was reading Frederic Henry Hedge's article on Coleridge and German idealism at this time and, undoubtedly, the influence of that reading is reflected in this letter (Sacks, *Understanding Emerson*, 78).

57. Emerson, *L* 1:413. For an informed discussion of the importance of this seminal concept to all Transcendentalists, as well as its sources in Coleridge, Kant, and others, see, Boller, *American Transcendentalism, 1830–1860: An Intellectual Inquiry*, 46–51.

58. Emerson, *JMN* 3:310. It is worthwhile to note here another interesting parallel with Jung, who came to look upon nature in the same light. As a young man, he states in his autobiography: "It seemed to me that the high mountains, the rivers, lakes, trees, flowers, and animals far better exemplified the essence of God." In nature, Jung concluded, "nothing separated man from God; indeed, it was as though the human mind looked down upon Creation simultaneously with God" (*Memories*, 45).

59. Emerson, *CW* 1:8, 38, 39.

60. Rank, *Myth*, 116–17.

61. Emerson, *JMN* 4:7.

62. Robert Richardson says of the incident, "He had to see for himself. Some part of him was not able to believe she was dead. He was still writing to her in his journals as if she were alive" (*Mind*, 3).

63. Emerson, *JMN* 3:325.

64. Emerson, *JMN* 4:27.

65. Ibid., 4:29.

66. Emerson, *JMN* 4:30. Once again, an interesting parallel occurs with Jung, who also came to see the Christian communion service as a hollow and meaningless ritual and thus experienced his own religious crisis of faith. Speaking of his reaction to his first experience with the sacrament, he describes his feelings of incredulity. "What was the purpose of this wretched memorial service with the flat bread and sour wine? Slowly I came to understand that this communion had been a fatal experience for me. It had proved hollow; more than that, it had proved to be a total

loss. I knew that I should never again be able to participate in this cere-
mony. 'Why, that is not religion at all,' I thought. 'It is the absence of
God; the church is a place I should not go to. It is not life which is there,
but death'" (Memories, 55).

67. Baker, Emerson Among Eccentrics, 13.

68. In referring to the "complex emotions stirred up by the death of
Ellen," Joel Porte states that, "It would not be unreasonable to suggest that
the breakdown in health and spirits that led Emerson to embark for Europe
on Christmas day, 1832 . . . was part of a crisis that was not only vocational
but also profoundly psychological" (Representative Man, 58). Gay Wilson
Allen describes Emerson's emotional/psychological distress at this time as a
"nervous breakdown" (Waldo, XII). Emerson's friend and sometime Transcendentalist, Frederick Henry Hedge, says of his resignation, "The sensation caused by this step was prodigious. Even friends were shocked by it.
Hints of insanity were not wanting" (Reminisces of Emerson, 97).

69. Jung observes that, in the artist, the psyche is "not merely a
question mark arbitrarily confined within the skull, but rather a door that
opens upon the human world from a world below, now and again allowing strange and unseizable potencies to act upon man and to remove him,
as if on the wings of the night, from the level of common humanity to
that of a more than personal vocation" "Psychology and Literature" in
Modern Man in Search of a Soul, 163.

70. Hodder, Emerson's Revelation, 65.

71. Emerson, JMN 4:67–68.

72. Ibid., 4:69–70.

73. Emerson, JMN 8:34.

74. Emerson, JMN 4:77.

75. Ibid., 4:117, 131, 157.

76. Emerson, JMN 5:109.

77. Emerson, JMN 8:182. Such passages confirm Barbara Packer's
assertion that, despite his reservations regarding its formal doctrines, "the
Roman Church possessed for Emerson all the attractions of Romance"
(Fall, 127). Indeed, this attraction would endure. In 1843, while lecturing
in Baltimore, he attended Mass at the cathedral there twice. Now known
as "The Basilica of the Assumption," the church is dedicated to the Vir-
gin Mary, whose richly ornate images decorate the dramatic interior. As
an expression of feminine divinity, the church must have been doubly attractive to Emerson. Later he wrote to his wife: "It is well for my Protestantism that we have no cathedral in Concord. . . . I should be confirmed
in a fortnight" (L 3:117–18). For an excellent discussion of Emerson's attitude toward Roman Catholicism over the years see Glen M. Johnson,
"Emerson and Isaac Hecker."

78. It is interesting to note that a later visitor to Europe from New
England who was also seeking faith in a time of chaotic change, Henry

Adams, had a remarkably similar experience. He relates in his *Education*, that while in Europe he "got drunk on his emotions," and that this part of his education was "only sensual" (74). Adams, like Emerson, would also fall in love with the great cathedrals and monuments of Europe and eventually would express that love in *Mount-Saint-Michel and Chartres* (1904, 1913).

79. Emerson *JMN* 4:84.

80. Ibid., 4:95.

81. Emerson, *JMN* 5:246.

82. Laura Dassow Walls indicates that, "By the time he returned from Europe [Emerson] was ready to be [a] true prophet—no less than America's philosopher of truth" (83). The striking change that overcame Emerson following the death of Ellen and his dramatic inward journey is described by Emerson's contemporary and Harvard classmate, Frederick Henry Hedge. In his "Reminisces of Emerson," he recalls that Emerson's brothers, Charles and Edward were considered the truly talented members of the family and that while at Harvard "Waldo as yet had given no proof of what was in him." After Ellen's death and Emerson's return from Europe, Hedge observes, "I saw him frequently during that winter & was much impressed with the intellectual progress he seemed to have made. . . . I felt as never before the overweight of his genius" (97–98).

83. Emerson, *JMN* 4:237. It is interesting to discover that in 1833 Emerson had reached his thirtieth year—the age at which it is traditionally believed Christ began his public ministry.

84. Ibid., 4:250, 278.

85. See Charvat, *Emerson's Lecture Engagement*, 15.

86. Emerson, *JMN* 4:272–73.

87. Brown, *LIFE*, 93.

88. Emerson, *JMN* 4:359.

89. Emerson, *CW* 154.

90. Jung maintains the energy of the unconscious compensates for the deficiencies of the conscious. "If anything of importance is devalued in our conscious life, and perishes—so runs the law—there arises a compensation in the unconscious. . . . No psychic value can disappear without being replaced by another of equivalent intensity." ("The Spiritual Problem of Modern Man," *Portable Jung*, 470). Robert Richardson makes note of this important development when he observes: "Not only does Emerson accept the Greek idea that the universe *is* beauty, *kosmos*, but he emphasizes the experience of that beauty as a wild delight. This inner wildness, this habit of enthusiasm, this workaday embracing of the Dionysian is quintessential Emerson. He is wild or he is nothing" (*Mind*, 229).

91. Emerson, *CW* 1:16–17, *Nature*. In light of these observations, it is ironic that Emerson is often held in relatively low regard by many eco-critics who feel he is not as immersed in nature as Thoreau.

92. Ibid., 1:17.

93. Emerson, *JMN* 5:19–20.

94. Ibid., 5:81, 274, 85.

95. Ibid., 5:107, 252.

96. Campbell, *HERO*, 36–37.

97. Emerson, *JMN* 4:325.

98. For information about Martineau's visit and her relationship with Charles and Waldo, see Gougeon, *Virtue's Hero*, 28–30.

99. Emerson, *L* 2:25.

100. Ibid.

101. Emerson, *JMN* 5:87.

102. Emerson, *L* 1:436.

103. Richardson, *Mind*, 436.

104. Emerson, *L* 7:34.

105. Emerson, *JMN* 5:297, 298. Emerson would later incorporate these thoughts into his lecture, "The Heart" (*EL* 2:283).

106. Emerson, *W* 9:92.

107. Emerson, *JMN* 11:213.

108. See, Ellen Emerson, *A Life of Lidian Jackson Emerson*.

109. Buell, *Emerson*, 24.

110. Eliade, *MYTH*, 75.

111. Erikson, *Childhood*, 249.

112. Emerson, *JMN* 5:255.

113. Ibid., 5:270–71.

114. Ibid., 5:271–72.

115. Campbell, *HERO*, 167.

116. Emerson, *CW* 2:160 [emphasis added].

117. Porter, *Emerson and Literary Change*, 74, 79. Robert Richardson points out that many of the key insights that Emerson presents in "Brahma" came from his reading and rereading of the Vishnu Purana and the Bhagavad Gita. From the first, he copied into his journal in the mid-1840s the lines, "What living creature slays or is slain? What living creature preserves or is preserved? Each is his own slayer or preserver, as he follows evil or good." He goes on to state that, "Emerson's absorption in Asian Religion and literature cannot be understood unless one sees that for him the East was proof—persuasive precisely because it was non-Western—that at the deep end of the pool, where it matters, Westerner and Easterner are profoundly alike, indeed identical" (*Mind*, 407–08). For our purposes here, the "deep end of the pool" is yet another representation of the collective unconscious in which all humanity is the same. For a further discussion of how Orientalism affected Emerson's later reform efforts specifically, see Gougeon, "Emerson, Poetry, and Reform."

118. Emerson's children and their birth years are: Waldo (1836), Ellen (1839), Edith (1841), and Edward Waldo (1844).

119. It should be stressed here that Emerson did not act "whimsically" and unilaterally on the promptings of the inner voice alone, as some of his contemporary critics have assumed. As evidenced throughout this study, he believed in the necessity of achieving a dynamic balance between the unconscious and conscious, the Reason and the Understanding. By maintaining a dialogue between the two, one might arrive at conclusions that are at once both heartfelt and reasonable.

120. Neumann, *CONSCIOUSNESS*, 174.

121. Emerson, *JMN* 5:322.

122. Ibid., 5:333–34. Emerson would later employ much of this passage in his essay "Spiritual Laws" (*CW* 2:90).

123. For an enlightening and detailed discussion of Emerson's intellectual and social development at this critical time, see, Kenneth Sacks, *Understanding Emerson*, 55–60. For an account of Emerson's 1837 antislavery address see Gougeon, *Virtue's Hero*, 38–40. For Emerson's "Letter to Martin Van Buren," see, *AW* 1–5.

124. Emerson, *JMN* 5:485.

125. Qtd. in Miller, *Transcendent Function*, 29.

126. Emerson, *JMN* 5:452.

127. von Frank, *Chronology*, 113.

128. Fuller, "Journal," 331.

129. Richardson, *Mind*, 240. For further elaboration of the complex nature of Emerson's emotional relationship with Fuller, see Charles Capper's excellent, *Margaret Fuller: An American Romantic Life*, 326 & ff.

130. Allen indicates that both Fuller and her young friend Caroline Sturgis eventually developed a love interest in Emerson that they would both find frustrating. He was clearly attracted to them both, but was also able to maintain a proper reserve in his relationships with them (*Waldo* 307, 388–89).

131. Emerson, *JMN* 5:326.

132. Ibid., 5:361.

133. Emerson, *JMN* 7:374. Some of this passage was later incorporated into his essay, "Montaigne," in *Representative Men* (*CW* 5:95).

134. Brown, *LIFE* 72.

135. Emerson, *JMN* 7:224. For a detailed and definitive discussion of the importance of oratory in the nineteenth century, and Emerson's contribution, see Lawrence Buell, "New England Oratory from Everett to Emerson" in his *New England Literary Culture*, 137–65.

136. Buell, *Literary Transcendentalism*, 30.

137. Emerson, *JMN* 7:338–39.

138. Jung observes, "Whenever the collective unconscious becomes a living experience and is brought to bear on the conscious outlook of an age, this event is a creative act which is of importance to everyone living in that age. A work of art is produced that contains what might truthfully

be called a message to generations of men" ("Psychology and Art," in *Modern Man in Search of a Soul*, 166). This was certainly the case for Emerson's art.

139. Campbell, *HERO*, 20.

140. Emerson, *JMN* 7:339.

141. Emerson, *JMN* 5:330.

142. Ibid., 5:411.

143. Merton Sealts, Jr., argues that Emerson consistently associated the concept of "heroism" with the role of the scholar, which is the role that Emerson himself would fill. See *Emerson on the Scholar*, 116 & ff.

144. Richardson, *Mind*, 263.

145. Allen, *Waldo*, 302.

146. Emerson, *JMN* 5:414.

147. Ibid., 5:420. Eventually, Emerson would include much of this material in his lecture and essay, "Heroism" (1841) where, once again, he would expand his own personal experience to the level of the universal.

148. Jung maintains that, "The archetypal image of the wise man, the savior or redeemer, lies buried and dormant in man's unconscious since the dawn of culture; it is awakened whenever the times are out of joint and a human society is committed to a serious error" ("Psychology and Literature," in *Modern Man in Search of a Soul*, 171).

149. Emerson, *JMN* 5:466.

150. Emerson, *JMN* 7:25, 28.

151. For an excellent discussion of Emerson's confrontation with the Unitarian church and its relationship to his spiritual evolution, see Geldard, *God in Concord*.

152. Allen, *Waldo*, 83, 321.

153. Barish, *Roots of Prophecy*, 152–53, 105–06.

154. Cayton, *Emerson's Emergence*, 177.

155. Myerson, "Convers Francis," 28.

156. Emerson, *JMN* 7:110.

157. Ibid., 7:224.

158. Steve Carter, while recognizing the similarities between Jung and Emerson, contends that, unlike Jung, Emerson's "emphasis is on the apollonian—on 'intellect' and 'law'—rather than on the dionysian" (22). Passages such as this, and Emerson's emerging role as a lawbreaker who "unsettles all things" would seem to refute Carter's position. Indeed, in one of the very earliest discussions of Emerson's psychology (1919), Regis Michaud argues against the notion that Emerson possesses a "heartless intellectuality." In contrast, Michaud insists that the intellectual quality in Emerson is counterbalanced by a "mystical" element. "For Emerson," he says, "as for our modern intuitionists, instinct and intuition are at the base of knowledge" (81).

159. Emerson, *CW* 1:145. Robert Milder argues convincingly that the period of Emerson's most radical thought is 1837–1841/2 and that the lectures he gave during this period "are philosophical and establish the broad historical context for revolutionary change" (51). Emerson's moments of personal ecstasy would certainly fortify this revolutionary urge. Joel Porte suggests that at the time of the "Divinity School Address," and in his Dartmouth Oration (both in the summer of 1838), "Emerson was trying improbably to combine the roles of revolutionary, social engineer, scholar, prophet, and martyr" (*Representative Man*, 105). Later, Emerson would deploy his revolutionary philosophy most fully in what would become a twenty-year campaign against America's greatest social curse, slavery.

160. Ibid., 1:31, *Nature*; 2:162, The Over-Soul; 1:180, Lecture on the Times.

161. Emerson, *CW* 2:317, The Poet.

162. Ibid., 2:103, Love.

163. Ibid., 2:103, 104, Love.

164. Ibid., 2:162, The Over-Soul. Emerson was often criticized by conservatives because of the "moonshine" quality of his transcendental thought and naturalistic philosophy. An article in the *Boston Transcript* in the 1850s refers to Emerson as "the great dreamer" who "like Fine-Ear in the fairy tale, lies upon the greensward and listens to the motion of each blade of grass, to the blossoming of flowers, hears the green leaves opening to the sunshine and the whole harmony of Nature's song, and then tells us—but not often in a language which all men comprehend—what he has heard the grass, and flowers and green leaves say." (The article is reprinted in *Transcendental Log*, ed. Kenneth Walter Cameron, 83–84.)

165. Emerson, *JMN* 7:270–71.

166. Emerson, *JMN* 5:337.

167. Wind, *Pagan Mysteries*, 212.

168. Richardson, in noting Emerson's deep interest in Neoplatonism, points out that he "was particularly struck by two Neoplatonic teachings: the idea of the world as emanation and the idea of the ecstatic union of the One. For Plotinus everything emanates, or flows out, from the One, the ultimate power and unity of things" (*Mind*, 348). Martin Bickman maintains that "Neoplationism stands only second to the design of biblical history in its influence and centrality both for Emerson in particular and for Romanticism in general (Bickman, *American Romantic Psychology*, 49). As indicated earlier, Vivian Hopkins makes this same point in "Emerson and Cudworth." Neoplatonism was an important influence for many of the psychomythic humanists as well.

169. Brown, *LOVE*, 23.

170. Ibid., 81.

171. Emerson, *JMN* 7:532.

172. Ibid., 7:544.

173. Ibid., 7:544.

174. Emerson, *JMN* 8:34.

175. Emerson, *JMN* 7:547. Not surprisingly, following his discussion of marriage, Emerson symbolically merges sexuality and art in a phrase that describe what is undoubtedly his own artistic goal. He states bluntly, "I want a spermatic book." Interestingly, in the balance of the entry Emerson also uses the term "spermatic book" to describe the writings of the Neoplatonist, Plotinus, as well as Plato and Plutarch, suggesting thereby that he saw them as "spermatic" writers and thinkers.

176. Fuller, "Journal," 330.

177. Emerson, *JMN* 8:193–94.

178. Jung, "The Spiritual Problem of Modern Man," in *Portable Jung*, 479.

179. Emerson, *JMN* 8:230.

180. Ibid., 8:356, 380. The fact that Emerson was raised in a household run by women, following the death of his father when he was only eight, might have rendered him more accepting of his own feminine side. Also, Edgar Wind points out that the hermaphrodite had mythical significance as a symbol of unity and harmony for Renaissance Neoplatonists. (See *Pagan Mysteries*, 211ff.).

181. Neumann notes, "Man's original hermaphroditic disposition is still largely conserved in the child. Without the disturbing influences from outside which foster the visible manifestation of sexual differences at an early date, children would just be children; and actively masculine features are in fact as common and effective in girls as are passively feminine ones in boys. It is only cultural influences, whose differentiating tendencies govern the child's early upbringing, that lead to an identification of the ego with the monosexual tendencies of the personality" (*CONSCIOUSNESS*, 112).

182. Richardson, *Mind*, 256.

183. Emerson, *L* 2:114, 115.

184. Emerson, *JMN* 7:132.

185. Emerson, *JMN* 8:163.

186. Ibid., 8:163.

187. Ibid., 8:165, 174, 179.

188. Ibid., 8:432–33. This expression of the triumph of life over death is also reflected in his poem "Brahma," as observed earlier.

189. Emerson, *CW* 1:16.

190. The poem appears in *W* 9:148–58.

191. As we shall see in chapter 4, Emerson makes this same association in the powerful and highly symbolic opening of his address at the Divinity School.

192. Emerson, *CW* 1:90.

CHAPTER 4: "THE DEVIL'S CHILD"

1. Woodbury, *Ralph Waldo Emerson*, 157; Matthiessen, *American Renaissance*, 3.
2. Emerson, CW 2:27.
3. Emerson, *JMN* 7:338.
4. Ibid., 7:270.
5. Emerson, CW 2:166; Walls, *Emerson's Life in Science*, 6; CW 2:160.
6. Ibid., 2:30.
7. Ibid., 2:149, Heroism. Sarah Wider points out that even in the twentieth century, critics like George Santayana, and representatives of the "Genteel Tradition" in American culture, worried that Emerson's "emphasis on the imagination could create an insurrection from beneath" that could mislead the unwary (85).
8. Buell, *Emerson*, 59.
9. Emerson, CW 1:63.
10. Emerson, CW 2:10, History.
11. Ibid., 2:27
12. Buell, *Emerson*, 58.
13. Emerson, CW 3:15, The Poet.
14. Buell, *Literary Transcendentalism*, 287–88, 289.
15. Emerson, CW 1:201; Campbell, *HERO*, 165.
16. Emerson, CW 1:7.
17. Porte, *Representative Man*, 76.
18. Ibid.
19. Neumann, CONSCIOUSNESS, 373.
20. Mott, *Strains of Eloquence*, 29.
21. Quoted in Gougeon, "Ellis Gray Loring," 42.
22. Neumann, CONSCIOUSNESS, 202.
23. Campbell, *HERO*, 257–58.
24. Cayton, *Emerson's Emergence*, 130.
25. Emerson, *Sermons* 4:193.
26. Emerson, CW 1:16, 8 *Nature*; Neumann, CONSCIOUSNESS, 359; CW 1:45; CONSCIOUSNESS, 110.
27. Emerson, CW 1:113, Literary Ethics.
28. Ibid., 1:158, Man the Reformer.
29. Ibid., 1:176, Lecture on the Times.
30. Ibid., 1:69.
31. Ibid., 1:10.
32. Tanner, "Unconquered Eye," 310.
33. Poirer, "Is There an I for an Eye?" 133.
34. Neumann, CONSCIOUSNESS, 115.
35. Emerson, CW 1:35.

36. Emerson, *CW* 2:156, Heroism.

37. Neumann, *CONSCIOUSNESS*, 211.

38. Thoreau, *Walden*, 216.

39. Emerson, *CW* 1:31. In speaking of the figure of Orpheus as it appears in Emerson's *Nature*, R. A. Yoder points out that in the myth, Orpheus made all reality fluid, and rearranged it around himself. "What proved to be the most important feature of the Orphic myth for Emerson," he states, was "the mythical fact of Orpheus taming nature or the wilderness—when he sang, all the rocks and trees and wild beasts arranged themselves in order around this central man" (XII). The creative vision of the poet is thus unlimited, exemplary, and centralizing. Vivian Hopkins asserts that "Orpheus became for [Emerson] . . . the master symbolist" ("Emerson and Cudworth," 84).

40. Emerson, *CW* 1:41–42, 42.

41. Paul, *Emerson's Angle of Vision*, 22.

42. Gelpi, *The Tenth Muse*, 81.

43. Campbell, *HERO*, 189.

44. Emerson, *CW* 2:71.

45. Ibid., 2:184. Sarah Wider reports that views such as these, and others, were often seen by critics as mystical and, therefore, irrelevant. Thus, a critic writing in the *Boston Morning Post* in 1838, following the "Divinity School Address," observed: "We cannot, however, believe that the peculiar views set forth with so much confidence and fascination by Mr. Emerson are likely to take a very deep root in the American heart. They are too dreamy, too misty, too vague to have much effect except on young misses just from boarding school or young lads, who begin to fancy themselves in love" (59).

46. Emerson, *CW* 2:188. Clearly, Emerson was determined to avoid the ironic fate of becoming a "terrible father" himself. As Buell observes, "More than any other writer, Emerson invites you to kill him off if you don't find him useful. This makes him one of the most unusual authority figures in the history of western culture, the sage as anti-mentor" (*Emerson*, 292).

47. Emerson, *CW* 3:17, The Poet. David Porter, in his revealing study of Emerson as poet, centers Emerson's poetics in a paradigm of process. He states that this process "allowed emergence into language of the intuited, paralleling the divine gift of speech and mirroring God's own language manifest in the visible universe." He insists that "the equation between God's creation and the artist's . . . is fundamental to Emerson's thinking about the poet" (46).

48. Campbell, *HERO*, 44.

49. Emerson was serious in substituting the poet for the priest. As Jeffrey Steele points out, for Emerson, "awareness of the failure of conventional religious and intellectual forms provides a spiritual vacuum

which faith in the unconscious fills" ("Interpreting," 91). It is from the unconscious that the poet-priest emerges.

50. Emerson, *CW* 3:11, The Poet.

51. Whicher observes that the "rock" upon which Emerson came to base his life "was knowledge that the soul of man does not merely, as had long been taught, contain a spark or drop or breath or voice of God, it *is* God." After this discovery, "his previous seemingly crushing disabilities evaporated into insignificance" (21).

52. *W* 10:325, Life and Letters in New England.

53. Barish asserts that "Emerson . . . was the first American thinker both to have the courage and finesse to recognize that he was facing an insoluble conflict, born as he was precisely at the time of the shattering of old beliefs, and to be able to accept that he could not force a new shape upon a patched-up creed" (8).

54. Emerson, *CW* 2:28, Self-Reliance.

55. Emerson, *CW* 1:89, 88.

56. Ibid., 1:88, 81, 83, 90. In his 1837 lecture "Religion," Emerson observes: "All attempts to confine and transmit the religious feelings of one man or one sect to another age, by means of formulas the most accurate or rites the most punctual, have hitherto proved abortive. You might as easily preserve light or electricity in barrels" (*EL* 2:92–93).

57. Porte, *Representative Man*, 115.

58. Cayton, *Emerson's Emergence*, 183.

59. Emerson, *CW* 1:199.

60. Emerson, *CW* 2:28, 30, 33.

61. Ibid., 2: 30, 33, 37, 38, 41, 51.

62. Emerson, *CW* 3:63.

63. Emerson, *CW* 2:149, 143.

64. Brown, *LIFE*, 23.

65. Emerson, *CW* 1:9, 10.

66. Ibid., 1:59.

67. Alan Hodder points out that "No American writer since Jonathan Edwards is more thoroughly steeped in the Christian Bible than Ralph Waldo Emerson" (7), and that its language dominates the style of *Nature*. While this is certainly the case stylistically, the substance of Emerson's belief, as we have seen, derives more from the content of his unconscious and its objective correlative and symbol, nature. As Sacvan Bercovitch observes that, "With all Romantics [Emerson] shifted the center of inspiration from the Bible to nature," *Emerson's Rhetoric*, 7.

68. Emerson, *CW* 3:43.

69. Albert Gelpi observes that the passage describes "a fall into the self-consciousness of the isolated ego," (71).

70. Emerson, *CW* 1:43.

71. Ibid., 1:42.

72. Emerson, *CW* 2:77–78.

73. Ibid., 2:168.

74. Ibid., 2:174

75. Campbell, *HERO*, 41. As noted earlier, in the "Introduction" to his collection, *The Transcendentalists*, Perry Miller describes this situation as a major factor in the evolution of Transcendentalism. He contends: "The Transcendental movement is most accurately to be defined as a religious demonstration. The real drive in the souls of the participants was a hunger of the spirit for values which Unitarianism had concluded were no longer estimable. It had, to all appearances irrevocably, codified into manageable and safe formularies appetites that hitherto in America had been glutted with the terrors of hell and the ecstasies of grace. Unless this literature [of Transcendentalism] be read as fundamentally an expression of a religious radicalism in revolt against a rational conservatism, it will not be understood" (2).

76. Emerson, *CW* 1:82.

77. Ibid., 1:84. Just a year before Emerson's address at the Divinity School, Norton had published *The Evidences of the Genuineness of the Gospel*, which argued for the divinity of Christ based on the fact that the historical Christ performed authentic miracles. It was exactly the kind of intellectual religious scholarship that Emerson condemned as the bane of all true faith.

78. Ibid., 1:77–78, 80.

79. Emerson, *CW* 3:167, New England Reformers (March 1844).

80. Emerson, *CW* 2:30, 29, Self-Reliance.

81. Brown, *LIFE*, 63.

82. Emerson, *CW* 1:56, 68, 69.

83. Emerson, *CW* 3:7, The Poet.

84. Brown, *LIFE*, 163, 297.

85. Emerson, *CW* 1:184, 185.

86. Wider points out that "reviewers unfailingly characterized Emerson's audience as 'young,'" and that "He was increasingly represented as a writer for one's youth and equated with the immaturity one discarded in adulthood" (59, 61).

87. In 1843, Emerson recorded in his journal the complaint that "Young men like H[enry]. T[horeau]. owe us a new world & they have not acquitted the debt" (*JMN* 8:375).

88. Emerson, *CW* 1:211.

89. Ibid., 1:156.

90. Ibid., 1:211, The Transcendentalist.

91. Emerson, *CW* 3:122–23.

92. Ibid., 3:154.

93. Emerson, *JMN* 5:411.

94. David Robinson, in his excellent and comprehensive study, *Apostle of Culture: Emerson as Preacher and Lecturer*, maintains that Emerson understood self-culture as "the evolving of the soul toward ultimate perfection" (4).

95. Emerson, *CW* 3:34, Experience.

96. Emerson, *CW* 1:36.

97. Emerson, *CW* 3:155, New England Reformers. Emerson states in his speech "John Brown" that, "the arch-Abolitionist, older than Brown, and older than the Shenandoah Mountains, is Love, whose other name is Justice," (*AW* 124).

98. Emerson, *CW* 1:62.

99. Ibid., 1:65.

100. Emerson, *CW* 3:163, New England Reformers.

101. Walls, *Science*, 224.

102. Emerson, *CW* 1:230.

103. Emerson, *CW* 2:39, Self-Reliance. As Brown observed earlier, the person who achieved such a balance "would not live in time" because the processes of the unconscious are timeless (Brown, *LIFE*, 93).

104. Emerson, *CW* 1:25.

105. Neumann, *CONSCIOUSNESS*, 108.

106. Emerson, *CW* 1:182, Lecture on the Times.

107. Campbell, *HERO*, 41.

108. Emerson, *CW* 2:162. As indicated in chapter 3 and later, because of his willingness to challenge "conventional" thinking, and also because of the distinctly mystical quality of some of his more oracular pronouncements, Emerson was often the butt of criticism and satire in the New England press. After he lectured in Salem, MA, in May 1843, the following article appeared in the Salem *Observer*.

> Ralph Waldo Emerson is like unto a man who saith unto all the children and dear middle-aged people of his neighborhood, "O come, let us go yonder and dance a beautiful dance at the foot of the rainbow. There will be treasures beneath our feet, and drops of all colors over our heads: and we shall be in the very presence of the mysteries of nature. And we and the rainbow shall be one—and the drops shall be usefulness—and the drops shall be righteousness and purity of heart—and mortality and immortality shall be identical—and sin and holiness—and labor and rest vulgarity and gentility—study and idleness—solitude and society,—black and white—shall all become one great commingled homogeneous and heterogeneous spot of pure glorification forever."
>
> Then all the children and the dear middle-aged people exclaimed, "beautiful, beautiful! Let us go yonder, and dance

beneath the foot of the rainbow." And they all go forth with
Emerson at their head. . . . At length, wearied and scattered,
they all returned to the humble village, and will be contented
with admiring the rainbow at a distance. (qtd. in Rosa, "Emerson and the Salem Lyceum" p. 80)

109. Emerson, *CW* 2:38.

110. Ibid., 2:3, 6, 20.

111. Neumann, *CONSCIOUSNESS*, xvi, xviii.

112. Emerson, *CW* 2:3, History.

113. Ibid., 2:160, The Over-Soul.

114. Ibid., 2:10, History. Other critics have noted this mythic, archetypal quality in Emerson. Most recently, Richard O'Keefe, without
considering the psychological underpinnings of such concepts, holds that
Emerson is a "literary artist, a writer who uses poetic devices and modes
and tropes," and that "Such devices, modes, and tropes appear in Emerson's work in the form of archetypes and myths" (2).

Maud Bodkin, in her classic study, *Archetypal Patterns in Poetry*,
speaks of human experience in terms similar to Emerson's. She refers to the
"concept of racial experience," as "all those systems or tendencies which
appear to be inherited in the constitution of mind and brain [that] may be
said to be due to racial experience in the past" (24). By this definition, the
mind is the repository of history whose patterns become archetypes.

Robert Richardson states, "Much of the masterwork, the literary
achievement of the American Renaissance, grows out of an overt interest
in myth" (*Myth*, 5). Jeffrey Steele suggests that in Emerson, "The unconscious energies embodied in myth" provide "the machinery of transcendence," ("Interpreting," 88).

115. Eliade, *HISTORY*, 13, 86.

116. Jung observes: "All the most powerful ideas in history go
back to archetypes. This is particularly true of religious ideas, but the central concepts of science, philosophy, and ethics are no exception to this
rule. In their present form they are variants of archetypal ideas, created
by consciously applying and adapting these ideas of reality" ("The Structure and Dynamics of the Psyche," in *Portable Jung*, 45–46).

117. Emerson, *CW* 3:46, Experience.

118. Emerson, *CW* 2:102.

119. Eliade, *HISTORY*, 157.

120. Emerson, *CW* 2:175, The Over-Soul.

121. Emerson, *CW* 1:16–17.

122. Emerson, *CW* 3:12; 1:17.

123. Emerson, *CW* 1:18, *Nature*.

124. Neumann, *CONSCIOUSNESS*, 294.

125. Brown, *LIFE*, 70.

126. Emerson, *CW* 1:19 *Nature*.

127. Porter, *Emerson and Literary Change*, 150.
128. Brown, *LIFE*, 70.
129. Emerson, *CW* 1:20.
130. Ibid., 1:20.
131. Emerson, *CW* 3:13.
132. Emerson, *CW* 1:20, *Nature*.
133. Brown, *LIFE* 58, 60.
134. Emerson, *CW* 1:21, *Nature*.
135. Ibid., 1:82.
136. Ibid., 1:301.
137. Ralph Rusk maintains that Emerson "pictured truth under what was for him the absolutely perfect figure of concentric circles. No act, no truth was final. A bigger circle would include the one just drawn" (*The Life of Ralph Waldo Emerson*, 283).
138. Neumann, *CONSCIOUSNESS*, 8.
139. Emerson, *CW* 1:12.
140. Albert Gelpi renders this notion in gendered and mythic terms. "Does [the Muse] shape the poem out of him [the poet], or does he shape her in the poem? Both; the father and the mother of the poem are one; the poet is Eros and Psyche" (77).
141. Emerson, *CW* 2:215, Art.
142. Buell, *Literary Transcendentalism*, 54.
143. Emerson, *CW* 3:20, The Poet.
144. Emerson, *CW* 2:218, Art; Emerson, *EL* 2:44.
145. Emerson, *CW* 3:20, The Poet; *CW* 2:216, Art.
146. Campbell, *HERO*, 41.
147. Emerson, *CW* 1:124, The Method of Nature.
148. Emerson, *CW* 2:213, Art; Emerson, *CW* 1:17, *Nature*.
149. Emerson, *CW* 1:117, *Nature*.
150. Emerson, *JMN* 8:246. It is interesting to observe that the figure of the uroboros was used by Margaret Fuller in the 1845 edition of *Woman in the Nineteenth Century*. It seems likely that Fuller saw the symbol as an expression of the unity of masculine and feminine qualities that figures so prominently in her work.
151. Such notables as F. O. Matthiessen have argued: "We can hardly assess Emerson's work in the light of his theory of language and art, since there is such disproportion between his theory and practice of it" (5). David Porter insists, however, that "The contrary actually seems to be true." Emerson's practice, he states, "if we will see it in its totality, bore out in a remarkably consistent way the theory he proposed" (137).
152. For a detailed history of this famous journal and its contributors see, Joel Myerson, *The New England Transcendentalists and the Dial*.
153. Buell comments on the "audacity" that is characteristic of these early writings, and less evident in the later essays, *Literary Tran-*

scendentalism, 295. Bronson Alcott's "Orphic Sayings" probably represent the extreme expression of the oracular, Transcendental style as represented in the *Dial*.

154. Emerson, *CW* 2:160, The Over-Soul.

155. Emerson, *CW* 1:31, *Nature*.

156. Ibid., 1:7, *Nature*. The contemporary expression, "What goes around, comes around," captures the same notion of compensatory circularity.

157. Ibid., 1:76.

158. Emerson, *CW* 2:179.

159. Ibid., 2:60, 71, Compensation.

160. Campbell, *HERO*, 89.

161. Emerson, *CW* 1:34–35.

162. For example, Arthur M. Schlesinger, Jr., in his influential study *The Age of Jackson* (1945) held that the Transcendentalists "from their book-lined studies, or their shady walks in cool Concord woods, . . . found the hullabaloo of party politics unedifying and vulgar." For Schlesinger, this "flinching from politics" was indicative of the self-reliant reclusiveness of Transcendentalists that, in his view, was "a failure they were seeking to erect into a virtue." He was particularly critical of Emerson for this presumed aloofness and asserted that the bard had "failed himself, and ignored the responsibilities of his own moral position" (382, 385). Coming after Schlesinger, the influential Emerson scholar Stephen Whicher would generally affirm this position. He asserted in his study, *Freedom and Fate: An Inner Life of Ralph Waldo Emerson* (1953) that Emerson, for the most part, lost interest in active efforts at social reform in reaction to the bitter controversy following his "Divinity School Address" in 1838. According to Whicher, after this event Emerson's "image of the hero-scholar, leading mankind to the promised land, steadily gave way to that of the solitary observer, unregarded and unregarding of the multitude" (76).

Some more recent scholars maintain that the social activities undertaken by so many of the Transcendentalists, especially Emerson, were in contradiction to the major philosophical tenets of the movement. Simply put, these scholars argue that the essence of Transcendentalism consists of its emphasis upon intuitively perceived moral truths, or "higher laws," and a corresponding moral and ethical self-reliance. Such a self-reflexive philosophical orientation, they contend, is essentially antithetical to organizations and institutions of all types, especially political parties and associations for social reform. Thus, John Carlos Rowe, in his study, *At Emerson's Tomb: The Politics of Classic American Literature* (1997), contends that "Emersonian transcendentalism and Emerson's political commitments from 1844 to 1863 are fundamentally at odds with each other," and that "Emersonianism is ill-suited to social and political reform" (25). Similarly, George Kateb, in his *Emerson and Self-Reliance*

(1995), describes Emerson's eventual participation in organized efforts at social reform as a "deviation" from the Transcendental doctrine of self-reliance (178). Similarly, Christopher Newfield, in *The Emerson Effect: Individualism and Submission in America* (1996) sees Emerson's active engagement in organized efforts at reform as a problematical compromise of Transcendental self-reliance.

163. Emerson, *CW* 1:59, The American Scholar.

164. Ibid., 1:211, The Transcendentalist.

CHAPTER 5: THE CALL TO SERVE

1. Emerson, *CW* 3:30, 35, 42, 46.

2. Ibid., 3:47, 49.

3. As he observes in "Self-Reliance," in America, the conservative element has "come to esteem the religious, learned, and civil institutions, as guards of property, and they deprecate assaults on these, because they feel them to be assaults on property" (*CW* 2:49).

4. Emerson, *CW* 1:185.

5. Campbell *HERO*, 353, 218.

6. Emerson, *CW* 2:179, Circles.

7. Ibid., 2:160, The Over-Soul.

8. Emerson, *CW* 1:188, The Conservative.

9. Campbell, *HERO*, 315, 316, 319.

10. Whipple, "Recollections," 106.

11. Emerson, *CW* 1:70, The American Scholar.

12. Emerson, *JMN* 7:342.

13. Emerson, *JMN* 5:479.

14. Emerson, *EL* 3:266.

15. In the New Testament, when Mary informed Christ that the hosts had run out of wine during the wedding feast at Cana, he replied: "Woman, what does your concern have to do with me? My hour has not yet come," (John 2:4).

16. Quoted in Gougeon, *Virtue's Hero*, 49.

17. Neumann, *CONSCIOUSNESS*, 173.

18. Richard, *"Gentlemen of Property and Standing,"* 12.

19. Gougeon, *Virtue's Hero*, 68–70.

20. Emerson, *JMN* 9:74.

21. Ibid., 9:62, 85.

22. Neumann, *CONSCIOUSNESS*, 174.

23. Allen, *Waldo*, 626.

24. Robinson, *Conduct*, 3.

25. Emerson, *CW* 3:48.

26. Rank, *Myth*, 128–29.

27. Buell also observes that the "later Emerson looks even more like the public intellectual than Transcendental Emerson, shifting from a predominant focus on great abstractions (such as culture, heroism, political theory) toward more focus on specific cultures (*English Traits*), historical figures (*Representative Men*), and specific reforms (for example, his discourses against slavery), which are put more under the sign of politics, or at least politics of culture" (*Emerson*, 42–43). Our argument here, of course, is that it is precisely the "Transcendental Emerson" that is manifested, and even fulfilled, in all of these areas. As Laura Dassow Walls states regarding Emerson's active commitment to the antislavery cause from 1844 onward, "It may have looked to others as if Emerson, in stepping into the public forum, was leaving his Transcendentalism behind, but really he is turning it outward. The inner law of the heart, the same heart that he implored the self-reliant individual to follow against the 'joint-stock conspiracy' of society, will rise up and bind all hearts by the gravitational pull of truth into masses of individuals, masses who will carry right before them in a true, moral revolution" ("The Higher Law of Science," 179).

28. Robinson, *Conduct*, 7.

29. For a detailed discussion of the Concord Female Anti-Slavery Society, and its activities at this time, see Sandra Petrulionis, "Swelling the Great Tide of Humanity."

30. Emerson, *LL* 2:23, 25.

31. Emerson, *AW* 10.

32. Ibid., 25, 26.

33. Ibid., 31.

34. Robinson, *Conduct*, 87.

35. As Emerson well knew, the Bible itself was frequently quoted in defense of slavery. For examples, see Mason Lowance, Jr., *A House Divided*.

36. Emerson, *CW* 1:62, American Scholar.

37. Emerson, *AW* 32. Emerson's statement here concerning the "oldest" and the "newest" philosophy is possibly a reference to Neoplatonism and Transcendentalism since both insist that "man is one."

38. Walls, *Science*, 186.

39. Emerson, *JMN* 7: 338–39.

40. All quoted in Gougeon, "Emerson's Abolition Conversion," 179.

41. Emerson, *AW* 77.

42. Neumann states: "Once the anima-sister has been experienced through the rescue of the captive, the man-woman relationship can develop over the whole field of human culture. The freed captive is not merely a symbol of man's erotic relations in the narrow sense. The task of the hero is to free, through her, the living relation to the 'you,' to the world at large"

(*CONSCIOUSNESS*, 202). Julie Ellison has noted this strong, emotional element in Emerson and observes that, while Emerson's essays are largely unemotional, "in other kinds of writing—poems, letters, journals, speeches—Emerson sympathizes with social and domestic events." This sympathy would be consistently expressed in the strong emotional content of his antislavery addresses ("Tears for Emerson," 158).

43. See Boller, *American Transcendentalism*, 137.

44. For a discussion of Transcendentalists' frequent references to the Declaration, see Gougeon, "Transcendental Warfare," 263–78.

45. Emerson, *Uncollected Lectures*, 40.

46. Emerson, *EL* 2:49.

47. Brown, *LIFE*, 63.

48. Emerson, *Uncollected Lectures*, 40.

49. Klonoski, "*Homonoia* in Aristotle's Ethics and Politics," 316, 315, 317.

50. Rusk, *Emerson*, 143, 158.

51. Kant, *Grounding for the Metaphysics of Morals*, 59. Interestingly, William James, who was significantly influenced by Emerson, describes a similar kind of subjective and intuitive sense of morality that he refers to as "a special and independent sort of emotion" that recognizes injustice ("The Moral Philosopher and the Moral Life," in *Writings*, 613).

52. Campbell, *HERO*, 319.

53. Garvey, "Emerson's Political Spirit," 15.

54. Ibid.

55. For more information on these and other provocative events in Emerson's antislavery career, see Gougeon, *Virtue's Hero*, passim, and *Emerson's Antislavery Writings*, "Introduction," xi–lvi.

56. Emerson, *JMN* 10:28.

57. For a discussion of the European scene at this dramatic time, see Larry Reynolds, *European Revolutions and the American Literary Renaissance*. For Margaret Fuller's firsthand experience of these revolutions, see Fuller, *Those Sad But Glorious Days*.

58. Emerson, *AW* 47.

59. Robinson, *Conduct*, 93.

60. Campbell, *HERO*, 365.

61. Emerson, *CW* 4:3, 4.

62. Ibid., 4:13–14, 18. Saundra Morris notes that, "All his life, Emerson's ideas tended to shape imaginatively into narratives about a messianic male poet figure, . . . who could cure the ills of the world." In these works, she notes, Emerson seeks "to tell symbolic narratives of the poet-hero within," a goal that Morris appropriately describes as "radically democratizing" (309).

63. Emerson, *AW* 134, 95, Lecture on Slavery.

64. For an informed discussion of the Fugitive Slave Law and its impact, see Gary Collison's *Shadrach* and Albert von Frank's *Anthony Burns*.

65. Gary Collison indicates that "more than a thousand black men, women, and children would be hunted down" and hundreds would be "sent back into slavery" under this law (2).

66. Emerson, *CW* 5:9.

67. Emerson, *JMN* 9:91.

68. Emerson, *AW* 65.

69. Eliade, *HISTORY*, 8.

70. Emerson, *AW* 67.

71. Ibid. Phrenology was a popular, nineteenth-century pseudo-science that held that a person's character could be "read" by examining the bumps on the head, which were thought to correspond to areas of "influence" in the brain.

72. Emerson, *AW* 166.

73. Ibid., 60, 59, 57, 60. For a more sympathetic portrait of Daniel Webster and his support of the Fugitive Slave Law and the Compromise of 1850 see, John F. Kennedy, *Profiles in Courage*, 55–71.

74. Emerson, *AW* 59.

75. Thoreau's classic statement on the topic is, of course, "Civil Disobedience." Gandhi was very familiar with Thoreau's essay and employed passive resistance as an instrument of revolutionary change. He believed very much in the efficacy of what has been called "soul force." His description of its source sounds remarkably Emersonian and Transcendental.

> All that appears and happens about and around us is uncertain, transient. But there is a Supreme Being hidden therein as a Certainty, and one would be blessed if one could catch a glimpse of that Certainty and hitch one's wagon to it. The quest for that Truth is the *summum bonum* of life. (Gandhi, *Autobiography*, 250)

Emerson, in his essay "Civilization" famously encouraged young idealists to "hitch your wagon to a star," (*W* 7:28). According to one biographer, for Gandhi, Emerson was one of the writers who "fed his inner intellectual and moral life," (Brown, *Gandhi*, 63).

Dr. King was influenced by Thoreau's "Civil Disobedience," as well as Emerson's writings. According to Anita Patterson, Dr. King "repeatedly and explicitly referred to Emerson in his speeches, lectures, and sermons," (177). The following passage from his famous "Letter from Birmingham Jail" makes an Emersonian distinction between *just* and *unjust* laws that is based on individual conscience.

You express a great deal of anxiety over our willingness to break laws. This is certainly a legitimate concern. Since we so diligently urge people to obey the Supreme Court's decision of 1954 outlawing segregation in the public schools, it is rather strange and paradoxical to find us consciously breaking laws. One may well ask: "How can you advocate breaking some laws and obeying others?" The answer is found in the fact that there are two types of laws: there are *just* and there are *unjust* laws. I would agree with St. Augustine that "an unjust law is no law at all." (293)

76. Douglass, as noted, was on the same program when Emerson gave his August 1, 1844 address in Concord. An early draft of this address, recorded in his journals, indicates that Emerson initially included Douglass as a living example of the heroic "anti-slave" (*JMN* 9:125).

77. Crane, *Race, Citizenship, and Law*, 113, 129.

78. The cultural "dialogue" that brought this change about could be seen a phylogenetic example of the "transcendent function," which Jung describes as a conversation between the conscious and the unconscious.

79. Emerson, *AW* 86–87, 84.

80. Emerson reports that when he referred to "Mr. Webster's treachery" in a conversation with an Episcopal clergyman, he replied, "Why, do you know I think *that* the great action of his life" (*AW* 54).

81. Brown, *LIFE* 311.

82. Emerson, *JMN* 11:351.

83. Emerson, *AW* 83,77.

84. Mott, "Emerson and Individualism," 91.

85. Emerson, *AW* 103, Lecture on Slavery.

86. von Frank, *Trials*, 97.

87. Buell, *Emerson*, 5.

88. See Gougeon, "Emerson and the Woman Question."

89. Emerson, *LL* 2:23.

90. See John L. Thomas, *The Liberator: William Lloyd Garrison*, 274–75.

91. Emerson, *LL* 2:25.

92. Ibid., 2:26.

93. Gougeon, "Emerson and the Woman Question," 590. See also, Clinton, *The Other Civil War* for more on the struggle for women's political enfranchisement.

94. Robinson, *Conduct*, 116.

95. Emerson, *AW* 81.

96. Ibid., 104, 105.

97. Ibid., 96.

98. Cole, "Emerson, England and Fate," 96.

99. Emerson, *CW* 5:131.

100. Robinson, *Conduct*, 118.

101. Weisbuch, "Post-Colonial Emerson," 213.

102. *Advertiser*, May 23, 1851.

103. Edward Emerson, "Emerson and Scholars," 27.

104. Emerson, *AW*, 107, The Assault on Charles Sumner.

105. Ibid., 118, Speech at a Meeting to Aid John Brown's Family.

106. Buell, *Emerson*, 34.

107. For a detailed discussion of the antislavery influence, see Barbara Packer's excellent "Historical Introduction" to *Conduct of Life*, *CW* 6:xv–lxvii.

108. Robinson, *Conduct*, 149.

109. Emerson, *CW* 6:1–2.

110. Ibid., 6:2.

111. Ibid., 6:23.

112. Ibid., 6:24.

113. Ibid., 6:28.

114. Ibid., 6:32, 33.

115. Emerson, *JMN* 14:363.

116. McPherson, *Battle Cry*, 232.

117. Emerson, *JMN* 15:111.

118. Neumann, *CONSCIOUSNESS*, 212.

119. Emerson, *CW* 1:67, The American Scholar.

120. Emerson, *CW* 3:23, The Poet.

121. Lawrence Buell observes that Emerson became "the spokesperson for American liberal democracy," and "an anticipator of a thoroughgoing democratic pluralism" (*Emerson*, 286, 287).

122. Emerson, *JMN* 15:182.

123. Because of his exposure to Transcendental philosophy early in his career through the writings of Emerson and Theodore Parker, and his consequent willingness to act on abstract ideals, Garry Wills refers to Lincoln as "a Transcendentalist without the fuzziness" (174).

124. Joel Porte describes this grand vision in detail in "Emerson and the Refounding of America."

125. Emerson, *LL* 2:311, Address at Dartmouth College

126. Ibid., 2:241, 242.

127. Ibid., 2:246, 247.

128. Ibid., 2:282.

129. McPherson, *Cause*, 20.

130. Ibid., 108.

131. McPherson, *Battle Cry*, 497.

132. Emerson, *LL* 2:300.

133. Qtd. in ibid., 2:288.

134. Emerson, *JMN* 15:210–11.

135. Emerson, *LL* 2:316.
136. In November, Emerson celebrated the heroism of the Fifty-fourth and their leader, Colonel Robert Shaw, in a poem, "Voluntaries," published in the *Atlantic Monthly*.
137. McPherson, *Battle Cry*, 565.
138. McPherson, *Cause*, 124.
139. Emerson, *W* 11:355.
140. For more on Emerson's support of Lincoln at this critical time, see Gougeon, "Transcendental Warfare."
141. Donald, *Lincoln*, 474.
142. Emerson, *AW* 140, 142, 153.
143. Emerson, *L* 5:387.
144. Emerson, *LL* 2:25. For a discussion of Emerson's influence on the modern Civil Rights movement, see Gougeon, "The Legacy of Reform."
145. Emerson, *CW* 1: 67.
146. Emerson, *LL* 2:344.
147. Campbell, *HERO* 345.
148. Emerson, *CW* 1:70.

EPILOGUE:
EMERSON, WHOLENESS, AND THE SELF

1. Neumann, *Great Mother*, 4.
2. Jung, *Modern Man in Search of a Soul*, 122.
3. Randall Fuller, "Emerson in the Gilded Age," 97.
4. Qtd. in ibid., 98.
5. James, "Emerson," 583.
6. Ibid., 586.
7. Mitchell, *Individualism*, 74, 75. Mitchell's study also notes extensively the work of several scholars who have argued persuasively for a strong Emersonian influence in James and Pragmatism generally.
8. Buell, *Emerson*, 181.
9. Allen, "Emerson and the Unconscious," 27. James M. Albrecht also makes a compelling argument for a similar Emersonian influence in James in "What's the Use of Reading Emerson Pragmatically? The Example of William James."
10. Qtd. in Mitchell, *Individualism*, 76.
11. Rosenweig, *Freud, Jung, and Hall*, 3, 81.
12. Qtd. in Bair, *Jung*, 598.
13. Smith, *Wounded Jung*, 110, 120.
14. Jung, "Civilization in Transition," 499.
15. James, Conclusions to the *Varieties*, 780.
16. In Jung, *The Structure and Dynamics of the Psyche*, 125.

17. Fuller, "Emerson in the Gilded Age," 98–99.

18. In her memorial essay published in the *Woman's Journal* shortly after his death, Howe wrote of him, "Among all of Mr. Emerson's great merits, we of this *Journal* must especially mention his loyalty to woman. . . . He was for us, knowing well enough our limitations and shortcomings, and his golden words have done much both to fit us for the larger freedom, and to know that it belongs to us." Qtd. in Gougeon, "Emerson and the Woman Question," 592.

19. For Storey, see Gougeon, "The Legacy of Reform." For Washington, Du Bois, and King, see Patterson, *From Emerson to King.*

20. Morrow, "The Bishop of Our Possibilities." *Time*, May 10, 1982, 124.

WORKS CITED

Adams, Henry. *The Education of Henry Adams.* Edited by Ernest Samuels. Boston: Houghton Mifflin Co., 1973 [1918].

Albrecht, James M. "What's the Use of Reading Emerson Pragmatically? The Example of William James." *Nineteenth-Century Prose* 20, Nos. 1–2 (2003): 388–432.

Allen, Gay Wilson. *Waldo Emerson.* New York: Viking, 1982.

———. "Emerson and the Unconscious." *American Transcendental Quarterly* 19 (1973): 26–30.

Anderson, Quentin. *The Imperial Self: An Essay in American Literary and Cultural History.* New York: Knopf, 1971.

Armitage, Angus. *The World of Copernicus.* New York: New American Library, 1947.

Bair, Deirdre. *Jung: A Biography.* Boston: Little, Brown and Co., 2003.

Baker, Carlos. *Emerson Among the Eccentrics: A Group Portrait.* New York: Viking, 1996.

Bargh, John A., James E. Uleman, and Ran R. Hassin, eds. *The New Unconscious.* New York: Oxford University Press, 2005.

Barish, Evelyn. *Emerson: The Roots of Prophesy.* Princeton, NJ: Princeton University Press, 1989.

Barnard, G. William. *Exploring Unseen Worlds: William James and the Philosophy of Mysticism.* Albany: State University of New York Press, 1997.

Bercovitch, Sacvan. "Emerson the Prophet: Romanticism, Puritanism, and Auto-American-Biography." In *Emerson: Prophesy, Metamorphosis, and Influence.* Edited by David Levin. New York: Columbia University Press, 1975.

Bickman, Martin. *American Romantic Psychology: Emerson, Poe, Whitman, Dickinson, Melville.* Dallas: Spring Publications, 1980.

Bodkin, Maude. *Archetypal Patterns in Poetry: Psychological Studies of Imagination.* London: Oxford University Press, 1963 [1934].

Boller, Paul. *American Transcendentalism: 1830–1860, An Intellectual Inquiry*. New York: G. P. Putnam's Sons, 1974.

Bosco, Ronald A., and Joel Myerson, eds. *Emerson in His Own Time: A Biographical Chronicle of His Life, Drawn from Recollections, Interviews, and Memoirs by Family, Friends, and Associates*. Iowa City: University of Iowa Press, 2003.

Brown, Judith M. *Gandhi: Prisoner of Hope*. New Haven, CT: Yale University Press, 1989.

Brown, Norman O. *Love's Body*. New York: Vintage, 1966.

———. *Life Against Death: The Psychoanalytic Meaning of History*. New York: Vintage, 1959.

Buell, Lawrence. *Literary Transcendentalism: Style and Vision in the American Renaissance*. Ithaca: Cornell University Press, 1973.

———. *Emerson*. Cambridge, MA: Harvard University Press, 2003.

———. *New England Literary Culture: From Revolution through Renaissance*. Cambridge: Cambridge University Press, 1986.

Burkholder, Robert, and Joel Myerson, eds. *Emerson: An Annotated Secondary Bibliography*. Pittsburgh: Pittsburgh University Press, 1985.

Cabot, James Elliot. *A Memoir of Ralph Waldo Emerson*. 2 Vols. Boston, MA: Houghton, Mifflin, 1887.

Cameron, Kenneth Walter. *Transcendental Log*. Hartford, CT: Transcendental Books. 1973.

———. *Emerson the Essayist*. 2 Vols. Hartford, CT: Transcendental Books, 1972.

Campbell, Joseph. *The Hero With a Thousand Faces*. Princeton, NJ: Princeton University Press, 1949.

Capper, Charles. *Margaret Fuller, An American Life: The Private Years*. New York: Oxford University Press, 1992.

Carpenter, Frederic. *Emerson Handbook*. New York: Hendricks House, 1953.

Carter, Steve. "The Poetry of Mind: Differences Between Emerson and Jung." *American Transcendental Quarterly* 49 (1981): 21–34.

Cayton, Mary Kupiec. *Emerson's Emergence: Self and Society in the Transformation of New England, 1800–1845*. Chapel Hill: University of North Carolina Press, 1989.

Charvat, William. *Emerson's Lecture Engagements: A Chronological List*. New York: The New York Public Library, 1961.

Cheyfitz, Eric. *The Trans-Parent: Sexual Politics in the Language of Emerson*. Baltimore: Johns Hopkins University Press, 1981.

Clark, Ronald W. *Einstein: The Life and Times*. New York: World Publishing, 1971.

Clinton, Catherine. *The Other Civil War: American Women in the Nineteenth Century*. New York: Hill & Wang, 1984.

Cole, Phyllis. *Mary Moody Emerson and the Origins of Transcendentalism*. New York: Oxford University Press, 1998.

———. "Emerson, England, and Fate." In *Emerson: Prophesy, Metamorphosis, and Influence*. Edited by David Levin. New York: Columbia University Press, 1975.

Collison, Gary. *Shadrach Minkins: From Fugitive Slave to Citizen*. Cambridge, MA: Harvard University Press, 1997.

Commager, Henry Steele. *The Era of Reform: 1830–1860*. Princeton, NJ: D. Van Nostrand Co., 1960.

———. *The Empire of Reason: How Europe and America Realized the Enlightenment*. Garden City, NY: Anchor Doubleday, 1977.

Cramer, Jeffrey, ed. *Walden: A Fully Annotated Edition*. New Haven, CT: Yale University Press, 2004.

Crane, Gregg. *Race, Citizenship, and Law in American Literature*. Cambridge: Cambridge University Press, 2002.

DeSantillana, Giorgio. *The Crime of Galileo*. Chicago: University of Chicago Press, 1955.

Doctorow, E. E. "Seeing the Unseen." *Discover* (December 2004): 40–45.

Donald, David Herbert. *Charles Sumner*. New York: Da Cappo Press, 1996.

———. *Lincoln*. New York: Simon & Schuster, 1995.

Douglass, Frederick. *Narrative of the Life of Frederick Douglass, an American Slave, Written by Himself*. New York: W. W. Norton & Company, 1997 [1845].

Eliade, Mircea. *Journal IV: 1979–1985*. Chicago: University of Chicago Press, 1990.

———. *The Myth of the Eternal Return: or Cosmos and History*. Trans. Willard Trask. Princeton, NJ: Princeton University Press, 1949.

Ellison, Julie. "Tears for Emerson." In *The Cambridge Companion to Ralph Waldo Emerson*. Edited by Joel Porte and Saundra Morris. Cambridge: Cambridge University Press, 1999.

———. *Emerson's Romantic Style*. Princeton, NJ: Princeton University Press, 1984.

Emerson, Edward Waldo. "Emerson and Scholars." In *Essays, Addresses, and Poems of Edward Waldo Emerson*. Cambridge, MA: Riverside Press, 1930.

Emerson, Ellen. *A Life of Lidian Jackson Emerson*. Edited by Delores Bird Carpenter. Boston: Twayne Publishers, 1980.

Emerson, Ellen Tucker. *One First Love: The Letters of Ellen Tucker Emerson to Ralph Waldo Emerson*. Edited by Edith W. Gregg. Cambridge, MA: Harvard University Press, 1962.

Emerson, Ralph Waldo, *The Complete Works of Ralph Waldo Emerson*. 12 Vols. Edited by Edward Waldo Emerson. Boston: Houghton, Mifflin Co., 1903–1904. (W).

———. *The Early Lectures of Ralph Waldo Emerson*. 3 Vols. Edited by Robert E. Spiller, Stephen E. Whicher, and Wallace E. Williams. Cambridge, MA: Harvard University Press, 1959–1972. (*EL*).

———. *The Journals and Miscellaneous Notebooks of Ralph Waldo Emerson*. 16 Vols. Edited by William H. Gilman, Ralph Orth, et al. Cambridge, MA: Harvard University Press, 1960–1982. (*JMN*).

———. *The Journals of Ralph Waldo Emerson*. 10 Vols. Edited by Edward Waldo Emerson and Waldo Emerson Forbes. Boston: Houghton, Mifflin Co., 1909–1914. (*J*).

———. *The Collected Works of Ralph Waldo Emerson*. 6 Vols. to date. Edited by Alfred R. Ferguson, Joseph Slater, and Douglas Emory Wilson. Cambridge, MA: Harvard University Press, 1971–. (*CW*).

———. *The Letters of Ralph Waldo Emerson*, 10 Vols. Edited by Ralph L. Rusk and Eleanor M. Tilton. New York: Columbia University Press, 1939, 1990–1995. (*L*).

———. *Emerson's Antislavery Writings*. Edited by Len Gougeon and Joel Myerson. New Haven, CT: Yale University Press, 1995. (*AW*).

———. *The Later Lectures of Ralph Waldo Emerson: 1843–1871*. 2 Vols. Edited by Ronald Bosco and Joel Myerson. Athens: University of Georgia Press, 2001. (*LL*).

———. *Uncollected Lectures by Ralph Waldo Emerson*. Edited by Clarence Gohdes, Jr. New York: William Edwin Rudge, 1932.

———. *The Complete Sermons of Ralph Waldo Emerson*. 4 Vols. Edited by Albert von Frank. Columbia: University of Missouri Press, 1989.

———. *The Poetry Notebooks of Ralph Waldo Emerson*. Edited by Ralph H. Orth, Albert J. von Frank, Linda Allardt, David W. Hill. Columbia: University of Missouri Press, 1986.

Erikson, Erik H. *Childhood and Society*. New York: W. W. Norton and Co., Inc., 1950.

———. "Reflections on the Dissent of Contemporary Youth." *Daedalus: Journal of the American Academy of Arts and Sciences* 99 (1970): 154–176.

Feidelson, Charles Jr. *Symbolism and American Literature*. New York: Oxford University Press, 1964.

Fiedler, Leslie. *Love and Death in the American Novel*. New York: Delta, 1966.

Frye, Northrop. *Anatomy of Criticism: Four Essays*. Princeton, NJ: Princeton University Press, 1957.

Fuller, Margaret. *Woman in the Nineteenth Century*. Edited by Larry Reynolds. Reprint 1845, New York: W. W. Norton and Co., Inc., 1998.

———. "Margaret Fuller's 1842 Journal: At Concord with the Emersons." Edited by Joel Myerson. *Harvard Library Bulletin* 21 (1973): 320–340.

————. *Those Sad but Glorious Days: Dispatches from Europe, 1846–1850.* Edited by Larry Reynolds and Susan Belasco Smith. New Haven, CT: Yale University Press, 1991.

Fuller, Randall. "Emerson in the Gilded Age." *ESQ: A Journal of the American Renaissance* 45 (1999): 97–129.

Gandhi, Mahatma. *Autobiography: The Story of My Experiments with Truth.* Translated by Mahadev Desai. Boston: Beacon Press, 1993.

Garvey, T. Gregory, "Emerson's Political Spirit and the Problem of Language." In *The Emerson Dilemma: Essays on Emerson and Social Reform.* Edited by T. Gregory Garvey. Athens: University of Georgia Press, 2001.

Geldard, Richard G., *God in Concord: Ralph Waldo Emerson's Awakening to the Infinite.* New York: Larson Publications, 1999.

Gelpi, Albert. *The Tenth Muse: The Psyche of the American Poet.* Cambridge, MA: Harvard University Press, 1975.

Gleason, William. "Re-Creating *Walden*: Thoreau's Economy of Work and Play." *American Literature* 65 (1993): 673–692.

Gougeon, Len. *Virtue's Hero: Emerson, Antislavery, and Reform.* Athens: University of Georgia Press, 1990.

————. "Introduction." *Emerson's Antislavery Writings.* Edited by Len Gougeon and Joel Myerson. New Haven, CT: Yale University Press, 1995, 2001.

————. "Adams in the Garden: Sex, Symbol, and Myth in *The Education of Henry Adams*." *Journal of Evolutionary Psychology* 7 (1986): 261–269.

————. "Emerson's Abolition Conversion." In *The Emerson Dilemma: Essays on Emerson and Social Reform.* Edited by T. Gregory Garvey. Athens: University of Georgia Press, 2001.

————. "Emerson, Poetry, and Reform." *Modern Language Studies* 19 (1989): 38–49.

————. "1838: Ellis Gray Loring and Journal for the Times." *Studies in the American Renaissance: 1990.* Edited by Joel Myerson, 33–46. Charlottesville: University Press of Virginia, 1990.

————. "'Fortune of the Republic': Emerson. Lincoln, and Transcendental Warfare." *ESQ: A Journal of the American Renaissance* 65 (1999): 259–324.

————. "Emerson and the Woman Question: The Evolution of His Thought." *The New England Quarterly* 71 (1998): 570–592.

————. "Looking Backwards: Emerson at 100." *Nineteenth-Century Prose* 30 (2003): 50–73.

————. "Holmes's Emerson and the Conservative Critique of Realism." *South Atlantic Review* 59 (1994): 107–125.

———. "*The Education of Henry Adams.*" In *American History Through Literature 1870–1920.* Edited by Gary Scharnhorst and Tom Quirk. New York: Charles Scribner's Sons, 2006.

———. "Emerson, Whitman, and Eros." *Walt Whitman Quarterly Review* 23 (2006): 127–147.

———. "The Legacy of Reform: Emersonian Idealism, Moorfield Storey, and the Civil Rights Movement." In *Emerson Bicentennial Essays.* Edited by Ronald A. Bosco and Joel Myerson. Boston: University of Virginia Press and Massachusetts Historical Society, 2006.

Graves, Robert. "Introduction." *New Larousse Encyclopedia of Mythology.* New York: Prometheus Press, 1968.

Green, Martin. "Review of Norman Brown's *Love's Body.*" *Commonweal* 23 (1966): 353.

Guthrie, James R. *About Time: Emerson's and Thoreau's Temporal Revolutions.* Columbia: University of Missouri Press, 2001.

Harding, Walter. *Emerson's Library.* Charlotteville: University Press of Virginia, 1967.

Hassin, Ran R. et al. *The New Unconscious.* New York: Oxford University Press, 2005.

Hedge, Frederick Henry. "Reminisces of Emerson." In *Emerson in His Own Time.* Edited by Ronald A. Bosco and Joel Myerson. Iowa City: University of Iowa Press, 2003.

Heller, Agnes. *Renaissance Man.* Translated by Richard E. Allen. London: Routledge & Kegan Paul, 1978 [1967].

Hodder, Alan. *Emerson's Rhetoric of Revelation: Nature, the Reader and the Apocalypse Within.* University Park: The Pennsylvania State University Press, 1989.

Hoffman, Daniel. *Form and Fable in American Fiction.* New York: W. W. Norton & Co., Inc., 1961.

Holmes, Oliver Wendell. *Ralph Waldo Emerson.* Boston: Houghton, Mifflin, 1885.

Hopkins, Vivian. *Spires of Form: A Study of Emerson's Aesthetic Theory.* Cambridge, MA: Harvard University Press, 1951.

———. "Emerson and Cudworth: Plastic Nature and Transcendental Art." *American Literature* 23 (1951–52): 80–98.

Hughes, Merrit Y. "Introduction." In *John Milton: Complete Poems and Major Prose.* Edited by Merritt Y. Hughes. New York: The Odyssey Press, 1967.

James, William. *The Writings of William James: A Comprehensive Edition.* Edited by John J. McDermott. Chicago: The University of Chicago Press, 1977.

Johnson, Glen M. "Ralph Waldo Emerson on Isaac Hecker: A Manuscript with Commentary." *The Catholic Historical Review* 79 (1993): 54–64.

Jung, Carl. *Modern Man in Search of a Soul*. New York: Harcourt, Brace & World, Inc., 1933.

———. *Psychology and Religion: West and East*. New York: Pantheon Books, 1958.

———. "On the Relation of Analytical Psychology to Poetry." In *The Archetypes and the Collective Unconscious*. Translated by R. F. Hull. New York: Pantheon Books, 1959.

———. *Civilization in Transition*. Princeton, NJ: Princeton University Press, 1967.

———. *Memories, Dreams, Reflections*. Edited by Aniela Jafee'. New York: Vintage Books, 1961.

———. *Psychology and Alchemy*. Princeton, NJ: Princeton University Press, 1968.

———. *Symbols of Transformation*. Princeton, NJ: Princeton University Press, 1956.

———. *Psyche & Symbol: A Selection from the Writings of C. G. Jung*. Edited by Violet S. DeLaszlo. New York: Anchor Books, 1958.

———. *Two Essays on Analytical Psychology*. Princeton, NJ: Princeton University Press, 1953.

———. "Psychological Factors in Human Behavior." In *The Structure and Dynamics of the Psyche*. Princeton, NJ: Princeton University Press, 1960.

Kant, Immanuel, *Grounding for the Metaphysics of Morals*. Translated by James W. Ellington. New York: Hackett Publishing Co., 1982.

Kateb, George. *Emerson and Self-Reliance*. Thousand Oaks, CA: Sage, 1995.

Kennedy, John F. *Profiles in Courage*. New York: Harper & Row, 1964.

King, Martin Luther, Jr. *A Testament of Hope: The Essential Writings of Martin Luther King, Jr*. Edited by James Melvin Washington. New York: Harper & Row Publishers, 1986.

Klonoski, Richard J. "*Homonoia* in Aristotle's Ethics and Politics." *History of Political Thought* 17 (1996): 314–325.

Kuhn, Thomas. *The Copernican Revolution*. New York: Vintage Books, 1957.

Larsen, Stephen and Robin. *A Fire in the Mind: The Life of Joseph Campbell*. New York: Doubleday, 1991.

Lawrence, D. H. *Psychoanalysis and the Unconscious and Fantasia of the Unconscious*. New York: Viking, 1960.

———. *Studies in Classic American Literature*. New York: Doubleday, 1951.

———. *The Symbolic Meaning: The Uncollected Versions of Studies in Classic American Literature*. New York: Viking Press, 1964.

Lebeaux, Richard. "Emerson's Young Adulthood: From Patienthood to Patiencehood." *ESQ: A Journal of the American Renaissance* 25 (1979): 203–210.

Lesser, Simon. *Fiction and the Unconscious*. New York: Vintage Books, 1957.

Levin, Harry. *The Power of Blackness: Hawthorne, Poe, Melville*. New York: Knopf, 1958.

Lewis, R. W. B. *The American Adam: Innocence, Tragedy, and Tradition in the Nineteenth Century*. Chicago: University of Chicago Press, 1955.

Lowance, Mason Jr., ed. *A House Divided: The Antebellum Slavery Debates in America, 1776–1865*. Princeton, NJ: Princeton University Press, 2003.

Lowell, James Russell. *A Fable for Critics* (1848).

Marx, Leo. *The Machine in the Garden: Technology and the Pastoral Ideal in America*. New York: Oxford University Press, 1964.

Matthiessen, F. O. *American Renaissance: Art and Expression in the Age of Emerson and Whitman*. New York: Oxford University Press, 1941.

McAleer, John. *Ralph Waldo Emerson: Days of Encounter*. Boston: Little, Brown, 1984.

McPherson, James. *Battle Cry of Freedom: The Civil War Era*. New York: Ballantine Books, 1988.

———. *For Cause and Comrades: Why Men Fought in the Civil War*. New York. Oxford University Press, 1997

Melville, Melville. *Correspondence*. Edited by Lynn North. Chicago: Northwestern University Press, 1993.

———. "Hawthorne and His Mosses." In *Moby-Dick*. Edited by Harrison Hayford and Hershel Parker. New York: W. W. Norton and Co., Inc., 1967.

Michaud, Regis. "Emerson's Transcendentalism." *The American Journal of Psychology* 30 (1919): 73–82.

Milder, Robert. "The Radical Emerson?" In *The Cambridge Companion to Ralph Waldo Emerson*. Edited by Joel Porte and Saundra Morris. Cambridge: Cambridge University Press, 1999.

Miller, Jeffrey C. *The Transcendent Function: Jung's Model of Psychological Growth Through Dialogue with the Unconscious*. Albany: The State University of New York Press, 2004.

Miller, Perry, ed. *The Transcendentalists: An Anthology*. Cambridge, MA: Harvard University Press, 1950.

Milton, John. *John Milton: Complete Poems and Major Prose*. Edited by Merritt Y. Hughes. New York: The Odyssey Press, 1957.

Mitchell, Charles. *Individualism and Its Discontents: Appropriations of Emerson, 1880–1950*. Amherst: University of Massachusetts Press, 1997.

Morgan, Edmund S. In "The Puritan Ethic and the American Revolution." *Puritanism and The American Experience.* Edited by Michael McGiffert. Reading, PA: Addison-Wesley, 1971.

Morris, Saundra. "Poetic Portals: Emerson's Essay Epigraphs." *Nineteenth-Century Prose* 30 (2003): 300–328.

Morrow, Lance. "The Bishop of Our Possibilities." *Time*, May 10, 1982, 124.

Mott, Wesley. *"The Strains of Eloquence": Emerson in His Sermons.* University Park: Pennsylvania State University Press, 1988.

———. "The Age of the First Person Singular: Emerson and Individualism." In *Historical Guide to Ralph Waldo Emerson.* Edited by Joel Myerson. New York: Oxford University Press, 2000.

Myerson, Joel. *The New England Transcendentalists and the Dial: A History of the Magazine and Its Contributors.* Rutherford, NJ: Fairleigh Dickinson University Press, 1980.

———. ed. *A Historical Guide to Ralph Waldo Emerson.* New York; Oxford University Press, 2000.

———. ed. *Ralph Waldo Emerson: A Descriptive Bibliography.* Pittsburgh: University of Pittsburgh Press, 1982.

———. ed. (with Robert Burkholder). *Ralph Waldo Emerson: An Annotated Secondary Bibliography.* Pittsburgh: Pittsburgh University Press, 1985.

———. ed. (with Ronald A. Bosco). *Emerson in His Own Time : A Biographical Chronicle of His Life, Drawn from Recollections, Interviews, and Memoirs by Family, Friends, and Associates.* Iowa City: University of Iowa Press, 2003.

———. "Margaret Fuller's 1842 Journal: At Concord with the Emersons." *Harvard Library Bulletin* 21 (1973): 320–340.

———. "Convers Francis and Emerson." *American Literature* 50 (1978): 17–36.

Neumann, Erich. *The Origins and History of Consciousness.* Translated by R. F. C. Hull. Princeton, NJ: Princeton University Press, 1949.

———. *The Great Mother: An Analysis of an Archetype.* Princeton, NJ: Princeton University Press, 1955.

Newfield, Christopher. *The Emerson Effect: Individualism and Submission in America.* Chicago: University of Chicago Press, 1996.

Norcross, John C., and James O. Prochaska. *Systems of Psychotherapy: A Transtheoretical Analysis.* Fifth ed. New York: Thomson, 2003.

Norton, Andrews. *The Evidences of the Genuineness of the Gospels.* 3 Vols. Boston: J. B. Russell, 1837–1844.

O'Keefe, Richard. *Mythic Archetypes in Ralph Waldo Emerson: A Blakean Reading.* Kent, Ohio: Kent State University Press, 1995.

Otto, Walter. *Dionysus, Myth and Cult.* Translated by Robert B. Palmer. London: Indiana University Press, 1965.

Packer, Barbara. *Emerson's Fall: A New Interpretation of the Major Essays*. New York: Continuum, 1982.

———. "Introduction." *The Conduct of Life, The Collected Works of Ralph Waldo Emerson*. Vol. 6. Edited by Douglas Emory Wilson. Cambridge, MA: Harvard University Press, 2003.

Patterson, Anita. *From Emerson to King: Democracy, Race, and the Politics of Protest*. New York: Oxford University Press, 1997.

Paul, Sherman. *Emerson's Angle of Vision: Man and Nature in American Experience*. Cambridge, MA: Harvard University Press, 1952.

Petrulionis, Sandra Harbert. "'Swelling the Great Tides of Humanity': The Concord, Massachusetts Female Anti-Slavery Society." *The New England Quarterly* 74 (2001): 385–418.

Poirier, Richard. "Is there an I for an Eye?" In *Ralph Waldo Emerson: A Collection of Critical Essays*. Edited by Lawrence Buell. Englewood Cliffs, NJ: Prentice Hall, 1993.

Porte, Joel. *The Romance in America: Studies in Cooper, Poe, Hawthorne, Melville, and James*. Middletown, CT: Wesleyan University Press, 1969.

———. *Representative Man: Ralph Waldo Emerson in His Time*. New York: Oxford University Press, 1979.

——— and Saundra Morris, eds. *The Cambridge Companion to Ralph Waldo Emerson*. New York: Cambridge University Press, 1999.

———. *In Respect to Egotism: Studies in American Romantic Writing*. Cambridge: Cambridge University Press, 1991.

———. "Emerson and the Refounding of America." *Nineteenth-Century Prose* 30 (2003): 227–249.

Porter, Carolyn. *Seeing and Being: The Plight of the Participant Observer in Emerson, James, Adams, and Faulkner*. Middletown, CT: Wesleyan University Press, 1981.

Porter, David. *Emerson and Literary Change*. Cambridge, MA: Harvard University Press, 1978.

Prochaska, James O., and John C. Norcross. *Systems of Psychotherapy: A Transtheoretical Analysis*. Fifth ed. New York: Thomson, 2003.

Rank, Otto. *The Myth of the Birth of the Hero, and Other Writings*. Edited by Philip Freund. New York: Vintage. 1932.

Reaver, J. Russell. *Emerson as Mythmaker*. Gainesville: University of Florida Press, 1954.

Reynolds, Larry. *European Revolutions and the American Literary Renaissance*. New Haven, CT: Yale University Press, 1988.

———. "Introduction." *Those Sad But Glorious Days: Dispatches from Europe, 1846–1850/ Margaret Fuller*. Edited by Larry Reynolds and Susan Belasco Smith. New Haven, CT: Yale University Press, 1991.

Richard, Leonard. *"Gentlemen of Property and Standing": Anti-abolition Mobs in Jacksonian America*. New York: Oxford University Press, 1970.

Richardson, Robert. *Myth and Literature in the American Renaissance.* Bloomington: Indiana University Press, 1978.

———. *Emerson: The Mind on Fire.* Berkeley: University of California Press, 1995.

Robinson, David. *The Unitarians and the Universalists.* Westport, CT: Greenwood Press, 1985.

———. *Emerson and the Conduct of Life: Pragmatism and Ethical Purpose in the Later Work.* Cambridge: Cambridge University Press, 1993.

———. *Apostle of Culture: Emerson as Preacher and Lecturer.* Philadelphia: University of Pennsylvania Press, 1982.

Rosa, Alfred. "Emerson and the Salem Lyceum." *Essex Institute Historical Collection* 110 (1974): 75–85.

Rosenzweig, Saul. *Freud, Jung, and Hall the King-Maker: The Historic Expedition to America (1909).* St. Louis, MO: Rana House Press, 1992.

Rowe, John Carlos. *At Emerson's Tomb: The Politics of Classic American Literature.* New York: Columbia University Press, 1997.

Rusk, Ralph. *The Life of Ralph Waldo Emerson.* New York: Columbia University Press, 1949.

Sacks, Kenneth. *Understanding Emerson.* Princeton, NJ: Princeton University Press, 2003.

Schlesinger, Arthur M. Jr. *Age of Jackson.* New York: Little, Brown, 1945.

Schliener, Louise. "Emerson's Orphic and Messianic Bard." *ESQ: A Journal of the American Renaissance* 25 (1979): 191–202.

Sealts, Merton Jr. *Emerson on the Scholar.* Columbia: University of Missouri Press, 1992.

Sherman, Stuart P. *Americans.* New York: Scribner's, 1922.

Smith, Robert C. *The Wounded Jung.* Evanston, IL: Northwestern University Press, 1996.

Steele, Jeffrey. "Interpreting the Self: Emerson and the Unconscious." In *Emerson: Prospect and Retrospect.* Edited by Joel Porte. Cambridge, MA: Harvard University Press, 1982.

———. *The Representation of the Self in the American Renaissance.* Chapel Hill: University of North Carolina Press, 1987.

Stevens, Wallace. *The Necessary Angel: Essays on Reality and the Imagination.* New York: Vintage Books, 1942.

Strawson, Peter, "Freedom and Resentment." In *Free Will.* Edited by Gary Watson. Oxford: Oxford University Press, 1982.

Tallis, Frank. *Hidden Minds: A History of the Unconscious.* New York: Arcade Publishing, 2002.

Tanner, Tony. "The Unconquered Eye." In *Critical Essays on Ralph Waldo Emerson.* Edited by Robert Burkholder and Joel Myerson. Boston: G. K. Hall, 1983.

Thomas, John L. *The Liberator: William Lloyd Garrison.* Boston: Little, Brown & Co., 1963.

Thoreau, Henry David. *Walden* (1854). Edited by William Rossi. New York: W. W. Norton and Co., Inc., 1992.

———. *Walden: A Fully Annotated Edition*. Edited by Jeffrey S. Cramer. New Haven, CT: Yale University Press, 2004.

Tillyard, E. M. W. *The Elizabethan World Picture*. New York: Vintage Books, 1961.

Tucker, Ellen Louisa. *One First Love: The Letters of Ellen Louisa Tucker to Ralph Waldo Emerson*. Edited by Edith W. Gregg. Cambridge, MA: Harvard University Press, 1962.

Uleman, James E., John A. Bargh, and Ran R. Hassin, eds. *The New Unconscious*. New York: Oxford University Press, 2005.

Van Cromphout, Gustaaf. *Emerson's Modernity and the Example of Goethe*. Columbia: University of Missouri Press, 1990.

von Frank, Albert J. *The Trials of Anthony Burns: Freedom and Slavery in Emerson's Boston*. Cambridge, MA: Harvard University Press, 1998.

———. *An Emerson Chronology*. New York: J. K. Hall & Co., 1994.

———. "*Essays: First Series* (1841)." In *The Cambridge Companion to Ralph Waldo Emerson*. Edited by Joel Porte and Saundra Morris. Cambridge: Cambridge University Press, 1999.

Walls, Laura Dassow. *Emerson's Life in Science: The Culture of Truth*. Ithaca: Cornell University Press, 2003.

Weisbuch, Robert. "Post-Colonial Emerson and the Erasure of Europe." In *The Cambridge Companion to Ralph Waldo Emerson*. Edited by Joel Porte and Saundra Morris. Cambridge: Cambridge University Press, 1999.

Whicher, Stephen. *Freedom and Fate: An Inner Life of Ralph Waldo Emerson*. Philadelphia: University of Pennsylvania Press, 1953.

Whipple, Edwin Percy. "Some Recollections of Ralph Waldo Emerson." In *Emerson in His Own Time*. Edited by Ronald A. Bosco and Joel Myerson. Iowa City: University of Iowa Press, 2003.

Whyte, Lancelot Law. *The Unconscious Before Freud*. New York: Basic Books, 1960.

Wider, Sarah. *The Critical Reception of Emerson: Unsettling All Things*. Rochester: Camden House, 2000.

Willey, Basil. *The Seventeenth-Century Background: Studies in the Thought of the Age in Relation to Poetry and Religion*. New York: Doubleday & Co., 1953.

Williams, Henry Smith. *A History of Science*. 10 Vols. New York: Harpers, 1904.

Wills, Garry. *Lincoln at Gettysburg: The Words that Remade America*. New York: Simon & Schuster, 1992.

Wind, Edgar. *Pagan Mysteries in the Renaissance: An Exploration of Philosophical and Mystical Sources of Iconography in Renaissance Art.* New York: W. W. Norton and Co., Inc., 1958.

Woodbury, George Edward. *Ralph Waldo Emerson.* New York: Macmillan, 1907.

Woodress, James. *Eight American Authors: A Review of Research and Criticism.* New York: W. W. Norton and Co., Inc., 1971.

Yoder, Ralph. *The Orphic Poet in America.* Berkeley: University of California Press, 1978.

Young, Gloria. "The Fountainhead of All Forms": Poetry and the Unconscious in Emerson and Howard Nemerov." In *Artful Thunder: Versions of the Romantic Tradition in American Literature.* Edited by Robert J. DeMott and Sanford E. Marovitz. Kent, OH: Kent State University Press, 1975.

INDEX

abolition, 105, 144; chapter 5 *passim*
abolitionists, 163, 169, 173, 178, 183
Adam: American, 205n61; and Eve,
  115; (Genesis), 31, 32; language
  of, 94, 107–108, 150; new, 23;
  and Original Sin, 52
Adams, Abby Larkin, 94
Adams, Abel, 94
Adams, Henry, *Education of Henry
  Adams, The*, 35–36; emotional
  attraction to Europe similar to
  Emerson's, 217–218n78
Adams, John, 174
African Americans: Emerson demands
  equal rights for, 186–187; racist
  attitude towards, 186
Albrecht, James M., 238n9
Alcott, Bronson, 230–231n153
Allen, Gay Wilson, 15, 55; on Jung
  and William James, 195
Anderson, Quentin, 201n25
animus mundi (world spirit), 47
antislavery, 105, 166; chapter 5 pas-
  sim; and women, 178–179
Aquinas, St. Thomas, 161
Archetypal Criticism, 38, 194
archetypes, 11, 38; defined, 22, 41;
  Emerson's use of, 114, 229; as
  history, 148, 229n116; and
  mythology, 148; power of, 193
Aristotle, 29; *Nicomachean Ethics*,
  170, 177, 185
Armitage, Angus, 204n49

art: and the idea of the soul, 89; and
  liberation of instincts 152; and
  nature, 97, 150; and religion,
  89,154; social significance of,
  72–73; as source of divine truth,
  169; as subversive of civilization,
  56, 142, 169–170; and the unconscious, 54–57
artist: as rebel, 56; as hero, 152, 153
Augustine, Saint, 5, 161, 236n75
Aurora (Boehme), 56

Babbitt, Irving, 37
Bacon, Francis, 25, 32
Baker, Carlos, 15
Barish, Evelyn, 62, 214n47, 226n53
Barlach, Ernst, 68, 164
Barnard, J. William, 203n53
Bercovitch, Sacvan, 226n67
Bhagavad-Gita, 172, 219n117
Bickman, Martin, 201n25, 206n70,
  222n168
bisexuality: psychological, 115
Blake, William: and the unconscious, 55
body: harmony with the soul, 89, 118,
  131, 155; opposed by ego, 132;
  importance for Emerson, 58,
  131–132; psychological impor-
  tance of, 47–50; repression of,
  97; resurrection of, 57–58
Boehme, Jacob: and revolutionary
  Christianity, 177; sensual language, 56; and unconscious, 55

Boston Vigilance Committee, 171
Brooks, Preston, 181
Brown, John, 181, 228n97, and Emerson, 181–182
Brown, Norman O., 9; antagonism between humanity and society, 142; and art as revolutionary, 170; and denial of the body, 47–48; and resurrection of the body, 57–58; and childhood as ideal, 51, 119, 138; and Christianity as revolutionary, 176–77; and collective unconscious, 22–23; and crisis of the modern world, 25; and Emerson, 199–200n25; and language and art, 54; *Life Against Death*, 46–58; *Love's Body*, 115; and mystical element of art, 13; and Original Sin, 31; and repressive culture, 49; and symbolism, 115–16; and timelessness, 96–97
Buell, Lawrence, 1, 17, 101, 108, 127, 128, 199nn2–3, 203n61, 215n49, 220n135, 225n46, 230n153, 233n27, 227n121; on Jung and William James, 195
Burke, Kenneth, 62
Butler, Joseph, *Analogy, The*, 80

Calvin, John, 93
Calvinism, 78, 85, 88, 144
Cambridge Platonists, 55
Cameron, Kenneth Walter, 33
Campbell, Joseph, 8, 46, 109, 197; and archetypal hero, 42; and artist as hero, 153; and Cosmogonic Cycle, 61; influenced by Emerson, 199–200n25; influenced by Freud and Jung, 23; and hero in history, 161, 165, 170–171, 172; *Hero With A Thousand Faces*, 58–62; and immortality, 30; and modern malaise, 24; and the "monomyth," 28–29, 58–59, 87, 91; and myth, 65; and the "supreme hero," 191; and the Terrible

Fathers, 18; and the unconscious, 58
Carlyle, Thomas, *Sartor Resartus*, 142; 200n25
Carpenter, Frederic, 15
Carter, Steve, 221n158
Cavell, Stanley, 197
Cayton, Mary Kupiec, 112, 136
centroversion: defined, 66
Chapman, Maria, 163
Cheney, Edna Dow: and Emerson, 207n71
Cherokees: and Removal, 16, 105, 162
Cheyfitz, Eric, 200n28
childhood: as psychological ideal, 47, 119; freedom of, 138; and hermaphroditic disposition, 223n181; as Messiah, 139
Christ: Emerson as, 130, 131, 163; and sacredness of the body, 131; paraphrased by Emerson, 112–113, 129–130; as hero, 161; and the Last Supper, 131; miracles of rejected by Emerson, 84; person of overemphasized, 140; as rebel, 63; and sentiment, 136; and reform, 177, 232n15
Christianity: as consciousness, 111; historical defects of, 140
Cicero, 175
circle: and Emerson, 229n137; as symbol of God, 161; as symbol of wholeness, 31, 73, 152–153, 186
Civil Rights Movement, 9, 38, 190; and Emerson, 197, 238n144
Civil War, 35, 164, 169, 173; begins, 184
Clark, Donald, 36
Clarke, Samuel, 80
Clarkson, Thomas, 166
Cold War, 24, 37
Cole, Phyllis, 180, 210n52
Coleridge, Samuel Taylor, 5, 45; meeting with Emerson, 63; quoted by Emerson, 87–88
collective unconscious, 11; defined, 41
Collison, Gary, 234nn64–65

Commager, Henry Steele, *Era of Reform, The*, 199n4, 205n58, 212n109
Concord Lyceum, 171
Concord Women's Antislavery Society, 164, 178
conscious/consciousness: as Christianity, 111; defined, 41; and Fall of Man, 139; masculine quality of, 41, 65; as realm of the fathers, 41; as repressive, 71, 80–81
Constitution, United States, 141, 176; Civil War Amendments, 190–91
Cooper, A. A. (Third Earl of Shaftesbury), 55
Copernicus, Nicolaus, 25, 32, 35, 205n49
Copperheads, 188
Crane, Greg, 175–176
critics: New Humanist, 36
Cromphout, Gustaaf Van, 210n40
Cudworth, Ralph, influence on Emerson, 55; *True Intellectual System of the Universe, The* 33, 49
culture: as a source of repression, 49, 70, 143; defined by Emerson, 110; revolutionary, 145
Cupid: and Eros, 214n37
Curtis, George, 168

Darwin, Charles, *Origin of Species, The*, 35, 36
Declaration of Independence, 28, 161; and reform, 177, 189; as Transcendental statement, 169–70
Deism, 34
democracy, 6; and Emerson, 173; informed by Eros and Love, 170; relies on the instinct of the people, 183
Descartes, Rene, 25, 32
Dial, The, 121, 154
Dionysus, 70–71, 113
Divinity College, Harvard, 78, 127, 164
Doctorow, Edgar Lawrence, 36
Donne, John, 32–33
Dos Passos, John, 9

Douglass, Frederick: and Emerson 70, 164, 167, 175, 187, 236n76; as heroic anti–slave, 69, 167, 236n76; and Higher Law, 175–76; mythic transformation of, 69; *Narrative of the Life of Frederick Douglass, an American Slave, Written by Himself*, 68–70, 175; raises funds for Massachusetts 54th, 187–88
Du Bois, William Edward Burghardt, 197

economics: and guilt, 52
Education of Henry Adams, The, 35–36
Edwards, Jonathan, 226n67
ego: and alienation, 136; 138; defined, 41; function of, 45–46; 60, 70; and opposition to the body, 132
ego-consciousness: associated with fate, 182; defined, 48; and loss of instincts, 152; repressiveness of, 60, 65; 61; and sin, 139; and suffering, 132
Einstein, Albert, 36
Eliade, Mircea, 8, 46, 101, 172, 197; and archetypes, 22; and the abolition of history, 64, 73, 83; and the abolition of profane time, 149; and destroying the evil of the past, 174; influenced by Emerson, 199–200n25; *Myth of the Eternal Return, or Cosmos and History, The*; 63–65; and the "terrors of history," 25
Eliot, Charles W., 2
Eliot, Thomas Sterns, 9, 21; "The Waste Land," 36
Elizabethan world view, 30, 32
Ellison, Julie, 233–34n42
Emancipation Proclamation, Preliminary, 186
Emerson, Charles, 1; death of, 18, 99
Emerson, Edward Waldo, 76, 181, 202n41
Emerson, Edward, 1, 42, 88; death of, 18, 99

Emerson, Ellen Tucker, 4, 79, 83, 100, 119; death of, 5, 17, 109, 122, 123, 140; and Emerson's emotional crisis, 79; Emerson falls in love with, 83–84

Emerson, Lidian Jackson, 100–101, 104 106, 117, 119

Emerson, Mary Moody, 5; and Jacob Boehme, 56

Emerson, Ralph Waldo: and abolition, 105; and abolitionists, resistance to, 163–164; and Adam in the Garden, 31; affective side of, 12–13; and African Americans, demands equal rights for, 186–87; and "Age of Reason," 77; and American culture, 196; and American Revolution, 161; and antislavery activity, criticized for, 181; and antislavery, chapter 5 *passim*; and archetypes, 193, 229n114; and Aristotle, 170, 177, 185; and theory of art, 150–58; and Asian religion, 219n117; and Augustine, Saint, 161; and "Bleeding Kansas," 181; and body and soul, unity of, 118, 155; and body, the importance of, 58, 131–32; and Boehme, 56–57; and Boston's Second Church, 1, 78, 79, 90, 123, 131; broad intellectual interests of, 206n71; and John Brown, 181–82; and Calvinism, 78, 88, 144; career as minister, 78–79; and cathedrals, European, 93; and Cherokee Removal, 16, 162; and Christ, 130, 163, 218n83, rejects miracles of, 84; and circle as symbol, 31, 150, 229n137, 152, 155; and collective social action, 178, 180; and communion service, rejection of, 90–91, 131; and conservatism, view of, 160–161; and cosmogonic power, 134; criticized as misty and vague thinker, 125, 181, 222n164, 225n45, 22829n108; and Ralph

Cudworth, 33–34, 55; and culture and repression, 110, 49; and death, 102; and democracy, 6, 173, 183–84; and desire for emotional intimacy, 104; as "Devil's child," 127, 136, 137; and Dionysius, 218n90; and direct revelation from God, 85; and Divinity College, Harvard, 78; and Divinity School address, reactions to, 111–112, 136–137; and divinity, personal experience of, 97; and Frederick Douglass, 70, 164, 167, 175, 187, 236n76; and the Emerson Centennial celebration (1903), 206n67; and Ellen Tucker Emerson, 79, 83, 85–91, 102, 122, 140, 214n47, 214–215n49, 217n68;140; and emotion, early distrust of, 77, 80; and emotions and affections, importance of, 17, 43, 75, 80, 81, 87, 89, 94, 100, 106, 107, 108, 111, 165, 169, 215n49, 217n68; and the English, 180; and "the establishment," 109, 136, 142; and Europe, departs for, 91, travels in, 92–95; European Revolutions of 1848, witnesses, 171; and Fall of Man, 31, 60, 139, 140; and father(s), rejection of, 62, 68, 76, 86, 104, 110, 136; and feminine self, 139, 169, 182; and Founding Fathers, 161; and freedom, 138–146; and the Fugitive Slave Law, 173–77; and Margaret Fuller, 106, 118; and Gandhi, 235n75; and genius, 128; and "the God within," 2, 92, 102, 112, 126, 134, 137, 166, 168, 172, 174, 177, 187; as one with God, 61, 132; and Harvard College, 27, 71, 76–77, 78, 105, 127, 164, 218n82; and Harvard Divinity School, 1, 57, 111, 112, 127, 130, 136, 164, 181, 222n159, 223n191, 225n45, 227n77, 231n162; and hermaphroditic ideal, 119; and hermaphroditic personality, 66, 115, 119; and hero as representative man and liberator, 172; and Higher Law, 4, 16, 141, 174–177, 190, 231n162; and history as archetype, 148; and history, concept of, 98–99; and Julia Ward Howe,197; and human centrality, 31; and imagination, 128, 153; and immortality, feelings of, 82, 140, 214n47; and influence on psychomythic humanism, 11,16–17, 37; and instinct, 13, 43, 71, 80, 82, 87, 89, 90, 92, 96, 104, 110, 132, 134, 142, 152, 155, 179, 183, 185, 221n158; and instincts as a source of knowledge, 82; inward journey begins, 91–92; and , Lydia Jackson marriage to, 100, 103; and William James, influence on 195–196; and journals, 75–76, 95; and Carl Jung, 27, 195–195; and Kant, 154; and Dr. Martin Luther King, Jr., 235–236n75; and language, 56–57, 83, 94–95, 98, 107–108, 150–151, 163–164, 222n164, 225n47, 230n151; as lecturer 95–96; lecture style, 162; life follows hero archetype, 18, 42, 102, 104, 128, 177; and Lincoln, 188–90; and love 145; and man as creator, 65; and marriage, view of 101, 116–118; and the Massachusetts 54th, 187–88; and Herman Melville, 3; and middle-class conformity, 1; and Milton, 32; and moral imagination, 80; and moral sentiment as key to reform, 141, 167, 172, 174–175, 185, 187, 195, 213n17; and mortality, early feelings of, 81; and mystical element, 221n158; and myth, 62; and Napoleon temperament, 105, 109; and Native Americans, 3, 15, 16,141,

162; and natural theology, 146; and natural world, importance of, 52, 57, 80, 89, 91, 93, 97, 108, 122, 138; and New Bedford Lyceum, 171; and Neoplatonism, 33–34, 55, 222n168; and Oedipal Revolt, 63; organic language, theory of , 107–08; and desire for passionate expression, 108; and Orphic poet, 133, 139; and Over-Soul, 28; and "party of property," critical of, 180; and personal rebirth, 92; and poet as hero, 133, 135, 152, 234n62; and poet as liberating god, 56; and "political spirit," 170–171; and pragmatic social action, move towards, 165; and Pragmatism, influence on, 238n7, 238n9; and problem of evil, 79, 102, 139; as prophet/redeemer/oracle/ reformer, 8, 18, 105, 109, 110, 111, 115, 123, 129, 137, 156,157, 159–160, 164, 169, 171, 184, 190, 193, 218n82; and psychic harmony, 102; and psychological ontogeny, 67; and racism, 168, 171; and reformers, criticism of, 158; and revolution, 111, 136; and revolutionary culture, 145; and role of poet, 8; and role of scholar, 7–8; and the Roman Catholic Church, 94 217n77; and Romantic revolution, 34–35; and the Second Church, Boston, 78–79, 91, 131; and self-culture, 4, 228n94; and self-reliance as key to reform, 177–78; and self-reliant hero, 127–28; and social fragmentation, 27; and the spiritual and sensual, 155; and Charles Sumner, support of, 181; as "supreme hero," 191; and symbols, theory of, 95, 115–116; and Texas annexation, 163, 171; and Henry David Thoreau, 227n87; and time and space, 64, 84, 114,

Emerson, Ralph Waldo (*continued*), 116, 147–149; and Transcendental philosophy, 18; and Transcendentalists, 143–44; and Transparent Eyeball, 61, 132, 134; unconscious as guide, 39; and unconscious, use of term, 51; and the Understanding and the Reason, 88, 98, 100, 102, 106; and Unitarianism, 1, 5, 6, 56, 62, 76–78, 80, 82–88, 94–95, 111–112, 123, 130, 144, 164, rejection of, 86–91; and the uroboros, 154; and visionary ecstasy, 17; and Waldo (son), 119–23; and wealth, 53–54; and Daniel Webster, 173–75; and "whim," the importance of, 114, 135; and women, 116, 141, 165, 166, 178, 179, 182, 197, 223n180; and women reformers, 166, 239n18; and women's suffrage, 179; as writer for youth, 227n86

Emerson, Ralph Waldo, works of, "Address at Dartmouth College," 184; "Address at the Dedication of the Soldier's Monument in Concord, April 19, 1867," 188; "Address at Waterville College, 188; "Address on the Emancipation of the Negroes in the British West Indies," 4, 166–169, 188; "Address to the Citizens of Concord on the Fugitive Slave Law," 174–176, 181; "American Scholar, The " 3, 6, 19, 27, 95, 105, 110, 132, 142, 145, 158, 162, 167, 182, 184, 190, 191; "Art" (essay), 154; "Art" (lecture), 153; "Assault on Charles Sumner, The" 181; "Beauty," 7; "Brahma," 103, 135, 223n188; "Books," 169–170; "Celebration of the Intellect," 185; "Character," 138; "Heroism" (poem), 138; "Circles," 21, 31, 82, 95, 135, 156, 161; "Civilization,"

235n75; "Compensation," 135, 157; "Concord Hymn," 194; *Conduct of Life*, 179–80, 182–83; "Conservative, The" 143, 160–161; "Politics," 144; "Divinity School Address, The" 4, 43, 105, 130, 140, 152, 155–156, 162; *English Traits*, 180–181; "Eros—October," 193; *Essays, First Series*, 18; *Essays, Second Series*, 18, 122, 135, 159; "Experience," 16, 121, 122, 159–160, 165; Fate," 182; "Fortune of the Republic," 189; "Fugitive Slave Law," 176–177, 179, 182; "Give All to Love," 1, 81, 101; "Heart, The" 219n105; "Heroism," 127, 138; "History," 148; 169; "Lecture on Slavery," 178, 179–180; "Lecture on the Times," 113, 132, 147; "Letter to President Van Buren," 162; "Life and Letters of New England," 136; "Literary Ethics," 132; "Lord's Supper, The" 131; "Love and Thought," 7; "Love," 84, 113, 114, 149; "Man the Reformer," 113, 132, 144, 159; "Method of Nature, The" 67, 154; "Moral Forces," 185–86; *Nature*, 6, 16, 18, 42, 54, 72, 83, 89, 95, 97, 110, 116, 121, 129, 131–132, 133–134, 138–139, 141, 147, 154, 156; "New England Reformers," 141, 144, 145–146, 167; "Nominalist and Realist," 45; "Ode to W. H. Channing," 3; "Over-Soul, The, " 14, 113, 114, 125, 126, 140, 148–149, 160, 161; "Perpetual Forces," 186–187; "Poet, The" 13, 56, 113, 135, 151, 184; "Power," 183; "Reforms," 163; "Religion," 226n56; *Representative Men*, 171–172, 173, 174–175, 176; "Resources," 190; "Self-Reliance," 4, 49, 63, 71, 113, 125, 126–128, 137–138,

141, 147, 232n3; "Speech at a
Meeting to Aid John Brown,"
181–182; "Spiritual Laws," 139;
"Voluntaries," 238n136; "Thren-
ody," 121–122; "Transcendentalist, The" 129, 158, 162; "Uses of
Great Men," 172; "Woman," 165,
178; "Young American, The" 146
Emerson, Waldo: death of, 18; and
Emerson, 119–124
Emerson, William, 78, 100
emotion: and the unconscious, 71;
importance of, 72; related to
instinct, 80
empiricism, 34,35, 71
England, 180–181
Enlightenment, 34, 58; displaced by
romanticism, 5
Erikson, Erik, 47; and Emerson, 84;
Childhood and Society, 102
Eros, 5, 101, 128–129, 165; abolishes
profane time, 149; as basis of democracy, 170; and the body, 40,
97; and Cupid, 214n37; defined,
6–7, 11; and erotic expression,
150; opposes fate, 182; as god,
43; and nature, 151; and Over-
Soul, 131, 147; as power of Love,
167; and soul, 155; and the
unconscious, 41, 43, 89, 131;
and unity, 117
*Essay Concerning Human Under-
standing* (Locke), 34
establishment, the: opposes hero, 68;
and Emerson, 109
Eucharist: combines body and spirit,
131
European Revolutions of 1848, 171
Eve: and Adam, 115

Fall of Man: and Adam and Eve, 115;
as Biblical archetype, 56, 59, 60,
101; as product of consciousness,
139, 151; as psychological phenomenon, 63–64
Feidelson, Charles, Jr., 38
Fichte, Johnn Gottlieb, 55
Fiedler, Leslie, 38, 68

First World War (World War I), 9, 24,
46
Fitzgerald, F. Scott, 9
Flugel, J. C., 60
Ford, Henry, 197
Founding Fathers: as liberating poets,
170; and "self-evident" truth,
175
Fox, George, 96
Francis, Convers, 112
Frank, Albert von, 178, 202n49,
214n47
Franklin, Benjamin, 212n109
Freud, Sigmund, 10; anticipated by
Emerson, 199–200n25; as influ-
ence on Archetypal Criticism, 32;
and art, 54; and Norman Brown,
46–58; and emotions, 13, 21, and
William James, 196; and D. H.
Lawrence, 207n72; and psy-
chomythic humanism, 37, 45;
distinguishes soul from body,
49–50; and symbolism, 116
Frost, Robert, 20, 197
Frye, Northrop, *Anatomy of
Criticism*, 207n72
Fugitive Slave Law (1850), 173–77
Fuller Margaret: and antislavery, 178;
and hermaphroditic psyche, 66;
106–107, 168–169; and marriage, 118; and uroboros,
230n150; *Woman in the Nineteenth Century*, 66, 230n150

Galileo, Galilei, 25, 32, 35
Gandhi, Mohandas, 175; influenced
by Emerson and Thoreau,
235n75
Garden of Eden, 31, 33, 35, 107, 114,
116, 151
Garrison, William Lloyd, 171
Garvey, T. Gregory, 170–171
Gea, 96
Geldard, Richard, *God in Concord*,
221n151
Gelpi Albert, 134, 201n25, 215n49,
226n69, 230n140
Gibbon, Edward, 142

Gilman, William, 76
God: expressed through the power of
    the unconscious, 135; considered
    dead, 140; symbolized by circle,
    161
Goethe, Johann Wolfgang von, 5; and
    the unconscious, 55
*Great Mother: An Analysis of an Ar-
    chetype, The* (Neumann), 193
Green, Martin, 199–200n25

Hall, G. Stanley, 196
Harper's Ferry: attack on, 181
Harvard College, 71, 105, 127, 164
Hawthorne, Nathaniel, 204n25
Hayes, Woody, 197
Hecker, Isaac, 217n77
Hedge, Frederick Henry, 199n1,
    217n68, 218n82
Hegel, Georg Wilhelm Friedrich: and
    the unconscious, 55; 204n30
Heller, Agnes, 30
Hemingway, Ernest, 9
Heraclitus, 135, 153
Herald of Freedom, 169
hermaphrodite: and childhood,
    223n181; and Neoplatonism,
    223n180; as symbol of whole-
    ness, 73, 115–117, 118–119, 119
Hero With a Thousand Faces, The
    (Campbell), 58–62
hero: as artist, 152, 153; creative
    powers of, 99; divine role of,
    165; and Emerson, 18, 42, 102,
    104, 127, 128, 177; and immor-
    tality, 61; as liberator, 172; as
    light-bringer, 67; as reformer,
    136; as representative man, 172;
    synthesizes conscious and
    unconscious, 71, 133; becomes
    tyrant, 161
heroism, 127–138
Hesiod, 7
Higher Law, 141, 174; and the Con-
    stitution, 190; and moral senti-
    ment, 187; as the product of the
    Reason and the unconscious, 175

history, 147–49
Hodder, Alan, 92, 226n67
Hoffman, Daniel, 38
Holmes, Oliver Wendell, 14, 210n33
Hopkins, Vivian, 34, 55
Howe, Julia Ward: and Emerson, 197,
    239n18
Hume, David, 80

Iamblicus, 55
immortality, 14, 28, 30, 48, 60–62,
    102, 134–135, 140, 147, 214n47,
    228n108
Industrial Revolution, 25–26
instincts: related to emotions, 71, 80;
    and art, liberated by, 54–55; and
    conflict, 57; related to the divine,
    13, 89–90; and Emerson, 13, 43,
    71, 80, 82, 87, 89, 90, 92, 96,
    104, 110, 132, 134, 142, 152,
    155, 179, 183, 185, 221n158;
    and knowledge, 82, 185; and the
    unconscious, 22
Ives, Charles, 197

James, William: influenced by Emer-
    son, 194–196, 238n7; on Emer-
    son's concept of the "Universal
    Soul," 195–196; on feelings as
    cognitive, 203n53; and intuitive
    morality, 234n51; as influence on
    Jung, 195–196, 199–200n25;
    meets Jung and Freud, 196–197;
    Varieties of Religious Experience,
    195
Jeans, Sir James, 36
Jefferson, Thomas, 174, 175
John the Evangelist, 138
Johnson, Dr. Samuel, 142
Jung, Carl, 9–10, 194, 199n25; and
    Archetypal Criticism, 38; and
    archetypal image of wise man,
    221n148; and archetypes, 22;
    and archetypes in history,
    229n116; and art and emotion,
    12–13, 21; and artist in society,
    220n138; and artistic psyche,

217n69; and the collective
unconscious, 22; and contrast between medieval and modern
world, 205n49; and crisis of
modern world, 27; and Emerson
on divinity, 27; and Emerson,
196–197; and emptiness of Communion Service, 216n66; and the
Fall of Man, 210–11n64; and
God in nature, 216n58; and
intuitive morality, 234n51; and
William James, influenced by,
195–196,199–200n25 and Herman Melville, 202n33; personal
breakdown resembles Emerson's,
215n50; on psychology as religion, 208n86; and psychomythic
humanism, 37, 45; and religious
experience, 196; and Romanticism, 206n70; and social significance of art, 72–73; and the
transcendent function, 105,
236n78; on the unconscious as a
guide, 39; on the unconscious as
compensatory, 218n90; and
unconscious as prophetic,
207n77; and unity of body and
soul, 118; and World War I, 24

Kames, Henry Home, Lord, 55
Kant, Immanuel, 5, 45, 55; and
    "moral feeling" as basis for law,
    170; as an influence in Transcen-
    dentalism, 206n62
Kateb, George, 16, 231–232n162
Kennedy, John F., 197
Kepler, Johannes, 25
King, Martin Luther, Jr., 175, 197;
    influenced by Emerson and
    Thoreau, 235–236n75
Klonoski, Richard, 170
Korean conflict, 9
Krishna, 172
Kuhn, Thomas, 29, 32

language: corruption of, 151; and
    emotion, 107–08; and erotic

expression, 150; as organic, 107;
    as sensual, 56; as symbol, 94–95,
    107, 98; and the unconscious,
    54–57
Larsen, Stephen, 199–200n25
Lawrence, D. H., 38, 200n25; influ-
    enced by Freud, 207n72
Lebeaux, Richard, 84
Leibnitz, 55
Lesser, Simon, *Fiction and the Uncon-
    scious*, 207n72
Levin, Harry, 38, 68
Lewis, Clive Staples, 197
Lewis, Richard, W. B., 38, 205n61
libido ballast, 109, 113, 133
libido charge (Neumann), 71, 130,
    131, 142, 143
libido: as power of God, 131
Lincoln, Abraham, 183, 184; and
    Emerson, 188–190; and Gettys-
    burg Address, 185; and Prelimi-
    nary Emancipation Proclamation,
    186; as Transcendentalist,
    237n123
Locke, John, and Emerson, 80, 126;
    and empiricism, 71, 77; *Essay
    Concerning Human Understand-
    ing*, 34, 35; on wealth, 53
Loring, Ellis Gray, 130
Lost Generation, The, 9, 36–37
love: as basis of democracy, 170; as
    function of the unconscious, 43;
    as principle of reform, 145,
    228n97
Lowance, Mason, 233n35
Lowell, James Russell, 15
Luther, Martin, 52, 96, 177

Magna Carta, 180
mandala: as symbol of wholeness,
    73
Marti, Hose, 197
Martineau, Harriet, 99
Marx, Leo, 38
Massachusetts 54th, 187–188
Matthiessen, Francis Otto, 14, 35,
    125, 230n151

McAleer, John, 15
McPherson, James, 188
Melville, Herman: on Emerson, 13; and Jung, 202n33
Mexican War, 175
Mexico, 163
Michaud, Regis, 221n158
Miller, Jeffrey C., 25–26, 28, 208–209n2
Miller, Perry, 5–6, 199n15; and Transcendentalism as religious movement, 227n75
Milton, John, 29, 32, 77, 88, 96; and human centrality in *Paradise Lost*, 33
Mitchell, Charles, 196
money: as symbol of guilt, 52
Montaigne, Michel Eyquem, 92
moral sentiment, 43, 141; and higher law, 187; as key to reform, 167, 174, 185; and James, William, 194
More, Paul Elmer, 37
Morris, Saundra, 234n62
Morrow, Lance, 197
Moses, 161
mother figure: and the unconscious, 60
Mott, Wesley, 177–78
muse, 7; and affections, 180; associated with the unconscious, 41
Myerson, Joel, 199n3, 230n152
myth: and the American Renaissance, 229n114

NAACP, 197
Napoleon I, 105, 109
Native Americans: and Emerson, 15, 16, 141, 162; oppression of in nineteenth century, 3; and Transcendental reform, 5; and vision of unified reality, 11
nature: as reflection of divinity, 89; as symbol of spirit, 150
neoclassicism, 34, 35, 58
Neoplatonism, 17, 32, 33–34, 115, 154; and Emerson, 55, 222n168; and the hermaphrodite, 223n180; influence on Romanticism,

222n168; and reconciliation of opposites, 157
Neumann, Erich, 8, 46, 87, 115; and abolition of time and space, 153; and centroversion, 66; and the circle as symbol, 152; and feminine as revolutionary force, 233–234n42; *Great Mother: An Analysis of an Archetype, The* , 193; and the hermaphrodite, 119; and integration of personality, 29, 183; and libido charge, 71; and modern malaise, 24–25; *Origins and History of Consciousness, The*, 65–74; and psychological balance of masculine and feminine, 119; and psychological ontogeny, 66; and reconciliation of opposites, 157; and repressive fathers, 163; and the task of the hero, 130–131, 133; and the Terrible Mother, 66; and the unindividuated state, 147
New England Women's Suffrage Association, 179
new humanism: Renaissance, 29
New Humanist critics, 36, 37
New Science, 17; rise of, 25, 32
Newcomb, Charles, 121
Newfield, Christopher, 231n162
Newton, Sir Isaac, 25, 33, 34, 36, 71, 77, 78, 212n109
Nietzsche, Friedrich, 200n25
Norcross, John, 201n26
North American Review, 107
Norton, Andrews: criticized by Emerson, 140; and miracles controversy, 227n77; as Terrible Father, 112; 137, 141, 174
Novalis (Friedrich von Hardenberg): and the unconscious, 55

Oedipal Revolt: and Emerson, 63
ontogeny, 23, 51–52, 67; and ego-consciousness, 148
Origen, 115

Origin of Species, The (Darwin), 35
Original Sin, 31, 52
Orpheus, 134, 168; as artist, 152;
    225n39
Otto, Walter, 70–71
Ouranos, 96
Over-Soul, 5, 6, 11, 147, 165; and
    Civil War, 184; defined, 28,
    42–43; power of, 156; and Emer-
    son's "political spirit," 171; tran-
    scendent nature of, 31; unity of,
    153

Packer, Barbara, 31, 201n28, 204n45,
    217n77, 237n107
Paradise Lost (Milton), 32, 33
parapsychology, 196
Parker, Theodore, 237n123
Pater, Walter, 104
Patterson, Anita, 235n75
Paul, Sherman, 134
Peace Party, 188
Petrulionis, Sandra, 233n29
Pharisees, 130
Phillips, Wendell, 171, 183
Philo, 115
phylogeny, 51–52
Plato, 29, 39, 55, 77, 223n175; and
    cosmos as living creature, 116
pleasure-principle, 47–48
Plotinus, 34, 55, 222n168, 223n175
Plutarch, 223n175
Poe, Edgar Allan, *Narrative of Arthur
    Gordon Pym, The*, 212n94
poet: abolishes time and space, 114;
    and Founding Fathers, 170; as
    hero, 133–134, 135; as liberating
    god, 56, 113; as priest, 135; as
    prophet, 169
Poirier, Richard, 132
Pope, Alexander, 77, 142; quoted,
    205n59
Porte, Joel, 38–39, 49, 129–30, 136;
    Representative Man, 62
Porter, Carolyn, 62–63, 201n25
Porter, David, 103, 150, 225n47,
    230n151

Pound, Ezra, 9
Pragmatism, 196; as influenced by
    Emerson, 238n7, 238n9
Proclus, 55
psyche: and bisexuality, 115; her-
    maphroditic quality of, 66, 119,
    223n181
psychomythic humanism, 9–12; emer-
    gence of, 21–44; Emerson's influ-
    ence on, 11, 16–17, 37; seminal
    archetypes of, 45–46; and Tran-
    scendentalism, 11, 88–89
Ptolemaic system, 30; Ptolemaic/
    Heliocentric controversy, 33
Puritan work ethic, 53

racism: attacked by Emerson, 168,
    171, 186; and New Bedford
    Lyceum, 171
Rank, Otto, 29, 154; *Art and Artists*,
    89; and role of divine hero, 165
rationalism: and the conscious, 71,
    127, 139, 140, 165, 174; associ-
    ated with sin and death, 13
reality-principle, 46–48, 54,151
Reason, the: associated with God, 102
    ; defined, 42, 88–89; 45, 59, 81,
    100, 102; equates with the un-
    conscious, 88, 97
Reaver, J. Russell, 16
rebirth: cycle of, 63–65
reformers: as "the Movement," 136
religion: and art, 154; and economics,
    52; as source of oppression, 72
REM sleep, 39
Renaissance (American), 30, 35
Renaissance (European): world view,
    17, 29–31
revolution: promoted by Emerson,
    111; 136; American, 161
Reynolds, Larry, 234n57
Richardson, Robert, 15, 56, 100, 106,
    110, 119, 214n49, 216n62,
    218n19, 219n117, 229n114
Rilke, Rainer Maria, 54, 56
Robinson, David, 17, 165, 167, 172,
    179, 180, 213n17, 228n94

Robinson, Edwin Arlington, 197
Roman Catholic Church, 94; Emerson's attraction to, 217n77; and Transubstantiation, 131
romantic movement: and Emerson, 79; as psychological phenomenon, 58; 67–68
Romantic Movement: displaces Enlightenment, 59, 63
romantic revolution, 59
Romanticism: American; and cycle of rebirth, 62; 62; and Emerson, 34–35; 39, 45, 48; and Jungian psychology, 206n70, influenced by Neoplatonism, 222n168; opposed to materialism, 52; and psychomythic humanism, 11, 37; and vision of unified reality, 11
Romanticism: European, 5, 34–35, 45
Roosevelt, Theodore, 2, 197
Rousseau, Jean Jacque, 34
Rowe, John Carlos, 16, 231n162
Rusk, Ralph, 14, 230n137

Santayana, George, 224n7
Sartor Resartus (Carlyle), 142
Schelling, Friedrich Wilhelm Joseph von: and the unconscious, 55
Schiller, Friedrich von: and the unconscious, 55
Schlesinger, Arthur M., Jr., *The Age of Jackson*, 231n162
Scott, Sir Walter, 77
Scribes, 130
Sealts, Merton, Jr., 221n143
Second World War, 9, 21
self-culture: defined, 228n94
self-reliance, 127–138
Shakespeare, William, 13
Shaw, Col. Robert Gould, 238n136
Shelley, Mary, 204n25
Sherman, Stuart P., 14
sin: as a construct of consciousness, 31, 139; original, 139; as self-alienation, 140

slave trade, 181
slavery, 6, 18, 52, 127, 145; chapter 5 *passim*
slaves, 166–167, women as slaves, 178
Smith, Robert C., 196
Song of Myself (Whitman), 48, 50, 60
soul: and art, 89; and body, 49, 89, 118, 131, 155; and cosmic energy, 155; as God within, 226n51; and unconscious, 28
space: and time, 113, 147, 148; abolition of, 153
Stael, Mme de, 206n62
Steele, Jeffrey, 27, 62, 200–201n25, 203n54, 203n57, 225n49, 229n114
Stevens, Wallace, 13
Stevens, Wallace, 197
Stewart, Dugald, 77
Storey, Moorfield, 197
Sturgis, Caroline, 107, 220n130
Sumner, Charles, 181
symbol: combines spiritual and sensual, 73, 108; Emerson's theory of, 95; and language, 98; and power of emancipation, 113; 116

Tallis, Frank, 39, 40, 204n35, 204n49, 208n86, 215n50
Tanner, Tony, 132
temperance movement, 144
terminology: note on, 19–20, 40–43
Terrible Father archetype, 18, 29, 70, 72; and Frederick Douglass, 69; as the Establishment, 136; opposes the hero, 68; and language of, 151; and Andrews Norton, 112; as the Slave Power, 163, 166–67, 190; and Daniel Webster, 174
Terrible Mother archetype, 66, 67, 70
Texas, 160, 163; annexation of, 171
Thoreau, Henry David, 3, 27, 31; and Artist of Kouroo, 64; and Emerson, 227n87; and Higher Law,

175; and immortality, 62; and opposition to materialism, 52–53; *Walden,* 49, 133; and time, 64, 65
Tillyard, E. M. W., 30
Timaeus (Plato), 116
time: abolished by poet, 114; 147–49; cosmic and profane, 63–65; as source of repression, 51; and space, 113, 147, 148, 153; and tragedy, 64; and timelessness, 96–97
tragedy: and historical time, 64, 100
transcendent function: defined, 41–42; 43, 87, 105, 236n78; and art, 108
Transcendentalism, 2, 45, 48; and antislavery movement, 178; and divinity of the self, 17, 35; and emotion 6; and immortality, 62; and importance of intuitive knowledge, 82, 104; and Lincoln, 237n123; and literary creativity as sacred art, 56, 153; opposed to materialism, 52; and psychomythic humanism, 11, 37, 88–89; and reform movement, 5–6, 10, 143–144, 158, 169, 233n27; as religious movement, 227n75; and self–culture, 145; and Unitarianism, 130; and withdrawal from society, 231n162
transubstantiation, 131
True Intellectual System of the Universe (Cudworth), 33
Tufts College, 185

Uleman, James, 39
unconscious: and contemporary psychological theory, 39; defined, 41; and divinity, 41, 43, 61; Emerson's use of term, 51; and feminine, 41, 65; as guide, 39; and immortality, 60–62; and language, 54–57; Campbell's use of, 58; as link to nature, 97; and mother figure, 41, 60; and soul,

28; and timelessness, 51; and childhood, 51
Understanding, the: defined, 42, 88–89; 45, 59, 100, 102; equates with consciousness, 88, 97
Unitarianism, 76, 85, 164; and Emerson, 86–91, 111, 123, 144; and miracles controversy, 84; and Transcendentalism, 130
uroboros, 67; and Emerson, 154; used as symbol by Margaret Fuller, 230n150; and hermaphrodite, 73; symbol of wholeness, 77

Van Buren, Martin, President, 162
Varieties of Religious Experience (James), 195
Very, Jones, 120
Vietnam War, 38
Vishnu Purana, 219n117
Voltaire, Francois Marie Aroute de, 34

Walden (Thoreau), 49, 64, 65
Walls, Laura Dassow, 26, 33, 34, 205n51, 218n82, 233n327; on Emerson's natural theology, 146
Washington, Booker T., 197
Weber, Max, 53
Webster, Senator Daniel, 173, 183; as "Defender of the Constitution," 175; 235n73, 236n80; as Terrible Father, 174
Weisbruch, Robert, 180
Whicher, Stephen, 15–16, 226n51, 231n162
Whitehead, Alfred North, 47
Whitman, Walt, 13, 48, 200n25; and sensual language, 57, 108; and opposition to materialism, 53; "Sleepers, The" 212n94; and unity of reality, 60; and unity of soul and body, 50
Whyte, Lancelot Law, *Unconscious Before Freud, The,* 54–55
Wider, Sarah, 12, 15, 214n38, 224n7, 225n45, 227n86
Wiley, Basil, 34
Wills, Garry, 237n123

Wind, Edgar, *Pagan Mysteries in the Renaissance*, 115, 223n181
Winters, Ivor, 16
Woman in the Nineteenth Century (Fuller), 66, 178
women: as reformers, 166, 178–79; subordination of in nineteenth century, 3; and Transcendental reform, 5, 178; women as slaves, 178
Women's Rights Movement, 38; and suffrage, 179, 190; and Emerson, 141, 179, 197

Woodbury, George, 125
Wordsworth, William, 63
World Parents, 67
World War I (First World War), 9, 24, 36
World War II (Second World War), 19, 21, 37
Wright, Frank Lloyd, 197

Yeats, William Butler, 204n18
Yoder, Y. A., 225n39
Young, Gloria, 201n25